Digital Passages: Migrant Youth 2.0

MediaMatters is a series published by Amsterdam University Press on current debates about media technology and practices. International scholars critically analyze and theorize the materiality and performativity, as well as spatial practices of screen media in contributions that engage with today's (digital) media culture.

For more information about the series, please visit www.aup.nl

Digital Passages: Migrant Youth 2.0

Diaspora, Gender and Youth Cultural Intersections

Koen Leurs

Amsterdam University Press

This book is published in print and online through the online OAPEN library (www.oapen.org).

OAPEN (Open Access Publishing in European Networks) is a collaborative initiative to develop and implement a sustainable Open Access publication model for academic books in the Humanities and Social Sciences. The OAPEN Library aims to improve the visibility and usability of high quality academic research by aggregating peer reviewed Open Access publications from across Europe.

This study was conducted as part of the Utrecht University Executive Board-funded High Potential project *Wired Up: Digital Media as Innovative Socialization Practices for Migrant Youth* (2008-2012).

This research was also supported by a Marie Curie Intra European Fellowship within the 7th European Community Framework Programme, project reference 332318 Urban Politics of London Youth Analyzed Digitally (UPLOAD) (2013-2015).

This publication was made possible by financial support from the Utrecht University Library Open Access Fund, Institute of Cultural Inquiry (ICON), seed funding by Cultures, Citizenship and Human Rights (CCHR) and a 2013 Royal Netherlands Academy of Arts and Sciences Council for the Humanities Stipend.

Cover illustration: C215 - Mirleft stencil image

Cover design: Suzan Beijer
Lay-out: Crius Group, Hulshout

Amsterdam University Press English-language titles are distributed in the US and Canada by the University of Chicago Press.

ISBN 978 90 8964 640 8
e-ISBN 978 90 4852 304 7
DOI 10.5117/9789089646408
NUR 670

Table of Contents

List of figures

List of tables

List of diagrams

Acknowledgements

First and foremost, with *much gratitude* I wish to *acknowledge* all informants for letting me in to their world. It was a great pleasure to learn more about digital practices from all the 1,408 survey participants. In particular, I felt greatly privileged to get to know the individual interviewees. Thank you Abdel, Abdelsammad, Anas, Amina, Amir, Ayoub, Badr, Bibi, Carlos, Faruk, Fatiha, Ferran, Hajar, Hatim, Ilana, Ilham, Inas, Inzaf, Kamal, Kenza, Khadija, Loubna, Mehmet Ali, Meryam, Midia, Mohammed, Mustafa, Naoul, Nevra, Oussema, Rachid, Ryan, Sadik, Safae, Sahar, Salima, Senna, Soesie, Soufian, SouSou, Tariq, Yethi and Ziham.

I am grateful to my colleagues and fellow students at Utrecht University and the London School of Economics for engaging with my work and sharing a passion. Special thanks to my mentors Sandra Ponzanesi, you made my rite of passage from student to scholar an enjoyable experience and Myria Georgiou, it's been a great intellectual journey exploring mediated cities from Singapore to London. Thank you Chiara Bonfiglioli, Babs Boter, Marianne van Boomen, Rosemarie Buikema, Thorsten Busch, Claudia Clemente, Feike Dietz, Niels van Doorn, Teun Dubbelman, Paul Gilroy, Jasmijn van Gorp, Berber Hagendoorn, Alison Harvey, Heather Hermant, Jay Lemke, Sybille Lammes, Lars Lundgren, Pramod Nayar, Levien Nordeman, Eva Midden, Geneva Murray, Dana Mustata, Domitilla Olivieri, Trude Oorschot, Valentina Rao, Sander de Ridder, Mirko Schäfer, Sanjay Sharma, Tamara Shepherd, Kevin Smets, Jacco van Sterkenburg, Florian Töpfl, Martine Veldhuizen, Nanna Verhoeff, Kim van der Wijngaard and colleagues at Radboud University, Innsbruck University and Johannes Gutenberg Universität Mainz.

This study was conducted as part of the Utrecht University Executive Board-funded High Potential project *Wired Up: Digital Media as Innovative Socialization Practices for Migrant Youth*, jointly carried out at the Faculty of Humanities and the Faculty of Social Sciences, in collaboration with Vanderbilt University, USA. It was a pleasure to work with the team: Thank you Mariëtte de Haan, Kevin Leander, Fadi Hirzalla, Fleur Prinsen, Lisa Schwartz and Asli Ünlüsoy. Thanks Manja Coopmans, Malin Grundel and Fayrouz Boulayounne for your assistance during fieldwork and data analysis. Thanks to the directors, teachers, and students of seven secondary schools across the Netherlands who generously enabled us to conduct fieldwork.

This book was shaped by feedback generously shared at various gatherings across the world including those organized by the Netherlands Research

School of Gender studies (NOG), InterGender, Centre for Humanities (CfH), the Postcolonial Studies Initiative (PCI), the Postcolonial Europe Network (PEN), the Japanese Society for Socio-Informatics International Workshop for Young Researchers, the International Communication Association (ICA), the Association of Internet Researchers (AoIR) and the European Communication Research and Education Association (ECREA). Manuscript reviewers and members of my dissertation committee: Lenie Brouwer, Radhika Gajjala, Frank Kessler, Lisa Nakamura and Liesbet van Zoonen, thank you for your critical feedback. Thanks Jeroen Sondervan at Amsterdam University Press – you assisted me in delivering this manuscript while we both welcomed a new baby into our families.

Finally, Stephanie and Xavier, thank you for your online and offline love, support and happiness.

Utrecht/London, March 2015

Introduction

Fig. 1: "Mocro's be like. Born Here," tweet @Nasrdin_Dchar (March 17, 2014)

> *I want to say one thing! I am Dutch and yes my parents are from another country, Morocco just to make it clear, and I'm proud of that!! Because I have been raised with two totally different cultures and I'm happy to have been able to experience that*
> – Meryam, fifteen-year-old (Facebook post, March 23, 2014)

"Do you want more or less Moroccans in this city and in the Netherlands?" This was the question Geert Wilders asked his audience during a party rally in The Hague. "Fewer, fewer, fewer!" chanted his supporters thirteen times before applauding. The audience had gathered on the occasion to celebrate municipal election results.[1] To this, the leader of the anti-immigration and anti-Islam Party for Freedom (Dutch: Partij voor de Vrijheid, PVV) smiled and made the promise: "then that will be arranged" (NOS, 2014). A storm of protest erupted, with several actions going viral online. On Twitter, using the hashtag #bornhere, Moroccan-Dutch celebrities such as the award-winning actor Nasrdin Dchar posted selfies showing their Dutch passports.[2] Many fellow Moroccan-Dutch people copied the tactic, #bornhere became a trending topic on Twitter, alongside other hashtags such as #spreadtheword, #bornthere, #leefhier (in English: living here), #ProudMoroccan, #mocro, #ookikbennederlands (in English: I'm also Dutch). In addition, more than 95,000 Facebook members liked the page "Ik doe aangifte tegen wilders" (I will report Wilders to the police) while 15,000 liked "Meer Marokkanen" (in English: More Moroccans). Eventually, more than 6,400 people reported Wilders's rally to the police, and a similar number of complaints was filed with Dutch antidiscrimination agencies. The Dutch Public Prosecution Service (OM) announced in December 2014 they will prosecute Geert Wilders "on suspicion of insulting a population group based on race and inciting hatred and discrimination" (OM, 2014).

This book considers how Moroccan-Dutch youth, mostly born in the Netherlands, navigate digital spaces to articulate their politicized identities in a time when claims over the failure of multiculturalism, anti-immigration sentiments and Islamophobia sweep across Europe. *Digital Passages: Migrant Youth 2.0* addresses not only to how these mostly second-generation migrant youth navigate across digital spaces, but also considers the digitization of key identity-formation processes, such as coming of age, rites of passage and the negotiation of offline/online gender, diaspora, religious and youth cultural expectations. For example, Meryam, a fifteen-year-old informant who also participated in the #bornhere protests, is a headscarf-wearing girl who is called a "*gangster*" in her school because she likes hip-hop. With her

1 Geert Wilders made these comments at the moment exit polls from local elections in The Hague revealed the PVV was running neck-and-neck with the liberal-oriented Democrats 66 (Dutch: Democraten 66, D66). The PVV ended up in second place with 14% of the votes after the D66 with 15%.

2 Born in the Netherlands from parents who migrated to the Netherlands from Morocco as guest workers, Nasrdin Dchar is famous for his acceptance speech for winning the Golden Calf for best actor at the 2011 Dutch Film Festival: "A few months ago I read an article in which Minister Maxime Verhagen said that having fear of foreigners is very understandable. Well, Minister Verhagen and Geert Wilders and all those people that stand behind you: I'm a Dutchman. I'm very proud of my Moroccan blood. I am a Muslim and I have a fucking Golden Calf in my hands."

Fig. 2: Geweigerd.nl website top banner (March 6, 2005)

Moroccan-Dutch friends, she posted selfies on Twitter, "Insta" (Instagram) and Facebook. Meryam mostly received positive comments and likes from coethnics, youth of other migrant backgrounds as well as ethnic-majority Dutch kids. However, in her Facebook post, she also addressed a few of her white Dutch classmates who had expressed sympathy with Wilders, writing she hoped they would change their minds: "*stop following someone who is so blind, you have to open your own eyes and think about what you say.*" To sign off she stated, "*the Netherlands is a free country so I wanna say, do whatever you wanna do.*" Inzaf, a fellow fifteen-year-old girl, shared "*I have filed a report myself. I have written that I'm of the opinion that he discriminates.*" She added, "*I have also had everyone I know file a report. You can do it online in no time.*" Geert Wilders's speech and the responses triggered illustrate that in the Netherlands a particular configuration of cultural difference, whiteness and (secularized forms of) Christianity has gained prominence. Through such discourses, binaries and borders are constructed. As a result, Muslim and migrant bodies may be feared and considered out of place. Many migrant and minority groups do not fit the norms and are therefore not seen to fully belong to nations like the Netherlands, yet they live inside them.

Fifteen years ago, Moroccan-Dutch digital media enthusiast Abdelilah Amraoui initiated a movement in the Netherlands called Geweigerd.nl (*geweigerd* in English: denied) in direct response to the discrimination among owners of club venues and discotheques that required bouncers to refuse people entrance based on their ethnicity, race or religion. Amraoui started the website because he beliefs that with access to the Internet "*you can now create media yourself in case you cannot find it elsewhere.*" The site invited young people who felt they were wrongfully refused entry to a venue to submit their stories of being refused access. Figure 2 displays the top banner of the Geweigerd.nl website, an animated GIF image which combines (in) famous Dutch club logos with stop-signs and the "top five of bouncer excuses" such as "this is not a multicultural event" and "there are already plenty of your sort inside." Personal experiences sent in by young people were published on the site. Collecting personal stories of mainly frustrated Dutch ethnic-minority youth, Amraoui hoped to engage in dialogue with those places of entertainment in order to renegotiate their admission policies. The issue received wider attention after Amraoui collaborated with the nationally famous Moroccan-Dutch rapper Ali B. in the release of the song similarly titled "Geweigerd.nl" that also scrutinized unfair and discriminating admission policies.

#bornhere and Geweigerd.nl illustrate how Moroccan-Dutch youth become 'digital space invaders.' The concept of digital space invaders builds on Nirmal Puwar's research on offline, institutionalized spaces where minority bodies are considered to be "out of place," upon successfully entering those they become "space invaders" of locations "which have not been 'reserved' for them, for which they are not, in short, the somatic norm" (2004, p. 1). The metaphor of space invaders is developed in this book to empirically, theoretically and politically consider what happens when Moroccan-Dutch youth articulate digital identities across digital spaces where they may not be expected or fit the norms. The argumentation draws mostly from extensive qualitative empirical data; however, descriptive quantitative data of 344 Moroccan-Dutch survey participants is used to contextualize the findings. The qualitative fieldwork consisted of in-depth interviews with forty-three mostly second-generation, Moroccan-Dutch migrant youth across five cities in the Netherlands and a virtual ethnography of Internet forums, instant messaging (IM), social networking sites (SNSs) and video-sharing websites. Theoretically, I connect and intervene in dialogues across new media, gender, antiracial and postcolonial studies, critical geography, migration and transnationalism as well as religious studies. The focus is on how Internet platforms are appropriated by Moroccan-Dutch youth to position themselves between cultures of origin, youth cultures and cultures of immigration and how issues of gender, ethnicity and religion are negotiated.

1. Online/offline space and power relations

The lens of space invaders will be developed to excavate dominant positions in/of digital media and their subversion. Similar to offline institutions, across digital space, templates, norms and interface decisions reserve certain dominant consumer, national, gendered, ethnic and racial positions. These socio-technical processes have uneven spatial effects, both online

Fig. 3: Google.nl search for *"Marokkanen"* (June 28, 2012)

and offline. Space dynamically materializes and structures behavior at the interplay of how hierarchical social relations distribute bodies and how bodies position themselves (Foucault, 1980; Lefebvre, 1991; Grosz, 1995; Puwar, 2004; Gilbert, 2010; Soja, 2010; Ahmed, 2012). As summed up by Raka Shome: "a focus on spatial relations of power enables scholars of communication and culture to understand and theorize the complex ways in which identities are being reproduced in our current moment of globalization" (2003, p. 39).

For example, Figure 3 displays the dominant positions that the Google Netherlands search engine associates with "*Marokkanen*" (the Dutch word for Moroccans). The auto-complete search query suggestions that Google provides appear automatically upon typing "*Marokkanen*" in the search field. The auto-complete algorithm offers query suggestions in a drop-down list, predicting behavior based on queries typed previously by Google users as well as generating items on the basis of traffic, page visits and recently crawled websites (Google, 2015).[3]

3 The search was carried out in a Mozilla Firefox browser, using the "Private Browsing" settings, whilebeing signed out from a Google account, with "Web & App Activity" turned off and without having searched for the topic earlier. The results do thus not present my earlier search behavior or that of my contacts.

The search query suggestions reveal some of the ways young Moroccan-Dutch people are allocated particular narrow gendered and racialized positions in digital space. From top to bottom they can be translated from Dutch as follows: "Moroccan jokes," "Moroccans must die" and "Moroccans and Polish people." The suggestions on "Moroccan jokes" provide results of websites that host offensive anti-immigration, anti-Islam and racist jokes. The second suggestion points the Google user toward discussion forums where right-wing extremists discriminate against ethnic others. For example, Google's third search result links toward a forum posting on MeetHolland.com where a user left the following comment about Moroccan-Dutch youth: "Those rotten bastards must die!!!!!!!!! Dirty, cowardly, disgusting, stinking cancer goats" (Wilders, 2005, my translation from Dutch). The third suggestion equates Moroccan-Dutch people with Polish guest workers arriving after the recent EU expansion. Simultaneously, without having pressed the search button, results are shown, including Google Image Search results. The four results are all stereotypical images of aggressive masculine street culture representing Moroccan-Dutch youth as dangerous loiterers and the inclusion of a policeman emphasizes Moroccan-Dutch boys as troublemakers.

The auto-complete algorithm (which is partly based on the search-term popularity among prior users) exemplifies sedimented ideas that emphasize particular associations and stereotypes of Moroccan-Dutch people – particularly those voiced by right-wingers rather than others. Spearheaded by the anti-Islamic Geert Wilders and the sensationalist press, young people of Moroccan migrant descent are often seen as a problem. Moroccan-Dutch boys are dismissed as strangers to Western democracies, possibly dangerous Islamic fundamentalists, terrorists or thieves while headscarf-wearing girls, in particular, are constructed as either un-emancipated and backward or oppressed by Muslim culture. In the context of the United States, danah boyd similarly argued that when, for instance, searching for the name "Mohammed" Google auto-complete suggestions provide suggestions related to Islamic extremism and terrorism. She defines this process as a form of "guilt through algorithmic association," as the search suggestions for Mohammed exemplify how people can be "algorithmically associated with practices, organizations, and concepts that paint them in a problematic light" (boyd, 2011a). Similarly, Eighteen-year-old Safae told me after her friend who covers her hair uploaded a picture on the Dutch social networking site Hyves, somebody sent her a message that stated "*we live in 2010, a headscarf is out-dated, and it's something of the past.*" Thus, digital spaces are not mere mute, neutral and external backdrops of identity formation, but distinct expressive cultures filled with ideologies, hierarchies and politics. These two examples remind us that digital space is not neutral but power-ridden: indeed, new digital divides are constructed this way.

Digital divides

Inequality in/of the Internet has first and foremost been considered with the digital divide metaphor. Scholarship on digital divides initially focused on making visible material divides across static geographic scales and across markers of difference. An uneven geographical distribution in terms of ownership of hardware and access to the Internet was noted: the rich, overdeveloped parts of the world were highly connected, while underdeveloped third countries were disconnected. Ownership and access was also unequally spread across different isolated axes of differentiation: younger and/or white and/or upper-class males were found to be more connected versus older and/or nonwhite and/or lower-class females. Used this way, the term "digital divide" is thus ideologically loaded, particular in its proposal that once the gap is closed, a "computer-revolution" will take place, spreading democracy, promoting equality and potentially ending poverty (Murelli & Okot-Uma, 2002). Emerging in the early 2000s, the second wave of scholarship on the digital divide shifted its focus from access and ownership toward skills and literacies. The gaps between "the information haves" and the "information have-nots" were again purported as operating at geographical and personal markers of difference (Selwyn, 2004). Policy makers and government institutions mobilized resources to provide the information have-nots with the skills for a more egalitarian distribution of knowledge.

Focusing on digital spatial hierarchies and their contestations, using feminist, postcolonial/antiracist, critical geography and Internet studies approaches this book contributes to a new wave of scholarship aiming to situate digital divides in everyday user contexts. There is an urgent need to acknowledge that so-called "have-nots" are people who are embedded in an intersectional web of power relations differentiated along axes including gender, race, religion and generation (Gilbert, 2010). As nonmainstream users, they may possess agency to appropriate digital spaces in order to counter or negotiate exclusion (Leurs, 2015). A grounded and intersectional perspective allows us to move beyond technologically deterministic utopian and dystopian renderings of social media use. On the one hand, promising alternative ways of being and the collapse of difference, postmodernism and neoliberal progress reconciled in a Californian ideology that framed cyberspace as a disembodied, equalizing, liberating, democratizing and empowering world separated from the offline world (Leurs & Ponzanesi, 2011a). On the other side of the spectrum, techno-pessimists have made sweeping dystopian remarks in response to utopian appraisal of the Internet. Most famously, Jaron Lanier warns that digital technologies make us lose democracy, devalue individuality and deaden creativity (2010) and Evgeny Morozov argues Internet activism is a delusion that makes us unable to recognize technologies are used for the purposes of propaganda, manipulation, censorship and surveillance (2011). These two perspectives, however, are not helpful to explain why migrant young people who encounter excluding practices online are still also heavy users.

So-called Web 2.0 Internet applications promise users to become active agents over their own representations. Internet applications such as blogs and SNSs signal the ongoing shift from people being represented by the media to people asserting self-presentation. Internet researchers have reached consensus in seeing the Internet as "an extension of life as it is, in all its dimensions, and all its modalities" (Castells, 2001, p. 118). As more users are promised to have a presence online, scholars need to start acknowledging the inherent unevenness in the ways in which they call all to make a contribution to digital culture (Graham, 2011). Unfortunately, Web 2.0 is no great equalizer, digital territories augment material, fleshy and concrete power relations of offline lives: indeed, "self-representation is actually a condition of participation in Web 2.0" (Thumim, 2012, p. 17). As audience members are increasingly also expected to construct a representation of themselves to sustain a public presence, Nick Couldry asked the question "are changing norms and expectations of presencing generating new types of political repertoire"? (2012, p. 51). The answer is yes, in tandem with offline locations, any digital space should be seen as organized around a durable but not fixed "habitus" of embedded hierarchical divisions (Kvasny, 2005; Freishtat & Sandlin, 2010; Leurs, 2015b; Papacharissi & Easton, 2013).

When considering Internet applications as platforms, their intricate functioning becomes more obvious. As an actual and symbolic stage from where to speak and perform actions, the "platform" is a semantic construct that combines computational and architectural fundaments with socio-cultural and political figurative imaginations (Gillespie, 2010). Digital practices increasingly take place in distinct spaces, resulting in a "platformed sociality" (Van Dijck, 2013, p. 5). Such platforms on the "Internet hails its audiences" in a way that is similar to how nondigital environments are intended for particular groups of people (Nakamura & Lovink, 2005, p. 61). As a result, there is a need to consider not only different levels of access but how through "differentiating practices" some digital identities are relegated to the periphery and some are privileged (Sims, 2013).

Repurposing Pierre Bourdieu's understanding of the habitus, online platforms can be considered as social structures where communities of practice engage in digital practices that cultivate habituated dispositions. Conceptually, a habitus dialectically emerges at the interplay of structure and agency, and continuity and change. In the words of Bourdieu, the habitus emerges around

> systems of durable, transposable dispositions, structured structures predisposed to function as structuring structures, that is, as principles which generate and organize practices and representations that can be objectively adapted to their outcomes without presupposing a conscious aiming at ends or an express mastery of the operations necessary in order to attain them. (Bourdieu, 1977, p. 72)

The user is both the creator and product of their habitus, and micro-politics resides in the individual, subjective strategies of meaning making that may challenge or reproduce organizational principles.

Across online platforms, habituated routines offer users a sense of stability, while everyday sociality is constantly evolving, most notably in the lives of the informants during their dynamic life phase of adolescence. For example, normative behavior on the social networking site Facebook is shaped and disciplined through the habitus of mainstream digital practice "in ways that are similar to the ways they perform in face-to-face interaction – policing the persona and actions of others within the social norms associated with those personas in particular cultural contexts" (Freishtat & Sandlin, 2010, p. 517). In contrast to Bourdieu, scholars have flagged that markers of difference such as gender, race and class impact upon habitual "embedded predispositions" of individuals and coconstruct digital taste preferences (Papacharissi & Easton, 2010, p. 177). However, so far little attention is paid to how these markers intersect in the everyday life of marginalized users across different locations where digital culture is expressed (Gilbert, 2010). The general lack of scrutiny of how intersecting power relations relate to spatial configurations of Internet applications is problematic because digital spaces are not neutral and/or innocent.

Internet platforms as passages

Building on the analogy of Internet platforms as passages and the notion of invasion of space I carve out a middle-ground position to account for how nonmainstream people in their everyday use are hailed and bound by but not fully determined by medium-specific characteristics, commercial incentives and user norms. First I will posit that Walter Benjamin's work on passages can be transposed to theorize social and symbolic meanings attributed to technological developments. In the mid-nineteenth century, arcades or pedestrian passageways ('passages' in French) emerged in Brussels, Bologna and Paris among other places. Historically, the term "arcade" refers to a pedestrian passageway that links two streets. Unlike public space, this glass, iron or brick roofed passage is open at both ends and concentrates a row of commercial establishments (shops, cafés, restaurants) in a small space. In the words of Walter Benjamin, arcades were "the most important architecture of the nineteenth century" (1999, p. 834). In parallel, it can be argued that nowadays, social media platforms play a fundamental role in the daily lives of millions of people.

Benjamin recognized that passages carried an ambivalent meaning, as objects of history they simultaneously contained a "dream and wish image of the collective." He observed the dialectic tension between collective desires and exploitative "ruins." Indeed, Benjamin urged to reflect on the social and technological imaginaries surrounding arcades by assessing whether technology users were truly "emancipated" (1999, p. 115). As a "technical organ of the collective," innovations such as the arcades were imagined as a "new nature": "these images are wish images; in them the collective seeks both to overcome and to transfigure the immaturity of the social product and the inadequacies in the social order." "Caught in a dream," Benjamin added "the new, in order to shape itself visually, always connects its elements with those pertaining to a classless society." The "new nature" furthering utopian imaginings remains "concealed within machines." Instead of these imaginations, Benjamin argued for the figuration of "ambiguity." The role of the arcade is double-faced, as Benjamin exemplifies: "during sudden rainshowers, the arcades are a place of refuge for the unprepared, to whom they offer a secure, if restricted, promenade – one from which the merchants also benefit" (1999, p. 31). Neither skepticism nor evangelism captures the dynamics of passages completely, and Benjamin argued for a consideration of its "constellation saturated of tensions" (1999, p. 475).

Although focused on the scrutiny of economic power relations in a striated modernizing society, the argument can be expanded to account for the ambiguous power relations with regards to politics and culture technologies sometimes conceal. Insights on ambiguous power relations in a modern, democratizing and urban mass society allow us to draw parallels to contemporary forms of exclusion, distinction, and contestation. Similarly in their scrutiny of Internet culture, critical media and feminist theorists have developed a creative, ambiguous middle-ground position between the utopian dreams and dystopian nightmare perspectives that were dominant in writings on digital embodiment, identity, and activism. For example, Judy Wajcman unravels the constellation of gendered technologies from the perspective of "mutual shaping," "where neither gender nor technology is taken to be preexisting, nor is the relationship between them immutable" (2007, p. 287; Van Doorn & Van Zoonen, 2009). In particular, I will empirically sustain how the situated negotiating of hierarchies and inequalities online may be an empowering experience.

Space invader tactics

My middle-ground perspective acknowledges early-twenty-first-century Internet platforms – analogous to nineteenth-century arcades – as ambiguous constellations full of tensions and hierarchies but with room for subversion. Power emerges at the interplay of top-down forces that Michel Foucault described as "the great strategies of geopolitics" and everyday subversion from below which he labels as "little tactics of the habitat" (1980, p. 149). Institutional and corporate power "strategies" may be negotiated by individuals or collectives through potentially subversive everyday life "tactics" (De Certeau, 1984). Accounting for both negative experiences of exclusion and positive experiences of agency and empowerment, digital practices are coconstructed by digital-space-specific user norms, application templates and interface decisions as well as their subversions. Spatial boundaries and hierarchies are not visible to those who can freely flow, they only show when bodies cannot pass and physically or metaphorically bang their head into a wall: "When a category allows us to pass into the world, we might not notice that we inhabit that category. When we are stopped or held up by how we inhabit what we inhabit, then the terms of habitation are revealed to us. We need to rewrite the world from the experience of not being able to pass into the world" (Ahmed, 2012, p. 176). This book documents such experiences as felt among young migrants in the digital realm.

During fieldwork, for instance, it became apparent that in video game culture, the tide of anti-immigrant feelings is perpetuated online. From the experiences of interviewees Ryan and Oussema, I learned that computer game culture is structured by mainstream Dutch normative and habituated ways of being. Fifteen-year-old Oussema shared that he often encounters racism and stigmatization in video games. He explained having similar experiences away from the screen. He mentioned, for instance, being frustrated when seeing people anxiously keep a firm grip on their purses upon encountering him in the supermarket. In the first-person shooter game *Counter-Strike*, players have the opportunity to talk to each other through their headsets and microphones. After saying, "*I am a Moroccan, I am a Muslim*," when asked to introduce himself by people in the game, Oussema sometimes finds ethnic-majority Dutch opponents cursing him out and calling him a "*terrorist*." In contrast, Fifteen-year-old Ryan explains that he feels accepted as a gamer, because he argues he does "*not look like a Moroccan*," in the sense that he is seen as "*very different from what normal Moroccan youth in my school do, they mostly use MSN, YouTube and listen to music*." He feels gaming is more "*Dutch culture*" and it is mostly "*Dutch kids who play games*." He is accepted, as a space invader tactic he backgrounds his Moroccan affiliations during in-game interaction using voice-chat programs like Skype or Teamspeak: "*When I talk I do not appear to be Moroccan*." On his Hyves SNS profile page he also subverts the dominant image of Moroccan-Dutch youth: "*When someone sees me there, they say I do not look like a Moroccan, but obviously I am one, but I do not let it show*." Masking his Moroccanness, Ryan passes as an ethnic-majority Dutch boy.

Ryan's act of passing acts offers self-protection but also reflects his desires to be accepted by the majority group (Sánchez & Schlossberg, 2001). Nakamura notes that "racial impersonation" is a form of passing that "reveals a great deal about how people 'do' race online." However, she argues that passing does keep the foundations of dominant exclusionary, white national identities intact (2002, pp. xvi, 37). The ambivalence of passing is elaborated by postcolonial theorists like Homi Bhabha, who recognizes processes of passing as "mimicry." Mimicry offers camouflage and can become a site of resistance and transgression. The other achieves "partial presence" by passing for something one is not and "becoming a subject of a difference that is almost the same, but not quite" (1994, pp. 122-123). Ryan does so by strategically employing dominant Dutch cultural repertoires and making less visible the ways he diverges from majority norms while emphasizing resemblances. These examples illustrate that digital terrains are hierarchical passageways, they are uneven geographies marked by material, symbolic and affective borders. Young, white, masculine and middle-class bodies participating in mainstream digital spaces produce and occupy certain habituated dispositions, ideal types and mainstream reserved positions, but young migrants can begin to destabilize representational hierarchies by using digital space invader tactics to manifest themselves across different online territories.

2. Digital identity performativity

> *I'm Muslim and all things considered I have decided to wear a headscarf. No one has directed or obliged me to do so, believe it or not, it's out of free will.... I am an adult woman who has tasted from all facets of live, and this is the direction I want to take... I do not force anything upon anyone, I function properly, I adapt myself and participate in Dutch society, but based on the fact that I wear a headscarf, people think they have the right to treat me as a second-rank citizen.... And believe me I do not have to be saved....*
>
> *What one considers as freedom is not the same for everyone. However, how I define it for myself is up to me, and myself only.... The next time when you see a girl, who covers her hair, please consider the other side of the story.... Islamization does not pose a threat to our society, but the growing intolerance against Islam does.*
> – Dunyahenya (2011, my translation)

In this section I theorize agency on the side of migrant youth as space invaders to become active agents in their own representation, for example, through articulating digital ethnic, religious and gender identifications. Above I included a blog post segment written by the Tunisian-Dutch blogger Dunyahenya to introduce how minority youth turn to digital spaces to perform alternative identifications. In her posting Dunyahenya states she is a well-educated conscious woman who has personally chosen to wear a headscarf. She emphasizes she does not need to be saved from Islamic oppression and questions people who take her veil as a pretext to treat her as a second-rank citizen. Dunyahenya publicly wrote about the implications of wearing a headscarf in the context of Dutch society, performing her identity as a young conscious Muslim woman. Being able to author and publish narratives about herself is a significant act for Dunyahenya and other minority youth alike to constitute themselves as specific individual beings. In contemporary multicultural Europe social institutions including the state and public opinion seek to interpellate and "resignify" everyday practices of wearing a headscarf as "inappropriate," reprieving those wearing them "from the power to define their own actions" (Duits & Van Zoonen, 2006, p. 103). miriam cooke coined the neologism "Muslimwoman" to critically reflect on the lumping together of such singular ascribed discourses that deprive female followers of Islam of their individuality, diversity and agency (2007). In the Netherlands, the headscarf is a heavily debated signifier often taken as a symbol that hails Islam as "Other" and that subordinates the subject to the (secularized/Christian) West (Said, 1979). The way its perceived inappropriateness is contested by Dunyahenya lays bare everyday mechanisms of inclusion and exclusion, appropriation and subversion across digital space (Leurs, Hirzalla & Van Zoonen, 2012, pp. 129-130).

Not swayed by the apparent apathy, laziness, and narcissism of young people, nor blaming neoliberal popular culture nor social media entertainment for their lack of interest in top-down parliamentary democracy, I feel it is urgent to consider (digital) identifications as processes with micro-political potential. Namely, it appears that

> most young people are engaged not by the "macropolitics" of politicians, and political parties, which are seen to be dominated by older generations and outdated cultural modes, but by the "micropolitics" of everyday life, single-issue campaigns, and so-called DIY (do-it-yourself) politics. (Banaji & Buckingham, 2013, p. 5)

I feel that this also holds for issues related to multiculturalism and migration in the lives of young people. Therefore, politics is here not taken to refer to the macro perspective of top-down governance of cultural diversity by politicians and policy implementation, but rather the micro-perspective of specifically located, everyday power struggles involved in becoming subjects by performing specific identities.

The micro-politics of everyday life will be considered by drawing on poststructuralist feminist's expansion of "the political" beyond traditional forms of politics. Inspired by the work of Michel Foucault – who has highlighted that "power is everywhere" (1978, p. 93): it is embodied, ubiquitous, distributed, diffuse and multidirectional – in this book I trace politics on the grounded level of subjects performing certain identities. I do so because I feel that identification, as an exercise of power, is a micro-political act, because in one's self-making (although it is not necessarily fully conscious) one can, for example, be held accountable for the ways in which one engages with other-ness and same-ness. The socio-cultural construction of identities is made possible and also bound but not fully determined by discursive frameworks. Following Foucault's approach to power, we can diagnose how subjects are dialectically produced and produce themselves within discursive settings. The room for action resides in between how discourses operate both as restricting power ("*potestas*") and empowering ("*potentia*") (Braidotti, 2006, p. 250). A certain degree of power is held over any subject, and one's action is limited and restricted, but there always remains room for maneuver, resignification and subversion as "points of resistance are present everywhere in the power network" (Foucault, 1978, p. 95).

Micro-politics

Identity stems from the Latin words "*identitas*" and "*idem*" that can be translated as sameness. Simply put, identification is thus an expression of being/feeling the same as someone, something or a community. Identification, however, operates in tandem with difference. Traditionally, reflexive self-making revolved around narrative practices such as, for example, diary writing (Braidotti, 2006, p. 250). Such narratives are constantly updated resulting from changes in one's context and are built on the basis of the choices offered and appropriated, as Anthony Giddens explained: "the reflexive project of the self which consists in the sustaining of coherent, yet continuously revised, biographical narratives, takes place in the context of multiple choice as filtered through abstract systems" (1991, p. 5). Such biographical narratives commonly include "stories that people tell themselves and others about who they are (and who they are not)" (Yuval-Davis, 2006, p. 202).

Children and young people increasingly face "the expectation" of seeking out their own rights and taking responsibility for their biographical "project of the self" (Livingstone, 2002, p. 300) requiring them to act upon and anticipate risks and insecurities in a context of diminishing traditional family and community support. Media play an important role in children and young people's "new responsibility to construct an explicit project of the self" especially because they are expected to "increasingly participate in explicit discourses of identity and identity construction" (Livingstone, 2002, p. 301). For example, Facebook, Twitter, Instagram and What's App mark "the emerging requirement in everyday life to have a public presence beyond one's bodily presence, to construct an objectification of oneself" (Couldry, 2012, p. 50). The recent explosion of social media use, especially among young people, and the constant stream of invitations users receive from platforms (think of Facebook prompting users to post status updates – "What are you doing now?") to make their identities explicit, resonate with the diagnosis Livingstone and Couldry made. The material infrastructure of the Internet has altered the ways in which reflexive narratives are constructed in a networked form of "mass self communication" (Castells, 2009), as online texts are increasingly networked, multimedial and shared with a wider audience.

Identifications performed on digital media platforms are tangible results of micro-political action. Action refers here to the performative power involved in being able to articulate identity alignments, for example, within, across or against axes of ethnicity, class, gender and religion. Following feminist poststructuralist theories on identity performativity, for example, performing gender revolves around a two-fold dynamic: a capacity to bring one's gender identity into being by carrying out (speech and other) acts, while relating to a normative set of prescribed rituals (Leurs & Ponzanesi, 2014a). Seeing the construction of identities and differences as performative acts can be traced back to John Austin, who theorized that speech acts are "doing something rather than simply saying something" (cited in Nunes, 2006, p. 12).

Judith Butler famously deconstructed the category of gender by foregrounding that gender identities are to be understood as something *we do* rather than something *we are*. She argues that identities are constituted through performative acts. There is no preceding or following gendered "I" that exists apart from performativity; rather, people come into existence through a matrix of gender relations. With her notion of performativity, Butler went beyond distinctions between dichotomies of materiality and embodiment. Gender identity performativity is the constitutive stylized repetitious process through which one acquires a gendered subjectivity (Butler, 2003, p. 392). In parallel with gender, "race as an identifier of difference is not in the body but rather made through the bodily acts" (Warren, cited in Rybas & Gajjala, 2007, p. 10). Similarly I understand other axes of differentiation such as class, religion, and generation also as *something people do* by carrying out certain acts, rather than *something they are*. The focus on the doing places emphasis on the dynamic character of identities, or rather identification, as identities are always in process.

In a similar vein, digital identity performativity, then, focuses not only on how identities are visible online but more specifically how they are executed (Cover, 2012). As Nakamura and Chow-White describe with regards to the identity category of race: "users don't just consume images of race when they play video games, interact with software, and program: instead, they perform them" (ibid., p. 8). Digital identity performativity is a "way of doing things" (ibid., pp. 8-9). By composing a nickname, posting a status update or making a profile photo people perform actions that bring into being race, gender and religious identities. Through digital identity performativity, such as liking a Facebook page dedicated to rap music a networked process is triggered that works as a "transformation" "transformation of some others into unlikeness ('not like me') and other others into likeness ('like me') (Ahmed, 2004, p. 355).

Intersectionality

In order to be able to make a meaningful cartography of situated digital identity performativity, it is important not to single out singular axes of identification such as ethnicity, diaspora or gender, but rather look at how they intersect across online/offline spaces (Gilbert, 2010). Migrant youth navigate a complex trajectory of belongings, as Meenakshi Durham explains

> the psychological transition of adolescence, already charged in terms of gender and sexuality is then imbricated with the conundrums of the other transition – the diaspora identity that demands delicate negotiations of race/ethnicity, nation, class, language, culture and history. (2004, p. 141)

Although I mention researching second-generation migrant youth, it is my intention not to separate out Moroccan-Dutch youth in order to reify a set of their stable essentialist traits. Rather, by taking an intersectional approach I take seriously the political value-ladenness of the label. This is necessary in order to be able to deconstruct, destabilize and make the label more porous. Making an intervention in dominant cultural essentialisms, it is my intention to uncover the variety of different positionalities, ambiguities and contrasts hidden behind the seemingly singular and closed-off category of Moroccan-Dutchness.

As a feminist theory and methodology, the perspective of intersectionality allows for a thorough analysis of the dialectic of oppression and empowerment in such multilayered identity-construction processes. Aimee Rowe (2008) developed intersectional theory in the field of communication studies, arguing that intersectionality allows one to scrutinize the "politics of relation." She argues that "differential belonging" or who/what people relate to is political. For example, she notes, when transracial alliances are formed across power lines of difference, "coalitional subjectivities" emerge (ibid., pp. 8, 15). In practice, intersectional thinking urges me to be reflexive and strategic in considering which connections to attend to, when, how and why. To explore the negotiation of multiple intersecting categories of difference the aim is to "situate subjects within the full network of relationships that define their social locations" while also pushing to "uncover the differences and complexities of experience embodied in that location" (McCall, 2005, p. 1781-1782). Digital identification practices, emergent from positionality and relationality, provide a window on everyday micro-politics. Online, identity performativity often becomes an explicit manifestation of the politics of relation, as connections within, across and against we-ness and otherness are published in the form of tweets, status updates and nicknames.

In sum, guided by intersectionality I can consider how identities are "embodied" digitally as material practices, "shifting, altering and realigning on a regular basis, and situated within multiple discourses of gender, race, ethnicity and sexuality" (Nayar, 2010, p. 81). Turning back to Dunyahenya's blog entry, "Muslimness," "Tunisian-Dutchness" and "womanness" are not social categories she possesses, but they result from the process of her (online) interaction with multiple, hyphenated communities of practice and engagement with normative expectations of in/appropriateness. Considering digital identities from the perspective of performativity and intersectionality sharpens the focus on differential representation and acknowledges how digital experiences of migrant youth may be empowering and restricting vis-à-vis the habitus of the platform in question. In the final section below, I specify what digital identities are made of.

Digital identities: Materiality, representation & affectivity

Digital identities are both material, representational and affectively felt performative connections articulated in distinct social media platforms. Throughout the book, my intersectional cartography of digital identity performativity unpacks "interlocking conditions of identity" by addressing "the symbolic, material, and affective connections through which a subject engages a particular discourse" (Hahner, 2012, p. 147).

Firstly, in contrast to the early myth of the Internet being somehow immaterial, I incorporate a "digital-materialist" perspective to consider "new media objects as material assemblages of hardware, software, and wetware" (Boomen et al., 2012, pp. 10-13). The material building blocks of digital identities demand a medium-specific analysis of the materiality of "digital infrastructure," "contents" and "context" (Miller & Horst, 2012, p. 25). Automated and user-generated data, algorithms, protocols, interfaces and default settings are examples how digital material works as "techno-cultural constructs" and "socioeconomic structures" (Van Dijck, 2013, p. 28). Together, these coconstruct the "affordances" of digital media platforms. Usually, especially when working smoothly, affordances remain invisible – black-boxed – in the experience of users, but as boyd emphasizes: "the architecture of a particular environment matters" (boyd, 2011b, p. 39). She adds, "affordances do not dictate participant's behavior, but they do configure the environment in a way that shapes participant's engagement" (ibid.). Affordances do not determine specific practices, but they do allow a specific radius of action, in terms of infrastructures, contents (hyperlinks, text, images, videos, audio) as well as contexts. These affordances are specific constellations of material characteristics (opportunities and limitations posed by interface properties), user cultures (how these properties are appropriated), perceptions (how affordances are experienced) and wider ideological processes of meaning making (norms that shape dominant discourses) (boyd, 2011b; Zhao et al., 2013). For example, users have negotiated the affordances of SNSs that blurred boundaries between private and public space for innovative forms of identity construction (Papacharissi, 2010).

Not in a linear or causal way, but certain material medium-specific configurations may hold a specific appeal for young people in comparison with adults, or migrants in comparison with nonmigrants. For example, young people find themselves in a state of becoming, beyond childhood; they have yet to reach the autonomy of adulthood. Digital platforms have become key spaces for young people to explore questions of identity, belonging and autonomy and to experiment with romantic relationships and sexuality (boyd, 2014). Scholars have, for example, recognized how social media have given new meaning to psycho-developmental "modes of adolescent connectivity" such as private self-identity formation and public social identity formation – these two resonate very well with private messaging and social networking, respectively (Boneva et al., 2006, p. 202). The concept of "polymedia" is useful to account for choices migrants make between technologies on the basis of the material, social, emotional and moral dimensions, for purposes such as transnational connectivity, the maintenance of relationships and identification (Madianou & Miller, 2012).

Secondly, in their tactics to negotiate infrastructural affordances, users coshape the representational symbolic content circulating on digital platforms. The generation of representational data results from "implicit" and "explicit" user participation (Schäfer, 2011). "Implicit" participation refers to the automated generation of data resulting from user action that is channeled by design and "explicit" user participation refers to how users become subjects as they use tactics to negotiate their presence on their own terms (Schäfer, 2011, p. 51). It is therefore of chief importance to "meld close interface analysis with issues of identity": the implications of medium-specific affordances and restrictions need to speak back to critical theories of cultural difference to raise more awareness of underlying ideologies (Nakamura, 2006, p. 35).

The construction of an online profile on, for example, a SNS is often "menu-driven" (Nakamura, 2002, p. 104). When designing a computer game avatar, users often have to choose from a restricted set of facial and bodily features, creating a "normative virtual body," which is "generally white, conventionally physically attractive, as well as traditionally gendered, with male and female bodies extremely different in appearance" (Nakamura, 2011, p. 338). SNSs are visually dominated by "Western standards of beauty" and the heterosexual male gaze persists: similar to offline space, digital space is "dominated by patriarchal, heteronormative belief, fueled by heterosexual masculine fantasy" (Donnelly, 2011, p. 174). Upon introduction, a new application such as the weblog is often discursively constructed as masculine and adult, marginalizing the activities of women and youth, while racialized bodies are still mostly absent as active agents in popular accounts of our globalized techno-cultural world, strengthening the myth of the technological lag of minorities (Everett, 2009, p. 133). Chicanos living in the Mexican-United States borderlands are, for example, often perceived in mainstream discourse as somehow being "culturally handicapped," displaying a "cultural unfitness" to handle technologies and contribute to digital cultures (Gómez-Peña, 2000, pp. 80-81). Indeed, it is important to remain aware of the "unequal (racialized, gendered) social life of information and its technologies where Euro-American 'sites' control the lives, labors, and identities of non-white races across the world" (Nayar, 2010, p. 162). The Eurocentric, Western and white ideologies that guide programming decisions and impact upon representational practices are profit-driven interventions that seek to monetize user-generated content (Schäfer, 2011; Gillespie, 2010; Andrejevic, 2011; Shepherd, 2014).

Thirdly, nonetheless, as space invaders nonmainstream users such as migrant youth continue to use these Internet applications. The #bornhere selfies posted in response to Wilders, transnational communication or the feeling that online one can be among likeminded people in a space of one's own (see Chapter 2 on forum discussions) illustrate positive affective experiences users have in articulating digital identifications. Affectivity is used here to address the ways in which interactions on a computer screen trigger certain responses in the body of a user. By being affected the emotional state of the user may change. In other words, affect concerns "the passage from one experiential state of the body to another," resulting from an encounter with another body, technology or text (Massumi in Deleuze & Guattari, 2004, p. xvii), while emotion "is the biographically specific meaning ascribed" to that passage (Jones, Jackson & Rhys-Taylor, 2014, p. 2). In particular, affect is produced through three interrelated processes: (1) *circulation*, which affect flows through people, text and objects across online and offline space, (2) *accumulation*, the affective sensation that grows through repetition, and (3) *endurance*, affective responses that can stick to people, texts and objects (Ahmed, 2004, pp. 45, 46, 91). In sum, digital identity performativity can therefore be considered as a multispatial process, taking place within and across socially produced spaces, each with their own habitus formed around their own material, representational and affective dynamics.

3. Moroccan-Dutchness in the context of the Netherlands

Migrant youth seeking to find their place in Europe have to negotiate public suspicions resulting from recent claims about the failure of multiculturalism, anti-immigration sentiments, Islamophobia and fears over urban unrest and riots. Perhaps an excessive example, Wilders's supporters shouting "less Moroccans" during a local election discussed in the opening of the chapter does illustrate the recent "Dutch backlash against multiculturalism," as policies and public opinion have shifted from toleration to repression (Prins & Saharso, 2010). In the Netherlands and elsewhere, parts of the majority population feel threatened by changes in their lives brought about by the forces of globalization that include migration, computerization, neoliberalism, increasing corporate influence, financial instability, consumerism and individualism (Essed & Hoving, 2014). Ethnic strife arises when ethnic-majority groups grow a "fear of small numbers" by distrusting newcomers and bestowing negative meanings upon ethnic minorities (Appadurai, 2006). Immigrant integration has steadily advanced, but Dutch discourse does hardly reflect such facts (Entzinger, 2014). This process can be explained because globalization cannot be countered "but you can attack minorities" (Jaikumar, 2011, p. 235). As Baukje Prins put it "the essential trait of Dutch identity is assumed to be its non-identity, its fluidity, its openness to 'others'." However, she added,

> by assuming that Dutchness is an unmarked (but actually Western, Dutch, white, etc.) category, a subject position that does not strike the eye because it does not differ from modern culture in general, it turns out to coincide with what is considered the norm or normal. Hence, everything non-Dutch gets marked as "other," as different from the norm. (Prins 1997, p. 126)

In the Netherlands, Moroccan-Dutch youth receive a lot of attention in media reporting, governmental policy making and scholarly research.

They are systematically stigmatized and made hyper visible by right-wing journalists and politicians, who frame them as anticitizens that pose a threat to Dutch society (Harchaoui & Huinder, 2003, pp. 7-11; Poorthuis & Salemink, 2011). Prior academic research has predominantly focused on elements of the so-called "Moroccan drama" (Jurgens, 2007), singling out issues like juvenile delinquency, radicalization, mental health problems and early school leaving. Of course, these issues are undeniably important and significant, but they present a narrow understanding of Moroccan-Dutchness. Things are going well for the majority of Moroccan-Dutch youth, but their realities remain largely invisible in contemporary debates. This study aims to contribute to an emerging strand of scholarship that considers everyday experiences of migrant youth in the Netherlands.

The first and most dominant strand of scholarship concerns juvenile delinquency and the overrepresentation of boys of Moroccan-Dutch descent in nuisance and petty crimes (e.g., Van Gemert, 1998; Werdmölder, 2005; De Jong, 2007). Secondly, anti-immigration politicians such as Geert Wilders emphasize that the traditions of the Netherlands, based on secularized Christian-Judaist belief systems are colliding with Islam. Islamic radicalization, in particular, is presented as a major concern after the murder of the controversial Dutch filmmaker Theo van Gogh by radical Moroccan-Dutch Muslim Mohammed Bouyeri in 2004, an event that can be understood in the wider context of Islamic fundamentalist attacks across the United States and Europe, including the September 11, 2001, attacks on the World Trade Center in New York City. The Muslim minority population is specifically singled out, as the Dutch researchers' focus is mostly on Islam and not on other religious extremisms (e.g., Slootman & Tilly, 2006). Recently, sensationalist media attention for the Charlie Hebdo murders in Paris (France), the arrest of home-grown Jihadi terrorists in Verviers (Belgium) and Dutch Muslims traveling to Syria and Iraq to fight for the Islamic State (IS) caliphate has added fuel to the fire. The study of mental health problems is a third focus. Second-generation Moroccan-Dutch youth are found to be at risk, as they have a greater chance of developing schizophrenia in comparison with ethnic-majority Dutch youth. Stress caused by stigmatization and culture/language barriers faced in Dutch society as well as specific Moroccan cultural, religious and societal factors are taken to explain this discrepancy. Scholars add that Dutch mental health institutions experience difficulties reaching Moroccan-Dutch people (e.g., Veen et al., 2010; Liberman & Williams, 2010). The fourth theme, early school leaving, concerns studies on uneven unemployment rates, problems in education and reliance on social security benefits (e.g., Heering & ter Bekke, 2008).

These studies all emphasize specific problems that pertain to a small segment of the Moroccan-Dutch community. Playing into the hands of Dutch right-wing anti-immigration parties when taken out of their contexts, these studies may be taken to paint a negative picture of the community as a whole. Scholars with other results have a difficulty of being heard, for instance, Frans Verhagen argues that in contrast to the dominant views of the failed integration of immigrants, the generation of descendants of migrants born in the Netherlands are rapidly advancing toward Dutch national averages in terms of education, language, employment, religion, marriage and birth figures (2010). Indeed, the rhetoric does not correspond with Dutch social reality; as a matter of fact, there is a "growing gap between facts and discourse on immigrant integration in the Netherlands" (Entzinger, 2014, p. 693). A focus on negative depictions may not only foster feelings of unbelonging but may also further worsen the situation by installing disproportionate anxieties over the Moroccan-Dutch community.

This book adds to a new strand of scholarship that aims to capture the rich textures of the everyday lives of Moroccan-Dutch young people. In this strand researchers have, for example, examined parenting styles and socialization patterns (Pels & De Haan, 2003, 2007), coming of age (Ketner, 2010), home making (Stock, 2014), gender relations (Buitelaar, 2007), religiosity (Nabben, Yeşilgöz & Korf, 2006), urban language accents (Nortier & Dorleijn, 2008), the popularity of kick boxing among girls (Rana, 2011), music and youth culture (Gazzah, 2009) and Internet use (Brouwer, 2006a). Below, I further deconstruct the label of "Moroccan-Dutchness" to provide a situated account of the experiences that informants may have.

Deconstructing labels

The category "Moroccan-Dutchness" needs to be unpacked carefully to recognize it is not an ahistorical, homogeneous, singular label. In this book, second-generation Moroccan-Dutch youth are considered as active agents, but I realize "agency is not individual, it is relational." For example, "children's actions and choices are codependent on the lives of others, particularly their family members" (Scott, 2014, p. 419). The social categories of ethnicity, language, gender, social stratification, education, living conditions, generation and religion may intersect very differently. Moroccan-Dutch people are the second-largest minority group in the Netherlands, following those of Turkish-Dutch background. With 374,996 people, the Moroccan-Dutch community amounts to 2.2% of the total Dutch population of 16.7 million (CBS, 2014a). Of this group, 45% migrated to the Netherlands from the 1960s onward as guest workers, while the other 55% were born in the Netherlands, after their parents had migrated (CBS, 2014a).

The 1960s form an important turning point in Dutch migration history, as the focus on colonial migration shifted toward guest workers the Dutch government recruited from various Mediterranean countries (Meijer et al., 2005, pp. vi-vii; Verweij & Bijl, 2012, p. 239). In the early 60s guest workers included Spaniards, Italians and Greeks mostly, while from the early 1970s, Turks and Moroccans outnumbered them. Estimates of the total number of Moroccans living in the diaspora range between 2.5 and 7 million (Loukili, 2007, p. 3). Both Moroccan migrants and the Dutch government expected guest workers to return to their countries of origin after working for a number of years. Especially after the 1973 oil crisis, guest workers increasingly sought to reunite with their family members in the Netherlands. Various factors played a role, such as: having a job while the economic forecasts in their countries of origin looked bleak; getting better accustomed to Dutch life and accruing more rights and realizing they would not be able to return back to the Netherlands upon their departure (Verweij & Bijl, 2012, p. 241).

The majority of guest workers who arrived in the Netherlands originate from the northern Morocco Rif area. They come from places like Al Hoceima, Berkane, Nador and Oujda and their surroundings where a Berber language is spoken.[4] Currently, 75% of Dutch people of Moroccan decent have ties with the Rif area. In Morocco, Berber languages hold an inferior status to the institutional Moroccan-Arabic (Darija) and French – a colonial remnant – that are dominantly used in urbanized parts of the country.[5] The Moroccan-Dutch population thus consists of Moroccan Berbers and non-Berbers, speaking a combination of a Berber language and/or French and/or Moroccan-Arabic and/or Dutch. The first language of their Dutch-born children is primarily Dutch (Cottaar & Bouras, 2009; Gazzah, 2010, p. 311).

4 Berber languages include Riffian/Tarafit spoken in the northern Rif Mountains, Tashelhit in the High Atlas and Anti Atlas in southern Morocco and Tamazight in the Middle Atlas in Eastern Morocco.

5 Since the seventh century Arab invasion in Morocco that brought Sunni Islam to Morocco, Amazigh cultures and languages have been marginalized by its rulers and authorities (Immigration and Refugee Board of Canada, 2000). Mohamed VI, the present king of Morocco, improved Morocco's human rights record and sought to expand the boundaries to what constitutes Moroccan national identity. Recognizing Amazigh as an official state language next to Arabic, he underlined Berbers are an integral part of the Moroccan social fabric (Maddy-Weitzman, 2011, p. 157).

Moroccan guest workers were mostly hired as manual laborers in factories, mines, harbors, textile industry and road construction, accepting jobs of low socio-economic status. The situation is slowly improving among their children, but Moroccan-Dutch people on average tend to live in small houses in relatively segregated, socially and economically deprived neighborhoods compared to the average in the Netherlands (Cottaar & Bouras, 2009; Van Praag & Schoorl, 2008). Moroccan-Dutch women on average also have more children in comparison with ethnic-majority Dutch women, although the generations born in the Netherlands have fewer children in comparison with those who migrated to the Netherlands (Schoorl, 2006, p. 9).

Nearly 50% of the second-generation youth obtain secondary education, and it must be emphasized that this is a remarkable accomplishment when considering a significant number of their parents were illiterate farmers who generally had received little schooling (CBS, 2012, p. 66; De Valk & Crul, 2008, p. 84). However, the educational achievements among Moroccan-Dutch youth are lower in comparison with ethnic-majority Dutch youth at this point. Dutch institutional structures, racist views as well as in-group dynamics form major obstacles to the educational development of Moroccan-Dutch students (Leurs & Ponzanesi, 2014b). Poor second-language training, together with particular selection mechanisms result in the fact that a majority of Moroccan-Dutch students are consigned to short, mostly vocational school tracks (CBS, 2012, pp. 75, 82). Unemployment is high among those graduating from these school tracks and Moroccan-Dutch youngsters are hard hit by discrimination in the labor market (Crul & Doomernik, 2003): youth unemployment in the among Moroccan-Dutch youth aged fifteen to twenty-four is a disproportionate 37% in comparison with one in ten among ethnic-majority Dutch youth (Dagevos, Huijnk & Gijsberts, 2014, p. 183).

It has been assumed that Moroccan-Dutch girls perform better in schools in comparison with Moroccan-Dutch boys (Verhagen, 2010, p. 220). In the last years, the number of Moroccan-Dutch girls graduating from educational tracks preparing for higher education and universities is growing at a faster pace in comparison with graduation rates of Moroccan-Dutch boys (CBS, 2014c). The schooling and employment dynamic is complicated further as Moroccan-Dutch fatherhood and motherhood have been found to sometimes operate a gendered "double standard" in the socialization of their children. Daughters are encouraged to pursue an education and to enter the job market but simultaneously parents are sometimes recognized to hold on to the male breadwinner model (Pels & De Haan, 2003, 2007).

Unpacking gender relations further, Moroccan parents are said to emphasize cultural and religious dictums of modesty especially toward their daughters, as boys are traditionally allowed a "wider radius of action outside the house" at the onset of puberty. Generational specificity is thus also gendered, as Moroccan-Dutch girls are sometimes seen as gatekeepers "to maintaining the family honour," and, Trees Pels and Mariëtte de Haan added, as "they still face the most restrictions, and they spend much of their leisure time with female family members and friends in domestic settings" (2003, pp. 52-61). Moroccan-Dutch parents are sometimes found to be more prohibitive about direct contact with the opposite sex than ethnic-majority Dutch parents. Under the supervision of their parents this contact may be monitored, for girls this may imply they have to avoid bringing shame on themselves in the presence of boys, "i.e. to behave timidly and modestly and to refrain from any looseness in appearance or expression" (Pels & De Haan, 2003, p. 58). Similarly, Moroccan-Dutch and Turkish-Dutch girls often spend a small amount of their spare time outdoors in public spaces, in contrast to Moroccan-Dutch boys who spend a lot of their time there (Nabben, Yeşilgöz & Korf, 2006, p. 27).

This observation has parallels with gendered spatial practices in Morocco. In Morocco, gender norms historically hierarchically govern space: "[S]pace boundaries divide Muslim society into subuniverses: the universe of men (the *umma*, the world of religion and power) and the universe of women, the domestic world of sexuality and the family" (Mernissi, 1987, p. 138). Although the situation is changing, Fatima Sadiqi notes these observations still hold as gender relations dichotomously structure space in Morocco, where public space (such as the street) is reiterated as masculine, as opposed to the private space of feminine domesticity (such as the kitchen) (2003, pp. 85-86).

Perhaps because they spend more time indoors, Moroccan-Dutch girls have been found to turn to the Internet more than boys (Nabben, Yeşilgöz & Korf, 2006, p. 46). Digital technologies are used among descendants of migrants to reinvent traditions while simultaneously seeking to assert their independence and circumvent family norms (Brouwer, 2006a; De Leeuw & Rydin, 2007; Green & Kabir, 2012, pp. 100-101; Alinejad, 2013). Coming of age concurrently with digital media, the literature suggests that these young people in their articulation of digital identities can subvert the gendered reputation-management dichotomy of masculine public versus feminine private space (Graiouid, 2005). Moroccan-Dutch girls sometimes lack access to outdoor informal meeting places, and scholars have observed that the Internet may offer viable alternatives.

In her study on Moroccan-Dutch girls' use of online discussion forums, Lenie Brouwer argues that these "girls are more restricted in their freedom of movement than boys, and thus, the Internet widens their horizons" (2006a). The broadening of their horizon occurs at the crossroads between cultural and religious concerns of their parents and the gendered norms and expectations of contemporary Dutch and global youth culture. For instance, in their dress, Moroccan-Dutch girls are expected to carve out a middle-ground position in choosing from the "headscarf" and "porno chic" clothes that dominate the wider spectrum of youth and fashion in the Netherlands (Duits & Van Zoonen, 2006). Moroccan-Dutch girls have been found to draw upon "multicultural capital" in negotiating chastity, virginity and obedience toward parents cherished within "Moroccan circles" and the peer norms of ethnic-majority Dutch youth. Moroccan-Dutch youth born in the diaspora in general have been found to stake out a middle ground between the specificities of "Dutch individualistic society" and "the collectivistic values" which are said to characterize "Moroccan" or "Islamic culture" (D'Haenens et al., 2004, pp. 73-74; see also Buitelaar, 2007; Leurs & Ponzanesi, 2014c). Finally, it must be noted that in comparison with the other major ethnic-minority communities in the Netherlands, a recent study found Moroccan-Dutch people are the "happiest," they largely feel "healthy," "at home in the Netherlands," "not often discriminated against" and are positive about "identifying with their country of origin" (CBS, 2014d; see also Gokdemir & Dumludag, 2011).

The rise of political Islam in majority Muslim countries, the September 11, 2001, attacks in New York City, and the growing visibility of Islam in Europe and the Netherlands "contributed not only to the sudden realization of the Dutch that their country now hosted a substantial number of Muslims, but also the identification of these migrants in religious, rather than ethnic terms. As a result, their culture was also understood and defined as essentially Islamic" (Peters, 2006, p. 3). However, although the majority of Moroccan-Dutch people present themselves as Muslim, the way religiosity is practiced differs widely. Descendants of Moroccan migrants attach less importance to the religious origins of their parents (Maliepaard, Lubbers & Gijsberts, 2010, p. 466-468; Phalet & ter Wal, 2004, p. 39). Islamic religious practices are becoming a more individual, symbolic and affective experience among Moroccan-Dutch youth (Leurs & Ponzanesi, 2014c).

A growing number of young people do not actively practice their religiosity by carrying out religious rituals or visiting mosques but they perform being Muslim as a part of their identity. Islam is performed as a "cool" cultural imaginary (Boubekeur, 2005, p. 12), which gets united with youth cultural music styles such as rap (LeVine, 2008). Islam is used as a cultural repertoire to give music, fashion, food and lifestyles "an Islamic touch" (Gazzah, 2009, p. 413). Islam is also a source of political struggle. Moroccan-Dutch girls have reportedly chosen to wear a headscarf in response to the politicization of Islam in the Netherlands (Gazzah, 2010, p. 312; Nabben, Yeşilgöz & Korf, 2006). In a recent survey among Muslim girls in the Netherlands, nine out of ten respondents stated to have proudly chosen to wear a headscarf, and one-third reported their headscarf is a "fashion statement" (Knaap, Stoepker & Wegloop, 2011, p. 40). Muslim women stake out their identities vis-à-vis two general prejudiced discourses that seek to discipline them (Piela, 2012, pp. 2-3). In the (neo)Orientalist discourse, Muslim women, especially those wearing the hijab, are represented as backward, irrational, silent and subjugated by Muslim male oppressors (Said, 1979; Afshar, 2008). In the conservative patriarchal Islamist discourse, women are also essentialized, albeit differently. This latter discourse foregrounds the role reserved for Western women as sex objects and places it in contrast to the rights granted to Muslim women within their families by Islam (Piela, 2012).

A focus on everyday practices offers much-needed nuance. For example, sixteen-year-old Naoul shared: "*I follow my own path.*" Similarly Loubna, a fourteen-year-old interviewee, illustrates that sweeping remarks should be treated with caution. She reports a variety of experiences in her personal autonomy and radius of action: "*In terms of culture, my background is Moroccan, but I do go out and visit the cinema, I go to the city and buy clothes. Those are things I also love.*" Digital practices allow for innovative negotiations of the specific intersection of gender, religiosity and generation experienced among second-generation migrant youth, as is evident from the Meryam's narrative:

> *I was born and raised here in the Netherlands, but my father emigrated to the Netherlands together with my grandfather when he was eighteen years old. He has taken Moroccan customs to the Netherlands and he uses them here. I think the habits of my parents are just very old-fashioned, even though they do try to learn the customs of the Netherlands. My parents were raised much stricter in terms of religion. My parents do teach me many things about our belief, but most of the time I go on and look up things about Islam myself. This is different from what they did: listening to the stories of their parents and copying those.*

Thus, it is impossible to speak of a singular and homogeneous label of Moroccan-Dutchness, as various divisional lines position individuals differently.

Similarly, I recognize that the ethnic-majority label of "Dutchness" must also be critically unpacked to reveal its constructedness around notions of Calvinism, secularized Judeo-Christian traditions, the Dutch language and whiteness (Essed & Hoving, 2014). The fierce debates spurred by a recent speech delivered by Dutch Princess Máxima, born in Argentina, reveal that the category of Dutchness is neither ahistorical nor homogeneous. In the speech she spoke about her personal search to find "the Dutch identity." Causing controversy she stated "*the* Dutch identity, however? No, I didn't find it." Rather, she emphasized her multilayered identity: "I have different loyalties and I am a citizen of the world, a European and a Dutchwoman" and claims "human identity and affiliation cannot be fenced off." She concludes by stating "the Netherlands is too complex to sum up in one cliché."[6] Princess Máxima was strongly criticized for claiming – from an elite position – that there is no singular, bounded Dutch identity. Having the luxury to be able to define her own position, she first deconstructs Dutchness and subsequently chooses her own categories. Criticizing Máxima's speech, right-wing anti-immigration politicians expressed their fears over Muslim migrants not assimilating enough into "the Dutch national identity" and changing the traditional fabric of Dutch society.[7]

6 These excerpts were taken from a speech Princess Máxima delivered on September 24, 2007, to celebrate the release of a study on Dutch national identities by the Scientific Council for Government Policy (WRR). In her speech, she foregrounds that people do not embody a singular Dutch identity but they rather identify with the Netherlands, a process that "leaves room for development. And for diversity." She explains her view by arguing her personal identification is multilayered: "I do not know what it is like to be a Dutchwoman.... Buenos Aires, New York, Brussels, The Hague, Wassenaar.... Different places and the people who live there have become a part of my life." She also stressed the economic potential of an ethnically diverse society. She emphasized the point that people in the Netherlands think too much according to divisional lines: "Birds of a feather flock together. But the Netherlands is not like the zoo Artis [Artis in Amsterdam is the oldest Animal zoo in the Netherlands]. Diversity and mixing give us strength" (my translations from Dutch, RVD, 2007).

7 Critiques of this speech also mark the gradual demise of earlier Dutch multicultural policies oriented toward welcoming newcomers by allowing them to retain their cultural heritage. Initially, different cultural affiliations were not seen as conflicting with one's ability to integrate and participate in Dutch society. Neorealist politicians dismissed this policy as a failure. Proponents of the earlier policies were increasingly framed as elite politicians who were unable to recognize the concerns and fears of "the Dutch people" about "strangers." The years between 1950 and 1970 have been recognized as a period of nonintervention. From the 1980s onward multiculturalism policies of "integration while retaining one's own culture" were oriented toward emancipation by improving the social, economic and legal positions of migrants. Policies have changed and newcomers now have to abide by strict requirements; they are increasingly forced to assimilate and relegate their ethnic/religious migrant cultural

In sum, in this section I argued labels such as "Moroccan-Dutch" and "Dutch" are inherently political and emerge from a variety of intersecting interests, including race, ethnicity, religion, gender and generation. Although Princess Máxima pointed at their socially constructed fabric, categories are often strategically used as each other's opposites. The terms are used to normalize a particular set of hierarchical power relations – for instance, right-wing anti-Islam politicians define ethnic-majority Dutchness by emphasizing that Islam cannot be a part of it. The power of definition is used to create an opposition between Dutchness and Islam.

4. The transnational habitus of second-generation migrant youth: From roots to routes

> Although this is still an underresearched topic, it is to be expected that studies of migrant children's use of ICTs will reflect the particular circumstances of the child as a young person growing up in a family and struggling to assert their independence.
>
> – Lelia Green & Nahid Kabir (2012, p. 101)

In this section I focus on how second-generation migrant youth use digital media to form a particular "transnational habitus" (Nedelcu, 2012) shaped by their parents who migrated themselves but also shaped by the society in which they grow up. Transnationalism is not a "one-generation phenomenon" (Mainsah, 2011, p. 203), rather the second generation develops distinct cultural repertoires, skill sets and social networks needed to navigate their local and transnational social fields (Levitt, 2009; Wessendorfer, 2013). Studies on acculturation show that people who have migrated themselves are primarily focused on acquiring a solid social-economic position, while identity issues play a large role for their descendants (Berry, Phinney, Sam & Vedder, 2006). However, in contrast to claims made by anti-immigrant politicians, having transnational connections do not mean migrants are excluded from their local host society: multiple identifications can be combined, "belonging, loyalty and sense of attachment are not parts of a zero-sum game based on a single place" (Vertovec, 2009, p. 78). Migrants' digital media use exemplifies this two-folded dynamic. Once understood

heritages to the private domain (Prins, 2010; see also Scheffer, 2007; Van der Stoep, 2009; Verweij & Bijl, 2012, pp. 240-245).

as doubly absent, as migrants were said to be not here, nor there (Sayad, 1999), they are noted to benefit from networking opportunities, allowing them to become "connected migrants"; enabled "to be here and there at the same time" they maintain local connections and connections with elsewhere (Diminescu, 2008, p. 572). In *ICT for the Social and Economic Integration of Migrants into Europe* Christiano Codagnone and Stefano Kluzer note that digital technologies "provide no 'magic bullet' solution to social exclusion" but more importantly, the authors empirically sustain the "mixed embeddedness" of many ethnic minorities that suggest technologies are both used as "bonding" social capital to link up with "coethnics" across the host society and diaspora, as well as "bridging" social capital to connect across communities (2011, pp. 10-12). This book provides further proof that second-generation migrant youth use ICTs to develop a "transnational habitus" that is distinct from their parents. Although they can be expected to socially reproduce to a great extent their parental dispositions, there are also many generation-specific "mechanisms through which migrants manage multiplicity and develop transnational and cosmopolitan skills whether emotional, analytical, creative, communication or functional" (Nedelcu, 2012, pp. 1345-1346). In particular, I focus on the generation-specific ways of being and culturally constructed social dispositions that include transnational engagements across large distances but also include local orientations toward cosmopolitan cohabitation.

On a theoretical level, combining orientations toward elsewheres as well as local contexts implies migrants have to balance two modes of cultural identification. The first mode includes cultural identification with one's "roots" (Gilroy, 1993a): a cohesive collective of coethnics, vital for feeling a sense of community belonging:

> The first position defines 'cultural identity' in terms of one, shared culture, a sort of collective 'one true self'.... within the terms of this definition, our cultural identities reflect our common historical experiences and shared cultural codes which provide us, as "one people," with stable, unchanging and continuous frames of reference and meaning, beneath the shifting divisions and vicissitudes of actual history. (Hall, 1990, p. 223)

"Routes," the second mode, acknowledges the processual character of cultural identification shaped by active encounters (Gilroy, 1993a). "Identity, in this second sense, is a matter of 'becoming' as well as of 'being.' It belongs to the future as much as the past. It is not something which already exists, transcending place, time, history and culture" (Hall, 1990, p. 225).

Transnational communication practices illustrate the workings of cultural identification with one's roots. These practices of dispersed people networking across distance have received most attention from media, communication and migration scholars. A pioneering study by Daniel Miller and Don Slater focused on the Trinidadian diaspora. They describe how "de Rumshop Lime," a collective online chat room, was used by young people at home and abroad to "lime," meaning to chat and hang out (2000, p. 88). Subsequently, for example, transnational communication among Basque (Oiarzabal, 2013), Chinese (Parker & Song, 2009), Greek (Georgiou, 2006), Filipino (Madianou & Miller, 2012), Indian (Mallapragada, 2006), Inuit (Christensen, 2003), Italian (Wessendorfer, 2013), Mexican (Byrne, 2008), Nigerian (Everett, 2009), Romanian (Nedelcu, 2009; Trandafoiu, 2013); Somali (Leurs, 2014a) and South Asian migrants (Gajjalla & Gajjala, 2008; Mitra, 2004) have been documented.

During my fieldwork, fourteen-year-old Loubna described how her whole family lives in Tetouan, northern Morocco, except members of her household and her two nephews. "*I cannot do without Morocco*" she shared. "*Everyday*" she has contact with her family members in Morocco. Together with her mother and siblings she sits in front of the computer: "*We talk to them using Skype, especially now that my grandmother is ill.*" Loubna and her household use Skype to sympathize with family members in the diaspora. Such practices are indicative of "ICT-mediated ordinary copresence routines" that enable transnational emotional support and care (Nedelcu & Wyss, forthcoming 2016). Copresence routines may affectively sustain feelings of "ontological security," a stable sense of continuous everyday being which provides "confidence" in "self-identity" (Giddens, 1990, p. 92). Myria Georgiou, in her study of transnational television viewing among Arab speakers in Europe, expressed that migrant "individuals have increasingly grounded their sense of ontological security on relational networks, which are often dislocated from the immediate locality" (2012, p. 307). Everyday affective forms of digital connectivity may become an emotional resource in the lives of migrants as they may accrue value in the form of "transnational affective capital" (Leurs, 2014a). It should be added that transnational communication, however, is appreciated mostly as a cheap and easy way of making do with difficulties involved in living at distance. It is not felt as a proper replacement for physically attending significant life events such births, deaths and weddings. Interestingly however, most informants did not engage in transnational communication themselves. Badr, a fourteen-year-old boy, explained his family has migrated from Morocco to countries across Europe, including Belgium, Germany, France, Spain and Denmark.

He described how he sometimes talks to his nephews who live in Belgium and Germany, but mostly his parents make use of Skype to talk to family members in the diaspora. They do not know how the program works, so he assists them in setting up the connection. Transnational communication was especially prevalent among parents and those interviewees who were themselves born in Morocco.

Second-generation migrants add a routed layer to transnationalism. Routed diaspora identifications result from ongoing processes "of movement and mediation" (Gilroy, 1993a, p. 19). Descendants of migrants appropriate transnationalism that can be symbolized and, for example, be digitally circulated as distinct markers of identification (Leurs & Ponzanesi, 2011b). For example, South Asian-Americans (and Brits), Japanese-Peruvian and Moroccan-Dutch youth branding themselves as "Desi," "Nikkei" and "Mocro," respectively, signal symbolic transnational affiliations grounded in their (nationally and globally) situated contexts. These affiliations do not concern actual transnational communication practices but concern symbolic representations of transnational diaspora ties: diaspora aesthetics. In the YouTube video *You Are Not an Indian*, Pharag Khanna describes the self-branding label of Desi: "You do not know the backstreets of Karachi or Bombay. Chances are if you go over there, they treat you as an American. You like to think of yourself as an Indian, but you are not, you are Desi, you are of South Asia not from South Asia" (Mallapragada, 2006). Youth of South Asian descent in the United States and the United Kingdom have been found to identify with the label "Desi" (Maira, 2002). Translated from Sanskrit, the word means "those from the homeland" (Mallapragada, 2006, p. 217). Instead of, or next to, having Skype conversations with South Asians in the diaspora, youth of South Asian origins living outside South Asia identify as Desi. Young people include the term "Desi" in their nicknames on social networking sites like Facebook, Instagram and Twitter. Others consume "Desi" youth cultural products such as music by M.I.A., the Sri Lankan Tamil urban recording artist from the UK. Secondly; the label "Nikkei" directs our attention to Japanese migrant youth in the diaspora.[8] Shana Aoyama found that the social networking site Hi5.com is taken up in Peru by young people of Japanese descent as an avenue for identity construction using the label

8 The word "Nikkei" originally related to a particular generation of Japanese-descended person in diaspora, at least in North America, terms like "Isei" and "Nikkei" refer to specific generations. There, Nikkei has a particular resonance inseparable from the experience in internment camps. However, over time and across space, the meaning of the term has been extended.

"Nikkei." She found both group confirmation based on the performance of Nikkei-ness as well as expressions of individuality (2007).

Similar to Desis and Nikkei, "Mocro" refers to another expression of binational consciousness. Mocros initiated a new branch in urban youth culture in Europe. Above I mentioned the term "Mocro" was used as one of the hashtags in the #bornhere Twitter campaign alongside tags like #proudmoroccan. The term was incorporated within mainstream Dutch youth culture After Ali B., a Moroccan-Dutch hip-hop recording artist, released a music single in 2005 called *Crazy Mocro Flavour* that reached the higher levels of Dutch music charts. The term "Mocro" originated on the streets of the Netherlands during the late 1990s and is now commonly seen as a Dutch honorary nickname for people of Moroccan-Dutch descent. "Moker," "Maroc" and "Mocro" are Moroccan-Dutch self-identification labels that are commonly used online (Boumans, 2002, p. 15). For instance, Amir, a sixteen-year-old informant, is a hip-hop fanatic who listens to Moroccan-Dutch artists like Ali B., Yes-R, Ree B. and Soesi B. He self-identifies as "Mocro"; in his e-mail address, for example, he combines his first name with the word "Mocro." Similarly, fifteen-year-old Meryam includes "mocrogirl" in her e-mail address. Across digital spaces like the Dutch social networking site Hyves and the discussion forum Marokko.nl, users go by nicknames such as "My own Mocro styly," "Mocro-licious," "Mocro-boy" and "Miss_MocroLady." A cursory glance at such nicknames displays how "Mocro" itself is often also already multilayered, as the term is often combined with age, gender, sexual preference, religious, sport, music, and generationally specific cultural affiliations. Chapter 3 further examines nicknaming practices from the perspective of intersectional digital identity performativity.

Desi-ness, Mocro-ness, and Nikkei-ness are common collective identification markers that are not just straightforward nationalisms. They refer back to different homelands, while simultaneously they also clearly mark one's situation of being routed outside of this homeland. Digital diasporas may no longer be understood simply in terms of having transnational conversations with people in the diaspora. Those born in the diaspora engage in digital practices of branding themselves by circulating diaspora aesthetics, which reshuffle traditional understandings of origin and belonging. Contemporary youthful digital diaspora identifications are therefore far more complex in their engagement with digital media than most existing theory allows: connections are hybridized, and affiliations are turned into practices of branding diaspora consciousness. When taken up, these labels signal in-between or "liminal" positions (Bhabha, 1994).

In postcolonial studies, in-between positions are recognized as a source of differential and multivocal cultural production. Liminal positions, for example, increasingly leave their mark on transnationally circulating cultural objects, such as food, cinema, music, and fashion. Second-generation Desi, Mocro and Nikkei youth, in their cultural production and identity constructions, innovatively articulate new imaged forms of digital diasporas. Digital diasporas can no longer solely be understood simply only in terms of how migrants connect to a clearly marked transnational community. Indeed, a contemporary understanding of diasporas and transnationalisms pays attention "to actual physical migration but makes room also for imagined, discursive, material, cultural, virtual and socially networked places and travels" (Knott, 2010, p. 79). Second-generation migrant youth are imagining affiliations through context-specific transnational representations of diaspora branding, which reshuffle traditional understandings of origin and belonging. Such networked branding includes expressing diaspora identities that are communal and individual but also situated locally, transnationally and globally. Their diaspora aesthetics are also shaped by multicultural encounters in the wider domain of global youth culture.

5. Hypertextual selves: Digital conviviality

As the cultural identifications among second-generation migrant youth are increasingly "routed" in their local, transnational and global contexts, the question arises to what they identify across cultural differences, and, in particular, how they do so using digital media? With this book, I aim to emphasize the societal and academic significance of analyzing youth cultures and digital space by zooming in on the everyday "conviviality" of cohabitation, bottom-up multiculturalism that understands "multiculture [as] an ordinary feature of social life" (Gilroy, 2005, p. xv). Youth cultures, in particular, are political since they foster hybridity at the crossroads of local, transnational and global orientations. Also, being organized around age and generation, youth cultures may challenge "the logic of racial, national and ethnic essentialism" (Gilroy, 1993b, p. 6). Beyond state-managed attempts at antiracism, everyday youth cultural interactions between people of different backgrounds may showcase conviviality and cosmopolitanism, generating potential for contesting racism and nationalism.

As is the case for most migrants, most of the informants live in urban centers in the Netherlands. As cities are always in process, subject to flows of people, goods, ideas, money, etc., its inhabitants have to learn to live together with people unlike them. City dwellers have to make do with living in the copresence and close proximity of racial, religious and cultural others. Building on Doreen Massey's concept, they have to negotiate a situation of "throwntogetherness": urban space can be characterized by the "contemporaneous existence of a plurality of trajectories," as inhabitants claim their position in the city, cultural difference is present in an intense "simultaneity of stories-so-far" (Massey, 2005, p. 11). As cultural identification increasingly takes place both offline and online, we can expect that online too a situation of "digital throwntogetherness" (Leurs, 2014b) will have to be negotiated. As personal trajectories are increasingly digitized, a great variety of stories is published across social media platforms by a growingly diverse user base. Therefore the micro-politics of presence, encounter and cultural difference also increasingly takes place online.

6. Structure of the book

The rationale of this book is to present a cartography of the performative practices of identification of Moroccan-Dutch youth across four different Internet field sites. In each of the four case studies one platform is singled out and grasped through a conceptual lens to account for the specificities of digital cultural identification processes and habituated dispositions of that particular space. Throughout the analyses, points of overlap, convergences, as well as differences across the spaces are noted. Following the preferences of the Moroccan-Dutch informants, four favorite spaces were chosen for analysis: forums, instant messaging, social networking sites and video-sharing platforms. The chapters are arranged in chronological order, the use of online discussion forums originated in the early 1990s, instant messaging began to take off in the mid-1990s, social networking sites became popular from the early 2000s onward, while video-sharing platforms like YouTube became fashionable after 2005. The emergence of a new platform did not lead to the fall of older applications, and the informants frequent these different digital territories next to one another. The four field sites do not exist in isolation but are inextricably connected. User practices travel and intertextually borrow from one another, facilitated by their digital formatting that include visual, textual and audio content and forms.

By emphasizing specificities of digital practices within and across these platforms, the continuities and changes that digital identity performances undergo over time and space are laid bare. My multispatial approach to identification therefore explores the different dimensions to how

Moroccan-Dutch youth become space invaders as they are positioned and interpellated but also strategically and tactically take up resources across applications to make multiaxial identity claims. Acknowledging that space invasion can be both a positive and negative experience, the case studies give more body to the middle ground perspective acknowledging digital identifications as specifically spatially hailed, situated and articulated.

In Chapter 1, methodological considerations are given and the empirical research process will be demystified. By outlining the creative collision of different methodological approaches I will locate myself within the continuum of social scientists' empiricism and humanities scholars' postmodern rejections of essentialism. Using quantitative and qualitative methods, different accounts of everyday identification through digital media use can be gathered. More specifically I introduce the decisions made and difficulties encountered in gathering and triangulating different sorts of empirical data. I combine large-scale surveys, in-depth interviews and observations of digital practices. These different partial, situated and contingent accounts allow me to construct a nuanced study. In the chapter I will present a reflexive account of the power relations I experienced. I will elaborate upon my efforts to avoid the pitfalls of speaking for the young informants and explain how I study digital practices and performativity of self with them.

In Chapter 2 I will argue how message boards such as Marokko.nl and Chaima.nl are taken up to narrate collective voices and identities. These discussion boards are used to maintain a national network of Moroccan-Dutch youth. The chapter zooms in on how informants discuss their gender, ethnic and religious positioning. First I consider the specific appeal among girls by considering how message boards are taken up to negotiate gendered issues of love, relationships, marriage and sexuality. Second, I consider what informants say about their experiences of power in reflecting and articulating their collective voice with regards to the situation of the Moroccan community in the Netherlands. Considering message boards as viable "subaltern counterpublics," these semi-hidden discursive safe zones display how hegemonic views are contested. Third, message boards are recognized as communicative spaces used to dynamically perform versions of Islam.

Chapter 3 provides a window into the private identities and personal engagements of Moroccan-Dutch teens with their peers on instant messaging (IM). Instant messaging remains a relatively understudied and undertheorized social media technology because data gathering within this private space is not straightforward. The medium-specificity of IM is recognized to structure the performativity of self both with display names in view of a full audience of contacts through which informants communicate communal ethnic, gender and youth cultural belongings to people they have added to their friend lists and as an under-the-radar activity of one-on-one chat conversations through which they articulate their individual, private and intimate identity expressions.

In Chapter 4 the focus is on selfies and hypertextual identifications on social networking sites. The chapter zooms in on two dimensions of visual representation. I address first how and why social networking site profile photos are imbued with gender and sexuality. As a way to brand the self, the particular ways of showing that get encouraged in profile photos signal specific power relations and expose forms of patriarchal subordination. Additionally I consider how hyperlinking – as a way to signal affiliations – offers the means to represent one's multiple self and belongingness. Hypertext is taken as an optic through which to address questions of identity differentiation and multicultural encounter. The perspective of hypertextual selves is elaborated further to innovatively map the ways in which Moroccan-Dutch youth mobilize various linked resources. Beyond institutional policies of multiculturalism, hypertextual selves exemplify how multiculture is a feature in young people's everyday conviviality of cohabitation.

In Chapter 5, the focus will be on affective dimensions of identification observable in interviewees' consumption of YouTube videos. In particular, the preference for two genres of YouTube youth culture will be considered. First, the affective engagement with diasporic videos shot in Morocco is unpacked. I discern the emotional workings of these videos as a form of affective transnational networking. Subsequently, accepting that viewing practices open up diverse subject positions, corporate music video clips are interpreted as resources to land global, transnational and national youth cultural flows. The analysis of the affective geographies of belonging the informants negotiate while watching YouTube videos presents another invocation of how identities become distributed, challenging essentialist representations of Moroccan-Dutch youth.

In the concluding chapter I synthesize the main findings, and consider broader consequences of quotidian multispatial digital cultural identification processes of Moroccan-Dutch youth. While navigating their selfhood between conflicting youth cultural, familial, gendered, religious and ethno-cultural motivations, digital practices expand the parameters of their social and physical worlds. By exploring whether digital forms of emancipation that I located in various corners of the Internet also cross over to the majorities in Dutch society, I consider wider implications for thinking about digital multiculturalism.

1. Methodological trajectory

> All scientific knowledge is always, in every respect, socially situated. Neither knowers nor the knowledge they produce are or could be impartial, disinterested, value-free, Archimedean. The challenge is to articulate how it is that knowledge has a socially situated character.
>
> – Sandra Harding (1991, p. 11)

Digital Passages develops the notion of space invaders to theorize migrant youth's identities in the context of digital spatial power relations; empirically analyze digital identification through spatial(izing) processes; and nuance understandings of digital multiculturalism. Below, I focus on space invaders as a mode of empirical analysis by reflecting on my methodological framework. Researching "digitally mediated identities" has especially been noted benefiting from a reflective "epistemology of doing" (Rybas & Gajjala, 2007). As part of my "everyday feminist research praxis" I aim to be transparent and reflexive (Leurs & Olivieri, 2014). In this chapter, I situate the knowledge I have produced and reflect on the power relations at play at the different stages of research. Philosophers of science and feminist theorists have lain bare that all academic paradigms have their own epistemologies, norms, procedures, expectations and assumptions of validity (Kuhn, 1970). Objects of study are constructed in specific ways by the theories and methods used to describe them, and thus knowledge is always situated, positioned and the result of a relational process (Haraway, 1988; Harding, 1991).

Pursuing "methodological cosmopolitanism" as a starting point in order to be able to acknowledge "the varieties of modernity and their global interdependencies," it was my aim to move beyond "methodological nationalism" (Beck & Grande, 2010). In particular, I have taken a mixed-methods approach, drawing from recent developments in "creative" (Gauntlett & Holzwarth, 2006), "participatory" (Gubrium & Harper, 2013) and "digital" (Rogers, 2013) methods. I join differently situated, but complementary "partial views" (Haraway, 1991, p. 183) on digital identification processes building on three subsequent phases of fieldwork conducted between fall 2009 and fall 2013: (1) quantitative survey data, (2) qualitative in-depth interviewing and (3) a virtual ethnography.

Table 1: Time frame of different fieldwork activities

Fieldwork activity	Period
Pilot in-depth interviews	Fall 2009
Pilot online surveys	Fall 2009
Pilot virtual ethnography: gathering instant messaging transcripts	December 2009-January 2010
Online survey in schools	Spring – Fall 2010
In-depth interviews	Fall 2010 – Spring 2011
Virtual ethnography	Fall 2011 – Fall 2012
Follow-up interviews	Fall 2011 – Fall 2013

The fieldwork was conducted in the context of Wired Up (www.uu.nl/wiredup), a high-potential Utrecht University board-funded interdisciplinary research project. It brought together humanities and social science scholars to study digital identification, learning and socialization of Moroccan-Dutch and Turkish-Dutch migrant youth in the Netherlands and Mexican-American migrant youth in the US. The survey was developed and conducted with team members, while the subsequent phases of fieldwork were my sole responsibility. The Utrecht University Faculty of Social Science WMO committee, which protects the rights of respondents under the Dutch Medical Research Involving Human Subjects Act, provided preapproval of the Wired Up fieldwork setup. With this preapproval, the study was exempted from other medical-ethical committee assessment. The temporality of data generation (see Table 1) will be addressed throughout the following chapters, by considering "what the Internet was like for these users at the time when the data were produced" (Hine, 2013, p. 83).

The structure of the chapter chronologically follows the fieldwork process. First, in Section 1.1, I reflect on the collision between quantitative and qualitative approaches. In Section 1.2, I reflect on developing, conducting and analyzing the large-scale survey in the context of the Wired Up research project. In Section 1.3, the dynamics of in-depth interviewing are considered, and I discuss the virtual ethnography in Section 1.4. In Section 1.5, I describe the politics of translation and introduce my approach to discursive analysis.

1.1 Empiricism versus constructivism

In this section, I locate myself within the continuum between hard-boiled empiricism and postmodern rejections of essentialism by outlining my creative collision of these different methodological approaches. When contrasting both fields, it can be noted that empiricist researchers hold positivist premises: by following a set of guidelines reality can successfully be captured in its essence. Following the key conventions of "good research" (rationality, verifiability, objectivity, falsifiability, reliability, generalization, large-scale quantification, neutrality and value-freeness of the researcher), a singular truth can be found (Griffin, 2011, p. 97). Quantitative social scientists maintain strict methodological procedures to ensure their research meets these standards. Empiricist epistemologies are dominant in scholarly knowledge production and they largely frame what constitutes valid knowledge.

Poststructuralist critical theorists operate on the other side of the spectrum. This humanities paradigm rejects empiricism and positivist truth claims for their essentializing tendencies. Building on critical philosophies of language, the epistemology of this tradition points to the social construction of knowledge. Scholars following its rules often do qualitative work that is attuned to theorizing the specific; they carry out in-depth critical close readings. At the level of micro-politics, they study how subjects come into being through multiple including and excluding discourses. Some, however, tend to black box their methodological considerations, making it appear as if their theoretical knowledge arises from unguided interpretation. For example, critical scholars in the humanities "have remained surprisingly silent about what it is that they do to achieve these results" (Griffin, 2011, p. 92).[1] However, a number of criteria can be distilled from this branch of research: interdisciplinarity, plausibility, reflexivity, and comprehensiveness (Griffin, 2011; see also Harding, 1991; Haraway, 1988; Buikema, 2009).

A dualism has emerged, opposing quantitative, positivist and empirical with qualitative, constructivist, theory-driven approaches (Lawson, 1995). Lorraine Code explains "quantification is still esteemed as the best method for achieving certain knowledge": objective, value-free, rigorous and hard quantitative methods are seen as superior scientific ideals, while theory-driven qualitative research is "frequently marginalized and dismissed as 'unscientific'" (1991, p. 160). Quantitative research is defined against qualitative research, a process through which the latter gets projected as mere opinion generating through subjective, irrational, flexible and soft interpretative methods. For instance, in some quantitative-oriented fields the use of "I" in publications is dismissed as an inferior style that conveys

1 Note for instance the lack of attention or blackboxing of methodologies in humanities doctoral dissertations or the absence of special sections on methodology in humanities journals.

subjectivity. However, poststructuralist feminist researchers, too, have perpetuated the dualism, dismissing quantitative methods as masculinist scientific rigor, which is ironic "because feminist scholarship has critiqued or broken apart many other dualisms in order to expose the process of othering that reinforces power relations" (Lawson, 1995, p. 451; see also Ramazanoğlu and Holland, 2002, pp. 28, 162). Negotiating the duality between positivism and reliability vis-à-vis social constructivism and relativism can be seen as a "greasy pole" dilemma: it is difficult to climb a pole while grasping both ends. One way to overcome this duality by articulating "partial visions" and situating produced knowledge (Haraway, 1991, p. 188). Quantitative and qualitative approaches to research are, however, not necessarily purely dichotomous, incompatible and/or mutually exclusive epistemologies.

Rather than seeing the two epistemologies as mutually exclusive, I strategically take an in-between position and make use of tools from both, while remaining sympathetic to the politics of feminism to locate and promote the transformation of social injustices. The quantitative data will be presented as descriptive information for contextualization purposes.[2] As such, this study is grounded within a normative framework to assess gendered, racial and other societal injustices. I explicitly want to avoid giving the impression that I am able to solve the tensions between the different epistemological traditions that I tap into. Instead I give a personal account of how I navigated between them, what my resources were and why and how I made certain decisions. Using survey, interview and virtual ethnography data enables me to join multiple considerations of the everyday digital experiences and identification of Moroccan-Dutch youth. Triangulating these different partial, situated and contingent accounts allows me to construct a multiperspectival and thus more nuanced study.

In this chapter, the value, dynamics and implications of the various approaches used are discussed. Quantitative and qualitative methods have their pros and cons: "[s]urveys are highly formal and standardized (we should be able to anticipate all pertinent questions); while fieldwork/ethnographic methods are informal and open to unexpected data (indicating little control over events)" (Lobe, Livingstone, Olafsson & Simões, 2008, p. 6). My combination of these approaches emphasizes the unconventional side of the study.

Indicative of my "everyday feminist research praxis" (Leurs & Olivieri, 2014), I mix methods that originate from different epistemological traditions,

2 Detailed statistical analyses such as correlation measurements go beyond the descriptives used in my argumentation; for such details, see Wired Up (2011).

but as a red thread I hold on to critical and reflective principles from feminist and postcolonial poststructuralist traditions. Although I take several participatory initiatives to share the power of definition and interpretation (Gubrium & Harper, 2013), I believe asymmetrical power relations between the researchers and the researched are impossible to be completely bridged. I depend on informants to share their voices to produce knowledge, but as the author, I have a final say. Below I account for how power relations impacted upon the different phases of the research, showing also how these relations do, however, not always remain purely oppositional.

1.2 The Wired Up survey

Knowledge always presents a view "from somewhere" (Haraway, 1991, p. 195), and feminists and critical scholars "can count from somewhere too" (Lawson, 1995, p. 452). The value of quantification for this study resides in its capacity to be able to map out trends and patterns in digital media practices of Moroccan-Dutch youth. These trends and patterns provide a solid focus for my subsequent in-depth interviewing and virtual ethnography. Survey research is a method for systematically collecting and analyzing social data via detailed and highly structured questionnaires in order to obtain information from large numbers of respondents presumed to be representative of a specific population. From early spring to late fall 2010, a survey sample of 1,408 secondary school students was established among seven schools in the Netherlands. After a Wired Up team member gave instructions, students were surveyed in a computer lab in their school. Most survey rounds took 30 to 50 minutes.

In this section I first reconstruct the development of the Wired Up survey and reflect on the power relations of survey research. Subsequently I describe the survey sampling procedure and reconstruct how we were able to secure access to respondents in seven secondary schools. Next, I reflect on administering the survey, before describing general personal dynamics and (digital) media use patterns among the group of Moroccan-Dutch survey participants that shaped subsequent research phases of interviewing and digital data gathering.

Constructing the survey

The Wired Up research project was conceptualized so that its eight group members (three project leaders: Mariëtte de Haan, Kevin Leander and

Sandra Ponzanesi; three postdoctoral researchers: Fleur Prinsen, Fadi Hirzalla and Lisa Schwartz; and two doctoral students: Asli Ünlüsoy and myself) would be able to make specific use of a collectively gathered central database of survey data. The survey document reached its final shape after an extensive, one-and-a-half-year-long process of negotiation, because it had to meet different research goals that ranged across different humanities disciplines such as gender and media studies and social science disciplines such as pedagogical sciences and learning sciences. Various stakes, expectations and requirements impacted differently upon its development, complicating and slowing down its conception. The survey was developed to learn more about how three key issues (identity, networking and informal learning) were practiced and experienced digitally among ethnic-majority Dutch, Moroccan-Dutch and Turkish-Dutch young people.

The survey approach was chosen to systematically produce generalizable data about digital identity, networking and learning among Dutch majority and ethnic-minority youth in the Netherlands. With the survey we aimed to make possible comparisons to find out about differences and similarities between groups, for instance, in terms of ethnicity, and within groups, for instance, in terms of gender. However, the three foci (identity, networking and informal learning) each demanded a particular emphasis in the survey. The latter two themes proposed by the social science members of Wired Up were oriented toward learning more about the potential of ego-networks for networked learning (Ünlüsoy, De Haan & Leander, 2012; De Haan, Leander, Ünlüsoy, Prinsen, 2014; Prinsen, De Haan & Leander, 2015). The theme of identity proposed by humanities members of the project was more geared toward capturing digitally mediated representational practices, such as self-profiling activities on social networking sites. Attention to person-to-person networking and learning with representational identity practices provide multisided, complementary views. However, reconciling these foci proved difficult, especially given the tight time constraints of a survey bounded by the short attention span of young people.

While reviewing the literature and searching for prior survey constructs we learned that our intended combination had never been brought together before. In particular, quantitative studies that go beyond addressing digital divides in terms of material access among young ethnic minorities users proved difficult to find: "empirical studies have not tended to survey users about their production of Internet content" (Nakamura, 2008, p. 177). Earlier and more traditional survey-based research primarily focuses on material access and patterns of media use (what applications are used and how often). In line with my plea to become attentive to uneven contributions to digital culture – this approach was extended to capture how young users continue their offline life online including socializing, seeking out and profiling their identities, finding information, building online networks, and learning from others. The final survey document consisted of six sections: the first section was designed to capture media use frequencies. The second section covered the conditions under which Internet use took place. The third section focused on identity markers. In the fourth section, learning and producing content was covered. In the fifth section, a number of socio-demographic indicators were covered. The final section built on a social network analysis (SNA) approach to study networking practices with five online contacts (see Leurs, 2012, pp. 313-324, to review the survey document).

Trained in new media studies and gender studies, I had to translate my interests in digital identity performativity into closed, formal, standardized questions to successfully meet the norms and principles of quantitative survey research. Many of my assumptions were principally theoretically informed but not empirically sustained elsewhere. Developing pioneering survey questions proved especially difficult when having to anticipate all questions and answers beforehand, therefore pragmatic solutions were sought. As I chose to focus in my study on the articulation of identities across digital media spaces, the survey would at least have to capture where young people move online. For the purpose of being able to map out spatial practices, a survey question was included in Section 1 that asked (using a timescale) the respondent's frequency of use of a selection of different platforms and applications. Also an open question was added to allow respondents to add other spaces they visit. Forming an additional indicator of importance, respondents were asked (using a three-point scale) to what extent they would miss the different Internet applications if they were not able to visit them anymore.

Section 2 covererd the context of digital practices, eliciting information on privacy, control, autonomy and freedom. Although the study approaches digital spaces as an extension of the offline world, I remained interested in the potentially transformative dynamics of the Internet. Therefore, respondents were, for instance, invited to answer whether there were topics they would rather talk about on the Internet than elsewhere.

Section 3 of the survey was designed to capture digital identification practices. I chose to focus on asking respondents what identity markers they upload on their personal profile pages. Presenting a list of items that I constructed on the basis of self-profiling options offered on Hyves and Facebook and member-checking during piloting, respondents were asked to answer what items they normally publish on their profile page. Respondents were also asked with what youth groups they identify. I sought ways to empirically capture multilayered identity construction, so multiple answers were possible for all questions in this section. The specific interests in "roots" and "routes" and the two-fold character of cultural and diaspora identification (Hall, 1990; Gilroy, 1993a) were translated into questions that captured the national, transnational and global dimensions of identification. Respondents were invited to think about whether they put up affiliations with food (Dutch food and/or migrant food and/or global food), celebrities (Dutch celebrities and/or migrant celebrities and/or global celebrities) and music (Dutch music and/or migrant background music and/or global music) on their personal profile page. Besides the ethnic specificities of their Internet-related activities, I intended to uncover gendered particularities. Therefore, respondents were, for instance, asked to choose, from a list of (gendered) self-presentational labels, three answers to reflect upon how they would show themselves in their display photo in order to be liked by their friends.

In order to make sure our survey would be attractive to youthful respondents, the decision was made to develop an online survey, making use of NetQ survey software. Online surveys have the advantage that they generate digital data that can readily be imported in data analysis software packages such as SPSS, and they allow for complex routing and skipping systems, enabling the respondent to participate in an inviting, individualized questionnaire. There are also disadvantages, as the survey software demanded us to translate our ideas in specific ways. We were, for instance, bound to the interface structure, but the option to include HTML and CSS programming enabled for a degree of flexibility. We had to make sure the survey would be understandable, largely self-explanatory but also attractive for students ranging from 12 to 18 years old. It was a complex task to design the survey in such a way so that it successfully addressed the youngest respondents without putting off segments of our intended older audiences. Furthermore, as we experienced during our extensive piloting phase and survey taking, it is difficult to design an online questionnaire that appears identical on different screens. Although screen resolutions, Internet browser settings and Internet transmission speeds differ, we sought for ways to present all respondents with a similar set of questions and survey design. This meant designing an accessible survey interface, with a clearly legible font, font color and template. We also had to make sure that questions would fit on different screens, even when they would be loaded on the smaller screens of laptops or even smartphones.

The power of definition

Asymmetrical power relations can be noted in the survey research process. The survey instrument steers respondents in a particular fixed direction and Wired Up team members held the power to define the answer categories with which respondents had to make do. However, respondents were invited to take an active part in the development of the survey. During periods of intensive piloting, the opinions of young people from the target population were gathered. An initial set of ideas, questions and multiple-choice answer categories was adjusted on the basis of feedback of a large group of young people who evaluated our questionnaire. In a first round, each survey question was discussed with fifteen young people individually. They were asked whether the questions and answer categories were clear, whether they missed answer categories and whether they understood the structure of the survey. Also their impressions of the length of survey were taken into consideration. Subsequently, the question-and-answer categories were refined on the basis of the first test round were checked with a group of twenty young people in a second piloting round. Respondents were involved in the realization of the survey; however, during the actual data collection, the instrument was not open to changes. Being temporarily fixed in this way, the survey forced respondents to squeeze their personal experiences and views in the offered answer categories as offered.

The following exchange I had with fifteen-year-old Ryan during one of the interviews reveals that respondents strategically manage the impression they want to make in giving answers:

> ***Ryan:*** *I thought to myself it was a bit of a boring survey.... but now all of a sudden there is an interview and I know it is taken very seriously....*
> ***Koen:*** *OK, well, because we have had a look at what kind of answers people have given.*
> ***Ryan:*** *Yes, yes, I have also given very genuine answers, I mean it!*
> ***Koen:*** *Because, of course, we can see from the results when people gave nonsense answers.*
> ***Ryan:*** *But, say with the question, "How much do you use the computer per day?"*
> ***Koen:*** *Yes?*
> ***Ryan:*** *I use the computer a lot, but in my answering I acted as if I don't use it so much. I did not want to show myself as a nerd or freak. You know, I did these kinds of things.... I admit.... I have lowered the time [in my answers on usage frequencies].*

Although the respondents, like Ryan, seized such opportunities to negotiate their presentation of self (Goffman, 1959), in the end, together with other Wired Up team members; I exercise definitional power when analyzing their answers. Aggregating data while controlling for and/or disregarding unreliable answers, I have the privilege of the final say over their representation. Constituting particular research subjects through categorizing, defining and naming practices is an inherently political and power-ridden process, because reality is structured according to a certain set of visions of the world (Foucault, 1980). It is our decision to choose what to represent and what to leave unnamed in the survey, and the analysis is guided by my personal decisions. Similar processes of naming occur during the interviewing and discursive analysis phases of the research as I make selections and inevitably hear and focus upon particular things, while ignoring and excluding others. In the following section, I continue my discussion of the Wired Up survey by describing the stratified sampling method and securing access to the research population.

Survey sampling and access

Given Wired Up's special research interests, the aim was to generate a sample with substantial groups of respondents stretching across ethnic-majority Dutch and ethnically diverse backgrounds.[3] For reasons of practicality, stratified sampling was chosen and schools with ethnically diverse student populations within roughly 1.5 hours of public transport travel from Utrecht were invited, creating a dataset with nearly one-third ethnic-majority Dutch young people and a remainder of ethnic-minority Dutch youth. We diversified the sample with regard to age, gender and education level. The average age of our respondents was 14.5 years and a little over half of them (53%) were

3 The Centre for Financial Institutions (CFI) is a Dutch Ministry of Education, Culture and Science organization that produces yearly overviews of student populations of all secondary education institutions in the Netherlands. The Centre also maintains overviews of ethnic compositions of schools. Although this data allowed us to decide which schools would be of interest for our research, their listings also need to be problematized. In the files CFI provided, figures are given for categorizations of people such as "%Autochth." for "Autochthonous," "%West." for "Westerners," "%Turk." for "Turkish," "%Moroc." for "Moroccan," "%Suri" for "Surinamese," "%Antil." for "Antillean," "%Nw-oth" for "New others" "%Unk" for "Unknown" (my translations from Dutch). These labels are value laden and politically charged. They are problematic in the sense that they do not allow room for any cultural hybridization, and they deny groups of people their Dutch nationality and identification. In addition, a binary opposition is created by listing Western students on one side of the line (that do not ask for further scrutiny) and on the other side of the line those who do not fit the category of "Western" are specified and separated out along national affiliations.

female. Some 52% of the respondents were following a lower preparatory school for secondary vocational training (Voorbereidend Middelbaar Beroeps Onderwijs, VMBO); 17% of the respondents were attending higher preparatory school for secondary vocational training (Voorbereidend Middelbaar Beroeps Onderwijs-Theoretisch, VMBO-T); 16% were attending general secondary education, preparing for vocational university (Hoger Algemeen Voortgezet Onderwijs, HAVO); and 13% of the respondents were attending academic secondary school, preparing for academic learning (Voorbereidend Wetenschappelijk Onderwijs, VWO, or *gymnasium*), which matches by and large the distribution of school tracks in the country (Wired Up, 2011, p. 9).

For this purpose, from late spring 2009 onward, twenty-five schools were invited to join our study. Contacts were established in four phases, starting with letters and e-mails, followed up with telephone calls and school visits. Eventually, after an extensive period of conversation and negotiation, the directors of seven schools granted us access to conduct our survey. This number includes two schools in both Utrecht and Amsterdam and individual schools in Gouda, 's-Hertogenbosch and Rotterdam. Access to schools was hindered and delayed by a heavy dose of research fatigue voiced by school directors, management and teachers. The rejection given by one Rotterdam school principal sums up the problem well:

Many thanks for your request to participate in the Wired Up research project.

However, we cannot join the project. The number of requests to carry out questionnaires, research, and projects is enormous with next to no advantages for school, or students. Also it still remains an invasion in our organization time and time again. The pressure from the [education] inspection to achieve good results continues unabated, and that thus remains our highest priority. There is no room for other affairs that do not support us in carrying out our educational program.

The Wired Up team took this feedback to heart, recognizing the vital importance of establishing a strong relationship with all communities involved, and ensuring not only the research team but participants too would be able to benefit from the study. For this reason, school directors, teachers and students received an explanation of the relevance of our research when inviting them to participate in our study, and in return we also asked what we could mean for everyone involved. Thus we aimed to take into account not only our own goals, but also ways to acknowledge how our research could become valuable for those participating as well. The school directors and teachers of all seven schools that participated emphasized that researchers cause severe disruptions to school dynamics upon every entry. It turned out that a large part of the research fatigue we noticed among gatekeepers when contacting schools appeared to have grown from frustrations with previous "hit-and-run" academics. Many researchers had entered their school communities to conveniently gather large data sets by administering questionnaires to their students, but after their departure they were never heard from again.

In dialogue with school directors and teachers, it was agreed that in return for granting the Wired Up team access to schools; we would communicate back our survey findings. For this purpose, seven school reports were written that contextualized and compared practices observed in individual schools with the other participating schools. The reports provided an overview of the state of the art of digital media practices in terms of networking, identification and learning among the students of the specific school. Also, the implications of digital practices captured in the survey for teaching purposes were sketched out. School directors, management and teachers were the intended audience for these school-specific reports. Some schools invited us to present the implications of the survey findings in a discussion meeting frequented by teachers and educators. Results were also communicated back to the students who participated in the survey themselves. Visually stimulating, oversized posters were printed to present students with a number of key characteristics, such as school-specific gender differences in frequency and attachment to Internet applications. The Wired Up team also presented findings in different school classes, using the printed posters or digital smart boards that were present in the classrooms. These presentations also enabled me to invite students to participate in the subsequent in-depth interviewing phase.

We aimed to provide educators greater insight in the digital practices of their school populations. One of the unintended consequences of communicating back findings to school management became apparent when Oussema, a fifteen-year-old interviewee, sent me a message through Facebook Messenger shortly after the Wired Up team shared the report with findings with his school: "*I think that's why Facebook, Twitter, Hyves etc. have been blocked in my school xD, when they learned which sites are used the most :P.*" One of Wired Up's key assumptions is that learning via the Internet and digital media can be incorporated in a positive way into contemporary education. While one of the motivators of our research was therefore to provide educators with ideas to connect with students through digital means, this example indicates how our findings also had some adverse consequences resulting, for instance, in a more stringent media policy in some schools, impacting heavily on the students' digital radius of action in school settings.

Conducting the survey

In a number of schools, school directors and teachers decided which classes of students would join the survey research; in others we pitched the research in front of classes, letting students decide for themselves whether they would want to skip class and join our study.[4] Each class was given two vouchers worth 7.50 euro, and the vouchers were given away to students in a lottery draw. In a short plenary presentation, all survey participants were briefly introduced to the aims and workings of the survey. We emphasized to every class of students that we were interested in learning their views about the relevance of digital media in their lives. Also, it was explained that their anonymity would be safeguarded, and that data would never be used to provide information to teachers, parents or government institutions about individual respondents. We also made clear that our analysis would only consist of reporting about patterns of user behavior, aggregated over groups of participants. By typing in a shortened website address that included the name of the school, students were redirected to the survey which was hosted on Utrecht University servers. During the surveys, the instructors remained present to supervise and monitor the survey process and answer any questions that arose.

The issue of trust showed itself to be of central concern, as was observable from remarks made by respondents. Comments and questions directed at me ranged from the content of the research – "*Why do you need this information?*" "*I'm not giving my real name,*" and "*What are you going to do with it? It will end up in the hands of the child protection board*" to the personal "*I think you like women with curly hair like the girls in this class, don't you?*" We also noticed that other students discussed the survey and gossiped about us behind our backs. Students were kindly asked to work on the survey individually, but some tried to establish a private backchannel of communication by starting up instant messaging alongside their Internet Explorer or Firefox Wired Up survey browser window. The survey takers assisted by teachers and engaged students, actively sought to keep sabotage practices to a minimum and ensured that the students completed the surveys individually.

Another example of such digital creativity shows how we, as outsiders and intruders to school communities, were challenged and tested in our

4 Meeting commonly accepted research standards in the Netherlands, an opt-out mechanism was followed; the seven participating schools distributed letters of invitation to parents of participating students. In the letter, parents were informed about the workings and aims of surveys. Parents could choose to opt out their children from our research. In every school, parents of a handful of children from the study made use of this option.

perseverance. For example, in one case, after finishing their questionnaires, students from a second-year class were allowed to exit the classroom and enjoy their lunch break. After finishing his survey, one student pulled off a clever prank, opening a video called *Farting Sounds* on YouTube shortly before switching off the power to his computer screen. So when all remaining students began breaking out in laughter with fart noises coming from one side of the room, it took some time to locate the computer that was producing the sounds from a row of black computer screens. A final example shows how stressful survey data gathering can be, when during the instruction to the survey we wrote the URL of the survey with indelible ink on a smart board while we were thinking we were writing on a white board that would allow us to easily wipe away our markings. The students stared at us without blinking and without saying anything, but began laughing at us when we had finished writing.

When these discomforting things happened, I tried my best to be a good sport and not let them bother me too much, and I found that by maintaining a friendly demeanor the students happily continued to participate in the survey (Sultana, 2007, p. 380). There were also plenty of occasions where students were genuinely interested in learning about our project, what it is like to work in the university, and finding out which academic trajectory we had completed. It also showed that our presence countered stereotypes of the University as an elite ivory tower disconnected from the real world, as one girl, for instance, expressed her amazement when she noticed we wore the same kind of sneakers, by shouting, *"I didn't know people in the university wore Nike Air Force Ones!"* My shoes became a sign of commonality, making me someone who could be empathized with.

In sum, besides documenting the process of conducting surveys in schools, this section also shows that quantitative fieldwork methods of survey research, often seen as a hallmark of objectivity, do involve very personal experiences and power relations that operate in different ways. A good introduction and an open, positive attitude of on the part of us survey takers proved most successful in ensuring the cooperation of the participants. I continue my discussion about hierarchies and power relations in fieldwork when reflecting on in-depth interviewing and discursive analysis.

Descriptive survey data about digital practices of Moroccan-Dutch youth

In this section I present a general overview of survey findings serving two purposes: they inform subsequent research phases and they introduce the reader to the group of respondents. First, general socio-demographics of

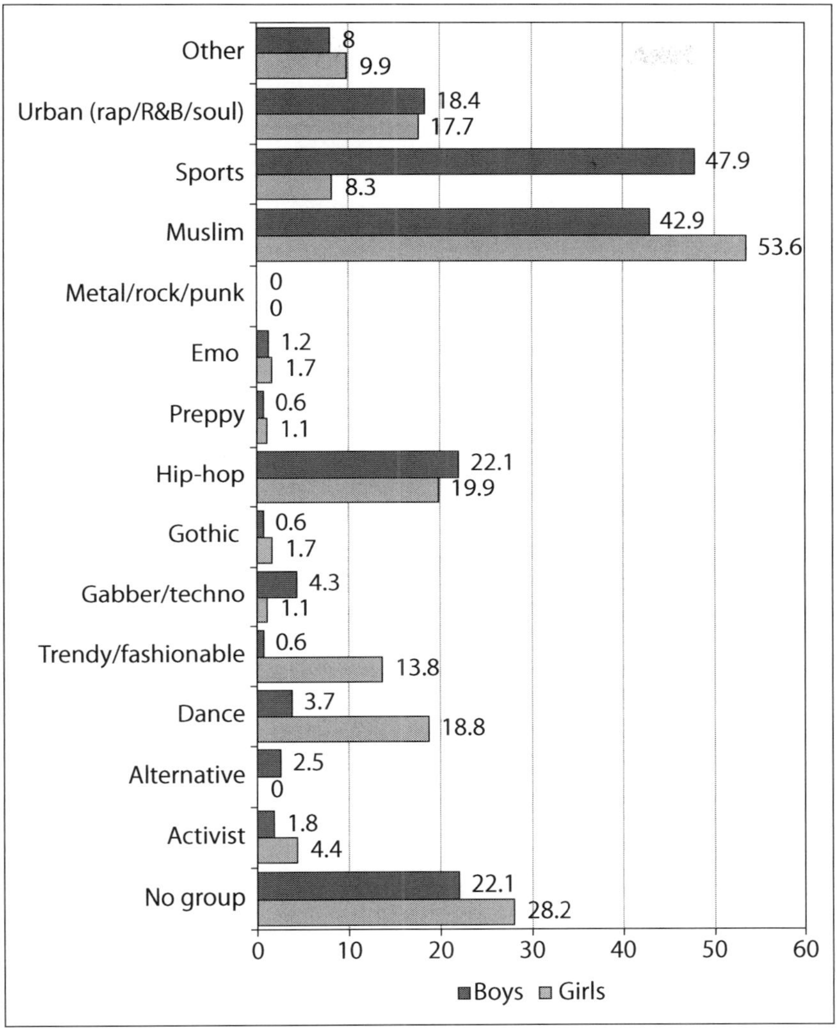

Diagram 1: Subcultural affiliations as expressed by the Moroccan-Dutch survey respondents (percentages, multiple answers possible, n = 344)

the Moroccan-Dutch survey participants are given. Secondly, I describe the gendered specificities of their media use, situate their practices in the context of usage and point out the digital spaces they valued the most.

From the total number of 1,408, 344 respondents described themselves as Moroccan-Dutch; this group consisted of 181 girls and 163 boys. On average they are 14.5 years old, and when prompted 98.5% describe themselves as Muslim. More than three-quarters (76.2%) of these young people speak Dutch at home with their parents. Two-thirds do this in combination with a

Berber language (66.9%) and half with Moroccan-Arabic (52.6%). We asked respondents which subcultural affiliations they would include on their personal SNS profile. Roughly half of the respondents reported belonging to a Muslim subculture and one-fifth saw themselves as urban and hip-hop. Gender differences become apparent; girls affiliated themselves more with dance music and being trendy and fashionable while boys saw themselves more as sporty (see Diagram 1).

For many Moroccan-Dutch youth, identifying with a Muslim subculture has become a more positive way to articulate one's postsecular identity as opposed to a top-down ascribed ethnic identity such as "You are an allochthone" or "You are a Moroccan cunt" (Leurs & Ponzanesi, 2014c). Next to hip-hop, urban, and the like, Moroccan-Dutch young people chose to be "Muslim online" (Buitelaar, 2008, pp. 244-247). During the interviews, informants expanded on religious elements they incorporated in their self-presentations. Underlining ethnic pride and wearing the headscarf as an important identity marker, thirteen-year-old Inas describes her construction of a personal profile page as follows: *"it's like, I'm wearing a headscarf. When I post a photo of me wearing a headscarf, you can so to say see that I have an Islamic background. And with my name and so on."* Furthermore, interviewees report to highlight their attachment to Islam by including religious acclimations such as "Inshallah" (God willing) in their nicknames or by showing they are a member of groups pertaining to Islam on their online profile page.

Table 2: Frequency of non-Internet media use among Moroccan-Dutch youth (percentages, n = 344)

	Never	1 Day per week	2/3 Days per week	4/5 Days per week	Daily	All the time
Reading newspapers and magazines	21.2%	40.1%	23.3%	7.6%	1.5%	
Reading books	27.9%	32.8%	17.4%	9.9%	6.4%	5.5%
Watching TV/DVD	0.6%	9.6%	13.7%	14.0%	24.7%	37.5%
Playing computer games on consoles	22.4%	16.0%	20.1%	8.1%	15.7%	17.7%
Using MP3-player/I-Pod	8.4%	7.6%	10.5%	16.0%	16.9%	40.7%

In this study, the focus is on digital media practices but these must be seen in the context of wider media consumption practices. Everyone watches TV, and using MP3 players is also very popular, while reading newspapers and

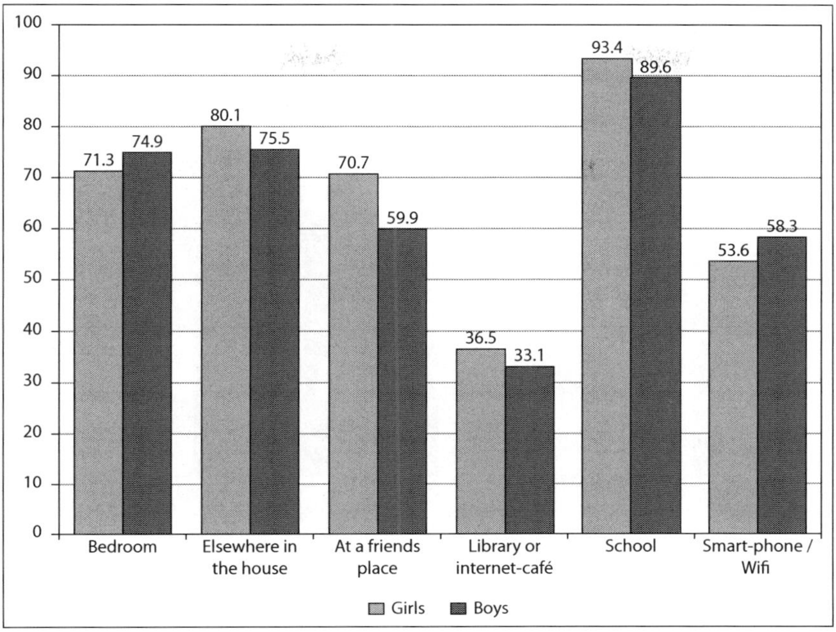

Diagram 2: Locations where Moroccan-Dutch youth connect to the Internet (percentages, n = 344)

playing computer games are also fairly common activities. Reading books is the least popular. In greater detail, on a daily basis, 8% of Moroccan-Dutch respondents read newspapers and magazines, 12% read books, 33.4% play video games on consoles such as the Xbox 360 or Play Station 3, 57.6% use their MP3 players or iPods and 62.2% of respondents watch TV or DVDs (see Table 2).

Computer ownership and Internet access is widespread, as 98.3% of Moroccan-Dutch girls and 96.9% of the boys report they have a computer in their homes with Internet access. These numbers are comparable to the 97% of males and 96% of females among the general Dutch population that own hardware and have Internet access in 2013 (CBS, 2014b). As shown in Diagram 2, the respondents connect to the Internet from various locations. Nearly three out of every four Moroccan-Dutch youth log on to the Internet using a computer in their own bedroom. Besides their own bedrooms, Moroccan-Dutch girls connect more frequently from a computer elsewhere in their house, at a friend's place, in the library or in an Internet café, or at school, while boys connect to the Internet via their smartphones more often. More than half of the participating young women and men use their smartphones to go online. Girls furthermore report sending more short messages using their mobile phones than boys (Leurs, 2012, p. 325).

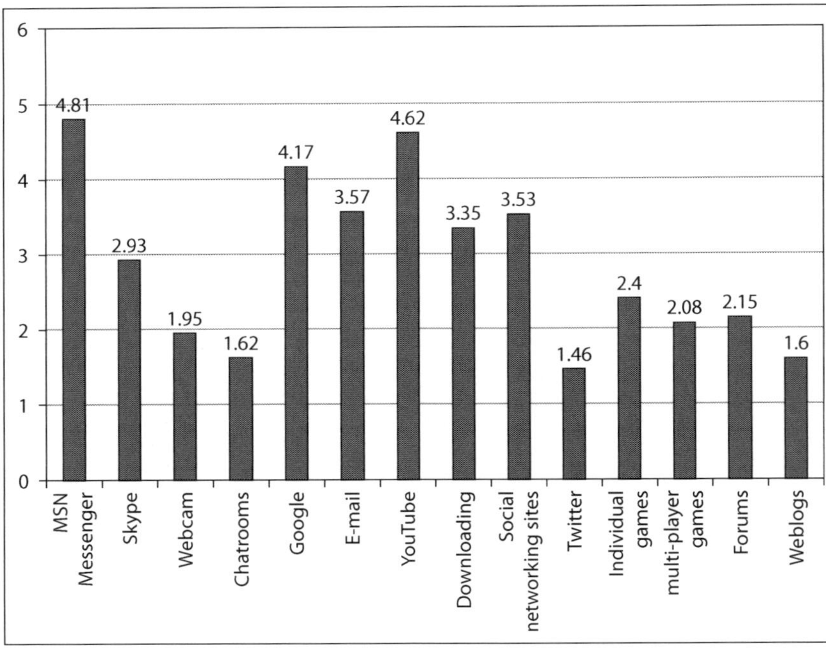

Diagram 3: Internet application user frequencies of Moroccan-Dutch youth (means, 5-point scale, n = 344)

Moroccan-Dutch girls report that they consider the Internet to be useful for searching for information and buying things that are difficult to get, while boys see the Internet as more useful for reaching organizations and finding help when they have problems (Leurs, 2012, p. 325). The majority of both Moroccan-Dutch girls and boys report experiencing great autonomy and limited restrictions in pursuing their own goals in their Internet use. This holds both for deciding what they download online, whom they talk to online and what they publish on their profile page (Leurs, 2012, p. 326). When controlled, Moroccan-Dutch youth are more monitored by their siblings, in contrast to ethnic-majority Dutch youth, who are mostly monitored by their mothers (Wired Up, 2011, p. 20).

Focusing on the frequency of use of various Internet applications, survey findings show that Moroccan-Dutch students mostly turn to MSN Messenger, YouTube, Google, e-mail, social networking sites, downloading, Skype, solo online games and discussion forums (Leurs, 2012, p. 326). This list of applications changes when considering practices students reported they would miss most if they were not able to do them anymore (see Diagram 4). In order of decreasing importance Moroccan-Dutch youth value the following applications most: MSN Messenger, YouTube, Google,

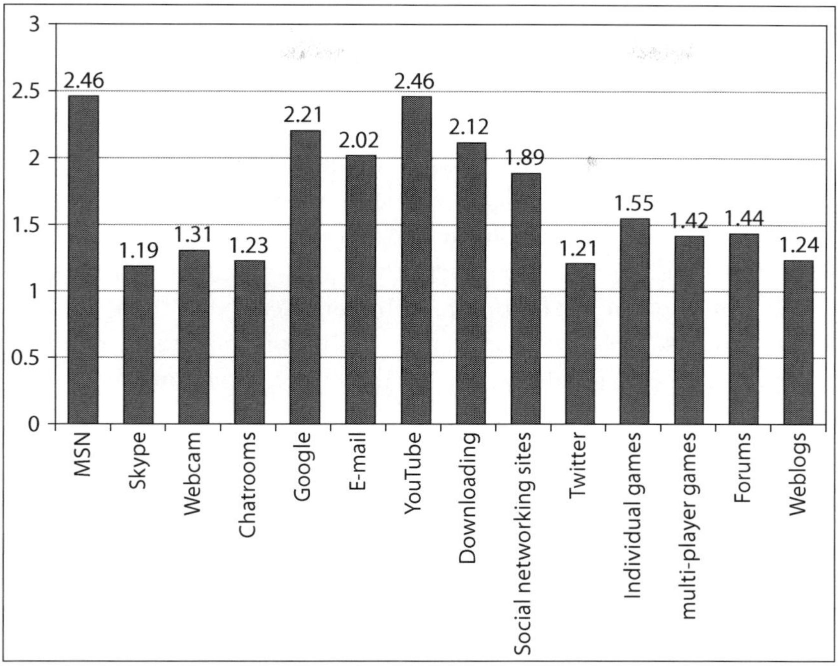

Diagram 4: The attachment of Moroccan-Dutch youth to various Internet applications (means, 3-point scale, n = 344)

downloading, e-mail, social networking sites and forums. When comparing boys and girls, it shows that YouTube, SNSs and MSN Messenger are equally valued among both groups, but it also shows that girls consider forums more important than boys, while boys are more attached to playing computer games, multiplayer games and using Twitter (Leurs, 2012, p. 326).

Even though they reported frequently making use of Skype, the great majority of Moroccan-Dutch youth themselves do not consider the application very important in their own lives. This difference between frequency of use and attachment can be explained by acknowledging that second-generation migrant youth often set up *Skype* connections to allow their parents engage in transnational communication with family and friends living abroad, in this case with Morocco and elsewhere in the Moroccan diaspora. As described in the introduction, Moroccan-Dutch youth themselves more often engage in representing their diaspora affiliations symbolically instead of connecting digitally with Moroccans living abroad.

In sum, the survey data was useful to introduce broad dynamics of the group under study, their digital practices and their Internet application preferences. Informants indicated multiple identifications as they reported belonging to multiple subcultural affiliations. Moreover, gendered specificities of Internet activities and user contexts were noted. These insights guided the subsequent interviewing and virtual ethnography phases. The survey findings provide a general but informative backdrop that assisted me in preparing questions pertaining to these digital spaces (MSN Messenger, YouTube, Google, downloading, e-mail, social networking sites and forums) that respondents considered important in their lives. Qualitative in-depth methods were chosen to critically reflect on how Moroccan-Dutch youth represent their identities across these different digital spaces. The survey played an additional important role, as a selection of the respondents was invited to participate in the in-depth interviews.

1.3 In-depth interviews

Besides large-scale survey research, I carried out semi-structured in-depth interviews. In addition to the descriptive statistics the survey data provided, the interviews were set up to enable a topological mapping, to work out how informants experienced practices across various digital spaces (boyd, 2010a). Based on the survey findings and my theoretical framework, I constructed an interview protocol and a series of topics that I wanted to get to with each interview, but then I also went where the youth wanted to go (see Leurs, 2012, pp. 328-330 for the interview protocol). In-depth interviews allow for capturing processes such as experiences, thoughts, perceptions, feelings and the production of meaning, self-positioning and attributing values that are impossible to capture with the survey approach. Instead of the closed yes/no questions asked in the survey, in-depth interviews allow asking the "wh" questions ("who/what/when/where/why) that elicit longer, more detailed and layered responses (Lobe, Livingstone, Olafsson & Simões, 2008, p. 10). Seeing the informants as experts on their everyday lives, I invited informants to share their personal experiences of self-positioning across digital spaces with me.

Similar to the survey data gathering, power relations were also at play during interviewing. Some critical/feminist scholars overconcerned with reflexivity, positionality and the issue of representation moved away from fieldwork completely and have turned to textual analysis. Moving away from fieldwork, they aim to avoid critiques of their research perpetuating unequal gendered and Eurocentric representations and speaking for women and other minorities (Sultana, 2007, p. 375). However, I do not want to paralyze myself in fear of such criticism. Below, I set out the efforts I took to avoid the pitfalls of speaking for the interviewees and explain participatory methods used to research digital practices, space and identity with them (Gubrium & Harper, 2013).

Below, I first describe how the interviewees were recruited. Second, I reflect on the dynamics of interviewer-interviewee positioning and asymmetrical power relations. Acknowledging spatial dynamics, I thirdly consider the implications of carrying out face-to-face interviews inside and outside school settings. Finally, I set out the rationale for conducting case studies of four digital spaces in particular.

Interview sampling

A selected group of survey participants was invited to join the interviewing phase of the study. The selection procedure consisted of the following steps: those participants who proved to have incompletely and/or unreliably filled in the surveys were filtered out from the SPSS database. In the next step, those cases where people reported they themselves or one of their parents migrated from Morocco and reported to be between twelve and eighteen years old were selected. Subsequently, in order to include youth who meet Wired Up survey user averages, respondents who reported they do not actively participate in a minimum of digital practices such as social networking sites, MSN Messenger and YouTube were excluded. Finally, from the resulting list, those who reported willingness to take part in follow-up interviews were filtered out.

School directors of two schools, one in Rotterdam and one in 's-Hertogenbosch, granted me access to reenter their schools. From these schools, forty-four Moroccan-Dutch students met my selection criteria, and they were all invited to join the interviewing phase. This was done after survey findings were presented in different school classes. Similar to the survey procedure, all students were sent a letter of invitation through the school administration, allowing parents to opt out their child from the research. Of those invited, fourteen students had either moved to another school, were sick at the moment of invitation, were not allowed to join by their parents or decided themselves against participating in the interviews. The thirty students that were willing to participate in the in-depth interviews consisted of sixteen students from one school in 's-Hertogenbosch (nine boys and seven girls) and fourteen students from one school in Rotterdam (six boys and eight girls). This group of informants was aged between twelve and sixteen years.

In order to include seventeen- and eighteen-year-olds and diversify the group of informants further, thirteen Moroccan-Dutch youth were contacted using snowballing methods in other cities. Locating the additional group of youth in Utrecht, Venlo and Eindhoven, the process was facilitated with the assistance of various gatekeepers, including Fayrouz Boulayounne, a research assistant of Moroccan-Dutch descent, other students and volunteering work contacts. Having fostered trust through personal references that vouched for me as well as the trustworthiness of the research, access to this supplementary group was granted relatively quickly. Parental consent was obtained for informants younger than eighteen who were invited through snowballing sampling.

A total of forty-three Moroccan-Dutch key informants participated in this qualitative phase of my research. Except for four interviewees, all informants can be considered as second generation migrant youth, as they were born in the Netherlands, from parents who migrated to the Netherlands. Mehmet Ali, Hatim, Kenza and Ziham, two boys and two girls, were born in Morocco and migrated to the Netherlands together with their parents at young age. Foreign-born young people who migrate before their early teens may be considered as members of a bicultural "1.5 generation" (Yi, 2009). It was my intention to include a variety of Moroccan-Dutch youth, aiming at an even distribution in terms of gender, age and school level. The group consisted of twenty-two young women and twenty-one young men. They range in age from twelve to eighteen years old; the average age of the informants is fifteen years (see Table 3).

Table 3: The interviewees; names are pseudonyms suggested by the informants

Pseudonym	City	Gender	Age	Generation	School year
Interviewees who participated in the survey					
Soesie	's-Hertogenbosch	female	13	born in the Netherlands	2 VMBO
Mohammed	's-Hertogenbosch	male	13	born in the Netherlands	2 VMBO K/T
Anas	's-Hertogenbosch	male	13	born in the Netherlands	2 VMBO K/T
Senna	's-Hertogenbosch	female	14	born in the Netherlands	2 VMBO K
Ayoub	's-Hertogenbosch	male	14	born in the Netherlands	2 VMBO K/B
Badr	's-Hertogenbosch	male	14	born in the Netherlands	2 VMBO K/B

Pseudonym	City	Gender	Age	Generation	School year
Mehmet Ali	's-Hertogenbosch	male	14	born in Morocco	2 VMBO K/B
Loubna	's-Hertogenbosch	female	14	born in the Netherlands	3 VMBO K/B
Meryam	's-Hertogenbosch	female	15	born in the Netherlands	3 VMBO K/B
Hatim	's-Hertogenbosch	male	15	born in Morocco	3 VMBO K/T
Hajar	's-Hertogenbosch	female	15	born in the Netherlands	3 VMBO K/T
Carlos	's-Hertogenbosch	male	15	born in the Netherlands	3 VMBO K/T
Ryan	's-Hertogenbosch	male	15	born in the Netherlands	4 VMBO-T
Nevra	's-Hertogenbosch	female	16	born in the Netherlands	4 VMBO-K
Amir	's-Hertogenbosch	male	16	born in the Netherlands	4 VMBO-B
Bibi	's-Hertogenbosch	female	16	born in the Netherlands	4 VMBO-B/K
Soufian	Rotterdam	male	12	born in the Netherlands	2 HAVO
Salima	Rotterdam	female	13	born in the Netherlands	2 VWO
Tariq	Rotterdam	male	13	born in the Netherlands	2 VMBO-T
Inas	Rotterdam	female	13	born in the Netherlands	2 VWO
Amina	Rotterdam	female	13	born in the Netherlands	2 VWO
Abdel	Rotterdam	male	13	born in the Netherlands	2 VWO
Ilham	Rotterdam	female	13	born in the Netherlands	2 VWO
Sahar	Rotterdam	female	14	born in the Netherlands	3 VMBO-T
Ziham	Rotterdam	female	14	born in Morocco	2 HAVO
Kenza	Rotterdam	female	14	born in Morocco	3 HAVO
Oussema	Rotterdam	male	15	born in the Netherlands	3 HAVO
SouSou	Rotterdam	female	15	born in the Netherlands	3 VMBO-T
Abdelsammad	Rotterdam	male	15	born in the Netherlands	2 VMBO-T
Faruk	Rotterdam	male	16	born in the Netherlands	3 VMBO-T

Pseudonym	City	Gender	Age	Generation	School year
Informants recruited through snowball sampling, who piloted the in-depth interview					
Inzaf	Eindhoven	female	15	born in the Netherlands	4 VMBO-T
Naoul	Eindhoven	female	16	born in the Netherlands	1 MBO
Yethi	Utrecht	male	15	born in the Netherlands	3 HAVO
Ferran	Venlo	male	17	born in the Netherlands	2 MBO
Ilana	Venlo	female	16	born in the Netherlands	1 MBO
Mustafa	Venlo	male	18	born in the Netherlands	2 MBO
Sadik	Venlo	male	17	born in the Netherlands	2 MBO
Safae	Venlo	female	18	born in the Netherlands	3 MBO
Informants recruited through snowball sampling, who piloted the survey and interview					
Rachid	Utrecht	male	13	born in the Netherlands	2 VWO
Midia	Utrecht	female	13	born in the Netherlands	1 VMBO-T
Kamal	Eindhoven	male	15	born in the Netherlands	3 VMBO-T
Fatiha	Eindhoven	female	17	born in the Netherlands	4 HAVO
Khadija	Eindhoven	female	17	born in the Netherlands	4 VMBO-K

In general, the interviewees live in small houses, in socially and economically deprived neighborhoods and they come from above-average-sized families. The majority of informants mentioned they know more about computers than their parents. In contrast to their parents, they are part of a generation that grew up with digital technologies. In my attempt to acknowledge all interviewees as distinct individuals, I introduce all forty-three interviewees individually in Appendix 1. Acknowledging individual autonomy of the informants themselves, all informants were asked to sign a consent form themselves during the interviews too. The interviewees were all awarded a 7.50 euro voucher in return for their time investment in the study. Interviews lasted between 45 minutes and two hours, and conversations with a number of interviewees continued via MSN Messenger, e-mail, and Facebook. This later process is further explained in Section 1.4. In sum, the in-depth interviewing phase of this study builds on conversations with forty-three key informants.

However, I intersperse my study with comments gathered from supplementary conversations. I held additional face-to-face, telephone and online interviews with others who help shape the digital spaces informants frequent, such as Abdelilah Amraoui, founder of Geweigerd.nl and the discussion forum Maghreb.nl; Rafik, founder of the "Imazighen" Hyves group; eMoroccan, who I interviewed about the videos he posted to YouTube; and Rafje, a cartoonist publishing on the discussion forum Marokko.nl. Also I have held conversations with parents, teachers, and school directors who at least partially shape the informants' experiences and perceptions of digital media practices.

Doing interviews using participatory techniques

By carrying out ethnography-inspired interviews, I employ a method that originates from the field of anthropology. Anthropologists use ethnographic interviews to learn more about unfamiliar cultural practices. Acknowledging its troubled past, it is of important to be transparent about the power hierarchies in ethnographic interviewing.[5] Feminist and postcolonial theorists have criticized those studying "the native informant" for disciplinary purposes of exercising authority and governance. The discipline has traditionally involved privileged, white, male Western intellectuals desiring to penetrate mysterious ways of life of those people classified as Others (Said, 1979; Spivak, 1993b, 1999). Immersing themselves in the lives of the people they study, they gain the point of view of an insider who is able to translate and represent indigenous and subaltern points of view to Western audiences. However, this process of translation and representation is not innocent. Rather, anthropological studies were used to justify the installment and perpetuation of hierarchies: "to assign a static ethnicity to the Other," writes Gayatri Spivak, "is to foreclose" (1999, p. 110). These foreclosed ethnic, gendered and religious hierarchies were subsequently used to warrant Western exploitation and dominance of the non-Western Other.

5 The history of ethnography-inspired interviewing is rooted in colonial anthropology. Preoccupied with knowing the Other, the discipline of anthropology was initiated during the era of European colonization (the seventeenth to the twentieth centuries) to further colonial and imperial exploitation of the colonies (Harding, 1991, p. 239).

In response, to overcome a "representational crisis" (Hine, 2013, p. 5) ethnographers increasingly reflect on their complicity with power relations (Sultana, 2007). And, by beginning to see "ethnography as critical theory in action" (Madison, 2012, p. 14), critical ethnographers are carrying out research in a deconstructive mode by including polyphonic and fragmented voices, discontinuous narratives, multiple perspectives and simultaneity (Olivieri, 2012, p. 145; Madison 2012). Postcolonial critiques have also made me attentive to the power relations of ethnography-inspired interviews and participant observation. Therefore, instead of uncritically ventriloquizing or appropriating informants' discourses, I reflect on the relationships between the interviewees and myself as a privileged researcher. Also I incorporated "creative" and "participatory" research techniques (Gauntlett & Holzwarth, 2006; Gubrium & Harper, 2013) and sought to incorporate a deconstructive, multilayered and multiperspectival stance in my discursive analysis of the narratives of informants (see Section 1.5).

One may wonder, why use ethnographic interviews at all? I strategically make use of ethnography-inspired interviews because they have been recognized as beneficial to the study of young people's own differential perceptions of childhood and adolescence (James, 2007; boyd, 2010a, 2014; De Ridder, 2014).[6] The perspective acknowledges that youth are the experts on their own lives, agency, memories, experiences, perceptions and thoughts, and its "goal is to understand the child's vantage point as valid and unique" (Saywitch, Camparo & Romanoff, 2010, p. 551). By eliciting explanations and elaborations from the young interviewees with open questions, instead of pressing directions with closed questions, and backgrounding one's views as an adult researcher, the interviewees can be encouraged to take the role of an expert. As the interviewer and informants take up these roles, the power differentials between children and adults can be decreased (Saywitch, Camparo & Romanoff, 2010). However, scholars have to "get round the un-get-roundable fact that all ethnographical descriptions are home-made, that they are the describer's descriptions, not those of the described" (Geertz, 1988, pp. 144-145).

By including participatory research techniques in my interview setup, I promoted informants to (at least partly) study with me their digital experiences and to become active agents over their own representations:

6 Just as gender and postcolonial studies matured from the 1960s onward by makings its tools more conceptually and empirically sophisticated by incorporating female subaltern voices and views, childhood studies should better understand the politics of childhood by listening to and considering children's own voices and experiences (James, 2007; Buckingham & Kehily, 2014).

> By participatory, we refer to methodologies, approaches, or techniques that afford the "subject," "community member," and/or "field site" greater narrative latitude when it comes to ethnographic knowledge production and a larger role in determining why and how research outcomes are produced and received by lay and academic audiences alike. (Gubrium & Harper, 2013, p. 16)

Inspired by Aline Gubrium and Krista Harper, I sought to afford the informants "greater narrative latitude" (2013, p. 16) in four ways. First, the names used throughout this study are pseudonyms suggested by the informants, so the informants had a say of how their voice would be included in the study. This was also intended to demonstrate my sincere interest in incorporating their voices in the study on their own terms.[7]

As a second mechanism for informants to participate in their own representations, they were asked how they would introduce themselves to others. The informants narrated complex narratives of selves, in line with Stuart Hall, who noted, "when I ask people where they are from, I expect nowadays an extremely long story" (Akomfrah, Gopaul & Lawson, 2013). These self-introductions already indicate a multiplicity that goes beyond singular understandings of identity. For example, fourteen-year-old Ziham described her individuality by noting "*everyone is different*," fifteen-year-old Carlos stated, "*most say that I look Dutch, but when I talk I look more Moroccan, because I am half Dutch, half Moroccan*" and thirteen-year-old Ilham, for example, described herself by stating "*I am Moroccan, Berber and Muslim, but as you can see with a Dutch nationality.*" Talking back to negative ethnic labels, thirteen-year-old Abdel emphasized he is "*a nice Moroccan boy.*" Sixteen-year-old Amir stated, "*I have my own personal style. I don't belong to any group – I'm just multiculti, I think.*" In terms of ethnicity, the majority of informants mentioned feeling attached to Morocco, while emphasizing they also feel Dutch. The hyphenated label "Moroccan-Dutch" is used throughout

7 For those informants who could not or did not want to come up with a name, I have chosen names that were somewhat popular among Moroccan-Dutch youth. For this purpose I used those that were mentioned in lively discussions taking place on the discussion forums Marokko.nl, Chaima.nl and Maroc.nl on the topic of popular Moroccan boys' and girls' names in the Netherlands. These discussions are also a lively reminder of the history of discrimination of Amazigh culture. Historically in Morocco, parents had to choose a name for their newborn from lists of officially allowed Arabic names. Names of Amazigh cultural backgrounds were not allowed. This rule also held for people in the Moroccan diaspora, who wanted their children to be able to apply for Moroccan citizenship. In 2010, the ban on Amazigh names was lifted (Human Rights Watch, 2010).

this study to reflect the hyphenated sense of ethnic identification that the majority of the informants narrate. This was the label that was most often mentioned. Also, when quoting their statements, I locate informants individually by including their self-introductions.

Thirdly, informants were repeatedly reminded of their roles as reliable sources of information about their experiences. For this purpose, I emphasized wanting to learn from the informant her/his perceptions and thoughts on digital practices. For instance, when I wanted to learn how fourteen-year-old Ayoub saw Facebook I asked him, "Of course I know a bit about the site, but imagine I do not know what Facebook is – Can you explain to me what happens there?" The question reveals how I had to strike a delicate balance between presenting myself as an expert and as ignorant. Informants did not take me seriously when I pretended to be unaware of the intricacies of digital culture, while they sometimes shied away from asserting their opinions when they sensed I had been studying it for a long time.

Finally, I asked interviewees to research with me their practices by letting them map out the digital spaces they participate in. Such creative methods are useful to explore mediated identities, they enable

> a kind of research which enables people to communicate in a meaningful way about their identities and experiences, and their own thoughts about their identities and experiences, through creatively making things themselves, and then reflecting upon what they have made. (Gauntlett & Holzwarth, 2006, p. 82)

New, creative approaches are needed in research with young people, as "most procedures for soliciting children's preferences do not reliably elicit information on their best interests and do not give children a meaningful voice in decision making" (Warshak, 2003, p. 373). For this purpose, at the beginning of the interviews informants were invited to draw a map of their view of the Internet on a piece of paper. The digital spaces included on their maps were used to structure the interview further. The task is an example of "image-based concept mapping," a participatory research technique which has been recognized as a successful way to capture the conceptions of networked information and communication technologies (Somekh and Mavers, 2003, p. 414). The idea to include the Internet mapping exercise came from initial face-to-face fieldwork experience but is also theoretically informed. During the piloting phase I learned that young informants found it difficult to think about issues that range across different applications; rather, they talked about how they made use of specific applications rather than the Internet in general. Theorists have also noted that in people's everyday life, "the internet will often not be experienced as a single entity and will have many different social meanings" (Hine, 2008, p. 5). Thus, considering different platforms as field sites in their own right is warranted, "it makes analytical sense to distinguish various *types* of social media" (Van Dijck, 2013, p. 8).

As an example, I discussed a map which listed my digital practices, mentioning my interest in looking up details about the latest basketball matches, YouTube highlight videos and blogs with basketball rumors; connecting with family and friends on SNSs, and torrent download websites to download TV series, art house movies and indie music. Informants were stimulated to think of their own way to map their digital practices. The description of this task doubled as a bonding exercise, letting the informant into my world as well. This warming-up phase was aimed at developing a rapport. Drawing the Internet map was an aid to recall practices (Lobe, Livingstone, Olafsson & Simões, 2008, p. 10), and I positioned myself through a formal introduction and revealed more about myself by discussing my own personal Internet map. The task proved to be a good icebreaker (Gubrium & Harper, 2013, p. 33). As they were drawing their maps, informants were researching digital practices with me. Interviewees were asked to map out their practices and add a short description. Figure 4 displays the map thirteen-year-old Soesie made. She, for instance, includes from the top left "*Watching pictures in my files*," "*MSN talking to friends*," "*www.Marokko.nl to*

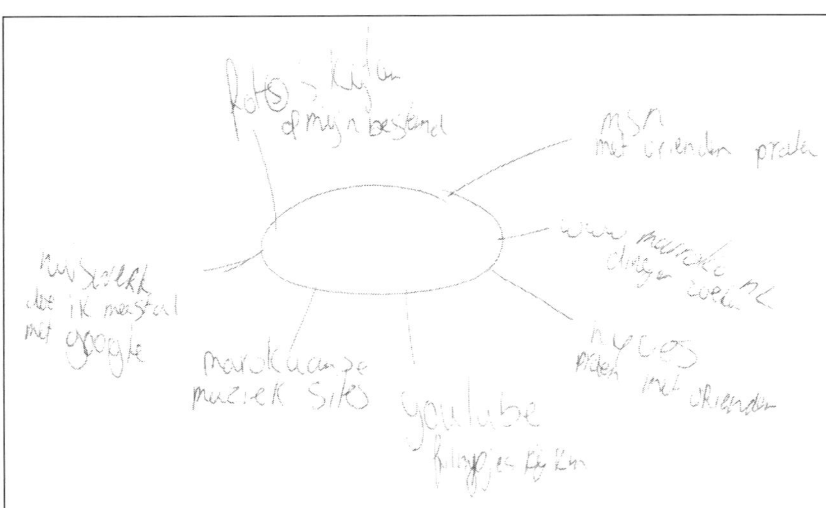

Fig. 4: Internet map made by Soesie, a thirteen-year-old girl

look up things," *"Hyves to talk to friends,"* *"YouTube to watch videos,"* *"Moroccan music websites"* and *"for homework I usually use Google."*

After informants finished drawing their Internet maps, one by one, all the different digital spaces informants listed were separately discussed in all interviews. Informants were, for instance, prompted to describe their frequency of use and to explain the features and usages of different applications. In my follow-up questions, I asked to what extent each space facilitated their presentation of self in terms of youth culture, gender, ethnicity and religion. Informants were asked about the commercial messages and advertisements they encountered in these spaces. Most importantly, the values, meanings and relevance attributed to each application were discussed, by considering which practices they found empowering, restricting, inspirational, discriminatory and troubling. During the mapping exercise, informants continued managing the impression they wanted to make on the researchers. While drawing the map, fifteen-year-old Oussema, for instance, said, *"Oh I have forgot one thing,"* hesitating to add another practice on his map he added, *"this may sound as if I am a nerd."* Drawing the Internet maps allowed the informants to take a moment to reflect upon their digital practices, which is important, as they commonly had not reflected on their usage before. When drawing her map, eighteen-year-old Safae shared the illuminating comment, *"You never really think about what you do online. This makes you think, like, 'What the hell do I do on the Internet everyday?'"*

The Internet map was useful for structuring the interview and eliciting personal narratives of passages, belonging and identification across digital spaces, and at the same time, the map enabled the informant to seize control over the directions the conversation would take. The mapping exercise also allowed room to consider directions the survey findings had not brought forward or that I had not anticipated before otherwise. Thus, informants assisted me in defining the contexts and boundaries of my research, which is of increasing importance when considering the great variety of Internet applications and the wide-range of offline contexts they interact with (Hine, 2008, 2013, 2015; Leander, 2003).

Reflexivity and power relations

> Fieldwork is meaningful as the encounter of two subjects who recognize each other as subjects, and therefore separate, and seek to build their equality upon their difference in order to work together.
>
> – Allesandro Portelli (cited in Wekker, 2006, p. 19)

In this section, I articulate my awareness of the ways in which interviewer-interviewee relationships cannot be taken for granted. I critically reflect on the personal presence of Fayrouz (who assisted in the fieldwork) and myself in the in-depth interviewing phase. As a university-educated interviewer, I hold the power to produce knowledge about informants. However, informants too exercise power in every research process, because but "for the grace, patience, and interests of the people involved, there would be little research" (Wekker, 2006, p. 4). Informants personally had the opportunity to accept or decline my invitation to participate in the interview, and they were also reassured that they were free to leave questions unanswered and they could always opt out from the research if they wanted.[8] Thinking through the role of power hierarchies, equality and difference in fieldwork, I sensed informants attributed credibility to me because I emphasized equality and displayed a sincere interest in the informants' everyday lives.

The issue of trust is again of vital importance. As I mentioned earlier, fifteen-year-old Oussema confronted me with being accountable for the knowledge that I produce. Having secured the trust of respondents, it turned out that the knowledge I produce could become harmful to the informants themselves. In the surveys, students enthusiastically listed their usage of various Internet applications. These findings made one school decide to block access to these digital spaces. In a sense, the trust the informant put in the research could have been damaged because of this development. However, in my interview with Oussema it showed that he did not felt betrayed by me, but by the school officials. As a matter of fact, he confided in me that he knew how to circumvent the newly imposed restrictions. Similar tactics of subverting technological limitations in the context of school came up frequently in different conversations. This indicates that I was not seen as a teacher, because I was an interested outsider judged to be trustworthy enough to be let in on secrets that breached school policies. As a researcher I entered into a social relationship with the individuals I studied. Being considered as different from teachers, and getting to hear personal stories also raises questions about the ethical implications of interviewing.

From the survey, as well as the presentation of survey findings and posters, informants had formed a general understanding of the research project before the interview. I am aware of the difficulties of discussing

8 No one opted out from the interviews during the process, but there were several who chose not to join the interviewing phase, as they said they were either too busy with school or their after-school jobs. One girl did not like it that no one else from her particular class was joining in the interviews, and opted out.

abstract notions such as identity or digital spatial inequality with young people. Floya Antias, based on her study with Greek Cypriotic-British youth, notes that "asking someone a question about their 'identity' often produces a blank stare, a puzzled silence or a glib and formulaic response. This is not only because research subjects have not understood the question, but also because they cannot easily provide answers" (2002, p. 492). In the interview, I therefore emphasize my interests in learning from the informant's personal experience about the role of the Internet in her/his life, and her/his views on youth culture, ethnicity, religion and gender issues and how they manifest across different Internet applications.

Continuously emphasizing how I would work to acknowledge the views of the informants as a serious source of knowledge, I noticed the rapport grow grew in my interactions. Informants also seemed to enjoy being at the center of attention. Notwithstanding the unequal power relations that remained in place when Fayrouz and I carried out the interviews, there were also different loci along which we as researchers aligned with the shifting identifications of the informants. When reflecting upon the relationship between interviewer and interviewee, shared interests and common ground are always to be found and "given the multiplex nature of identity, there will inevitably be certain facets of self that join us up with the people we study, other facets that emphasize our difference" (Narayan, 1993, p. 680). Similar to how we tried to read our informants during the interviews, informants were also trying to read us (Wekker, 2006, p. 10).

Some of my individual identity facets such as being adult, white, university-educated, male, secular, raised Roman-Catholic, speaking with a hint of southern (Brabant)-Dutch accent might be taken to emphasize difference from the informants. However, other affiliations might be taken to emphasize commonality that work to bridge gaps between us. Axes of similarity in some interviews included me being online since around age twelve, being a man, my knowledge of slang and urban jargon, fascination with forms of youth culture, music, video, sports, clothing brands and the anchorage of digital practice in our lives, as well as my outspoken commitment to antiracism and social justice. Some young female informants emphasized difference when breaching the personal subjects of romance and love, while others seemed to easily speak about these topics to me exactly because they perceived me as an outsider.

Similarly, adult and university-educated Fayrouz who speaks with traces of a southern (Limburg)-Dutch accent also secured common ground. Informants displayed alignment with Fayrouz in terms of shared womanhood, parental migration history, Muslim religious affiliations, and speaking

Arabic and Berber. For instance, thirteen-year-old Ilham became very curious to learn more about the migration background of Fayrouz. Ilham asked her about her descent, and Fayrouz explained her father and mother grew up as members of two particular Berber tribes in northern Morocco. Fayrouz also noted how interviews were more fluid as she could switch between Dutch and Arabic/Berber to clarify informants' statements. When informants used some Darija[9] (Moroccan-Arabic) and Berber words they found more telling to explain certain settings or behavior, they presumed Fayrouz knew the meaning of these words, while I had to prompt interviewees for further explanation.

For instance, when Fayrouz asked whether there are also non-Moroccan-Dutch participants on the discussion forum Marokko.nl, Ilham said, "*It is dot nl, not dot Morocco, so, yes it is for everyone. Everyone is* marhbabikoum." Ilham used the Arabic word "*marhbabikoum*" to indicate everyone is welcome to join discussions on the site. While in her conversation with fifteen-year-old SouSou, being a woman and speaking Moroccan-Arabic and Berber, Fayrouz was able to cover the difficulties of voicing taboo or "*hchouma*" [10] topics within the context of the household, and the opportunities to do so online. Fayrouz noted informants expressed a sense of ethnic commonality by using terms like "*hchouma*" and "*marhbabikoum*." Besides these advantages, having an insider position also has cons. On the one hand, by having Fayrouz interview informants, a shared ethnic descent and gender background contributed in some instances to a more open and relaxed attitude and created an environment in which girls shared more than they would have shared with an outsider like me. On the other hand, with being situated in an insider position one might more easily take things for granted, as a reflective distance is more difficult to achieve. In another case, a young male informant became less talkative during an interview when he got to see Fayrouz as someone he considered to be too much of an insider.

These examples illustrate how Fayrouz and I could be simultaneously an insider as well as an outsider to the worlds of our informants, and that both

9 Darija covers varieties of Arabic spoken in the Maghreb, which includes Algeria, Libya, Mauritania, Morocco and the Western Sahara in northwestern Africa. Darija includes many loanwords from the languages of Maghreb's past rulers, such as Turkish, Spanish and French (Ennaji, 2005, pp. 58-60).

10 As I will elaborate in Chapter 2 on online discussion forums, "*hchouma*" refers to the label used to discuss practices that are considered taboo and transgressive in Moroccan culture. Without the presence of Fayrouz in the research process, I would not have been able to incorporate a discussion of the intricacies of this notion in this book.

dimensions triggered contradictory responses from the informants (Gilbert 1994; Mullings, 1999). Various interview setups were explored to make sure we understood the different implications of interviewer-interviewee positioning processes.[11] Fayrouz's assistance ultimately proved valuable; as without her these complex dynamics would not have manifested themselves so evidently. And of course it would be naïve to think that the informants became close friends, and I understand they have only granted me partial access to their worlds. However, two researchers – who both bring different personal backgrounds into the research – working together in interviewing construct knowledge from different, partial and personal perspectives. This process also became evident when I transcribed interviews conducted by Fayrouz and vice versa.

Inside and outside school: The dynamics of interview settings

Thirty interviews were carried out in two schools, fourteen in Rotterdam and sixteen in 's-Hertogenbosch. These interviews were carried out as a follow-up to the questionnaires, and school directors, teaching coordinators, as well as teachers, teaching assistants, library personnel and janitors, supported fieldwork access. They facilitated my contact with the students, as the directors allowed me to reenter the school communities to present the findings of our survey and to invite potential interviewees. Teaching coordinators and teaching assistants offered assistance by providing me with personal class schedules of individual informants. In large part, interviews took part during school hours and teachers in some cases allowed students to miss parts of their class, allowing me more time to carry out my interviews. The total of thirty interviews that took place in Rotterdam and 's-Hertogenbosch were conducted on school premises, and janitors and library personnel helped me to find proper locations to carry out the interviews. Locations where interviews took place included classrooms, study halls, meeting rooms, school libraries, multimedia centers and computer labs. In most cases, these locations allowed me to talk one-on-one with interviewees, or in some cases I carried out an interview in one end of a room, while Fayrouz carried out an interview in the other end of the room.

11 For instance, as a male interviewer I interviewed male informants, while Fayrouz interviewed female informants. This setup was also reversed, with me interviewing female informants and Fayrouz interviewing male informants. Also, as a duo we jointly interviewed individual informants and we tried out jointly interviewing two informants as well. I have included who conducted the interview for each interviewee in Appendix 1: Meet the informants.

These are not neutral locations, and I recognize that carrying out in-depth interviews within the school settings poses both opportunities and constraints. I noticed that interviewees are accustomed to these locations. Conducting interviews in their familiar everyday spaces of socialization enables interviewees to feel secure (Saywitch, Camparo & Romanoff, 2010, p. 552). Informants knew that the school directors and teachers had provided me access to the school; they saw my presence validated by them. As a relatively unfamiliar face (interviewees only saw me once or twice before when they filled in the questionnaire and when I presented our survey findings), I was an intruder into their regular space of education. To a certain extent, the space made them feel at ease taking away a part of their nervousness, while the setting was new and unfamiliar for me, making me feel nervous myself as well.

Recognizing a distinct set of norms and expectations connected to the setting of the school, I would emphasize that the interview should not be seen as a test, in the sense that I would not mark anything they would share as either a right or wrong answer. Also, I ensured informants their views would be anonymized and treated confidentially. Finally informants were informed that for the purpose of transcription and analysis, the conversation would be audio-recorded. Bringing out either a Sony audio-recording device or my Apple iPhone 4 to record the interview served to focus the conversation on digital practices by prompting all kinds of discussions about mobile devices, including the benefits of accessing the Internet from a BlackBerry or Apple smartphone (Shepherd, 2010).

The school institution has its particular "normative ways of being" (Puwar, 2004, p. 116). This is a material and symbolic space where certain behavior is promoted and other practices are dismissed through objects, gestures and bodies (Leander, 2003, pp. 212-213). During the interviews, it became apparent, for instance, that some schoolteachers saw everyday digital media practices as a waste of time. Investing time in digital practices was considered to be detrimental to students' homework and assignments.[12] I noticed I had to subvert this way of thinking during the interviews in order to have informants open up and describe their experiences using Internet applications. Thirteen-year-old Amina, for instance, voiced her surprise about the research project, stating, "*You are quite interested in*

12 Seeing homework and digital practices as oppositional and competing with each other in terms of time investment, most teachers do not acknowledge the fluid relation between the two that most informants noted. The majority of the informants, for instance, mentioned they commonly used instant messaging to talk about homework.

what we and other youth do" on the Internet, "*We would never even think about that adults and students could be interested in these things.*" They had not met any adult before us that showed a similar level of sincere interest in their digital practices. After emphasizing wanting to learn more about their everyday practices from their viewpoints, I was surprised at how open informants became, sharing personal narratives on topics ranging from the context of school such as homework, to those pertaining to their life beyond school including friendships, love, family as well as romantic relationships, sexuality, religion, holidays, fights, bullying, racism, hobbies, sports and passions.

In terms of atmosphere in the school setting, the school bells, buzzing teachers' voices and student conversations in hallways, the humming of a photocopy machine in the library and the typing sounds coming from computer labs not only took away uncomfortable silences, they also added to the air of familiarity for the informants. For instance, my interview with SouSou took place in a partly separated space in one end of a computer lab. While 25 meters away, a group of students were doing computer assignments, she shared her personal feelings. She described that most people in her school "*say that I am smart*" but she added she felt "*a lack of self-confidence*" and found it "*difficult to make friends.*" I include her voice here to illustrate she felt comfortable enough and felt a sufficient level of trust to speak about these difficult topics. The proximity of fellow students also had its drawbacks, however, making some informants cautious about sharing their personal feelings. During my interview with Fourteen-year-old Mehmet Ali this became apparent. A teaching assistant led Mehmet Ali and me to a study hall, a big, bright place with large windows. Through the windows one could oversee different classrooms and a computer lab. At the beginning of the interview, Mehmet Ali was speaking quietly, giving brief answers. At a certain point, he began to speak more loudly, telling enthusiastically about his digital practices. Only then I realized that a girl who had been doing her homework in peace in another corner of the room had left the study hall.

To ensure that I would be able to include those personal narratives that might be more easily shared outside the context of school, the interviews with thirteen Moroccan-Dutch youth contacted through snowball sampling were purposefully conducted outside their institutional education settings. I chose to conduct these interviews outside of the informant's homes, because Moroccan-Dutch youth do not always seem to feel more secure speaking to researchers in their home spaces as they may struggle to deal with another normative community than their family peer community there (Pels &

De Haan, 2003, p. 83). I held additional interviews in nonthreatening and permissive environments ranging from a university cafeteria, a university office shared with a dozen other graduate students, a museum café, a lunchroom, and a hotel lobby.

Selecting field sites

Earlier I described how the Internet maps served as an icebreaker at the beginning of interviews, and how they provided a structure to map out the intensities and particularities of informants' digital practices across different spaces. However, I have also considered them all together to narrow down my focus and make a selection of which spaces to study more in-depth on a case study basis. In order to make an informed selection on the basis of informants' preferences, I used the website Worldle.net to generate a word cloud by combining all the Internet applications that informants included in their personal Internet maps (see Figure 5).

The size of the platform names in the figure indicate how frequent they were included in the Internet maps informants drew. The figure shows the key digital spaces Moroccan-Dutch youth frequent: (1) MSN, an instant messaging application; (2) the video-sharing platform YouTube, (3) the social networking sites Hyves and Facebook, and (4) the online discussion forum Marokko.nl. The Internet maps guided the decision which Internet applications to study more in-depth, in this book, I have focused on these four digital environments as key "field sites" (Boelstorff, 2010; Hine, 2013). Although these platforms are interconnected and interdependent, digital experiences increasingly revolve around distinct forms of "platformed

Fig. 5: Word cloud based on all Internet applications included in the Internet maps of the informants

sociality" (Van Dijck, 2013, p. 5). I contrast the four field sites, because Internet scholarship "has yet to engage thoroughly with the Internet qua medium (or, more correctly, a diverse bundle of information and communication technologies each with distinct possibilities for content)" (Press & Livingstone, 2008, p. 191). Of course, platforms may have some features, content and user populations in common and "ongoing boundary ambiguities" between applications may arise (Marshall, 2010, p. 12). They also do not exist in isolation from offline power relations. Nonetheless, they do deserve attention as distinct locations of fieldwork, as they each hold a distinct material, symbolic and affective appeal for the informants. In the following section I reflect more on the virtual ethnography I conducted across these different field sites.

1.4 Virtual ethnography

> Reaching understandings of participants' sense of self and of the meanings they give to their online participation requires spending time with the participants to observe what they do online as well as what they say they do.
>
> – Lori Kendall (1999, p. 62)

The survey provided general information on the kinds of digital practices Moroccan-Dutch youth engage in. The interviews served the purpose of mapping out how informants think about various platforms by eliciting their personal experiences, perceptions and thoughts. This section details how I was able to get a sense of how informants perform their identities online across these spaces. I was interested in observing online practices and capturing digital data. Virtual ethnography is a methodology that allows the researcher to be attentive to how a social media platform as a field site acts both as a "culture" and a "cultural artifact," which is "variously constructed by users with quite different interpretations of what it means for them" (Hine, 2013, p. 138). In my virtual ethnography of the four field sites of instant messaging, discussion forums, SNSs and YouTube, I combined participant observation with qualitative "digital methods" for data gathering (Rogers, 2013). Digital methods, "a methodological outlook and mind-set for social research with the web," aims to capture "medium-specific" dynamics on platforms in a way that "follows the medium." Instead of drawing from pre-Internet era methods, "natively digital objects" are studied as meaningful objects. This way it becomes possible "to diagnose cultural change and societal conditions by means of the internet" (Rogers, 2013, pp. 4, 19, 21).

Capturing digital practices is a troublesome enterprise as researchers still "barely know how to track their 'texts' given the three-fold problems of overwhelming volume of material, temporary existence and its 'virtuality'" or its "hypertextual" character. These are the reasons why, in the field of new media studies, "few textual studies of content favored by children been undertaken" (Livingstone, 2003, p. 150). Aiming to address this void, I asked informants permission to observe their construction of digital identities across the four field sites. Informants were also invited to share their digital practices with me. For the purpose of the virtual ethnography, I gathered contact details of those interested in follow-up research during the in-depth interviews. Some informants gave their e-mail addresses, others their mobile phone numbers or SNS profile page nicknames. In this section I reflect on gathering ethnographic data in the different field sites, and I especially contrast the difficulties I experienced on publicly accessible and closed platforms (Leurs, 2013). I situate my approach in Internet research ethics.

Publicly accessible digital field sites

Being publicly accessible, the digital materials informants engage with on online discussion forums and video-sharing sites were gathered by asking informants about their favorite topics and rubrics as well as their favorite videos. I would subsequently browse these spaces to look up conversations and videos. My personal observations were recorded by writing field notes and by saving, printing and archiving discussions and saving videos. By detailing personal research experiences on online discussion forums I ground Internet research ethics further.

After I posted a job vacancy for a research assistant under the nickname Wired Up on Yasmina.nl, an online message board popular among Moroccan-Dutch girls, several people responded to the topic with questions and inquiries. However, there were also users who questioned my intentions. A mere 7 minutes after I posted the job advertisement, I was shocked when I read one user had written, "*do not respond, this is a lover boy who is recruiting*" (Wired Up, 2010a). In the Netherlands and Belgium the term "lover boy" refers to pimps who coerce girls into prostitution or other forms of illegal forms of sexual exploitation. I had a similar experience when I initiated a discussion under the same nickname on the online message board Maroc.nl about different language influences I encountered while studying instant messaging. While some Maroc.nl participants enthusiastically assisted me in translating words and phrases I did not understand, others questioned my intentions. One user, for example, asked, "*are you hustling a Moroccan girl somewhere?* " (Wired Up, 2010b).

Before me, there had been other students, researchers and journalists taking public message boards as a starting point to learn more about Moroccan-Dutch youth. User HaasHaas shared his unease and frustrations with again seeing outsiders coming to the message board to study the Moroccan-Dutch community.

> *Ow god, those snobs are turning to us again as if we are a living laboratory. Go research yourself one time or so something like ooh we from the university are going to put something under a microscope because we do not have anything better to do. Pff.* (Wired Up, 2010b)

The frustrations HaasHaas voiced may be attributed to the dominant scholarly and journalistic focus on problems within the Moroccan-Dutch community. Studies focusing on a particular problematic segment of any community may be taken to paint a negative picture of the community as a whole. Difficulties of overcoming suspicion and gaining access to the community result from earlier scholars' focus on issues such as juvenile delinquency, mental health problems, radicalization and Islam (see the introductory chapter). Understandably, such studies may lead Moroccan-Dutch individuals to regard scholars with due suspicion (Bel Ghazi, 1986, p. 10). Other users continued to make efforts to make me feel welcome, typing for instance, "*HaasHaas, be ashamed of yourself. Let this man carry out his work.*"

My experiences resonate with fundamental debates over Internet research ethics. Research ethics demand that scholars conduct research while respecting human dignity, autonomy, anonymity and safety. Internet research, in particular, raises dialectic questions concerning ways of guaranteeing informants' anonymity versus crediting authorship, corporate and individual ownership of data, blurring of boundaries between publicity and privateness, asking or assuming informed consent, considerations of vulnerability and contextual harm of research subjects and mechanisms for securing digital trust (Hine, 2013, 2015; Kozinets, 2010; AOIR, 2012). Throughout the study, when referencing publicly accessible digital materials of people proven to be adults, I credit the author with the nickname she/he uses. In my conversation with YouTube user eMoroccan, for instance, he made it clear that he wanted me to refer to his nickname when I included his material and statements in my writing. However, by crediting his authorship, his nickname can be traced back to his online presence that, in turn, might provide easy ways to locate further personal details. Such issues complicate traditional research standards aimed at ensuring anonymity. Nonetheless, although widely accessible and easily retrievable, people participating in online discussion forums may perceive or consider the content they have contributed as private or sensitive information. HaasHaas's remarks suggest that he participates in what he feels is his own online community, complicating the complex blurring of online boundaries between public and private. Although strictly publicly accessible, the messages posted on discussion boards I frequented have a specific intended audience.

I took HaasHaas's remark seriously, because it reveals how some people may experience unequal power relations when privileged outsiders such as researchers, students and journalists write about their community in particular ways and exclude the vast majority of everyday voices. I therefore took this criticism to heart and always made sure to explain my intentions when observing everyday digital practices. In addition, I reflected on my positionality at the beginning of all conversations, both online and offline. Furthermore, as reading public forum discussions sometimes gave me the feeling of eavesdropping on a personal conversation, I chose to refrain from being a passive lurker, but participated and actively made my presence known. However, HaasHaas reminded me that – unlike other face-to-face methods I used, such as survey taking and interviews – by conducting virtual ethnographies, information is used that is not always confidentially given specifically to the researcher by an informant (Kozinets, 2010, p. 143). Scholars have recognized the changing reputation mechanisms and credibility assessments young people make while using digital media (Metzger & Flanagin, 2008). I sought to foster digital trust by clearly positioning myself as a researcher and by providing hyperlinks to the Wired Up research project and my personal website. However, I should add that most of the people I interacted with online already knew me from face-to-face encounters, as I largely limited my online participant observation and data gathering of online forums and YouTube to those topics, threads and videos that my informants specifically spoke about with me or shared with me.

Accessing closed digital field sites

HaasHaas was also critical of how I had gathered data in the private space of instant messaging. In response to my questions about Moroccan-Dutch words on the discussion forum Maroc.nl he posted the following:

> *How did you actually collect those conversations? Do those young people know about it? Or did you just look at the chat history on MSN? Are you allowed to do that? Or is it because young people made use of a computer that is owned by a school or the government, enabling you to research it?* (Wired Up, 2010b)

In this subsection I reflect on data gathering on digital field sites that are not directly accessible to researchers. Starting off with face-to-face contact proved invaluable in addressing the issue of digital trust in the private digital spaces of instant messaging and social networking sites. These two Internet applications are largely closed off from the eyes of onlookers. The majority of the interviewees have set their profile page settings to private so that other social networking site users outside their list of friends cannot view their personal profile pages. By sending out friend requests to those informants that provided their social networking site contact details, and asking them permission to study their self-profiling practices, a number of personal profile pages were opened up to me. Fourteen-year-old Ayoub, thirteen-year-old Anas, thirteen-year-old Midia, thirteen-year-old Mohammed, fifteen-year-old Oussema and fifteen-year-old Yethi provided me access to their personal profile pages. Furthermore I have carried out contextual face-to-face and e-mail interviews with eight group page founders and moderators.

In instant massaging, too, users are able to maintain the boundaries of their digital space by deciding whom to include on their buddy list. Only those that are included on this list can see the display pictures and display names that individual users have chosen, while one-on-one conversations are personal and even more inaccessible. Here, I discuss how I gathered instant messaging transcripts at greater length to illustrate the intricacies of carrying out participatory forms of research in a private digital space. The data-gathering process reveals additional ways I sought to have informants study their digital practices with me.

Following the example set by Gloria Jacobs (2003) and Shayla Thiel-Stern (2007), informants were invited to save instant messaging conversations to the hard drives of their computers. All forty-three interviewees I spoke with used MSN. A smaller group of six informants eventually granted me access to their personal MSN communication network by saving and sharing conversation transcripts. These six participating young people were requested to ask their contacts permission to save the transcript in the beginning of their conversations for research purposes. Only conversations that were agreed upon by contacts to be saved and shared were included in my analysis. Asking permission was done, for instance, as follows:

> ***El Hoceima is the bom, that's the place where i come from so just tell everyone thats the city number ONE says:*** *I participate in a research on msn and I have to copy and paste conversations and send them to them would you allow me to use this conversation?*
>
> ***~..ღ. n O u я я.ღ.. ~ says:*** *yea course sweety ♥.... hahaha its bout nothing anyway*

Informants Fatiha, Naoul, Midia, Kamal, Khadija and Inzaf responded to my call to submit IM conversation transcripts. They were invited to save IM conversations to the hard drives of their computers between December 2009 and February 2010. This process of data gathering was skewed, as the group of six people sharing transcripts consisted of five girls and one boy. Interested informants were asked to save IM transcripts of conversations they held with five people of their choice. From their collection, I asked the young people to select five transcripts consisting of at least ten turns, which they deemed fit for me to read.

I stressed in my invitations that I did not mind with whom informants spoke or what their conversations were about. I welcomed everyone and all topics. In total, I received twenty-six transcripts, ranging in length from ten sentences to over three pages. Participants sent in IM logs of conversations with friends ranging from thirteen to twenty-two years old. All interviewees said the transcripts they sent in were talks with friends that they knew from outside the Internet, for instance, through school, work or from their neighborhood. In total, twenty of the talks were with women friends, and six with male friends. Interview narratives were used to provide a more gender-balanced supplementary interpretative context.

This approach has its obvious limitations and I recognize that participants chose conversations to construct a self that they wanted me to see. First, although it became apparent from the survey and the interviews that MSN was widely used to engage in intimate or romantic conversations I mostly received transcripts of friendly conversations between two boys or two girls. Secondly, those who shared transcripts with me estimated that 10% of their contacts live abroad. Informants explained how they assist their parents in initiating MSN webcam conversations with family members who live abroad. Interviewees shared their personal accounts with them, as some parents were unable to manage MSN on their own. However, transcripts of such exchanges were not shared with me and transnational conversations could therefore not further considered in the analysis. Even though very rich, the transcripts provided thus only offered a partial view on their everyday private digital identity positioning.

In addition, the informants' ability to self-select the material was integral to ensure that they were taken seriously as experts over their own messaging practices. In Chapter 3, I include excerpts from these instant-messaging transcripts. By doing so, together with using the pseudonyms and labels informants suggested themselves and by choosing to study those platforms that their Internet maps revealed to be most important, I aimed for informants to become, to some degree, active participants in this text. In the next section I account for the dynamics of representation further by describing the analytical precautions I take while scrutinizing informants' narratives through a lens that is attentive to the discursive distribution of power, a process in which I also take part.

1.5 Analyzing informants' narratives

After the surveys, in-depth interviews and virtual ethnography I found myself with a large volume of empirical data. In this section I set out how I analyzed informants' narratives that were collected through interviews and the observation of digital practices. These data are not value-neutral facts and they do not speak for themselves about digital identification processes among second-generation migrant youth. Rather, these narratives are open to multiple readings and my "representations are interpretations" (McRobbie, 1982, p. 51). My focus is on unraveling how the narratives reflect informants' navigation through structural parameters that are social, gendered, ethnic, generational, religious and youth cultural and their negotiations of agency within these structures. Grounded theory and discursive analysis were used to generate meaningful patterns from the narratives gathered in online and offline in-depth fieldwork. In this way, I justify the interpretative knowledge claims I make and stay away from textual appropriation of informants' narratives (Ramazanoğlu and Holland, 2002, pp. 160-161). My textual analysis consisted of a phase of systematic coding, exploring various themes in the data and a phase of theoretical reflection through the discursive analysis of power relations flowing through the narratives. Before discussing these two phases, I assess the politics of translating interviewees' narratives.

Politics of translation

Throughout my argument, I include direct quotations to have informants speak for themselves. However, to open up the study to a larger audience, the voices of the informants were translated into English. The process of translating informants' digital practices and interview narratives needs to be problematized. In her essay "The politics of translation," Gayatri Spivak argued that Western translators of subaltern discourse – next to maintaining its contents and tone with dignity – have the responsibility to make the influence on the texts they produce visible (1993b, p. 181). Transferring texts from one language to another is not neutral; rather, as a process of (re)narration, translation should be considered as an analytical act. This holds true both for translating spoken interview recordings into a written language as well as translating Dutch recordings and gathered digital narratives into English.

When writing about digital practicesof participants, we Internet researchers "literally reconfigure these people when we edit their sentences, because for many of them, these messages are a deliberate presentation of self." In addition, in their publications, researchers in their "texts construct the essence and meaning of the participant, as perceived and responded to by others" (Markham, 2004, p. 153). My translation process of instant messaging narratives can be taken as an example of the impact made by rewriting. IM is a social media application that allows individuals to privately exchange short messages and socialize in real time. Reading the instant messaging transcripts informants shared with me, I was confronted with a distinct genre and expressive culture consisting of multilingual out-of-school literacies. Consider the original exchange between thirteen-year-old Midia and her friend:

> ***Schaakmat schatj zegt***: haha heb je die foto gezien zij en yasminaaaaaa
> ***mevrouw mocro zegt:*** die kus?
> ***Schaakmat schatj zegt***: wuhaha jhaa
> ***mevrouw zegt:*** tfoee man die hoer
> ***Schaakmat schatj zegt***: aisha staat dr 3ed leuk op maar
> yasminna
> jongee man
> ***mevrouw mocro zegt***: k haat yasmina egt he
> wollah nii normaal
> ***Schaakmat schatj zegt***: I KZAG HAAR VANDAAG
> hahaha
> vbijdaand

In my attempt to include the specificities of such conversations in my translations, I only translated into English the Dutch words that were used. Words and sentences typed in (Latinized) Moroccan-Arabic and Berber were not translated into English in the running text. Rather explanations are given between brackets. By leaving these words untranslated I aimed to have readers witness the original forms of multilingual IM communicative exchanges. Furthermore, although for outsiders of this new genre of writing this may look as a messy writing style full of typos, abbreviations and misspellings, it is important to realize this is partly a decorative and creative writing style for insiders. Such decorative, creative spellings were carried over into English, and I also included in my translations the ways sentences were usually divided over multiple turns.

> ***Triumph sweeti says:*** haha did you see that picture her and yasminaaaaaa
> ***miss mocro says:*** that kiss?
> ***Triumph sweeti says:*** wuhaha jhaa
> ***miss mocro says:*** tfoee man that whore [*tfoe*: dirty]
> ***Triumph sweeti says:*** aisha looks 3ed good but [*3ed*: still, however]
> yasminna
> oh boyy
> oh man
> ***miss mocro says:*** i hate yasmina fo sure
> wollah noot normal [*wollah*: with Allah, I swear]
> ***Triumph sweetie says:*** ISAW HER TODAY
> hahaha
> eneemy

The conversation moved from an opening greeting sequence to Midia ("Triumph sweeti") informing whether "miss mocro" was on speaking terms with Aisha. After finding out they were still quarreling, Midia added fuel to the fire by gossiping about the selfie Aisha used as her IM display picture. Aisha is a girl the conversationalists both knew, both from outside the world of instant messaging ("*I saw her today*") as well as from within ("*did you see that picture*"). In the photo another girl, Yasmina, was apparently kissing Aisha. While Aisha looked "*3ed good*" in the picture, the appearance of Yasmina irritated both girls. Miss mocro called her names adding "*tfoee*" ("*tfoe*" is a word that occurs both in Berber as well as in Arabic) to dismiss her: "*man that whore*" and typed she really hates her. She put extra emphasis on her assertion by adding the Arabic/Berber term "*wollah*," meaning with Allah. Midia, using capitalized letters, shouted she saw their opponent (their "*eneemy*") that day.

I employed a similar strategy in translating interview transcripts, incorporating non-Dutch words in the running texts. Nonetheless, the choice, explanation and contextualization of translated segments included in my argumentation reflect my personal coding decisions and interpretation. By placing in italics the quotations taken from informants' narratives, I set aside their voices from my own reasoning and flag the constructedness of the translations.

Coding

In this section, I reflect on the way I coded interview transcripts and other forms of collected empirical data. The three levels of abstraction recognized in "grounded theory" are helpful to explain the procedures I followed (Strauss & Corbin, 1998). In the first phase of open coding, I read all the empirical data extensively to develop a coding tree. I inductively looked for structures, categories and themes to sort the data rather than superimposing a preformed framework. Secondly, I assigned categories and themes a position, gradually refining the coding tree by assessing and connecting the various codes. This way, I increasingly ordered and interconnected the codes in a specific way. Concepts can be formulated by finding patterns, similarities and differences within categories and between themes. In the third phase, I compared the different themes and took the analysis to a more abstract theoretical level.

Using NVivo, a qualitative data analysis software package, I coded interview transcripts and digital practices using separate database files (Bazeley, 2007). NVivo assisted me in my interpretative coding creativity. For example, it helped me to keep an overview of all the interview transcript files, allowing me to search these files at once, and to bring them all together in a coding tree. In line with how informants drew maps of their favorite Internet applications, the first phase of coding consisted of categorizing parts of the narratives according to the various field sites. The field sites shaped the major branches of the coding tree. Secondly, reading through all the texts relating to the individual spaces, my theoretical touchstones guided me in specifying the various sub-branches of the coding tree, coding discussions related to the key topics of the study, such as: identity performativity; medium-specific characteristics; language use; gendered, ethnic, migration, religion and generational issues; youth culture; transnational networking, online-offline dynamics, obstacles; boundary-making; publicness and privateness; and visibility and invisibility. Thirdly, I started looking for points of convergence and divergence when comparing the practices and meanings attributed to the different spaces. I used critical discourse analysis to consider the larger context of hierarchical but unstable power relations.

Feminist poststructuralist critical discourse analysis

The collected narratives are not necessarily self-evident for my argument. As Ien Ang specified: "it is only through the interpretative framework of the researcher that understandings of the 'empirical' come about" (1996, p. 46). In this final subsection, I reflect on my specific engagement with the collected textual materials. I conducted a critical discourse analysis to unravel both dominant and alternative meanings of the intersections and intertextuality of gender, ethnicity, religion and youth culture encoded in interview transcripts and digital data. Also, I remained attentive to the field-site-specific configurations of agency and subordination, studying how digital spaces give rise to specific normative ways of being. This way the method is used to filter the themes that arose from the interpretative coding process through the lenses of new media, feminist and postcolonial theories. I employed discourse analysis by connecting it with my theoretical grounding in poststructuralism and intersectionality.

A variety of discourse analysis approaches can be distinguished. Nelson Phillips and Cynthia Hardy categorized four different orientations (see Figure 6). The vertical axis distinguishes between levels of focus; ranging from scrutinizing linguistic structures and functions of text to the contextual embedding of texts, while the horizontal axes discern the critical and constructivist approaches. Social constructivists tend to work on a micro-level, exploring how specific social realities are constructed,

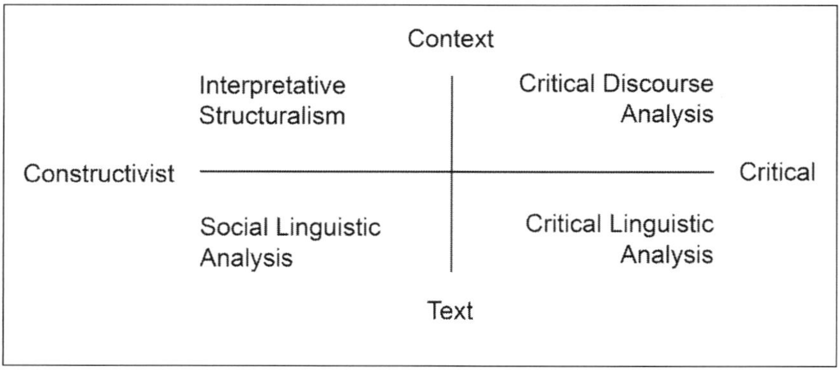

Fig. 6: Four different approaches to discourse analysis (Phillips and Hardy, 2002, p. 20)

while critical discourse analysts focus more on the discursive embedding of power dynamics, knowledge distribution and ideological assumptions (Phillips and Hardy, 2002). Moreover, approaches analyzing the internal cohesion of texts can be discerned from critical approaches that focus more on contextual connections made in texts (Buikema, 2009, p. 312).

In my analysis, I take cues from critical discourse analysis but operationalize it differently. Critical discourse analysis references a Foucauldian theory of language as a disciplinary form that produces subjects, a process which can simultaneously be countered to reveal agency: it "is centrally concerned with analyzing patterns in language use in order to uncover the workings of ideology or investment within/through it, and thus to be able to resist it" (Griffin, 2011, p. 98). I take a stance informed by poststructuralism, understanding language use as a discursive locus of power, where meaning can be imposed and contested. As Foucault noted, individuals are always "simultaneously undergoing and exercising this power" (1980, p. 98). He specified power as a "productive network" by arguing, "what makes power hold good, what makes it accepted, is simply the fact that it doesn't only weigh on us as a force that says no, but that it traverses and produces things, it induces pleasure, forms knowledge, produces discourse. It needs to be considered as a productive network" (Foucault, 1980, p. 119). "Power exists only when it is put into action," Foucault wrote, emphasizing its performative character (1982, p. 219). Specifically, power dynamically operates in two ways: it is normalized and "exerted" over people and it gives them the "ability to modify, use, consume or destroy" its homogeneity (ibid., p. 217). The two-sided relationship between power and subjectivity reveals people are "subject to someone else by control and dependence" while also struggling to manifest their "own identity." Struggles, Foucault recognizes, are often aimed "against forms of domination (ethnic, social, and religious)" (ibid., p. 212).

The emancipatory ideals of feminism and poststructuralism can be brought together in carrying out feminist poststructuralist discourse analysis. Judith Baxter listed the aims of this approach as follows: "analyzing intertextualised discourses in spoken interaction and other types of text," which builds on poststructuralist principles "of complexity, plurality, ambiguity, connection, recognition, diversity, textual playfulness, functionality and transformation" (2008, p. 245). Building on feminist theories of intersectionality, I combine poststructuralist understandings of discursive power with a focus on the convergence of multiple axes of domination and differentiation including gender, ethnicity, religion, age and generation.

In practice, carrying out a critical discursive analysis that speaks back to critical theory begins with deconstructing gathered texts: "to reinscribe and resituate meanings, events and objects within broader movements and structures" (Eagleton, 1986, p. 80). Such an intersectional deconstruction promotes "to ask the other question" to consider how performed identities and relations are multiply located by different discourses: How does racism operate in tandem with patriarchy, sexism, heterosexism, homophobia and/or class-issues? (Matsuda, 1991, p. 1189). Understanding discursive power as productive, I not only focused on intersecting forms of domination but also took an agency-sensitive approach. This way I carried out a discursive analysis of interview transcripts and digital practices by being attentive to how the informants' field-site-specific narratives revealed their embeddedness in unequal, intersecting power relations but I also acknowledged multispatial micro-politics of power subversion. Thus discursive analysis was taken up to deconstruct how intersecting axes of differentiation among my informants in their process of identity performativity across digital spaces perpetuated and/or contested hierarchical power relations. This method allowed me to answer the plea for a critical ethnographical stance that incorporated reflexivity and multiperspectivism to remain attentive to polyphony and fragmentation in informants' narratives.

1.6 Conclusions

In this chapter, I have reflected on how I translated the theoretical framework of space invaders into an empirical methodological approach to analyze Moroccan-Dutch youth identity practices across digital spaces. I have demystified the research process of gathering and analyzing empirical data by reconstructing my unconventional but strategic journey through quantitative-empirical and qualitative-theoretical methods. Discussing the politics of gathering and analyzing data through large-scale surveys, in-depth interviews, virtual ethnography and feminist poststructuralist critical discourse analysis, I specified the grounds on which to judge between and combine different epistemologies that give different accounts of reality.

I reflected on how knowledge produced in one research phase was used to structure subsequent phases: survey findings shaped my focus in the interviews, and the Internet maps drawn by the interviewees in turn helped me to select the four field sites of online forums, instant messaging, online social networking sites and YouTube. Selecting these four for in-depth case studies also directed my virtual ethnography efforts.

Writing in a reflexive mode (for instance, by discussing the power relations at play in data gathering and by describing some personal fieldwork experiences), I illustrated the value ladenness and situatedness of knowledge production. And although I used several participatory techniques to have informants at least partly decide over their own representations in the research, the power of definition largely remained in my hands. In sum, I accepted that all forms of research embed some kind of bias and specific political commitments. Knowledge is always a social construction; it is impossible to attain a singular, absolute truth. Rather, different methods construct differently situated knowledges. As I continuously move between and evaluate different bodies of data this book combines various partial perspectives on second-generation migrant youth and their everyday construction of identity across digital spaces.

2. Voices from the margins on Internet forums

It is a sort of support. As a process of feeding [your emotions], by sort of reacting to each other. You'll have everyone who backs you up. It's like everyone is on the same side. You kind of become more sure of yourself. You just know, yes look we are not the only ones who think this way and so on. Thus you can express your opinion and just put everything up and you hear that others are similar to you.
– Ilham, a thirteen-year-old girl

In this chapter, Internet forums as frequented by Moroccan-Dutch youth are considered as safe arenas to form counterpublics and exert agency. Ilham eloquently described the emotional support she receives from being able to secure speaking power on the online discussion forum Marokko.nl. Message boards, also known as Internet forums, are digital spaces where users can engage in conversations by publicly posting messages in response to each other. Ilham shared her self-confidence grows from being able to publish her opinions and connect with other like-minded people. She has the agency to publish her own opinions, in contrast to being positioned in certain ways by others elsewhere. On the forum, she can speak for herself and see others positively acknowledge her presence. This way, she can self-consciously claim membership in an alternative supportive community consisting mostly of second-generation migrant youth like her. Feeling heard, she receives confirmation that other Moroccan-Dutch peers share her joys, doubts and frustrations of negotiating contradictory youth cultural, ethnic, gendered and religious discourses. Forums show how a "digital architecture" may "promote particular forms of storytelling and invite others to listen in through specific practices" (Papacharissi & Easton, 2013, p. 178).

In Latin, the word "*forum*" refers to the open, public space at the center of Roman cities. This space functioned both as a marketplace and gathering place. In particular, I consider the online formation of Internet forums as digital "subaltern counterpublics" (Fraser, 1990, p. 67). Nancy Fraser developed this notion in extension of Jürgen Habermas's ideal-type of the "bourgeois public sphere." In Habermas's philosophy, society resolved around a singular, all-embracing public sphere. Fraser rightly posits this conceptualization does not allow one to capture the reality of contemporary stratified societies. Rather, she recognizes that a multiplicity of competing publics provide arenas for subordinated groups. By circulating "counter discourses" these people can engage in "discursive contestation" (1990, p. 62). Online discussion forums provide subordinated groups with particular counterpublics, away from the mainstream they can be seen as safe "hush-harbors" where hegemonies can be scrutinized and group cohesion can be fostered (Byrne 2008, p. 222). I argue Moroccan-Dutch youth appropriate the medium-specific particularities of Internet forums to shape counterpublics, through which they forge community relations and establish their own shared space to counteract, subvert or engage with dominant spheres of state-based secular culture, defiant public media reports and parental versus peer expectations with their imposition of dictums and norms about proper behavior. Online discussion forums allow for the proliferation of alternative voices in the digital public domain. More specifically, I focus on how online forums are taken up among the informants as counterpublics to (re)construct their identities at the crossroads of ethnicity, gender and religion. Motivated by the heuristic perspective of space invaders to consider digital spatial power relations as simultaneously enabling and restricting, I also scrutinize how forum discussions remain subject to disciplinary processes of regulation and control.

Although in everyday life experiences axes of differentiation operate simultaneously, for analytical purposes I separate out digital ethnic, gendered, and religious identity performative practices in my argumentation. First, focusing how ethnicity is renegotiated I observe the dynamics of "digital multiculturalism" on forums (Leurs, Midden & Ponzanesi, 2012). Countering mainstream negative news framing, I map the powerful feelings informants experience while voicing their alternative opinions about the Moroccan-Dutch community. However, this does not mean these pages are immune to negative exposure by intruding non-Moroccan-Dutch outsiders. Secondly, I consider how informants renegotiate gender relations to stake out their own individual gendered positionality. Discussing issues such as love, relationships, marriage and sexuality, the reflections the informants shared reveal how they navigate the expectations of their peers, Islam, Dutchness, Western European stereotypes and "*hchouma*" (Skalli, 2006, p. 96), the gendered moral order of their parents and the wider migrant community. Third, I analyze the workings of "digital postsecularism" (Leurs & Ponzanesi, 2014c) by considering how religiosity is renegotiated on Internet forums. Internet forums are used as a space to negotiate between "halal" (codes of conduct allowed in Islam) and "haram" (conduct forbidden in Islam) practices.

The chapter is structured as follows. I first introduce the use of forums among Moroccan-Dutch youth. Additionally, I introduce the discussion boards that informants most frequently visit: Marokko.nl and Chaima.nl. In Section 2.2, I theorize the ways in which message boards may function as counterpublics for minority groups. In the remaining empirical part of the chapter, I analyze three different forms of digital counter practices, focusing, respectively, on ethnicity, gender, and religion.

2.1 Internet forum participation among Moroccan-Dutch youth

In the Netherlands and worldwide, scholars have argued online discussion forums hold a specific appeal to ethnic and religious minority groups. Over the last two decades, they have remained popular among minorities including Moroccan-Dutch youth (Brouwer, 2011; Borghuis et al., 2010; Byrne, 2008; D'Haenens et al., 2004; De Koster, 2010; Elahi, 2014; Geense & Pels, 2002; Mamadouh, 2001). Wired Up survey findings corroborate this distinct preference: Moroccan-Dutch youth reported visiting online discussion boards more than ethnic-majority Dutch youth. Moroccan-Dutch respondents also reported a higher level of attachment to online discussion boards than ethnic-majority Dutch youth. Additionally, Moroccan-Dutch girls participated more in forum discussion than Moroccan-Dutch boys (Leurs, 2012, pp. 123, 327; Wired Up, 2011). Also, Moroccan-Dutch girls reported feeling more attached to the communicative space than Moroccan-Dutch boys did (see Table 4). This distinction was also evident from the interviewing phase; out of the total of forty-three interviewees, seventeen girls and five boys included Internet forums in their Internet maps and spoke to me about their use of these forums.

Table 4: The importance of online discussion forums in the lives of Moroccan-Dutch youth (percentages, n = 344)

Would you miss online discussion forums if you could not use them any longer?	*Completely not*	*Somewhat*	*Very much*	*Total*
Girls	58.6%	23.2%	18.2%	100%
Boys	76.7%	19.0%	4.3%	100%

Marokko.nl and Chaima.nl

> *Marokko.nl is a website where especially Moroccans come, so to say. You talk about all kinds of things – for example your Eid or just nonsense or politics or something like that. Those kinds of things are discussed and you see how others think about things.*[1]
>
> – SouSou, a fifteen-year-old girl

For SouSou, Marokko.nl is a space to hang out with other Moroccan-Dutch teenagers away from the mainstream of Dutch society. She finds others to share in celebrating Eid, the conclusion of the fasting-month of Ramadan. Also, she expresses her views on political issues. But most of all discussants get the chance to anonymously put forward what SouSou calls *"just nonsense."* "Just nonsense" topics can in fact be of great importance in the lives of the young people, as in practice, these include personal prosaic experiences, trivial thoughts, banal ideas and everyday issues that all enable peer-verification as users learn what others feel about their personal meanderings. Through collaboratively sharing these conversations with the whole public of the site, youth establish a distinct Moroccan-Dutch community. As Naoul, a sixteen-year-old girl, notes: Marokko.nl is a community, *"it is your own circle, with all those Moroccan things"* that are discussed, and *"the people there are like you, that's nice."* Similarly, Inas, a thirteen-year-old girl, explains: *"You have the feeling you get nearer to each other, you feel connected. For instance, someone from Amsterdam posts something about fashion, and I like that posting. Subsequently I will start speaking with that person, with her or him."*

Moroccan-Dutch people first established Internet forums in the late 1990s to express dissatisfaction with the one-sided coverage of their demographic in Dutch media (Geense & Pels, 2002, p. 13). Ranging in interests and incentives, a wide variety of forums – such as Amazigh.nl, Bladna.nl, Chaima.nl, Maroc.nl, Maroc.nu, Maghreb.nl, Maghrebonline.nl, Marokko.nl, and Zoubida.nl have been created and are frequented by second-generation Moroccan-Dutch youth. Marokko.nl was recognized as "the most popular online discussion board among allochthonous young people" (Knijff, 2009); it was also the most popular forum among the interviewees.

1 Eid ul Fitr: festivities to celebrate the conclusion of the dawn-to-sunset fasting month of Ramadan.

This chapter focuses on Marokko.nl and to a lesser extent Chaima.nl, because those twenty-two informants who spoke about their engagement with Internet forums all reported frequenting Marokko.nl. Five girls mentioned they also turned to Chaima.nl. Using gender-stereotypical terms, thirteen-year-old Amina distinguished the two as follows:

> *There is one site, which is called Marokko.nl, and I'm serious it's buzzing with Moroccan youth there. Also people from other cultures and origins, but Moroccan youth are the majority. They have founded the site themselves. It is very active, everyone goes there to talk to one another, and there is something for everyone there.*
>
> *Chaima.nl, that is a very pleasant site as well. It's for girls. The site is made up completely in pink, with [discussions] about nails and those kinds of things. It offers you a space where only girls gather, but sometimes also boys go there to [talk about] sensitive topics and explore what girls are up to. For instance, topics like fashion are discussed, and love and marriage. You'll read about girls who are about to get married. I believe a Moroccan[-Dutch] girl also founded the site. But also others are welcome, you know.*

On September 30, 2014, on Marokko.nl almost 207,000 accounts were registered, 1.3 million topics were opened and 36.6 million comments were left. On Chaima.nl 62,000 accounts were set up, 120,000 topics and 3.4 million comments were published. The amount of lurkers (anonymous readers who do not post) is expected to be much higher. Marokko.nl is estimated to reach a remarkable 75% of Moroccan-Dutch people in the age category between 15 and 35, roughly one-third of the total Moroccan-Dutch population visit the site on a weekly basis (Knijff, 2009; Motivaction, 2007). Anyone with access to the Internet can read messages that are posted; however, in order to contribute one has to become a member by registering with an e-mail account and one's date of birth.

To give an impression of the topics, the following discussion rubrics are most active on Marokko.nl: "Moroccan youth and current events," "Tea lounge," "Nonsense corner," "Moroccan youth, love and relationships," "Fashion and beauty care," "Moroccan weddings in the Netherlands and Belgium," "The world of the Moroccan woman," "Islam and I," "Sports," "Moroccan pop culture" and "Story rubric." On every page on the forums of Marokko.nl, the slogans "virtual community" and "*La maison du Maroc*" (French for "The home in Morocco") appear. Upon opening the site, one of a number of different background images appear, including romantic pictures of deserts, ancient cities and beaches that appeal to its visitors' image of Morocco. The site owners make use of the Dutch "*Kijkwijzer*" rating system to indicate that information on the site might be considered offensive. Developed by the Netherlands Institute for the Classification of Audio-visual Media, *Kijkwijzer* is a media classification scheme that makes use of pictograms to characterize media content. Prominently on the bottom-right of Marokko.nl, pictograms are placed as cautionary reminders indicating discussions may include violence, fear, sex, discrimination, drug and/or alcohol abuse and coarse language.

Initially launched in June 2006, Chaima.nl is a more modest site that targets Moroccan-Dutch girls, in particular. The main color used in its interface is pink, and other stereotypical feminine symbols appear, such as pictures of roses, high heels, nails, jewelry, dresses, and make-up. Showing some overlap with Marokko.nl, the following rubrics are most active there: "News," "Introduce yourself," "Chill corner," "Fashion and clothing," "Love and relationships," "Marriage and engagements," "Quran, Hadith and prayer," "Music club," "Poems," and "Stories."

When registering on Chaima.nl, users have to agree "to refrain from posting obscene, rude, sexually oriented, hateful, threatening or messages that are otherwise forbidden by law," and accept "Chaima.nl's right to delete, manipulate, move or close any discussion" (Chaima.nl, 2011). Upon registration to Marokko.nl, users have to accept that the board owners forbid "disrespectful messages, including racism, sexism, dirty language or swearing," "user advertisements," "publishing personal contact details" and "pornographic materials." Should they encounter any discrimination on the site, users have the duty to actively report it. Moreover, the site outlines its code of conduct as follows: "the language of communication is Dutch. Messages in English, Arabic and/or Tamazight are accepted. Messages in other languages are not allowed, except for when they add to the discussion and users explain them in Dutch." The site also forbids certain usernames: "Sharon, Bush, bin-laden, el_qaida, terrorist, or something which smells of it are not allowed." Users also have to accept that "they transfer ownership over all messages published on Marokko.nl to Marokko.nl." In terms of age requirements, the site requires users to guarantee that they are at least sixteen years old, or that they have parental permission (Marokko.nl, 2011a).

In contrast to the volunteer-based model of Chaima.nl, Marokko.nl's owners display an apparent commercial incentive. The forum users and the user-generated content circulating on the site are exploited as a niche market with great potential for advertisers. The site also holds a particular appeal to government agencies. The content is owned by a company called Urban Connect, which specializes in "ethnic marketing, online communication with urban youth, market research and intercultural advertisements" (Urban Connect, 2011b). The company sells advertisers access to 50,000 youth who visit Marokko.nl on a daily basis, selling announcements that can appear next to the 50,000 messages and 1,500 topics that are left each day (Urban Connect, 2011a). In it's branding, Marokko.nl presents itself as "virtual community," that

> is frequently visited by 75% of all Moroccan-Dutch youth and it has a great societal and commercial value. A virtual community offers an accessible opportunity to discuss all sorts of topics. But we offer you more. From the discussions that take place themes arise that our visitors often encounter, such as the care for their parents or questions around Islam and sexuality. We offer online services directed on our target group, that they may be able to employ in their real life to avoid problems. (Urban Connect, 2011b, my translation)

The company strategically sets up a distinction here between the "virtual community" and "real life," selling corporations access to a relatively untapped market of ethnic minorities in the Netherlands. Additionally, governmental institutions are invited to buy into the opportunity to manifest themselves on the forum, to be able to connect with a specific target group who might otherwise not be reached but who need governmental assistance to avoid real-life problems.

On both message boards, users can perform their identities in distinct ways. Users can choose a nickname and add a signature they like (although they do have to abide by the protocols of the platforms). Common nicknames include age, gender, ethnicity, diaspora, religion, race, youth cultural and sports affiliations. Fourteen-year-old Sahar describes the Moroccan affiliations in nicknames: "*people, for instance, add little Moroccan, or their name, or a town in Morocco, where they are from.*" Amina, a thirteen-year-old girl, notes that on Marokko.nl, users add distinct signatures to their posts "*they add their whole life-story, or write about the people that they miss. Or people just write about what they are like.*" Individuals have the opportunity to include text-based and visual signatures to their postings, often consisting of a religious saying or a reference to contemporary events. Also, users can include an avatar, a small graphic that represents something about a user's character. Eighteen-year-old Safae attests that these are chosen "*to get people's attention, to get them to react on your postings. When you add a nice photo you get more attention from the people you don't know.*"

Finally, users can create a personal profile page on both sites using text boxes where they can write about their "biography," "interests," or "occupation/education." On Marokko.nl, "gender" and "roots" are also available categories through which users can describe themselves, while Chaima.nl provides a box for "city of residence." Distinct reputation management systems are at work in these profile options. For example, numbers of posts users have contributed to the sites as well as the date of registration indicate their standing in the community. Also, users can give other posters credits if they like their contributions to the site: the more credits users receive, the more green lights appear under the poster's nickname shown next to every comment posted. On Marokko.nl and Chaima.nl, users themselves can flag messages as inappropriate, and subsequently site moderators decide whether to remove the comment and ban the user from accessing the site. In the next section, I theorize how user contributions can lend Internet forum discussions the status of (counter)publics.

2.2 Theorizing Internet forums as subaltern counterpublics

A community will evolve only when a people control their own communication.
– Frantz Fanon (cited in Kahn & Kellner, 2007, p. 17)

In this section, I map the academic debate on minorities' and migrants' use of Internet forums for voicing their identity, forming publics and counterpublics. Internet forums began as digital replacements for physical bulletin boards, used to provide notices and information, announce events and advertise things for sale. Originating in the early 1990s, message boards are a web-based technological evolution of the 1970s dial-up bulletin board system (BBS), newsgroups and electronic mailing lists. Currently a great variety of Internet forums are used by millions of people across the globe. They are set up to cater to the different, and specific, interests of groups of users, ranging from hacking and activism, to white-supremacy, computer games and anime. Famous examples of forums include 4chan.org, a site where users can post images anonymously (members of the international hacktivist group Anonymous are said to gather there); stormfront.org, a white-nationalist and supremacist neo-Nazi Internet forum; steampowered.com, an online game community; and gaia-online.com, a forum dedicated to anime videos.

"The social structure in society tends to be reflected in the social structure of the Web forums" (Van Stekelenburg, Oegema & Klandermans, 2011, p. 257). Marianne van den Boomen explains that message board communities are engrafted onto real-life communities, besides geographical affiliations, they may be based on "biographical identities: women, parents, gay's, children, elderly, handicapped, ill, blacks" (2000). In contrast to early cyber utopian expectations, it was first noted in the study of Internet forums that race is made as relevant online as it is offline. Byron Burkhalter countered the revolutionary expectations of technology by noting that in Usenet (a predecessor to contemporary Internet forums), in the absence of physical cues, race was textually "achieved, maintained, questioned, and reestablished" similar to the offline world (1999, pp. 63-64). In sum, as online discussion forums can be used by majority and minority subjects to define their own identities in their own space, forums constitute "highways" and "byways" across digital territories (Franklin, 2003, p. 486). Over the course of the last decade, scholars have sought to explain the popularity of message boards among migrants through various case studies including Internet forum use among Polish migrants in the UK (Galasińska, 2010); Chinese in the UK (Parker & Song, 2006; 2009); Asian-Americans, Mexican-Americans and African-Americans (Byrne, 2008); Indians in the US (Mallapragada, 2006); South Asian women (Mitra, 2004; Mitra & Watts, 2002); migrants in Germany (Androutsopoulos, 2007); and Russian LGBTs and queers in Israel (Kunstman, 2008).

In the United States, AsianAvenue.com, MiGente.com, and BlackPlanet.com are online discussion boards that represent Asian-American, Mexican-American, and African-American digital "public spheres" (Byrne, 2008). A shared racial identity serves as a common ground and determines who can participate in these spaces (Byrne, 2008, p. 18). These sites are frequented by millions of users. Its evident there is a great demand for such "dedicated sites," Byrne writes, because these spaces are sources for a sense of collective identification and ethnic pride. Online discussion boards highlight how "ethnic communities construct, stabilize, modify, and challenge individual and community senses of identity over a relatively long period of time." Besides identification, she adds, forums are used to develop and promote alternatives to mainstream, institutionalized ideologies. Also, they allow for the development of a shared insider consciousness of "racially, and often gender-appropriate behaviors" (2008, pp. 17, 29-31).

The Indian diaspora in the United States gathers on forums such as Drumnation.org, Madhavi Mallapragada observed how middle-class, Hindu-centric "gendered nationalism" is constructed, but she also noted users performed "alternative ways of imagining identity, belonging and community in their current location in the US" (2006, p. 225). SAWNET, a website for women of South Asia, has been argued to enable dispossessed individuals "to find a voice in the public sphere" (Mitra, 2004, p. 492). Forums arguably enable migrants to voice themselves, by doing so they might be enabled to contest biases in the "traditional structures of speaking power," through digital practices they might find "a place at the table" (Mitra & Watts, 2002, p. 489).

David Parker and Miri Song studied Britishbornchinese.org.uk and Barficulture.com, forums set up by British-born Chinese and South Asians. They read these sites through the notion of "reflexive racialization," highlighting the ability taken up by migrant users "to host a self-authored commentary on the issues faced by racialized minorities in a multicultural context" (2006, p. 583). In another study, the authors examined BritishChineseonline.com, arguing that such sites serve to pluralize senses of civic cultures. They recognize the imperative among second-generation British Chinese "to speak for themselves for the first time," while rearticulating their cultural inheritance to British and Chinese aspects of their backgrounds (2009, pp. 600-601). Jannis Androutsopoulos concerned himself with German-based diasporic websites, arguing these are instances of "media activism," as people who claim membership of specific ethnic groups assume responsibility for "maintaining a public space for fellow diasporians." He, however, also notes the commercialization of diasporic websites, as banners and advertisements are included to promote "products and services related to the respective ethnic group" (2007, pp. 343-344). In her ethnography, Adi Kunstman's highlights how forum discussions of queer Russian migrants in Israel displays the "performance of borders" (2008, p. 270) through which unwanted others are excluded.

From these case studies, we learn that Internet discussion forums are spaces where minorities can assert their voice, contest speaking power and assert alternative ideologies and identities. Online, I see voice as the material, representational and affectively embodied process of "giving an account of oneself" (Butler, 2005). Voice matters, because it reveals reflexive agency: although unevenly distributed, voice remains "irreducibly plural," allowing people to emerge as subjects who make sense of their life as it is embedded in multiple settings (Couldry, 2010, p. 7-10). Those who feel excluded may appreciate forums for resistance and intervention in their forming of "alternative public spheres and oppositional subcultures" (Kahn & Kellner, 2007, pp. 18-19). Digital self-representations constitute a complex genre with many elements coshaping the ways in which users can tell their own story and speak for themselves (Thumim, 2012).

These dynamics can be theorized further by drawing on Nancy Fraser's notion of "subaltern counterpublics" (1990). She theorized that minority subjects may form alternative publics in response to the dominant public sphere, in "parallel discursive arenas where members of subordinated social groups invent and circulate counter discourses to formulate oppositional interpretations of their identities, interests, and needs" (1990, p. 67). This notion extends Jürgen Habermas's ideal-type of the "bourgeois public sphere."[2] In Habermas's view, society resolved around a singular, all-embracing public sphere. Fraser rightly recognized that a multiplicity of competing publics provides arenas for subordinated groups (1990, p. 62). I approach the public sphere as performative, which is as much about discussion as it is about voicing a cultural style through which one imagines the self and demarcates one's own group.

For example, Jacquelien van Stekelenburg, Dirk Oegema and Bert Klandermans counted the number of words dedicated to immigration and integration issues that were published after major news events on

2 In 1962 Jürgen Habermas assessed conversations taking place among members of the bourgeoisie in Britain's coffee houses, France's salons and Germany's *Tischgesellschaften* in the eighteenth century as the idealized conception of a "bourgeois public sphere" at the interface of society and government: "between the two spheres, as it were, stands the domain of private persons who have come together to form a public and who, as citizens of the state, mediate the state with the needs of bourgeois society" (2002, p. 95). Fraser updates this notion of the public sphere by grounding it in reality, recapturing its value as an analytical lens to assess contemporary developments. I briefly describe three assumptions Fraser reconsiders that indicate the relevance of the concept for the argument in this chapter. First, she critiques Habermas's idea that interlocutors in the public sphere would speak "as if" they were equals. By merely bracketing difference, Fraser argues, inequalities are not eliminated, and bracketing difference mainly works to the disadvantage of subordinates (1990, p. 64). Moreover, in his conceptualization of the public sphere, he equated the public with being male. To foster participatory equality, Fraser notes, social inequalities need to be addressed in order to be dissolved. Secondly, she saw that a singular view on public deliberation obscures the view on alternative, competing publics constituted by subordinated groups. Thirdly, Habermas restricted the public sphere to discussions of "public matters," however, according to Fraser, distinctions between private and public matters made by the majority do not necessarily acknowledge minorities' interests, and only "participants themselves can decide what is and what is not of common concern to them" (ibid., p. 71).

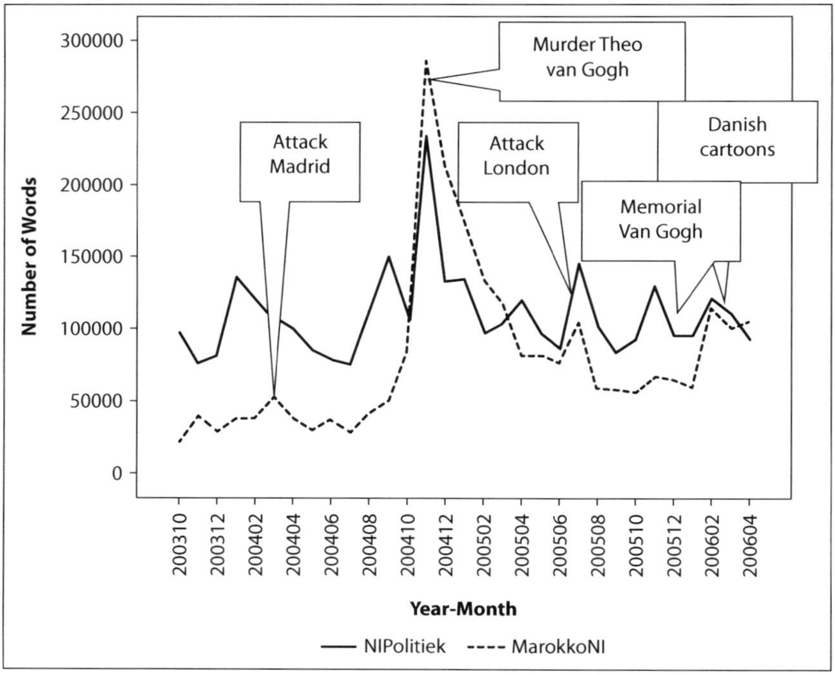

Diagram 5: Attention for major news events on nl.politiek and Marokko.nl (adapted from Van Stekelenburg, Oegema & Klandermans, 2011, p. 263)

both Marokko.nl and the ethnic-majority Dutch-oriented Internet forum nl.politiek. Diagram 5 captures how these forums serve as platforms to actively contribute one's voice in public debates. Events plotted include the Islamic extremist March 11, 2004, train bombings in Madrid and the July 7, 2005, bombings in the public transport system in London, and the controversy over the publishing of cartoons of the Islamic prophet of Muhammad in the Danish newspaper *Jyllands-Posten*, which all spurred substantial debate. But above all, the murder of Dutch filmmaker Theo van Gogh sparked considerable discussion. Shortly after Van Gogh directed his polemic film about the repression of Muslim women by Muslim men, he was murdered by a young Moroccan-Dutch extremist and in revenge, right-wing racists burned Dutch mosques and Islamic schools. Reflecting this turmoil, the graph shows a peak of words published dedicated to integration and immigration issues on Marokko.nl. In the sense that young Moroccan-Dutch people were able to share their voices on the matter, Marokko.nl appears as a space to air frustration and learn to cope with these developments.

In everyday practice, the forums show how Moroccan-Dutch youth embed themselves in a local community of young people who share ties with Morocco: "what these websites keep together is not the transnational but the national network of Dutch Moroccan youth" (Brouwer, 2006b, p. 1167). Both "roots" and contemporary "routes" identifications (Gilroy, 1993a) take place. On the one hand, Internet discussions among second-generation Moroccan-Dutch youth "can be seen as a virtual way of keeping alive the image of Morocco" (Brouwer 2006b, p. 1153). Similarly, Maroc.nl, a predecessor of Marokko.nl, was described as a digital, communal "Moroccan living room." The makers of that site were convinced forums were also of great value for ethnic-majority Dutch people, as reading forums offered them a glimpse of Moroccan-Dutch life that would often "test and unmask their prejudices" (Stichting Maroc.nl, 2001, p. 9). On the other hand, the boards offer rich resources for identification processes that allow youth to attune themselves not only to Moroccan affinities but also to Dutch everyday realities (De Waal, 2003). The main language used is, for example, nearly always Dutch, but posters do make use of Berber and Moroccan-Arabic insertions. As in offline speech, these insertions "function as a mode to express bilingual identity," but they are also markers of "style" (Dorleijn and Nortier, 2009, pp. 137, 140).

The medium-specific, relatively anonymous character of message boards is said to hold a specific appeal for Moroccan-Dutch youth: "young Dutch Moroccans are more likely to discuss and dispute Moroccan and Dutch traditions in the safe encounter of quasi-anonymous forums than in face-to-face contacts with relatives, peers or teachers" (Mamadouh, 2001, p. 271). This is not unique to migrant users, as similar relevant merits are recognized in Internet forum participation among other disenfranchised groups. For instance, in his study on sexual minorities (Dutch orthodox Protestant homosexuals), Willem de Koster noted a comparable double function. For those "struggling with stigmatization" in offline life, Internet forums are appreciated as a "refuge." They provide a "springboard" for those learning to improve their offline lives by digitally negotiating practical everyday questions about being gay and faithful in the context of orthodox Protestantism (2010, p. 572).

The two-fold dynamic of "ethno-cultural positioning," as a process of both position allocation and position acquisition (Van Heelsum, 1997), is an entry point to understand the performative construction of a subaltern counterpublic. On the one hand, bottom-up position acquisition refers to "the extent to which members of a given group look upon themselves primarily as members of a specific group and/or act as such," while on the other hand, top-down position allocation refers to "the extent to which (the bulk of) society considers them primarily as representatives of a specific group and/or treat them as such" (ibid., p. 24). Next to ethnic positioning, the dynamic of position allocation and acquisition also holds true for and is intrinsically connected with gender, sexuality, youth culture and religious positioning. In every offline and online setting, a particular configuration of material, representational and affective structures orders the available youth cultural, religious, ethnic, sexual and gendered subject positions. However, there is always room left for the stretching, negotiation and subversion of these allocated positions, through processes of bottom-up position acquisition on message boards (Leurs, Midden & Ponzanesi, 2012).

Scholars have conceptualized and empirically grounded the possibilities for using the Internet to develop a public sphere (Dahlberg & Siapera, 2007; Papacharissi, 2009). I provide more nuances in the debate by considering how migrant youth use Internet forums as an alternative counterpublic sphere. The literature suggests that message boards are taken up by migrants to articulate their voices and identities in an attempt to stake out a community on their own terms. Seizing the opportunity to speak for themselves on message boards, ethnic-minority forum users self-consciously claim membership to an alternative public, while using ethnicity as a marker to determine who is entitled to participate. I intervene in the debate by exploring how norms of gender, generation, nationalism, diaspora and religion intersect with ethnicity in users' articulation of voice and identity (Leurs, Ponzanesi & Midden, 2012).

Furthermore, earlier research has failed to address how outsiders – who do not meet ethnic identity norms – perceive Internet forums set up and frequented by minorities. Scholarship so far has stopped at the "euphoric celebration of this emergence of voice from thus far marginalized groups" online, and has not yet considered fully their impact on existing power structures (Gajjala & Birzescu, 2010, p. 74). Although documenting how Moroccan-Dutch youth become space invaders – as they assert themselves in Internet forums and articulate alternative normative ways of being that subvert the digital status quo – is important, scrutinizing how their processes in turn are accepted or contested in the wider context of existing power hierarchies is more relevant. Below, I first assess the ways in which Moroccan-Dutch youth seek to acquire alternative ethnic positions using Internet forums. Second, I explore how the informants negotiate gender issues on message boards. Thirdly, I analyze how Islam is dynamically performed in these spaces.

2.3 Digital multiculturalism: "Not all Moroccans are the same"

Fig. 7: "Average Moroccan boys look like this," forum user Mocro_s contesting Moroccan-Dutch masculinity (Mocro_s, 2007a)

> *It's all negative. But there are also Dutch people who do so [commit crimes] and why aren't they mentioned in the news? It's only the Moroccans. Okay, they are right in the sense that there are a number of Moroccans who do it [break the law] – we are not hypocrites. All right, but not all Moroccans are the same. Because you have it in every culture, there is also a part that is not – there are good, nice people. There are the ones who do things like stealing and so on, but with what they say about someone, they judge a group of Moroccans. They form an opinion about the whole community, the whole Moroccan culture, seeing it only this way and they just shouldn't do that. [On Marokko.nl] you can discus the topic, like "I think it's this way," or, "No, I don't think you are right."... Thus, you express your own opinion and so on. Do you get my point?*
>
> – Bibi, a sixteen-year-old girl

Bibi emphasized she felt Moroccan-Dutch individuals who break the law in Dutch are painfully over exposed in mainstream press. She shared she felt the whole Moroccan-Dutch community is dominantly framed as one homogeneous criminal group. One bad apple receives all the attention, ruining the whole bunch. Bibi and other interviewees felt bad that only this side of the story gets told. The focus on the small minority of criminals collapses the category of Moroccan-Dutchness, even though of course not all Moroccan-Dutch people are the same. Informants reported that Marokko.nl is better suited to match their interests of voicing other narratives. I illustrate with Figure 7 that a great deal of discussion is about the stereotypes and counter-positioning of Moroccan-Dutch youth in the Netherlands. A boy is shown who meets the stereotype of the young Moroccan-Dutch rascal boy. A smoking, bearded young man wearing a cap and sports clothes is depicted to extend a greeting in Moroccan-Arabic, "*Ewa sahbi.*" He also asks whether someone wants to smoke a "*shisha*" or waterpipe. In addition to not speaking Dutch, the boy can be said to signify alterity, as he is wearing clothes and sneakers in the colors of the red and green Moroccan national flag. However, as a symbol of peace the boy is making a V-sign hand gesture, making an attempt at conciliation.

Moroccan-Dutch youth are often seen as irreconcilably different from homogenous white, secular Dutch culture and identity. In response to such narrow framings of difference, it is urgent to reconsider multiculturalism by rethinking "difference" (Modood, 2007). As Bibi's statement indicates, cultural differences are not just constructed from within a minority group, but also from the outside group, resulting from its treatment and representation. As a result of being treated differently, minority groups are perceived as different. From this perspective it is important to note that people who are collectively targeted as others, may logically respond as a collective as well. Or to put it differently, following Tariq Modood there are two forms of difference at play in multicultural societies: "negative difference" (stigmatization, racism and discrimination against groups) and "positive difference" (identifications and the understandings that groups have of themselves) (2007, p. 37). Moroccan-Dutch youth navigate this double-faced character of difference on a day-to-day basis. Negative difference refers to how they are seen as incompatible Others by, for example, right-wing politicians, while Bibi's narrative illustrates an example of positive difference that can be found in how Moroccan-Dutch youth digitally voice themselves on message boards. The question arises whether positive difference can be actively foregrounded to counter the negative difference they experience resulting from the racialization of their religion that singles out Islam as outside of the frame of modernity (Balibar & Wallerstein, 1991). This question remains pertinent, considering, for example, the feelings Soufian, a twelve-year-old boy, shared: *"I think that nonbelievers, not all of them, are very much discriminating in their thinking and talking about my belief, and that makes me very sad."* He added, *"We live in a multicultural society and I am of the opinion you should accept every human being as he or she is and treat his [or her] religion with respect."*

Users appreciate discussion sites such as Marokko.nl because they can communicate with their own circle of people and share or hear alternative voices regarding Moroccan communities in the Netherlands. Eugenia Siapera observes that "the existence of minority media reflects the exclusion of minorities from the mainstream media, and to some extent it reflects the need for minorities to have their own mediated space" (2010, p. 94). Their corner of the Internet is often used to discuss and reframe dominant images circulating in news media. Echoing Bibi, thirteen-year-old Salima described mainstream news media in this way: *"They speak about Moroccans very often. If it would be a Turk or someone else, than it is not immediately news or so, but when there are Moroccans involved, it is immediately like: all right, these are Moroccans, instantly on the news."* Ideally, national news media reflect the broad dynamics of a society, including the multicultural dimension of that society, however, in the Netherlands, ethnic minorities feel as though coverage is skewed (D'Haenens et al., 2004, p. 69). Fourteen-year-old Senna remarked that, *"On Marokko.nl you also get news, news is discussed, it is more about Moroccan news and so on. That you do not find in de Telegraaf."* *De Telegraaf* is the largest daily newspaper in the Netherlands, especially known for its populist and sensationalist reporting. Sixteen-year-old Nevra found that *"different stories"* are shared on Internet forums, where *"there is often negative talk about Moroccan youth [in the newspapers]. I find that youth there can say what they want, showing it is not all bad."*

Away from the cultural hegemony of mainstream media, users can engage in ideological struggles through discursive contestation with mainstream media by speaking for themselves, instead of having to witness being spoken for again and again. Contestation of the black-and-white depiction is a key organizing principle of the forum. Online users realize this, according to Ilham, a thirteen-year-old girl: *"everyone is not the same, yes not all as one."* Young people feel safe enough to be able to disrupt stereotypes, *"because yeah, you can defend yourself and say whatever you want, it is your opinion, and you can just give your view there."* Moroccan-Dutch youth are critical consumers of Dutch-language news coverage, carefully assessing the information presented on issues relating to Morocco and the Moroccan community (D'Haenens et al., 2004). As the narratives of the informants illustrate, they are dissatisfied with the news offerings of mainstream Dutch press, as they report to feel offended by the way news items are negatively framed. Online forums are seen as a viable alternative to discuss issues left uncovered there and positive cultural difference can be acknowledged and appreciated.

Hush harbors

Although message boards are in principle publicly accessible to all Internet users, the informants perceive Marokko.nl as a welcoming space to publish and read alternative voices. Fourteen-year-old Senna stated, "*I think that half of the [Dutch] people does not even know that it exists.*" Message boards' perceived hidden character, tucked away from the mainstream, has been acknowledged as a main reason why minority groups become attracted to them. Dara Byrne describes message boards frequented by minorities "fly well below the mainstream radar" with the term "hush harbors," a notion previously used to describe spaces in which slaves gathered away from supervision from their white masters (2008, p. 17). Hush harbors are also important spaces in contemporary American society, semi-public spaces such as barbershops and beauty parlors provide safe spaces "where Black folks affirm, share, and negotiate African American epistemologies and resist and subvert hegemonic Whiteness" (Nunley, 2004, p. 222). As a space to negotiate unequal power relations, such hidden sites have played an important role throughout history for African Americans to be able to "untie their tongues, speak the unspoken, and sing their own songs to their own selves in their own communities" (Nunley, 2004, p. 223).

The hushedness of Internet forums is valuable for developing cohesion and a shared sense of belonging. Because a shared ethnicity is the organizing principle of ethnic forums, they are "relatively free of *mass* participation by ethnic outsiders" (Byrne, 2008, p. 17). In line with this principle, Bibi (sixteen years old) said she feels at home on the page, because there she says she can experience "*that really Moroccan atmosphere,*" as everyone, for example, uses "*those Moroccan words, you know.*" In focusing on message boards as the digital formations of hushed counterpublics, it becomes apparent that informants recognize Internet forums as safe loci for discursive contestation in response to exclusionary practices prevalent in Dutch society.

> *The main topic more concerns Geert Wilders and so on. He of all people can say things about Muslims. While we, for instance, cannot talk about the*

> *Jews, because then we are the racists. About those things, we say "Why is he allowed to do it," and to be honest, everyone thinks he is a retard, a dog; we do not like him at all.* (Bibi, a sixteen-year-old girl)

Interviewees shared heated debates over the controversial Dutch anti-Islamic Member of Parliament Geert Wilders on Marokko.nl. The informants feel Geert Wilders can say whatever he likes, while everything Moroccan-Dutch youth say is put under the microscope. Feeling enabled to share their stories on the forum, as creators and products of a habitus particular to this digital space, the interviewees feel more secure and confident to speak out. The counterpublic provides a sense of freedom from the tensions in society stirred up by the Party for Freedom (Dutch: Partij voor de Vrijheid, PVV) and other examples of right-wing populism. Following the hush harbor rhetoric, the informants all assume that the white master is not present on the site. Fifteen-year-old Oussema, for example, said: *"I don't see Wilders having a look at the site, I cannot imagine that."* The absence of non-like-minded others makes the site feel more welcoming, fifteen-year-old Meryam described: *"there are very many youth, Moroccan youth, who go on Marokko.nl.... It is about Geert Wilders, for instance, and then everyone joins in and you can see reactions posted by others, how they think about it."*

The carnivalesque

Unlike the social networking site Hyves, which, as I note in Chapter 4, is characterized by a situation of "digital throwntogetherness" (Leurs, 2014b), as views from across the socio-cultural-political spectrum are expressed in one single space, Marokko.nl is considered as a hush harbor where people agree upon a shared set of assumptions. From the narrative of fifteen-year-old Inzaf it becomes clear that Marokko.nl can assist Moroccan-Dutch youth to cope with negative difference. She insists that unlike other digital spaces, on Marokko.nl members are bound together because they all dismiss the polarizing brought forth by Geert Wilders and the PVV:

> *We speak about various Moroccan things, but we agree about one thing. For instance, about Geert Wilders – all of Marokko.nl agrees that he is no good, or that he lost his mind. On Hyves it would be different; everyone would have a different opinion. You have very few people who have a totally different opinion. Everyone would think something like, "Yeah, if I see him on the streets, I will shoot him dead," and then you have a few people who would say something like, "No – Why? He is not doing anything wrong."*

Seemingly perpetuating extremism, at first glance the statement by Inzaf demonstrates how forum contributors are complicit in perpetuating negative difference and the othering of the Moroccan-Dutch community as a whole. However, the statement is only a polemic mimicry of extremism. It should be understood in the interpretative context of the cultural repertoires of street language and hip-hop youth culture. Her way of expressing her feelings about the debate in the Netherlands can therefore be interpreted as a "diss," in global hip-hop linguistics, "to diss" is short for dismiss, disparage and/or disrespect. Instead of an actual death wish, her statement is a strong carnivalesque polemic voiced in a context with its own conventions and community norms.

The carnivalesque refers to "peculiar folk humor that always existed and has never merged with the official culture of the ruling classes" (Bakhtin, 1984, p. 474). It may include "ridicule of officialdom, inversion of hierarchy, violations of decorum and proportion" (Brandist, 2001). As a theatrical form of parody, carnivalesque acts may offer resistance to hegemonic form: "carnivalesque discourse breaks through the laws of a language" as a political and social protest (Kristeva, 1986, p. 36). Inzaf's statement is a part of a verbal duel expressed as a culmination of feelings of discrimination, injustice, and subordination. As physical battle is transferred to a verbal duel, "a substitutional relationship between real and verbal violence" is formed: this function has a long history in rap. In the global flows of hip-hop youth culture, "the-violence-as-verbal metaphor" is a significant example of a particular politics of language (Newman, 2009, p. 200).

For example, Inzaf statement may be seen as dialoguing with another example of carnivalesque ridicule: the controversial song "Hirsi Ali Diss" (2004) by the Moroccan-Dutch rappers DHC from The Hague. In the song, the Somalian-Dutch prominent Islam critic Hirsi Ali was similarly dismissed: "We are busy preparing for your liquidation / Bomba action, against Hirsi Ali / That is my reaction for the unrest she is making / Talking on TV about *integration.*" In this song coarse language of the street, assertive dissing and the demand for respect come together in a reaction on the Dutch debate on integration. Verbally threatening Hirsi Ali in the song is DHC's way of forming a response to being mistreated (De Koning, 2005).[3]

3 During the interviews, the informants equated PVV perspectives with the mainstream. This view should be problematized, because the anti-immigration and anti-Islam stance of extremists is not the same as the Dutch political norm. Although it must also be admitted that the situation is complicated, as the party received 15.5% of the votes during the 2010 Dutch general election, giving them 24 of the 150 seats in the House of Representatives. And although the PVV formally was not a part of the governing coalition, the coalition depended on a Parliamentary Support

Inzaf shows how deep the feeling of being disrespected by right-wing extremists runs among Moroccan-Dutch youth. Her carnivalesque "diss" reflects on and expose her sense of the dominant power order. Symptomatic of the social injustice inflicted on the Moroccan-Dutch community, they reveal a great deal about their perception of the Dutch political and societal centers of power. Inzaf's assertion can be seen as an "unspeakable" narrative that may only be voiced in a space perceived as safe and private. Moroccan-Dutch teenagers turn to message boards where they can express their – perhaps unconscious – feelings of oppression. Writing about his own sense of identity, Stuart Hall comments on the unspeakable in relation to identity by arguing: "identity is formed at that point where the unspeakable stories of subjectivity meet the narratives of history, of a culture" (1996d, p. 115). Resisting being muted and taking the opportunity to speak the unspeakable is of major importance: "hitherto excluded from the major forms of cultural representation, unable to locate themselves except as decentered or subaltern, [they] have acquired through struggle, sometimes in very marginalized ways, the means to speak for themselves for the first time" (Hall, 1997b, p. 183). The problem remains that, although masked in a carnivalesque narrative, the unspeakable gets asserted in public. The line between publicness and privateness is blurred online; the Moroccan-Dutch participants perceive the boards as private and hushed from the mainstream, while in fact they are publicly accessible.

Networked power contradictions

In articulating a self-defined ethnic identity in a self-contained space, migrant Internet forum users may be able to succeed "in overcoming some of the hierarchical structures of traditional broadcast media" (Karim, 2003, p. 13). Ilham thinks that ethnic-majority Dutch people do not mind these discussion boards as long as they are not bothered with them: "*I think they just say something like: If they don't terrorize the Internet, so to say, just let them happily stick to their little corner, all Moroccans and so on.*" However, acceptance and normalization of alternative views and knowledge circulating on Marokko.nl is far from straightforward. The problem for Marokko.nl is that speech norms of different communities may collide, as the digital space is also accessible to non-Moroccan-Dutch participants.

Agreement with the PVV to reach a majority in parliament. The Dutch coalition collapsed in spring 2012, and losing twelve seats during the 2012 elections, the PVV also lost a substantial part of its influence.

In recent history, subaltern subjects have voiced themselves, inserting "alternative styles of political behavior and alternative norms of public speech" to the mainstream, while in response the mainstream "excoriated these alternatives" (Fraser, 1990, p. 61). Fraser further explains this process by stating, "unequally empowered social groups tend to develop unequally valued cultural styles" (1990, p. 64). The troubling result is that when ethnic minorities find the opportunity to voice themselves, their contributions are marginalized. This process is also visible when considering how journalists and politicians frame Marokko.nl. Public news media link discussion sites frequented by Moroccan-Dutch individuals such as Marokko.nl to extremism and radicalism, with newspaper items such as: "Cut-and-paste Islam: How young Muslims in the Netherlands compose their radical worldview" (Oostveen, 2004). Forums are dismissed as the underbelly of the unknown, as segregated ghettos, and as grimy spaces disconnected from the mainstream: "Ghettos on the web: On the Internet, every group creates its own truth" (Hulsman, 2005). Carnivalesque disses like the one by Inzaf analyzed above are misinterpreted as examples of verbal abuse: "Forums where verbal abuse is allowed" (Pietersen, 2008). Possibly aiming to sell their messages to larger audience – through selling fear – such news items echo widespread Islamophobic us-versus-them discursive strategies. Marokko.nl site cofounder Khalid Mahdaoui criticized journalists for selectively taking quotes from the site, lifting them from their original contexts, in order to juice up news reports (Labovic, 2005, p. 27).

A recent governmental decision also signals how these contradictory power relations in the media have ramifications for sites like Marokko.nl. In his position as Dutch Minister of Housing and Integration Eberhard van der Laan cut funding for the site. He ironically stated this decision was not related to a study his department released accusing the site of publishing discriminatory statements that incited hatred (Rijksoverheid, 2009). Internet sociologist Albert Benschop expressed concerns about the research, wondering why only sites frequented by Moroccan-Dutch youth (Marokko.nl, Islamwijzer.nl and Maroc.nl) were included in the investigation, while right-wing populist sites like GeenStijl.nl were not included (Knijff, 2009). Mahdaoui states that Marokko.nl actively tries to discourage discrimination by deleting 20,000 comments and 150 members on a weekly basis. He admits that moderators are having difficulties assessing the daily flow of 50,000 messages, however, he adds that only around 5% of the messages cross the line of what is lawfully permitted (Pietersen, 2008). This small number of deviant postings should be seen in perspective. The increased monitoring and critique can be traced to the growth of extreme right-wing politics: with every demonstration, although very well organized, something offensive is shouted. These remarks used to dissolve in the masses, however, once online, they leave material traces. Right-wing extremists tightly monitor the site in search for offensive behavior as "they have their eyes set on discrediting the site" (Benschop cited in Pietersen, 2008, my translation).

Furthermore, as the site has no control over who subscribes and posts, right-wing users are also present on the site. An estimated 20% of Marokko.nl visitors comes from the right-wing blog Geenstijl.nl or are supporters of the PVV, and Benschop notes: "Those visitors sometimes set up a profile like Mohammed21 and discredit the site with extremist statements," after which, they will complain about the site (Knijff, 2009, my translation). The hush harbor, where users thought they could voice their views inaudible from the white master and other like-minded people, has thus been compromised. Whenever subaltern subjects are able to voice themselves online, their actions are often disciplined in return: "as the individual begins to feel empowered by the ability to speak up and back in such networks – there is a quick and simultaneous appropriation occurring that swiftly *places* this voice into a slottable position" (Gajjala & Birzescu, 2010, p. 77).

Although the informants perceive the forums as safe zones where they can articulate alternative ways of being, their acts of invading digital space simultaneously remain subject to tight scrutiny and control. Reflecting on disciplinary mechanisms, Mahdaoui wonders whether Moroccan-Dutch youth are expected to make a greater effort than ethnic-majority Dutch people. He asks why Moroccan-Dutch people have to behave better than ethnic-majority Dutch people, and adds that after Theo van Gogh was murdered, Dutch ethnic-majority users were behaving very indecently on his forums: "As long as law allows it, it is allowed on our site. When someone shouts Bin Laden is his hero, we keep it online. It will spur discussion and that is valuable. The Internet does not cause radicalization, but it is an outlet" (Mahdaoui, cited in Labovic, 2005, p. 27, my translation).

Marokko.nl moderators are trained to consciously leave insulting messages in order to spur debate: "What is incredibly insulting for one, falls under the right of free speech for the other. We provide the space for discussions. We believe in the self-cleaning capacity of the community. This is the way it has been for years: they correct one another." This way, Wilders's followers that flock to his site also get the chance "to shout whatever they want," he says. Furthermore, he concludes that journalists and politicians should not forget that a lot of members are fifteen or sixteen years old, and he asks, "What is scary about their writings?" (Mahdaoui, cited in Pietersen, 2008, my translation). In their search to attract corporate funds, the founders further began to commercially exploit the potential of the site by selling advertisers access to a relatively untapped ethnic-marketing niche. Yet despite outsider scrutiny and this increasing commercial presence, the desire among Moroccan-Dutch youth to articulate their own position and claim speaking power persists.

2.4 Digital "*hchouma*": Renegotiating gender

Figure 8 captures voicing gendered identity, the theme explored in this section. The figure shows a stylish, tidily clad girl carrying an expensive handbag in one hand and talking to her friend on her BlackBerry smartphone with her other hand. The girl shares that she is upset to have found out her boyfriend sent a message with a heart emoticon to another girl. Looking for vengeance, she set up a date with her ex-boyfriend. In the figure the girl speaks to her friend on the phone, stating:

Fig. 8: "Average Moroccan girls look like this," forum user Mocro_s contesting Moroccan-Dutch femininity (Mocro_s, 2007b)

> Hey Sam, it's me! My god, I'm angry! I had a fight with my boyfriend yesterday. He sent Amanda – you know, that cheap whore – a message with a heart. Idiot! Pff. I almost had to cry, I went crazy! Yes, I know it because 24/7 I'm logged in to the Hyves of my boyfriend because I have a BlackBerry. In revenge I will date my ex! Nooho, I won't kiss him.... Oh, he is here. I'll talk to you soon, Sweetie, love you. Kiss kiss.

Discussing issues such as love, relationships and sexuality happens in private, away from their parents' eyes. As shown in Diagram 2 (see p. 67) the majority of Moroccan-Dutch youth connect to the Internet from their bedrooms. Nearly three out of four Moroccan-Dutch girls, for instance, log on from their own room and connect to the Internet at their friends or families' homes. These findings suggest that Moroccan-Dutch girls might be able to enjoy a significant level of privacy while engaging with the Internet. During the interviews, informants also explained they can strategically negotiate more freedom in choosing where they log in to the Internet. Thirteen-year-old Soesie explains, "*It depends on where I take my laptop. When I am in my room, nobody will enter. When I'm sitting downstairs, on the couch, and my mother sits next to me she will occasionally have a glance* [*at the screen*]."

Online, anonymity-fueled disinhibition may grow when users feel they can violate norms without risking sanctions, repercussions or disapproval: "both because one is free of the expectations and constraints placed on us by those who know us, and because the costs and risks of social sanctions for what we say or do are greatly reduced" (Bargh et al., 2002, p. 34). Although anonymity of course also has its downsides, disinhibition fostered through anonymity has been recognized as a positive feature for Internet forum users. In "discussion threads, anonymity may provide a cover for more intimate and open conversations," and in addition the perception of anonymity may allow for more "experimentation with new ideas" (Bernstein et al., 2011, p. 6). From the safety of their own or their friends' bedrooms where parents are not allowed to enter, girls note they turn to discussion forums where they find it easier to discuss "*hchouma*" topics. Loubna Skalli defines this notion as setting the limits to "what may or may not be said, done, looked at, or even hoped for" in Moroccan gender relations:

> *Hchouma* is a label applied to virtually everything considered transgressive, taboo, unconventional, provocative, or progressive by the cultural order in Morocco. Slightly more charged than the concept of "shame," *hchouma* is the master socio-cultural code into which the Moroccan

> individual, and women in particular have been and still are socialized. (2006, p. 96)

The *hchouma* mechanism is based on social obligations, Islamic rules of conduct and familial norms. This moral order governs reputations, disciplining subjects by installing in them a "fear of losing face in front of others" (Sadiqi, 2003, p. 67). The informants considered online discussion forums a good space to address gendered taboo issues that might transgress the limits of dominant community standards. Bibi (sixteen years old) reported that she turned to Marokko.nl to discuss issues of intercourse and sexuality in the context of marriage. She shared she would rather turn to the online community instead of bringing it up with her parents. With such topics, she shared, *"you don't dare to go to your parents, because you find it really embarrassing"*:

> *Yes, for example, about [pause] sex or something and marriage and then they say... Yes, because in the Muslim faith, when you have [sex] the first time you are not to oppose your husband and [you should] just do "it." And [about] these things I'm definitely not going to my parents[to ask], "Mom, Dad, listen, is that the case?" Yes, it is* hchouma, *you know. I am shy about [talking to] my parents about these things.*

Participating in online forums, girls report experiencing a greater sense of freedom to discuss the sometimes-stringent social-cultural codes of socialization of their parents and wider community. Spending more spare time indoors, "Dutch-Moroccan girls are more restricted in their freedom of movement than boys, and thus, the internet widens their horizons" (Brouwer, 2006a). Moroccan-Dutch girls turn to message boards to engage with topics such as health, meeting new friends, intimacy, romantic relationships and sexuality (Leurs, Hirzalla & Van Zoonen, 2012).

Daring to break taboos: "I just want to know what 'the real deal' is"

> *You perhaps dare to say more on the Internet. You know, you do more; usually you are anonymous, if you want to at least, so you share your experiences. At home you can usually not talk about these things, otherwise you would have done that long ago. Then you can tell it online. And you see what people on the Internet have to say about it. And that might help you.*
>
> – Amina, a thirteen-year-old girl

Amina summarized the relevance of online message boards in the lives of Moroccan-Dutch girls. On Internet forums, some Moroccan-Dutch girls shared feeling less restricted and because of that they dare to bring up personal experiences they struggle with and cannot share elsewhere. Having a space to discuss issues that are difficult to broach in conversations with parents is of the utmost importance. This enables Moroccan-Dutch girls to express themselves and discuss behavior that is not possible in their usual social-cultural spheres. The barriers such as sanctions and repercussions to disclosing *hchouma* aspects of the self for family honor, for example, are not as strongly felt on message boards.

Sixteen-year-old Nevra holds a similar opinion: "*It is nice, because at home you cannot talk about them, and now you can talk about them* [*online*]. *Also, you can learn more about the topic.*" New ideas and insights are shared that may benefit the personal development of the young persons involved. Fifteen-year-old SouSou describes, "*You have a special section about sexuality and those kinds of things* [*laughs*].... *Yes, these things – you normally don't talk about them.*" Among the informants, message boards are used to discuss and share views on intimacy and sexuality. SouSou describes further: "*Especially when something has happened or so, yes you can talk about it, just as an anonymous person. You get all kinds of reactions and so on, that is fun* [*laughs*]." Issues that are difficult to discuss in face-to-face contexts are more easily considered in the digital realm. This holds true for conversations with parents but also with peers. On the message boards, as thirteen-year-old Inas thinks, girls are less inhibited in their conversations in comparison with discussing their experiences with friends outside of the Internet: "*If you have a problem, and you would like to talk about it with someone. I think it is easier than like* [*talking*] *with my girlfriend, because people usually give a different name....* [*Online*] *they talk about these things more casually.*"

For instance Loubna (fourteen years old) spoke about how one forum participant asked the community for help, asking support as to whether she dealt with domestic violence in the right way.

> *For real a girl revealed much about herself on Marokko.nl and said something like "Yes, my husband beats me," and so on. And "I am divorced," and everyone said "Yes, that is good," and so on. Than one girl said something like, "No, if your man was good and handsome, then you had to just stay with him." I don't know.... Yes, I did not really like that. Yes, I really found that....* [*silence*]. *That was really stupid.*

There is another dimension to the popularity of discussing *hchouma* aspects of the self on Internet forums such as Marokko.nl and Chaima.nl, as research has shown that Moroccan-Dutch teenagers do not always feel addressed by sex education initiatives in the Netherlands. Compulsory sex education in Dutch secondary school settings is not always considered appropriate by (religious) minorities and migrant groups (Borghuis, De Graaf & Hermes, 2010). Digital sex education initiatives aimed at Moroccan-Dutch youth miss their target as they "feel their voice is not heard; they cannot identify with the sites but rather feel repulsion and rejection" (Borghuis, De Graaf & Hermes, 2010, p. 235). Internet forums are taken up as an alternative space for circulating knowledge and education pertaining to sexuality. Bringing sexuality into the public digital space of discussion forums, they demonstrate how to successfully breach the dichotomy of masculine public and feminine private space that is noted to exist in Morocco (Mernissi, 1987; Graiouid, 2005; Sadiqi, 2003).

Ilham (thirteen years old) stated, "*It is fun to know for me what people have to say when I have put something online.*" But, learning from others is also of great importance, especially receiving peer-group verification from other girls, which is central during adolescence. Ilham explained, "*I just want to know what 'the real deal' is so to say, but, for instance, when I have put something on Marokko.nl I want to know what people think of it.*" Fellow discussion board participants offer advice, support, and information, all from the relative safety of their computer screens. They assist a number of our informants to decide upon action. "*If you want to get something of your chest, yes if you want to know something, than you just open [a topic]... and everyone reacts and they can give you advice*" (Loubna, fourteen years old).

An imagined comfort zone atmosphere established by anonymity and moderation contribute to the experience. In the words of fourteen-year-old Senna, especially, "*Chaima.nl is for girly girls. You won't find any boys there. If you look at the names there, all you see is girl, girl, girl.*" Ilana, a sixteen-year-old girl, confirmed: "*It is a good thing, to have all those girls together so they can really talk about girlish things.*" Khalid Mahdaoui, cofounder of Marokko.nl states that the majority of visitors are female: 60% (Van der Zee, 2006, p. 53). Some overestimated the absence of boys: "*In my opinion there are almost no guys on Marokko.nl. I think it is more something for girls*" (Meryam, fifteen years old). The bottom-line, however, is that girls feel comfortable enough to discuss very serious issues on the site. As such, Internet discussion forums as a form of anonymous Internet communication may also lead toward forming personal relationship and greater intimacy among contributors. As Amina notes:

> *Yes, you also make new friends there. Even though you don't know them. Most of the time they are girls. You don't trust them immediately or something like that. But you get a bit closer by also sending private messages to each other. "Hey, how are you?" "Which school do you go to?" "How old are you?" and so on. I have met girls who were similar to me like that.*

Everyday sexual practices and experiences are discussed from the bottom up. Online message boards make it possible for young Moroccan-Dutch girls to discuss and ask questions not just about sexuality in general, but also in connection to Islam. The forums provide participants with a supportive vehicle to renegotiate their relationship with their sexualities and their Islam, as Meryam (a fifteen-year-old girl) attests:

> *There are also many stories about Moroccan girls who behaved badly and who have improved their behavior, who have returned to their faith, Islam, and they have worked very hard to achieve that.*

These statements corroborate the assumption that message boards are especially popular among Moroccan-Dutch girls to voice the struggles they experience in their efforts to "demonstrate counterviews toward the dominant Western image of Muslim women as well as to their own communities" (Brouwer, 2006a). Girls may find in message boards a space with particular socio-cultural dynamics that allow for acquiring new positions vis-à-vis certain notions (of gender relations) upheld by their parents or fellow community members and in dialogue with both Western and mainstream Dutch conceptions of sexuality and relationships. Articulating an in-between position, subaltern subjects can find agency to mark out "an interstitial future" (Bhabha, 1994, p. 313). Online discussion forums assist Moroccan-Dutch youth in staking out a position in-between claims of rooted familial, religious and community norms and routed youth cultural expectations. The next section considers this process further by analyzing how informants perform their religiosity.

2.5 Digital postsecularism: Performing Muslimness

Figure 9 introduces the third theme: the performative renegotiation of Islamic codes of conduct. A fashionable headscarf-wearing girl is depicted wearing pink lipstick and carrying a handbag. The girl confidently states

Fig. 9: Forum user Mocro_s contesting Moroccan-Dutch religiosity (Mocro_s, 2007b)

she feels attractive and smart but criticizes fellow Muslim girls who do not cover their hair. Also she feels smoking cigarettes cannot be reconciled with the principles of the Muslim faith, gossiping about Asma as a "*Tfoe kehba*" (Moroccan-Arabic for "dirty whore") because she saw her smoking with Mo. A text balloon presents us with her thoughts:

> Long live public transport. I'm still in MBO, but that does not matter? I feel hot and I am smart. I have EVERYTHING. I hate those showing their curly hair by not wearing a headscarf. *Tfoe.* What kind of Muslims are they? I never gossip. Oh, by the way, do you know Asma? Yes her from [Amsterdam] West,. She SMOKES. Yes, I swear it. I saw her yesterday with Mo!!!!!!! *Tfoe kehba.*

This section explores how forum discussions are used among like-minded Moroccan-Dutch Muslim youth to connect and insert in the public sphere alternative configurations of believing. Like elsewhere in Europe, in the Netherlands, democracy and Islam are often presented as "irreconcilable discursive categories" through emphasizing a binary view between secular "good people" and postsecular Muslim "bad people" (Sunier, 2010, p. 125). Digital practices provide insights on how postsecularism is actually lived and experienced. These practices can be taken to counter the conservative reactions in contemporary debates on the revival of religion, which tend to isolate Muslims as the locus of the return of religion as a challenge to democracy, secularism, and progress. Contesting the association of religion with backwardness, or straight foreignness, Moroccan-Dutch youth appropriate Islam, not an essentialized and static category, removed from other markers of identity and belonging. Participating in online forums fosters agency through a democratization of belief systems and religious authority and resisting hegemonic renderings of Moroccan-Dutchness and Islam. On forums, being Muslim is a public and private everyday practice that is deeply embedded in digital affordances (Leurs & Ponzanesi, 2014c).

During our interview, fifteen-year-old Meryam mentioned the habits of her parents were "*just very old-fashioned.*" They were raised much "*stricter*" in terms of religion. In contrast to how her parents learned about Islam through copying "*the stories of their parents,*" she "*looks up things about Islam herself.*" Meryam also spoke about *Het Handboek voor Moslimvrouwen* (*The Handbook for Muslim Women*), a book that she had in her handbag. She shared that she liked to keep a book like that with her at all times. "*I read those, because it gives you a lot of rules and how you can do your best to become a good Muslim woman.*" These books give her something to hold on to, offering guidance in making everyday decisions. For similar purposes, she turns to Marokko.nl to read about personal stories that people have shared. The book, she notes, was bought "*at the mosque and it gives you rules to abide by.*" While "*on Marokko.nl, I type 'Islam' and many different pages appear. And I look at those. Some rules are not in the book, but they might be available on the Internet.*" Meryam added how she "*noses around*" in forums on Islam. Meryam's narrative illustrates how Moroccan-Dutch youth engage in forum discussions to align "strict Muslim demands placed on them with liberal youth culture" (Brouwer, 2006a). The tension between being provided with meanings by authorities such as the imam and her parents and taking the opportunity to articulate personal religious interpretations themselves lies at the heart of this section on digital postsecularism and performative Islam.

Internet forums frequented by religious people have been recognized as manifesting the tension over religious authority. Online discussion forums such as Marokko.nl have been likened to "digital minarets" (Brouwer, 2002). The site includes an image of a minaret in its logo. The minaret is a sign which conveys its meaning as a distinct element of Islamic architecture. It has become a universal symbol of Islam and Muslim community but it also provides a vantage point for making the call to prayer (Bloom, 1989). By using a logo with a minaret, Marokko.nl signals it also provides vantage points for Islamic prayer as well as giving a visual cue for congregating Muslims.

Digital reconfigurations of religious authority

Though the relation between religion and media (both old and new media) has received attention in recent studies (Couldry, 2003; Højsgaard and Warburg, 2005; Hoover, 2006; Nynäs, Lassander, and Utriainen, 2012; Sedgwick, 2015), the link to (new) media studies, and the way in which "religion" is manifested and reconfigured online, has not been sufficiently elaborated upon. In her recent *Digital Religion* (2012), Heidi Campbell argues, for example, that different religious communities negotiate complex relationships with new media technologies in light of their history and beliefs. This begs the question of how religious practices, are lived, articulated, and performed online, responding to public debates as well as to intimate needs.

Collaborative, bottom-up, peer-to-peer networking through social media "has led to a complex reconfiguration of religious authority models" (Bunt, 2009, p. 17). Digital media, it is argued, fragments religious authority in the Muslim world in the Middle East by opening up "a marketplace of ideas, identities, and discourses" (Eickelman and Anderson, 2003, p. xii). And this process goes beyond metaphor: "It is a reality that decisively shifts forms and resources of such discourse and its practices in favor of middle-class actors" and it "feeds into new senses of a public space that is discursive, performative and participative, and not confined to formal institutions recognized by state authorities" (2003, p. 2). Charles Hirschkind observed an Islamic counterpublic in Egypt that is partly fed by cassette-sermons as an alternative to the televisual and press media promoted by the state (2006). The recent revolutions across the Middle East and North Africa have also partly been attributed to the distinct role of digital technologies to organize protests and air alternative voices (Allagui & Kuebler, 2011). Nadirsyah Hosen identifies a democratization of religious authority in Indonesia as middle-class Muslims actively "shop around" in locating Islamic guidance and legal opinions ("*fatwas*") they find suitable to their lifestyle by browsing different Islamic websites (2008).

Such practices can lead to a subversion of the top-down authority over interpreting Islamic principles and practices. Carmen Becker acknowledges, "a broader decentralizing tendency within Islam" in Europe, as she notes Salafi Muslim activists in Dutch online spaces engaged in "meaning-making activities that tell people how to behave and how to 'be in the world'" (2009, p. 79). Moroccan-Dutch youth are said to turn to message boards to guide themselves through the maze of Dutch norms and values with Islam as a frame of reference (Van Summeren, 2007, p. 291). Furthermore, medium-specific disinhibition may provide a valuable "opportunity to submit sensitive questions about Islam to a cyber-Imam or to peers" among Moroccan-Dutch youth (D'Haenens, 2003, p. 411). In sum, a diversity of performative Islamic practices are made visible to other users, opening up visibility on the multiplicity of ways Muslims connect with Islam beyond the parameters of traditional networks and communities.

Voicing Muslimness

> *Marokko.nl is easy. You can easily find out about things when you want to know something. On the site, there are many Moroccans, most of them are Muslim – just almost everyone, I believe. Thus you can really read their stories and you can really express your sincere interests.*
>
> – SouSou, a fifteen-year-old girl

The informants assess the value of being able to discuss one's interpretation of Islam in various ways. Some informants note that the Internet has enabled them to learn about topics that used to be left untouched. As Amina, a thirteen-year-old interviewee, describes it: "*religion – for that I often go to Chaima.nl and I am also active on the topics about Islam. Where people [discuss] how they see Islam, and how I see Islam, so to say. This way you also make the differences smaller.*" She pointed toward the positive potential of social media, as people can draw upon personal religious interpretations of other individuals they encounter online. These processes of knowledge production and consumption have been described as a form of "cut-and-paste Islam," highlighting its eclectic character where people shop around for their religious preferences (Buitelaar, 2008, pp. 248-249). As different views on Islam are brought together in one space, a generational-specific "Islamic habitus" or way of life and set of "Muslimness" dispositions may be coshaped at the crossroads of top-down and bottom-up performances and socializations (Sedgwick, 2015, p. 3).

Being able to articulate and narrate a personal relationship with Islam is highly relevant as Buitelaar and Stock learned in their interviews with Moroccan-Dutch Muslims. They feel externally pressured in Dutch society to take sides: "the spatial metaphor 'to take sides' occurs frequently in the narrations of our interlocutors." They feel "caught between a Muslim and a non-Muslim 'camp' that both claim definitional power" over them (Buitelaar & Stock, 2010, p. 170). Public TV is not considered as a solution in bridging those two camps, as apart from the negative framing of Moroccan-Dutch boys as rascals and thieves informants noted the lack of recognition of Islam as a viable institution in the Dutch mainstream press. "*Yes, public broadcasting is there for everyone, but it doesn't focus on, for instance, Islam* [*in a positive way*]" (Ilham, a thirteen-year-old girl).

Fig. 10: Cartoon *Overvaren* (in English: *Sailing Across*) (Rafje.nl, 2011)

Forums offer an alternative. In my interview with Rafje, an artist whose provocative statements are published on Marokko.nl regularly, he shared he aims to capture the tendencies and ambivalences in Dutch multicultural society. Noteworthy is his reworking of a traditional Dutch children's song and play in which toll has to be paid to a skipper who will take people across one of the Dutch rivers (see Figure 10). Rafje clearly renders visible the hermetic division – instigated by "Skipper" Wilders and his followers – between good (read secular) people and bad (read Muslim) people in this statement: "Wilders, will you let me sail across? Yes or no? If so, should I hate Islam? Yes or No?"[4] Away from the Dutch mainstream, message boards are used to acquire a self-narrated religious position.

As another invocation of a (counter)public sphere our informants report engaging in similar religious meaning-making activities. Sixteen-year-old Ilana states that in the rubric *"'Islam and me,' many things about Islam are discussed also the rules of Islam."* Sahar, a fourteen-year-old girl, also participates in this rubric and adds people exchange ideas, *"about things you should and you shouldn't do."* Informants told me that when negotiating the (sometimes strict) Muslim demands with Dutch liberal youth culture, many people discuss whether certain things are "halal" (allowed in Islam) or "haram" (forbidden in Islam).[5] Ferran, a fourteen-year-old boy, provides an example: *"whether you may have a boyfriend and so on."* Not everyone appreciates bottom-up interpretations of what is haram or halal. Some see disadvantages in online performances of religion. As Nevra (sixteen-year-old girl) observes: *"You now see that people who are engaged with their faith, they actually make a personal version of their faith. They do things that they aren't allowed to do, because many people do them [and share their actions online]. They say, you can do it, too."* Inas, a thirteen-year-old informant, also voiced her skepticism about online discussions on Islam: *"I do not try to find too many things about it."* She chooses to uphold her own conceptions about Islam. *"That's my own opinion. And someone else should not change my opinion."* Nonetheless, fifteen-year-old Inzaf notes that converts might

4 "Skipper, will you let me sail across, yes or no? Do I have to pay toll, yes or no?," as originally in Dutch: *"Schipper, mag ik overvaren, ja of nee? Moet ik dan ook tol betalen, ja of nee?"* The children's play centers around one child, the skipper, who sets the terms for other children in the play to cross a path she or he chooses.

5 "Halal" and "haram" form the twofold distinction between what is seen as lawful and what is seen as forbidden. Eating ritually slaughtered beef is, for example, halal while consuming alcohol is considered haram. There are three intermediate categories between the two poles that complete a five-part scale: *"mandub"* for what is recommended, *"mubah"* for a neutral permissible and *"makruh"* for what is objectionable and repugnant (Leaman & Ali, 2008, pp. 46-47, 72).

find in Marokko.nl a space of support: *"Those who have converted to Islam ask about what they should do, where they should go. The people on the site help them and say what they can do best."*

In their contribution to forums, together with references to Islam, for instance, Bibi chose a picture of the Amazigh flag, while Nevra includes a photo of her hands covered in henna and Meryam includes Taourirt, her nickname, and also the town where her parents where born in Morocco. Performing one's Islam through discussions, nicknames and avatars is a personal, micro-political example illustrating how definitional power may be appropriated beyond the camps of mainstream Dutch society and religious authorities. Prior research shows Moroccan-Dutch youth use signatures and nicknames to perform religious affiliations on Maroc.nl, one of Marokko.nl's predecessors. To signal their belonging and gain further recognition among other participants, Maroc.nl posters used nicknames such as "Dutch Muslim" and "Muslima25" and signatures such as "Servant of Allah" or "May Allah give a heart to the heartless and then fill the hearts of the people with peace, brotherly love and tolerance" (Van Summeren, 2007, p. 285). Religious positions are acquired on Internet forums, and defining oneself by expressing "I am Muslim" for many Moroccan-Dutch youth has become a more positive way to articulate one's individual identity as opposed to an ascribed ethnic identity such as "You are an allochthone" or "You are a Moroccan cunt". Next to hip-hop, urban and the like, Muslim youth can chose to be "Muslim" online (Buitelaar, 2008, pp. 244-247). As I show in more depth in Chapter 3, interviewees combine religious, youth cultural and ethnic affiliations in their instant messaging nicknames and avatars.

2.6 Conclusions

In this chapter I focused on how young Moroccan-Dutch become space invaders by using Internet forum discussion pages. Marokko.nl and Chaima.nl are the national networks of Moroccan-Dutch youth. Discussing how informants digitally renegotiate multiculturalism, gender relations and postsecularism I gave three examples of how Internet forums can function as counterpublics. Although performed in commercial, socio-cultural structures of power, informants feel they can publish narratives of "positive difference" (Modood, 2007, p. 37) in their digital space, instead of being identified as a member of an imposed group. In this way, the agency of Moroccan-Dutch youth becomes apparent. This form of agency must be seen in the light of the politics of difference, recognizing how individuals are located in multiple positions of subordination. Doubly marginalized Moroccan-Dutch girls may work against both simplistic stereotypes of Muslim girls as being passive and oppressed that persist in Dutch society while they also negotiate their individual gendered positionality in the context of the sometimes strict demands of Islam, their parents and their families.

The struggle over allocated and acquired subject positions can be further explained by considering Michel Foucault's writings on power and knowledge. As two sides of the same coin, he distinguished two sides to the organization of power. On the one hand, Foucault writes, people are inscribed and subjected to power, as their range of action is restricted, for instance. On the other hand, individuals are the subjects of power as they have the ability and capacity to make changes (Foucault, 1982). Knowledge acts as a regulatory mechanism, those in power exercise their command by defining, labeling and categorizing people. In a similar vein, Moroccan-Dutch youth are allocated subordinate positions. Moroccan-Dutch contributors use Internet forums to exercise their speaking power and narrate their self-acquired positions. In voicing themselves they are able to strategically foreground alternative collective ethnic, gender and religious identities and voice the essentials of their belongings in their own terms (Spivak, 1990, p. 11). The grasped opportunity for resignification is a significant form of agency. By voicing themselves, they take the opportunity to speak for themselves, instead of being positioned by Dutch societal, Moroccan-Dutch community and familial social norms as well as religious authorities. Forums are perceived also a safe space to practice piety and alternative forms of religious agency, not necessarily in conflict with the dictums of the secular host society which label religion, and Islam in particular, as blocking youth from integration and girls, in particular, from their path to emancipation

Moroccan-Dutch youth will not be able to overthrow the unequal power structures in Dutch society by voicing themselves on message boards, however, such actions give hope for future change. They might feel empowered when they feel safe enough to voice their in-between identities, as they expand the discursive space beyond the "negative difference" (Modood, 2007, p. 37) of top-down allocated gender, ethnic and religious positions circulating in the settings they move through. Although imagined as a "hush harbor" where informants feel safe, my discussion of journalists' ghettoization and politicians' regulation of Marokko.nl reminds us of the disciplinary and control mechanisms that remain at play both online and offline. If these acts of repression would get the upper hand, Moroccan-Dutch youth might be left with feeling excluded and unwelcome. Informants, however, felt they have the final say over their space and their position in digital practices of multiculturalism.

Although Moroccan-Dutch youth become the majority, thirteen-year-old Ilham invites ethnic-majority Dutch youth to visit their space: "*It is dot NL, not something like dot Morocco, so it is for everyone – everyone is mar7hbabikoum [welcome], everyone can come.*" Most importantly, as fifteen-year-old SouSou notes, message boards like Marokko.nl are spaces where one can feel heard and feel appreciated by like-minded people: "*You can pleasantly talk with fellow Moroccans about all kinds of stuff, where you can read beautiful stories. There, you can just be with other Moroccans.*" The narratives of the informants showcase how they give an Islamic touch to their everyday digital practice without resorting to violence or public defiance. At the same time, Islam is revisited from new perspectives. Judging from how they appropriate discussion forums as a safe and supportive digital counterpublic, Moroccan-Dutch youth show they aim to renegotiate multiculturalism, gender dictums and the postsecular revival of religion to eventually coshape a more inclusive, cosmopolitan public sphere attuned to the everyday needs of a growing multicultural youth generation.

3. Expanding socio-cultural parameters of action using Instant messaging

The time is 8:30 p.m. on a Saturday evening in late January 2010, when classmates Khadija and Nadia, two eighteen-year-old Moroccan-Dutch girls, have a private conversation over MSN Messenger. The conversation below follows an exchange about a school assignment that the two classmates have to prepare. The girls agree to sit down after the weekend to finish their presentations about fashion. The girls also talk about a holiday trip that Khadija's parents made to Dubai. Her parents' holiday was "*chill.*" They took nice pictures and bought a PSP (PlayStation Portable) as a holiday gift for her brother. She herself received Dubai souvenir t-shirts, Mexx blouses and "*expensive fabric for a Moroccan dress.*" Nadia types "*besaha*" to congratulate her in Latinized-Arabic for these gifts.

-- ___Ms. Laouikili ♥, Some people!!!- Li Tmenit Lqito Fik says:___ ah well
im going for a nice swimm tomrw
really feel like going
*___Porque es el destino. says:___ Haha thats good!! Good dont drown he hahaah
-- ___Ms. Laouikili ♥, Some people!!!- Li Tmenit Lqito Fik says:___ no no I have nough love handles
*___Porque es el destino. says:___ hahahahahah Silly
-- ___Ms. Laouikili ♥, Some people!!!- Li Tmenit Lqito Fik says:___ haha yea true
*___Porque es el destino. says:___ Swia swia [shwia shwia: calm down, calmdown]
tina was doing a diet of some sort [*tina*: you]
-- ___Ms. Laouikili ♥, Some people!!!- Li Tmenit Lqito Fik says:___ hahaha
yeah, ze3ma [*ze3ma*: expressing doubt]
I have started to eat les and so
but it is quite difficult
the temptation is too strong
especially here at home
*___Porque es el destino. says:___ hahahha
I believe so for sure
with that little chef
eee we havvve
soon
-- ___Ms. Laouikili ♥, Some people!!!- Li Tmenit Lqito Fik says:___ haha
*___Porque es el destino. says:___ eat that dish of your mama

-- ***Ms. Laouikili ♥, Some people!!!- Li Tmenit Lqito Fik says:*** yes i just told herr tha
****Porque es el destino. says:*** tina have to learn me
-- ***Ms. Laouikili ♥, Some people!!!- Li Tmenit Lqito Fik says:*** we hadnt had tha in a long time
-- ***Ms. Laouikili ♥, Some people!!!- Li Tmenit Lqito Fik says:*** yes i have to lear it myself
tina should come make t yema with me [*yemma*: mother]
****Porque es el destino. says:*** Yes inshallah [*inshallah*: God willing]
-- ***Ms. Laouikili ♥, Some people!!!- Li Tmenit Lqito Fik says:*** inshallah

In the transcript, Khadija talked about how she is planning to go swimming the next day. Nadia jokingly urged her to be careful not to drown. Half jokingly, Khadija replied her "*love handles*" will keep her afloat. Nadia turned to Arabic, stating "*schwia schwia*" or in English: "calm down, calm down" to downplay this last remark. She then asked about the diet Khadija was following. Khadija explained that the cooking skills of her mother made it difficult to pursue the diet. Nadia in return typed she wants to learn from Khadija and her mother how to prepare good food. Nadia and Khadija ended their conversation in Arabic wishing "*Inshallah*" or God willing,[1] they will soon learn to cook together. It can be observed how Khadija stated she "*ze3ma,*" meaning "with doubts," "*started to eat les and so.*"[2] In typing the word "*ze3ma,*" the number three is used to write the Arabic letter ع. This is the eighteenth letter of the Arabic alphabet, which has no equivalent in the Latin alphabet. When using a Latin alphabet keyboard to type Arabic, this letter can be represented with a 3. Ending their conversation, Khadija and Nadia expressed "*inshallah,*" God willing, they would get together to learn to cook from Khadija's mother ("*yema*"). In all these cases, the Latin alphabet was used to write a specific dialect, Moroccan-Arabic or Darija.[3]

The MSN conversation excerpt sheds light on the private side of one-on-one conversations and the more public side of broadcasting one's affiliation to one's list of contacts. Socio-technologically, the medium configured the ways users can narrate their identities in these two ways. In this chapter, I explore these two dimensions further to better understand the popularity

1 *Insha' Allah, inchAllah* or In šā' Allāh is an Arabic phrase (إن شاء الل) that can be translated into English here as "If it is God's will," or "God willing."
2 The word "*ze3ma*" is a discourse marker used among Europeans of North African descent to express uncertainty: "perhaps it is so" (Boumans, 2003, p. 1).
3 Darija covers varieties of Arabic spoken in the Maghreb.

of instant messaging (IM) among informants. First, considering that Nadia and Khadija used IM software to discuss personal struggles over dieting, the excerpt illustrates that IM established a safe communicative space they used to discuss intimate matters among themselves. On the private side, or "backstage" of instant messaging (Jacobs, 2003, p. 13), the informants were primarily engaged in under-the-radar, iterative identity formation processes. Therefore I assess how IM was valued as a relatively safe personal networked territory, where youth can receive a validation of their feelings and cement their relationships. Second, on the more public side that consists of one's IM contacts, words from various languages (Dutch, English, Spanish, and Moroccan-Arabic) were used in the display names. Khadija used the display name "*Li Tmenit Lqito Fik*" (Moroccan-Arabic for "what I hoped I found in you"), illustrating how various affiliations are circulated in IM expressive culture. Khadija expressed multiple belongings with this display name that was broadcasted to everyone in her friend list. Therefore, I assess how interviewees – in the more public "onstage" of IM that goes beyond the one-on-one conversation (Jacobs, 2003, p. 13) – used display names that represent multiaxial identification.

It should be noted that the social media landscape has tremendously changed since my fieldwork. Microsoft had shut down the standalone application Windows Live Messenger (MSN's successor) on October 31, 2014, but many of the arguments put forward in this chapter remain valid because in different shapes and forms the service of instant messaging has been incorporated in platforms such as the social networking site Facebook (Facebook Chat) and the video-chat application Skype. In the lives of adolescents, the role of MSN has, in particular, been taken over by the immensely popular smartphone messaging applications such as BlackBerry Messenger (Davis, 2012) and WhatsApp Messenger (Church & De Oleveira, 2013). Although critical masses of users have migrated from one platform to another, the underlying communicative and symbolic principles of instant one-on-one exchanges are largely comparable.

In this chapter I argue that IM was actively made into a communicative space of their own among Moroccan-Dutch youth, where they negotiated personal and social identities at the crossroads of national, ethnic, racial, age and linguistic specificities. Instant messaging can be understood as a private territory where individuals in specific material-embodied spatial contexts perform everyday, but very meaningful, discursive interaction. Instant messaging remains relatively understudied and undertheorized because data gathering within this private space was and is not straightforward; users control who they let into their network and exchanges are not stored in a publicly accessible environment online but on the computers or mobile phones of the users. In this chapter I make an empirical contribution to the performance of self in the field site of IM while also aiming for theoretical refinement of the understandings of the medium-specificity of instant messaging and distinct processes of adoption by its users. Drawing from Wired Up large-scale survey findings, in-depth interviews, and IM transcripts sent in by six informants – Fatiha, Naoul, Midia, Kamal, Khadija, and Inzaf – I set out how gender, diaspora, youth culture and technologies intersect and influence each other in this communicative space (Leurs & Ponzanesi, 2011c, p. 56).

This chapter is structured as follows. In Section 3.1, I ground the IM use of Moroccan-Dutch youth in Wired Up survey findings and explain the key characteristics of MSN in the words of my interviewees. In Section 3.2, I bring together insights from computer-mediated communication (CMC) and digital literacies scholarship by turning to instant messaging as a discursive practice with an emphasis on postcolonial intersectionality. Earlier work on IM mostly centers on white American teenagers; I diversify this scholarship by focusing on the intersectional performance of identity of adolescent, Moroccan-Dutch youth. Subsequently, I explore two dynamics of MSN expressive culture that arose during my analysis of the corpus of interviews and chat transcripts. The focus in Section 3.3 is on the backstage of IM, where I highlight how our interviewees negotiated ownership over their IM territory and engaged in intimate and personal identity formation. In Section 3.4 the focus is on the *onstage* of IM through which more public identifications are expressed. First I analyze the use of gendered selfies as display pictures. Second I discuss the semi-public expressions of collective local, transnational diaspora and global youth cultural orientations. As forms of social identification among their peers I analyze whether Moroccan-Dutch youth act against ethnic absolutist labels by authoring multiple selves and expressing diverse social belongings.

3.1 Moroccan-Dutch youth using instant messaging

> *When I get home, I go online. I press "busy" and I go downstairs. I grab something to eat and I go and pray a bit. Then I go back upstairs and have a look at who has talked to me. I have a look what's going on and talk about homework. And about, "Have you heard about this?" – you know, gossip, just to keep up to date about everything that is going on.*
>
> – Bibi (a sixteen-year-old girl)

In this section I introduce main patterns of usage my informants noted. IM was very popular among the Moroccan-Dutch young people who participated in the 2010 Wired Up survey. In line with US and Dutch adolescent user patterns (Lenhart, Rainie & Lewis,2001; Duimel & De Haan, 2007), the great majority of girls (97%) and boys (93%) used the technology at least once per week, while 53% of participating girls and 43% of boys reported logging in more than once daily. Respondents also expressed their attachment to IM; almost-three quarters of the participating Moroccan-Dutch girls and half of the boys reported that they would miss IM very much if they were not able to use it anymore. More specifically, 95% of the girls versus 82.5% of boys would miss it at least somewhat if they were not able to use it anymore (see Table 5).

Table 5: The importance of instant messaging in the lives of Moroccan-Dutch youth (percentages, n = 344)

Would you miss MSN if you could not use it any longer?	*Completely not*	*Somewhat*	*Very much*	*Total*
Girls	5.0%	32.2%	62.8%	100%
Boys	17.5%	32.5%	50.0%	100%

The interviewees corroborated the survey findings, as eighteen-year-old Safae confessed, "*I think you can call it an addiction, because automatically I go on MSN, every day,*" while thirteen-year-old Amina laughingly shared "*MSN? I use it every day. I have been online this morning, and yes tonight again. I just have to check my MSN.*" I learned, for instance, from Fatiha that she used IM "*every day at least two hours.*" Major motivations behind IM use include connecting with her friends, as she stated: "*All of my friends use MSN*" and "*It is a free way of talking to your friends and family.*" Naoul agrees and added, "*It is convenient in the case you need to reach somebody.*" Thirteen-year-old Soesie noted, "*When you have nothing to do, you go and enjoy yourself on MSN.*" Night after night, IM was bustling with activity. Fourteen-year-old Inas stated that "*especially in the evening, when everyone has finished doing homework, I also go online.*" Now that young people increasingly own mobile phones with Internet access, they are also on MSN more often. Fourteen-year-old Senna noted that she is nearly always online: "*I'm on MSN almost every day. The whole day. When I have my mobile with me, then I'm online.*"

Figure 11 shows a screenshot of an instant messaging conversation I held with Soufian, a twelve-year-old boy, during the summer of 2011. The

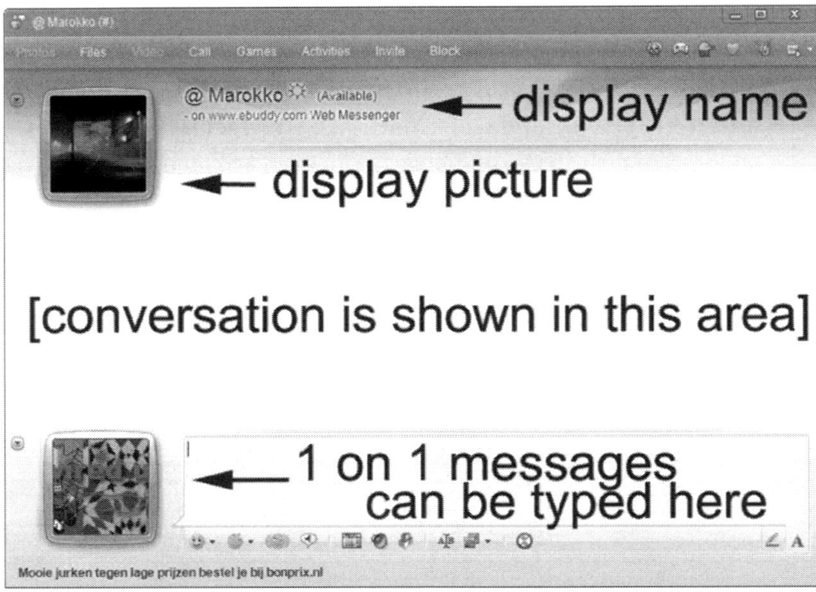

Fig. 11: Screenshot of an MSN Messenger conversation with twelve-year-old Soufian (July 22, 2011)

example is included here to set out the various analytical dimensions to the medium-specific performativity of self in IM I aim to unpack. At the top of the conversation screen, Soufian's display name "@ Marokko ☼" appears. Logging in to MSN, he indicated in his display name that he was on holidays in Morocco at that moment and the sun was shining. As Soufian logged into MSN using eBuddy.com Web Messenger, an automatic second name is added below his display name. eBuddy allows users to have conversations with MSN contacts without having to install any software on a computer. The application does not store any conversation history on the computer, unlike the Windows Live Messenger software that archived exchanges by default. Soufian used a display picture showing the blue, green and yellow Berber flag next to the green-starred red Moroccan national flag. Soufian's display name showed up in friend lists of people who have added him, together with the names of all other people in their lists. The display picture appeared on the screen of the conversation partner upon initiation of a one-on-one conversation. At the bottom of the conversation screen, a box is shown where users can enter messages to the conversation partner. A small smiley emoticon appears in the bottom. When clicked, a drop-down menu appears from which users may insert a smiley in their conversation. At the bottom, a commercial message appears: "Beautiful dresses for low prices you order at bonprix.nl."

IM is distinct from profiling practices on social networking sites such as Hyves and Facebook, which I discuss in Chapter 4, as it is considered as a more intimate space, said fifteen-year-old Hajar: "*On Hyves it's less personal, because everyone can see it, on MSN it's more personal and you can share things.*" Meryam, also fifteen years old, added: "*MSN, I find it totally different from Facebook. Facebook is more to horse around while MSN is to have a chat. More serious.*" The medium-specificity youth recognize in IM as a space that is not publicly accessible – allowing for greater personal autonomy in circulating personal information among a selected group of friends – is, however, not always acknowledged by adults, said sixteen-year-old Naoul:

> *My mother thinks that MSN is like chat. That you are chatting with the weirdest people from across the globe. But that's my mother, I can explain it to her one thousand times, and she still does not understand it. She will see a picture of me on the screen and she will say, "Do not put any pictures on the Internet," and I will say, "No, this is not the Internet, this is a picture on MSN, only the people in my personal list can see it." She will say, "No, this is the Internet." I can explain, but she won't take note of it. So I keep it to myself.*

MSN was a private communicative space. In thirteen-year-old Midia's words, MSN "*is for your self, nobody sees who and how many contacts you have in your list.*" Relationships and affiliations that were built within this space could be kept personal; they are only for the eyes of the individual users. Naoul and Midia suggest MSN was taken up to negotiate processes of coming-of-age where identity-in-the-making can be observed. However, IM was largely kept shut off from parental supervision and from other onlookers. Its private character has, for instance, caused concern among some parents. Declining our invitation to participate in the study, a mother who migrated from Morocco to the Netherlands voiced her concerns over the computer use of her three children (aged eight, eleven and thirteen): "*occasionally I have seen the [IM] conversation history and the conversations between the kids did not charm me very much. Many girls had a webcam and did their very best to look attractive.*" She eventually decided to prohibit her kids from using IM and online social networking sites: "*I am of the opinion that too much dirt and nonsense is sold and spread through these media and the disadvantages outweigh the advantages*" (e-mail conversation held between December 21 and 29, 2009).

Although not fully publicly accessible, informants nevertheless noted staggering numbers of people in their personal contact lists. Fourteen-year-old Ziham had 789 contacts, fifteen-year-old Carlos brags he had "*something like 900*" contacts, and thirteen-year-old Soesie listed 328. As ready knowledge that informants listed from off the top of their heads, such numbers seemed to mean much. For some, large numbers of friends were a status symbol. Thirteen-year-old Rachid, however, commented:

> *I have something like 50 friends in my MSN list. I am unlike some people who have I don't know 500 people in their list. They just add people that they don't even know, just to get a long list. But I don't think it's cool to have so many people in my list.*

A friend list was a status symbol that allowed young users to show off how many people they know. Wired Up survey findings showed that young people with a migration background had more people in their IM contact lists than ethnic-majority Dutch youth. Moroccan-Dutch young people listed an average of 231 contacts and ethnic-majority Dutch youngsters listed 205 contacts (Wired Up, 2011). The higher average number of contacts among migrant youth can partly be explained when considering that migrant teenagers also maintained contact with family and friends in the diaspora using IM. For instance, sixteen-year-old Faruk described he had family members living in the Netherlands, France, Spain and Morocco in his list. However, as I argued in the introduction, like most other informants I spoke with, Faruk did not really communicate with contacts in the diaspora himself but he mainly brokered access to contacts from abroad for his parents:

> *We just use MSN. My parents do not really know how it works. Yes I log in for them; I will click on my aunts' name when she is online. I set it up for them. I will put my parents in front of the webcam and have them communicate. Actually I enjoy it because my mother eyes the webcam with a real look of amazement on her face. It's nice because in the past I can say they would have never been able to do that. They are astounded.*

Sixteen-year-old Naoul, for instance, said: "*The children have to start up everything, and my dad will sit in front of the camera and he will talk. He does not know how to do it.*" Informants noted that parents had difficulties managing IM on their own. These statements by Faruk and Naoul reveal a generational divide in ICT knowledge and skills that may exist in some Moroccan-Dutch families. Moreover, it should be noted that some parents – especially Moroccan mothers of Berber descent who migrated to the Netherlands – were illiterate or had received little formal education at the moment of immigration (Pels & De Haan, 2007, p. 72). Having grown up with technologies such as MSN that their parents are unfamiliar with, Moroccan-Dutch youth may act as technology brokers as they assist their parents to cross a digital divide by brokering diasporic IM connections. Complicating intergenerational relations, the roles of parents as educators and children as learners get reversed (Leurs & Ponzanesi, 2013). This practice resembles other instances of invisible work multilingual migrant teenagers may have to engage in such as "culture" and "language brokering" when having to translate for their parents across private (e.g., filling in financial documents) and public domains (e.g., dealing with medical consults) (Orellana, 2009, pp. 19-21; De Haan, 2012). As the possibility of having conversations with contacts in the diaspora does not fully explain its value in the lives of Moroccan-Dutch youth, the question arises as to which other identity performance roles were invested in the communicative space of IM. Below I discuss scholarship in the traditions of CMC (computer-mediated communication) and digital literacies to theorize instant messaging as a power-laden discursive practice that displays how identities are performed across axes of differentiation.

3.2 Theorizing instant messaging as a way of being in the world

Forms of computer-mediated-communication come and go. The online social networking site Facebook has, for instance, largely superseded blogging sites from the early 2000s such as LiveJournal and Xanga. Instant messaging, on the other hand, has been around for almost two decades. Instant messaging is now available on various platforms such as the recent smartphone apps like What's App and it has been subsumed in larger applications such as Skype and Facebook. The practice of instant messaging, available online as a standalone platform since the 1990s, remains important in the lives of many adolescents. IM has been established as "fact of life, a way of being in the world" (Lewis & Fabos, 2005, p. 470). In the 1990s scholars recognized that instant messaging software was used as a supportive technology in the workplace. However, since the start young people have also used IM. They became space invaders as they appropriated the technology to further their own goals (Grinter & Palen, 2002). IM became a regular evening activity among adolescents when it "replaced the long telephone conversations between friends that used to be so frequent in adolescence" (Albero-Andrés, 2004, p. 112). The importance of IM can be grasped by comparing it to offline gathering places such as shopping malls and schoolyards. Mostly away from close adult supervision, such spaces are important to fend off boredom, "hang out" in groups and engage in various "friendship-driven" activities (boyd, 2010b, pp. 80-84). By logging on to IM, young people are able to connect with groups of friends who are "always-on" (Baron, 2008).

Being a fundamental part of everyday communication, IM has been studied from a variety of perspectives (Leurs & Ponzanesi, 2011a, 2011c, 2012). CMC scholars argue that "computer mediated written language often has speech-like characteristics" (Hård af Segerstad & Hashemi, 2006, p. 56). In instant messaging, these speech-like characteristics are represented through a distinct writing style with its own "Internet-speak" norms, consisting of abbreviations, apparent misspellings, ungrammatical and incorrect uses of typed language. Unlike the hypervisual dynamics of Facebook and Hyves (see Chapter 4), IM is mainly about typed narratives. Journalists, teachers, policy makers and parents have expressed their concerns about these linguistic features of IM. Often dressed up in moral panic rhetoric, IM applications and the informal speech circulating there are seen as a challenge to written culture. The practice is suspected of corrupting formal writing skills among young people and causing harm to print culture institutions (Thurlow, 2006). Discussions of IM by educators and journalists conflate "language change" and "language decline" when arguing that IM is "destroying language" (Baron, 2008, p. 161). IM is not leading to "linguistic ruin" and more importantly this digital practice can be acknowledged for "its own unique style" (Tagliamonte & Denis, 2008, p. 3). Appropriating the digital space, youthful users constitute alternative language norms that differ from official norms imposed by the state and accepted ways of speaking (Bourdieu, 1991, p. 45).[4] From the perspective of performativity of self, the question is not whether IM is detrimental to language, but rather, what process of meaning making lies behind its unique style for youth, and young people with a migration background in particular? Messaging users "don't just 'send' messages as an action ('message' as verb) they *are* a system of messages ('message' as noun); they are both constituted by and productive through messages" (Hartley, 2010, p. 23). Therefore I am interested in the meanings that can be attributed to the dynamic, expressive culture circulating in IM; for instance, that of the display names that appear in friend lists of users. Additionally, IM expressive culture includes sending short messages, exchanged by users to express themselves, using a

4 Pierre Bourdieu noted that official languages are linguistic laws that are bound up with state-formation processes: "Obligatory on official occasions and in official places (schools, public administrations, political institutions, etc.), this state language becomes the theoretical norm against which all linguistic practices are objectively measured" (1991, p. 45).

"full range of variants from the speech community – formal, informal, and highly vernacular" (Tagliamonte & Denis, 2008, p. 24).[5]

Scholars in the new literacy studies (NLS) tradition have examined digital literacies that have evolved in IM. Eva Lam recognizes that "to perform different voices and versions of one's self dependent on the audience has come to characterize the aesthetics and epistemology of IM" (2009, p. 380). The communicative space of IM sheds light on two "modes of adolescent connectivity": private self-identity formation and the more public social identity formation (Boneva et al., 2006, p. 202). In the first mode of adolescent connectivity, teenagers engage in "person-to-person communication" for purposes such as comparing themselves "to similar others and to receive verification for his or her own feelings, thoughts and actions" (ibid.). In their personal conversations youth "'decipher' the self" and negotiate their being in the world. Besides private self-identification, IM is used for "one-to-many communication" which is a second mode of adolescent connectivity. "Crucial to their social identity formation," this allows adolescents to express their "connectedness to a group that creates a feeling of group belonging" (Boneva et al., 2006, p. 202). Display names are examples of more public one-to-many forms of communication in IM. By naming themselves in distinct ways, users show affiliations, for instance, with peer groups.

The distinction between the onstage and backstage underlines the distinct ways instant messaging is taken up. Building on Erving Goffman's dramaturgical understanding of the everyday theater of the performance of self (1959), Gloria Jacobs describes the IM practices of Lisa, a white, American middle-class adolescent girl: "the backstage conversations [synchronous, dyadic IM exchanges] are where alliances are formed, problems are discussed and solved, and plans are made beyond the hearing of others.... The onstage places [display names] are where alliances are declared and social positions and presence are established" (2003, p. 13). The distinction between what is collectively made visible onstage by IM users such as display pictures and

5 As is also apparent from the excerpt of the IM conversation between Khadija and Nadia included at the beginning of this chapter, conversations have specific compositions that may be seen as a new genre of writing. The transmission style of messages includes the breaking up of single utterances into several lines of chat. Naomi Baron gives three reasons why users employ this particular style. Her first reason is technological. To maintain the attention of the interlocutor, utterances are often broken up into smaller pieces. By pressing enter while continuing to write an utterance, the conversation partner can begin reading the message, while the sender types the remainder. Her second reason refers to the readability of the message. Conversations are easier to follow when messages consist of short lines instead of larger chunks of text appearing on the screen. Finally, users reported to her that in their division of utterances over multiple turns "they are consciously attempting to make the results visually resemble a poem" (2004, p. 417).

display names, and what is negotiated in the backstage in personal conversations corresponds with the two modes of adolescent connectivity of public and private identity formation. In the backstage, IM can be used to "rehearse different ways of being before trying them out offline," as Deirdre Kelly, Shauna Pomerantz and Dawn Currie learned from their interviews with Canadian girls (2006, p. 3). In the onstage, IM can be used to signal affiliations and claim memberships. Thus, IM is to be considered as "multi-voiced," as it can be taken up to "perform a version of self" that can be shifted for different audiences (Lewis & Fabos, 2005, p. 493). These findings are, however, mostly based on the study of North American white, middle-class teenagers.

Recently, scholars have begun to focus on IM practices of American minority young people. Youngjoo Yi, for instance, studied IM identity construction among Korean-American adolescent youth. Her interviewees embraced IM as a safe space in which they "were becoming active, participatory social agents who constructed their own transnational and transcultural community." They were "'re-makers' of the textual, technological, linguistic, and cultural resources available" (2009, p. 123). Lam conducted an in-depth case study of instant messaging multiliteracies of Kaiyee, a Chinese-American adolescent girl. She traces the IM networking of Kaiyee with the local Chinese immigrant community, her translocal network of Asian American contacts and transnational connections with peers in China (2009). Yi focuses mostly on the performance of transcultural identifications, while Lam focuses on the issue of adolescence and migration. In both cases, isolating one of multiple axes of signification means that others might have been overlooked.

As I have noted in the prior chapters, with an intersectional lens I aim to make visible the ways the informants are differentially positioned and position themselves in specific ways in particular situations, because gender, generation, diaspora, religion and youth culture as well as issues of stereotyping complicate their processes of coming-of-age. This way, I consider the multilayered identification and complex intersecting journeys of children of immigrant groups. In the wider Dutch discourse on migration and integration, Moroccan-Dutch people are seen as the "absolute other" and females with a migrant and Islamic background especially run the risk of being isolated as "unemancipated others" (Ghorashi, 2010, pp. 75-81). In the introductory chapter I have set out how gender and other categories of difference such as age, generation, diaspora and youth culture, are material, representational and affective acts. In this chapter I consider intersecting symbolic grammars of difference as constituted through performative instant messaging practices.

Within the structure of IM, performative acts of, for instance, age, gender, ethnicity, generation and diaspora in instant messaging include the updating of one's display name, display pictures and abiding by IM speech conventions of emoticons, exchanging short utterances and using opening and closing conventions. By acknowledging the fluid and complex dynamics of socio-technological networks like IM I once more underline my theoretical aligning with feminist technoscience approaches that go beyond "gender essentialism" and "technological determinism" (Wajcman, 2007, pp. 294-296). Employing this perspective, as Meenakshi Gigi Durham posited: "The Internet then can be seen as an 'unformed place,' which depends to some degree on its use to find its structure. It is at the interface of user and technology that socialization instills order to the disorder of the Internet" (2001, p. 37).

Similar to other platforms, everyday exchanges on MSN are bound but not fully determined by interfaces, algorithms, corporate interests and discursive norms. Technological, linguistic and social norms give order to the performance of self in IM, but also leave room for resignification in the ways individuals and collectives of users adopt the medium (Leurs & Ponzanesi, 2011a, pp. 206-208; Leurs & Ponzanesi, 2012, pp. 440-441). In sum, in my analysis of IM, I combine CMC and digital literacy perspectives and remain aware of symbolic grammars of difference that intersect in our interviewees' performance of self in the digital realm (Leurs & Ponzanesi, 2011c, pp. 58-62).

Everyday discussions of personal issues, emotional support, fights, gossip and flirting took place on MSN. Such activities generated a fascinating window into the private and personal engagements of teens with their peers mediated through the performance of self in a digital space. However, as I discussed in Chapter 1, entrance to this private space was not straightforward (Jacobs, 2005; Thiel-Stern, 2007). I believe this is why in-depth studies examining the expressive culture of instant messaging including What's App, BlackBerry Messenger and Snapchat are scarce, while the more publicly accessible platforms such as social network sites like Facebook and microblogs such as Twitter have attracted scholars from a wide variety of disciplines. Below I firstly focus on the various ways ethnic-minority youth negotiate their ownership and perform the boundaries of their personal space. Secondly, I analyze the more public micro-politics of updating display names and display pictures.

3.3 The private backstage

The importance of being able to negotiating ownership over IM can only be understood when considering what was discussed there. The IM transcript below is an example of boy talk. Seventeen-year-old Fatiha was in conversation with her twenty-two-year-old Somalian-Dutch classmate Owsark. Owsark makes sure that nobody can eavesdrop on the conversation by asking Fatiha whether she was sitting behind the computer all by herself. Once they are both convinced that they had the privacy to talk, the girls turned to the sensitive topic of boys. This IM gesture can be compared to offline settings when it sometimes is desirable to make sure nobody can overhear a personal conversation:

> ***owsark says:*** ohyea theres something are you alone
> ***Show remorse!!........Allah (swt) will accept it from you and inchAllah will offer you goodness!! says:*** yes
> why
> ***owsark says:*** hha well
> i was at fatima
> on the laptop
> and i saw a photo
> in her pictures folder
> guess who
> ***Show remorse!!........Allah (swt) will accept it from you and inchAllah will offer you goodness!! says:*** who?
> ***owsark says:*** that one guy i told you about
> i told her what are these photos doing here
> ***Show remorse!!........Allah (swt) will accept it from you and inchAllah will offer you goodness!! says:*** which ones?
> ***owsark says:*** she know him
> the guy in school
> our the one you interviewd
> ***Show remorse!!........Allah (swt) will accept it from you and inchAllah will offer you goodness!! says:*** oooh khalid
> hahahaha
> ***owsark says:*** yes that one
> wallah saw [wollah: with Allah, for extra emphasis]
> a picture of him

The exchange was about something that happened when Owsark visited Fatima, a mutual friend. There, stored on Fatima's laptop in the personal pictures folder, she discovered photos of a boy she likes. It appears from the text that Owsark got somewhat jealous. She wanted to know from Fatiha how she thought the photographs got there. She quickly fired a series of short questions about the girl: does "*she know him,*" "*the guy in school*" and "*the one you interviewd*"? In this section I first discuss the main conversational topics informants discussed in IM. Next I analyze how informants became gatekeepers over their own, networked territory in their use of physical and digital processes of boundary making. Subsequently I assess the risks and opportunities involved when using IM to get to know boys and girls without having to meet face-to-face.

Conversational topics

When I asked what fifteen-year-old Inzaf and her friends usually do on IM, she reported that girls gossip "*mostly about boys with whom they are in love with or about other people*," while sixteen-year-old Naoul added, "*girls talk about*

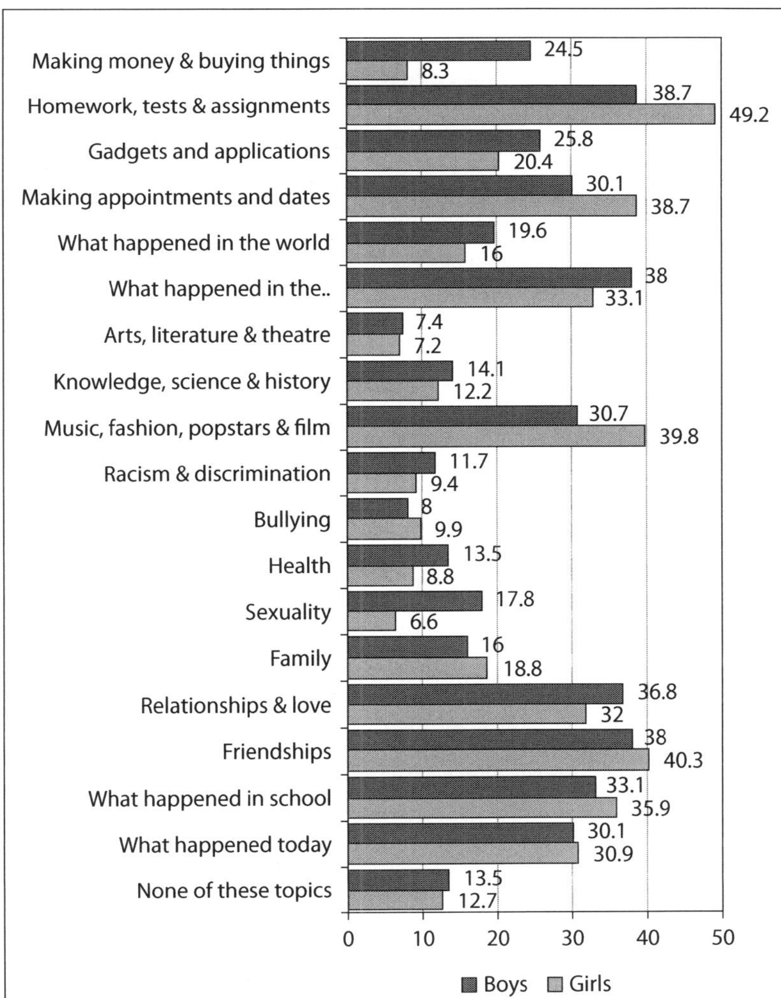

Diagram 6: Topics Moroccan-Dutch youth report to discuss (graph shows percentages, n = 344)

things such as shopping, school and some girls talk about boys." In the Wired Up survey, respondents were asked what topics they prefer to talk about online rather than face-to-face. The three most frequently mentioned topics among Moroccan-Dutch girls are "homework," "friendships" and "music, fashion, pop stars and film." Moroccan-Dutch boys list "friendships," "what happened in the neighborhood" (38%) and "homework" most frequently. Furthermore, important topics for both girls and boys are "relationships and love," "what happened today," and "what happened in the school." For the girls who participated in the survey, "making appointments and dates" is done more frequently than boys, while boys report the topics of "sexuality," "making money and buying things" and "new gadgets and applications" more often than girls. One out of every three boys and girls list the topic "relationships and love." It shows that using MSN to make appointments and dates is mentioned by almost 40% of Moroccan-Dutch girls (see Diagram 6).

Topics such as "friendships" and "relationships and love" resonate with private self-identity formation, the first of two modes of adolescent connectedness, next to more public social identity formation. Processes of private self-identity construction can be understood as backstage performances of self. Following Erving Goffman's use of theater metaphors to describe everyday interaction (1959), Jacobs argued that "backstage behavior," beyond the observation of power holders, is often done in IM to "build and test social ties." "Once operating within the safety of the backstage," her informants "use a variety of discourse cues and conventions to signal closeness, to build meaning and to work through misunderstandings" (2003, pp. 8, 31). With these characteristics, IM appears to be used as a playground for establishing (romantic) relationships.

Boundary making

> *I do have a laptop of my own, but my brother has changed the password, so I can't log in. He only lets me use it for school. He controls what I have done; he looks at the [browser] history, which he forbids me to delete. He checks whether I only do school work, instead of going on Hyves or so on. But I also have the Internet on my phone. Mostly I use my BlackBerry, because my brother doesn't allow me to go on sites like MSN, that's why I use my mobile.*
>
> – Ziham, a fourteen-year-old girl

Ziham revealed that she strategically negotiates access to her IM contacts by logging in on her BlackBerry smartphone. This way she circumvented the restrictions her brother placed on her Internet use. The backstage was consciously safeguarded from unwanted onlookers. Sixteen-year-old Naoul made sure she talks to the right person by phoning her friend: "*It can always also be someone else on MSN, so if I call her I know for sure it is her.*" Surveillance by older brothers and sisters also can be denied said sixteen-year-old Nevra: "*My brother sometimes comes and takes a look at what I'm doing. But I click everything away.*" She considered IM as a space of her own. When he wanted to check her online behavior, she closes "*every screen. It is none of his business. He does not need to know.*" Various informants, similar to Soufian in Figure 11, engaged in IM conversations using the web-based messenger service eBuddy.com. Conversing with IM contacts with this service has its advantages over the standard Windows Live Messenger as it did not leave traces of personal conversations stored on the computer, so they did not have to worry about conversation histories being read by family members or siblings. Thirteen-year-old Inas logged on to IM when she knew her parents were away:

> *I usually do it when they are not around, otherwise they will look at what I'm doing. And I don't like that. Because when I'm, for instance, talking to a boy, I do not want my mother to be standing behind me, you know? My mother will know what I say to that guy.*

American adolescent girls in Shayla Thiel-Stern's study considered IM a private space where adults are literally shut out. Using codes such as "mh" for "Mom's here" and "brb" for "be right back" girls keep conversations private, and they make sure they can share their thoughts on personal, compromising and embarrassing topics on IM. IM users can quickly close the chat window when unwanted onlookers, such as parents or siblings, approach the computer (2007, p. 52). The American teenagers in Rebecca Grinter and Leysia Palen's study emphasized the advantage of being able to operate IM "below the radar": "use can be unobtrusive, go unnoticed, or even be covert" (2002, p. 26). Much the same, my informants described their MSN conversations as very intimate and personal; as thirteen-year-old Midia claimed, IM "*is for yourself. Nobody sees who and how many contacts you have in your list.*"

On the platform itself, territories were also digitally bounded and maintained by codes and conventions. The lack of visual cues of regular face-to-face communication in IM has lead users to be creative and develop a cultural repertoire with a distinct writing style that includes smileys to convey emotions and manage impressions. Linguistic practices become meaningful for users themselves and others through a citation and reconstitution of norms and repertoires. IM requires skills that are not fixed or pregiven. These skills demand continuous investment, as the norms are not static. Midia explains that "*you see by the way someone talks on MSN whether he always uses it or sometimes.*" As the excerpt included in the beginning indicates, among our informants, IM writing style includes interethnic language use. In the opening of a conversation Midia asked Soad how she felt:

> ***I am Crazzy in love with you .. my feelings for you cannot go away says:*** Eey, darling whatsup??
> ***Checkmate sweetie says:*** hmdl with youu sweetyy? [*hmdl*: short form for Praise to Allah]
> ***I am Crazzy in love with you .. my feelings for you cannot go away says:*** good good hmdl keep it tat way hea zinaa xxxx [*zina*: beauty]

Midia "*hmdl*" felt good and Soad responded with "*hmdl*," she was okay. Midia wished Soad "*hmdl*" kept it that way, sharing "*xxxx*" for her "*zinaa*." With the abbreviation "*hmdl*," the word "*alhamdoelilah*" was inserted, which can be translated into "all praise is due to Allah." "*Zina*" is a word used in Moroccan-Arabic and Berber that can be translated as "beauty." Thus, Soad wished that Midia with the help of Allah would keep healthy, called her a beauty and offered her kisses.

Such dynamic language and social norms served as exclusionary and inclusionary mechanisms, determining who is part of the in-group and who is not. The desire for personal autonomy during adolescence might partly explain the medium-specific appeal of platforms like IM. Karen Bradley explains, "adolescence is marked by the desire for autonomy and independence" and recognizes that "the Internet offers adolescents social, moral, recreational, and intellectual experiences that are not mediated by adults" (2005, p. 62). Beyond the control of adults IM users have an active say over their space, as Faruk, a sixteen-year-old boy, described:

> *MSN is something different. You can say many things there that you do not easily say in the streets, because you might be embarrassed. For instance, when there is a girl standing in front of you, you can blush and so on. While on MSN, you can just type without her seeing it. On the Internet, you can actually be yourself more, than outdoors. You can talk freely and be a bit looser.*

A sense of greater autonomy seemed to result in feeling less inhibited about expressing one's intimate feelings and approaching potential partners.

Faruk was of the opinion that you could "*be a bit looser*" while on MSN. Having to type emotions is experienced as easier than sharing them otherwise. Fourteen-year-old Mehmet agrees: "*On MSN you dare a lot more, you dare to do and say more.*" It should be noted that IM was not primarily used to get in touch with strangers. The majority of informants only spoke to people they knew from elsewhere and learned more about them using IM. Using IM, Moroccan-Dutch youth note feeling less easily embarrassed, as using text to communicate does not show whether one is blushing or not when talking about sensitive and personal topics. According to fifteen-year-old Kamal "*when you are typing, difficult things can be said more easily*" because "*the words don't have to come out of your mouth.*" One can keep up one's appearance: "*On MSN you also never stutter, and when you make a mistake you can correct it, for instance, when you have typed something wrong*" (sixteen-year-old Amir). This was not only true for boys. Fourteen-year-old Sahar agrees she sometimes felt ashamed when talking about relationship issues away from the computer "*but on MSN, you do dare to say it. Because you are just on your own, and you do it more quickly.*" Fifteen-year-old SouSou explained IM "*usually makes it easier to talk*" and she felt less inhibited because "*you don't have to look at each other*" face-to-face. This observation also may help to understand why in one study on young people in the US, over one-third of participants reported having said something over IM they would not have said elsewhere (Lenhart, Rainie & Lewis, 2001, p. 22). Youthful users thus dare to share more on private platforms like IM, as they feel less inhibited sharing their feelings.

Unstable boundaries: Risks and opportunities

Perhaps informants felt less inhibited because they could maintain the boundaries to IM themselves by deciding who is added to and banned from their contact list. Fatiha described negative experiences with boys who demanded that she show herself on her webcam; she said that IM turned bad "*when the other directly asks whether you can turn on your cam,*" leading to an avoidance of those contacts. Midia spoke about her straightforward solution when people she did not know "*stalked*" her. "*You just have to block them and delete them off your list.*" This technical feature enabled users to keep out unwanted outsiders. Furthermore, female informants noted they could verbally counter boys better on IM than offline.

For example, thirteen-year-old Inas typed it is easier to talk back to guys on IM: "*When I'm in a fight with someone, I don't go to him, but I go on MSN. I like that better [than] to quarrel with someone. It's easier there. Maybe I regret it later on, but it is easier on MSN.*" Fourteen-year-old Kenza similarly felt IM allowed one to be more outspoken: "*When you say something personal, you maybe have to cry. On MSN you don't really have to cry.*" This, however, lead fifteen-year-old Meryam to note: "*Things can get pretty rough on MSN*"; it is not all rosy "*because you can type whatever you like and nobody will stop you.*" Kelly, Pomerantz & Currie studied adolescent girl practices in Canada and learned these girls stop boys and men from harassing them by blocking them off their friend lists (2006). The authors recognized the significance of girls being able to block "boys who were mean": "this power to respond to insults is significant in light of research showing that girls and women still appear to be more vulnerable to sexual insults, because boys and men have more diverse sources of strength and status" (Kelly, Pomerantz & Currie, 2006, p. 22). On the micro-political level of negotiating gender relations, girls may seize the opportunity to counter mean boys. However, IM is not a realm disconnected from real life, and intimate conversations spilling outside of the space of IM may have very serious consequences.

There remains a danger of exposing oneself in the backstage of IM because the Internet is not a social vacuum. In the case of IM, the line between private and public was unstable. Most informants noted the danger of private conversations getting copied and pasted to other contacts. Fourteen-year-old Mehmet Ali explained: "*When you talk to someone about personal things, that person can copy and paste and show it to everyone.*" During the interview with Inzaf and Naoul, they reflected on a bad IM sexual-harassment experience of a girl they both know. Their friend was pressured into showing parts of her body to a boy using a webcam on instant messaging. He forced her into undressing, stating he would spread other revealing pictures of her if she would not cooperate. Eventually she exposed herself in front of her webcam, which had very serious consequences. After their relationship ended, the boy broke the codes and conventions of MSN space and circulated outside of the space the webcam images he saved. The images became a new instrument of power, used to seek revenge.

Koen Leurs: Do you see any dangers or unpleasant things in MSN?
Naoul: Yes the webcam
Koen Leurs: Why do you feel it's dangerous?
Naoul: For girls that have lots of contact with boys, they can do things they will regret later. For instance, they will go camming and the boy will press printscreen. A girl I know she did a really stupid thing with a boy and the boy pressed printscreen and sent it to the whole city. This will make you get a reputation. That is really dangerous and you have to be really careful....

Naoul: Parts of her body, she showed to the cam and that boy took a picture and he sent that to everyone in our city. And at a certain point it got to her nephew, and he beat her up badly.
Inzaf: Yes terrible, she ended up in the hospital.
Naoul: For two days she was in the hospital, I believe, and at a certain point her dad found out and she got beaten up again. She spent a week or so in the hospital.
Inzaf: She showed me her bruises [pointing to her neck and shoulders].
Naoul: She really got hit in the neck.

The exchange over "*camming*," slang for webcamming which often implies cybersex, reminds us that girls can remain very vulnerable in the digital realm, and it illustrates how familial, ethno-cultural and religious norms regulate the partly overlapping but also partly divergent spaces of IM and the offline world. Perhaps the continuing attachment to IM can be explained by taking into account again that within their families, Moroccan-Dutch girls are sometimes more restricted in their movements than boys, as they are perceived as gatekeepers of "the family honour" (Pels & De Haan, 2003, p. 61). Inzaf, for instance, noted that her parents were worried over her conversations with members of the opposite sex on IM: "*my parents do know what MSN is, but they say, 'Yes, you should not have too many boys in your list and this and that,' but [I don't mind]*." In the introduction I argued that contradictory gender discourses circulate in youth cultures and informants' family circles.

Requirements from the two domains can clash. In some families values such as honor and chastity prevail and are especially expected of girls. Familial social norms require some informants to remain modest in their contacts with boys. Such differential expectations also color their digital practices. My study of Internet forums has revealed how public digital spaces are taken up collectively to relatively anonymously nuance and counter gendered, religious and ethno-cultural expectations, and IM offers further insights on how personal digital spaces are assumed to meander between contradictory assumptions. Fourteen-year-old Loubna mentioned she protects her reputation by deleting digital traces of her exchanges in IM: "*You can always have the conversation history retrieved by someone in your home.*" IM was used by some interviewees to extend the parameters of their physical and social worlds, although they recognized the dangers of being found out (Leurs & Ponzanesi, 2011c, pp. 70-71).

Fourteen-year-old Mehmet Ali thought that MSN was more popular among girls than among boys, as he felt girls are more confined to the home "*as a girl when you are not allowed to go out, you can still talk with your friends.*" IM enables young people to be connected away from adult supervision, while being confined to their homes; IM is a "quiet technology" that can be "used to talk with friends outside the times that would be allowed either by natural constraints or by socially-determined constraints" (Grinter & Palen, 2002, p. 26). For some Moroccan-Dutch girls, the Internet sometimes "functions as a protected meeting place," as it is not always considered "appropriate for a Muslim girl to go to a café to meet the opposite sex" (Brouwer, 2006a). Sixteen-year-old Bibi illustrated that MSN is appealing for Moroccan-Dutch girls to get in touch with boys, away from the watchful eyes and scrutiny of her community:

> *In any case you are at home. You are in your room. Nobody from the community is around.... For instance, concerning the topic of love, when I like someone I don't dare to say to someone at first things like, "Yes, I love you." On MSN it is easier, because that someone is not standing in front of you.*

IM was used to circumvent restrictions placed on Moroccan-Dutch girls by parents and siblings, enabling users to get in touch with other people. Wired Up survey findings showed that almost 40% of participating girls use IM to schedule meetings and dates. The interviewees reported that girls can, for instance, exert agency in setting up dates. Inzaf is hesitant about it: "*I don't know but I think there are many girls who think it is easier.*" Midia on the other hand told me: "*Well, I think that every girl first talks to a boy on MSN to get to know each other better and then tries to schedule a date.*" Because familial and community control over their freedom remains a key issue, Naoul found "*it is easier to approach a boy via MSN via the Internet than a boy who would walk by here, especially for girls who are a bit shy.*" In the words of Fatiha: "*You get the chance to get to know somebody better without having to be with somebody face to face.*" IM seemed to be used as a space to get acquainted and develop a bond. These findings add another layer to the study by Kelly, Pomerantz and Currie who argued that use of instant messaging among girls they interviewed "allowed them to rehearse different ways of being before trying them out offline." They also used instant messaging to practice taking the initiative in (heterosexual) relationships in IM (2006, pp. 3, 20).

Having the blocking feature at hand, IM was used to try out private conversations. Although Inzaf raised the issue of her friend getting beaten up after showing herself on a webcam using IM, she felt IM remained a safer option: "*It is a greater risk to approach a stranger on the street just like that. You never know what that person is like – he could be aggressive.*" If the conversation goes wrong, or a contact demands intimate webcam images, the interviewees reported that they will block and delete the contact from their buddy list. Naoul told me about what can go wrong, but she still used instant messaging "*because it is a fun way to spend your free time.*" Perhaps this distinct preference can be explained because, "women participate more actively and enjoy greater influence in environments where the norms of interaction are controlled" (Herring, 2003, p. 209). The different ways users take pleasure in staking out their own private communicative space resonates with the notion of "jammer girls." Debra Merskin claimed that, facilitated by sociological and technological changes and informed by third- wave feminism,[6] "jammer girls" negotiate their worlds by making use of Internet applications to "enjoy a sense of freedom and a sense of control" over their own communication in order to securely be able to "validate their feelings" (2005, pp. 57, 64). Notwithstanding dangers that remain, part of the power of IM is that it was a space where young people, away from unwanted onlookers, were found to have fun, rehearse personal identifications and experiment with intimate relationships. In the next section, I discuss the onstage of IM use, where informants performed their identities by actively remixing different cultural affiliations.

3.4 The more public onstage

Besides a key topic of IM conversation, love and affection was also commonly expressed in the display names that interviewees and their friends use. For instance, Souad, Midia's thirteen-year-old girlfriend, used the display name "*I am Crazzy in love with you* ♥*... my feelings for you cannot go away* ☹" to share her crush with her friends. Fifteen-year-old Inzaf also shared that she wrote "*short poems*" in her display name "*When I, for instance, am in love with someone, I will create those.*" Achmed, Fatiha's twenty-one-year-old conversation partner, went by the display name of "*Only when the fiish stop swimming I will stop looking for giirls;-).*" In this section, I shift my focus from the backstage of private one-on-one IM communication to the second important mode of adolescent connectedness of one-to-many social identification. Besides publishing romantic feelings, "onstage" IM behavior accommodates different ways of being. Display names and display

6 Moving away from essentialism and embracing ambiguity, third-wave feminism is concerned with the micro-politics of multiple oppressions, but also the opportunities for agency in the everyday life of women (Mack-Canty, 2004).

pictures are "a way to take the stage for a select audience" and they can be dynamically used to perform various versions of themselves (Jacobs, 2003, p. 26). In updating display photos and articulating display names, digital labor is performed to gain status and grab the attention of peers. Below, I first interpret display pictures by locating them in the context of youth cultural industries. Second, I explore display names as a form of multilayered bricolage and discuss how being able to include interethnic language use in IM cultural repertoires is significant for the informants.

Display pictures and gender stereotypes

Display pictures, which are often distinctly gendered selfies, are important means of performing an onstage presence (as is also elaborated in Chapter 4 where display pictures on social networking sites are analyzed). Kamal, for instance, wanted to look "*cool*" in his MSN display picture while Khadija wants to appear "*friendly*" and "*fashionable*" in hers. Inzaf suggested that girls show "*most of the time pictures of their lips or of themselves,*" while boys show "*pictures of themselves with their friends and sometimes of their six-pack.*" Seventeen-year-old Fatiha added that girls use "*mostly nice sensual or emotional images,*" while boys used "*mostly tough looking pictures.*" These remarks indicate a dominant localization of commercialized global youth discourses: a perpetuation of the dichotomy of clear-cut masculinity versus complementary femininity as sensuality and emotionality versus rough-and toughness. Salima, a thirteen-year-old girl, confirmed "*a girl I know added 'sweet' in her name, while a boy named himself 'coolboy',*" thus "*guys want to act tough, something like 'I am the best,' while girls want to look nice in pictures, so everyone will like them.*" Used as digital self-portraits of their bodies, display photos as such can be seen as virtual real estate for marketing the self, in an ongoing verification of complementary feminine and masculine conventions. Young people sell their gendered selves to each other in their gendered peer attention economy (Leurs & Ponzanesi, 2011a, p. 208).

Furthermore, the fragmentation of the body into sexualized objects – showing seducing lips for girls and well-muscled abdomens for boys – reflects idealized stereotypical images of adolescent girls and boys. Preoccupations with physical beauty myths are typical for Western adolescents and their consumption of perfect sexual body discourses. These, for instance, find resonance in the literature on American adolescent girls' messenger use (Thiel-Stern, 2007; Durham, 2001). American adolescent girls have been found to consume ideals of culturally defined female identities on IM: "IM is a space as guided by corporate and commercial discourses as any magazine or television show" (Thiel-Stern 2007, p. 97). Throughout my virtual ethnography, in the months of January and February 2010 I especially looked at the "MSN today" pop-up screen that automatically appears when signing in. The pop-up screen provided an overview of newsworthy articles for MSN users. It can be seen as a piece of virtual real estate used by corporations to attract IM users to their advertisements, with common topics such as dieting ("lose wait like Beyonce"), celebrity gossip ("Brad and Angelina break up," "Dinand honest about cheating") and sex-tips ("Prima Donna's in porn"), all of which play into stereotyping gender, sexuality and body-myths. Corporations are seeking entrance to the private space of IM. Pop-ups, IM bots (automated IM partners added to one's contact list offering information about banking, shopping, etc.) and commercials appeared within the personal space (Thiel-Stern, 2007, p. 100). As another invocation of culture jamming, informants generally reported paying little attention to these advertisements in MSN. Fatiha, for instance, told me: *"I ignore those commercials and they do not bother me."*

Beyond a stereotypical gendered performance of self, other axes of differentiation were also highlighted in display pictures. As already shown in Figure 11, Soufian included the Moroccan and Berber flag in his display name. Other informants similarly exerted affiliations with Morocco in their pictures. Fourteen-year-old Kenza signaled being proud of her ethnic background by showing the Moroccan flag: *"I put the flag of Morocco there, so people will know that I am Moroccan."* Thirteen-year-old Tariq added that next to showing being proud, the flag is also a way to stake out one's individuality: *"I have chosen a photo of the flag of my country. It shows my descent. Not many people do that. I do it to show I'm proud of it."* Fourteen-year-old Senna noted that next to the Moroccan national flag the Amazigh flag is also used, because *"it is a part of them, a Moroccan part"* that Moroccan-Dutch Berber users want to show. Performing oneself as Moroccan was, however, not done by only publishing ethnic signifiers such as the Moroccan national flag or the Berber movement flag. For example, fifteen-year-old Meryam stated *"I wear a headscarf, so when I put my picture up on MSN, others will know that I am Moroccan,"* signaling religious markers indicating membership in the Moroccan-Dutch community are also in included in display pictures.

Display names and bricolage

The crafting of an appealing display name is another example of identity work that is communicated from one-to-many. These names not only appear in person-to-person conversations, but also in the buddy list of IM contacts. By double-clicking on someone's display name in one's list of friends, users can start conversations. By making references to specific inspirations and showing orientations to friends, display names are similar to display photos used to demarcate and manage an online presence. And they are used to attract the attention of potential conversation partners. The young people who participated in the study of Cynthia Lewis and Bettina Fabos were constantly monitoring their buddy lists, as friends in these lists regularly changed their display names. They concluded that the buddy list is used as a means of surveillance (2005, p. 489). Young people keep an eye on the various ways in which their friends (re)author themselves. Analyzing display names in the gathered transcripts reveals that this naming is gendered but also displays hybrid forms of religious, ethnic, and youth cultural belonging.

In the words of interviewee Noual, a display name "*as a matter of fact tells a sort of life story.*" The interviewees remix various linguistic symbolic grammars of difference in their onstage display names. Thirteen-year-old Ilham was of the opinion that updating display names on IM is in a way similar to publishing Twitter status updates: "*Sometimes when I'm, for instance, doing my homework, I will change my status to 'ssht, I'm busy doing my homework.' Actually that's just like Twitter only I don't use Twitter.*" The updating of a display name can be understood as a digital ritual. Being increasingly online people turn to networked rituals such as updating display names, statuses and posting tweets to give order to their lives. Rituals, Kevin Hillis wrote, can accommodate different ways of being in the world: "ritual allows participants to performatively enact or rehearse strategies to cope with the crucial changes they may undergo" (2009, p. 56).

The habitual updating of display names covers one of its dimensions, its bricolage character highlights another. Jacques Derrida noted that readers of texts engage in bricolage. He recognizes readers actively participate in meaning production, and become engineers of texts by deconstructing language structures through their linking of them with concepts beyond and behind the text. In this way, readers decenter texts by recombining them with other materials (Derrida, 1978). Dick Hebdige, in his analysis of punk as a subcultural style, argues that bricolage refers to signature style elements that are used to mark distinctiveness: "it is basically the way in which commodities are used in subculture which mark the subculture off from more orthodox cultural formations" (1979, p. 103). In the digital context, the concept can be taken to grasp the combination and juxtaposition of materials to create new meanings. Jannis Androutsopoulos commented on diasporic groups' online multilingualism in Germany: "being marked off as a personal territory, screen names and signatures allow their bearers to engage in cultural bricolage, appropriating resources from various domains" (2006, pp. 539-540).

Illustratively, fifteen-year-old Oussema explained that he lists his name, together with "*mocro*," which he says "*just means Moroccan boy*" and as a second nickname he added a reference to the hajj his parents made "*because I am proud that my parents have gone to Mecca, I typed 'Mom and Dad have gone to Mecca'.*"[7] Fifteen-year-old Meryam articulated her nostalgic imagination of Morocco: "*I always type 'Morocco is the country to dream of.' Because I think Morocco is really a beautiful country and I really would like to stay there all the time. But it's impossible! This way people know that I am crazy about Morocco.*" Display names in the corpus reveal affective ethnic affiliations, often used in combination with gendered articulations. Examples include the use of "*Maroc,*" referring to the French word for the country of Morocco, "*mocro chick,*" "*mocro girl*" and "*mocro boy.*" Inzaf informed me such names are common. She told me, "*mocro boy means I am from Morocco and I am a boy,*" and she thought names such as these are written in English "*to sound cooler.*" Interestingly, migrant users in Germany have also been found to perform their ethnic identities through English language nicknames, mostly in combination with gendered expressions, "as in Persian Girly, PersianLady, prince of Persia, and sexy greekgirl, GreEk Chica, greekgod19" (Androutsopoulos, 2006, p. 540).

References to ethnic ties were among the markers of difference expressed in display names. Inzaf logged in to MSN using a display name written in English: "*El Hoceima is the bom, that's the place where I come from so just tell everyone thats the city number ONE.*" The rhyme combines rap vernacular, informed by global youth culture, with an expression of diasporic belonging. Inzaf told me she stumbled upon something similar on a website and she felt it was something for her so she altered her display name accordingly. She added that "*it rhymes in English*" and she felt it's "*nicer to say it in English than in Dutch.*" Explaining its significance she shared: "*It means a lot to me because that is the town in Morocco where I am from and I want to show that I am proud of it.*" The name represented her attachment to the city of Al Hoceima in Morocco: "*I was not born there but my father is from El Hoceima.*" Her father supported her identity performance, Inzaf mentioned, "*When I was using it, he saw my name and he thought it was good*" (Leurs & Ponzanesi, 2011c, p. 73).

In the introduction I argued that identification among diasporic subjects concerns an ongoing marking of difference and sameness, as people in

7 Hajj refers to the pilgrimage to Mecca, Saudi Arabia. As the fifth pillar of Islam, hajj is a religious duty for every Muslim who can afford it. Hajj is the largest pilgrimage in the world (Raj, 2007, p. 137.

changing settings affiliate with where they came from in combination with what they want to become (Gilroy, 1993a; Hall, 1990). These junctures are also digitally mediated, in this case through the bricolage of display names in IM by Moroccan-Dutch youth. Fourteen-year-old Kenza, for instance, said, "*this way I show people what I am like.*" The display name of Inzaf displayed the emotional influence the migration experience of her father had on her life. However, there is another layer to this marker. The display name also illustrates her mediation of contemporary orientations. Turning to English, she signals her affiliation with contemporary global youth culture.

In IM, as Jacobs argues, "spellings indicate membership in an online community" (2003, p. 35). For instance, in my research, I came across the display name of a girl who crafted a netspeak translation of the Arabic name Nour, "ღ *n O u я я* ღ," and also the display name of a boy consisting of both Latin and Arabic characters, "*Mø* محمد *BadBoy.*" In the latter netspeak, Mø, is combined with Arabic alphabet characters to write the name Mohammed. The name also integrates a connection to mainstream global hip-hop culture by referencing Bad Boy Records, the American record label set up by the rapper Sean "Diddy" Combs. The take-up of CMC-specific writing styles in display names reveals another dimension to the ways in which our interviewees become active agents over their own representation: they author multiple selves and express diverse social belongings. These display names appear on the screen over and over, every time a new line is typed and the enter button is pressed. By choosing to name themselves in these specific ways they come into being as gendered, ethnic and youth cultural beings in the context of IM. Through a repetitive performance of these names, IM installs the user's differential identity.

Besides netspeak and English, the informants also tapped into Latinized Arabic. Khadija in the conversation excerpt included at the beginning of the chapter listed "*Li Tmenit Lqito Fik,*" Moroccan-Arabic for "what I hoped I found in you," while Fatiha logged in with the display name showing religious orientations: (partly translated from Dutch) "*Show remorse!!........ Allah (swt) will accept it from you and inchAllah will offer you goodness!!*"[8] During my interview with Khadija, she made it clear that this statement is used to express her commitment to Islam: "*I am a believer and what is in my name is a sort of phrase taken from the Quran.*" Similarly, sixteen-year-old Nevra logged in with the display name "*Allah ou akhbar.*" Fourteen-year-old

8 Here, "swt" is the acronym for "*Subhanahu wa ta'ala*" meaning "may He be glorified and exalted."

Senna noted that Moroccan-Dutch IM users might "*have something Moroccan in there, a word. For instance, 'Ana Maghrabia'.*" "*Ana Maghrabia*" can be translated as "I am from the Maghreb" in Dutch. The interviewees thus not only turn to English to express their affiliations. Display names that include Moroccan-Arabic written in the Latin alphabet appear widely.

A funky, informal writing style

By writing Arabic while using the Latin alphabet, IM users can claim membership to specific peer groups, but also enjoy this "funky" everyday informal writing style that generates "peer-group prestige" (Palfreyman & Al Khalil, 2003). David Palfreyman and Muhamed al Khalil analyzed the representation of Arabic in IM conversations in the United Arab Emirates. Similarly to the examples discussed here, their interviewees, female university students, combined characters from the Arabic alphabet with characters from the Latin alphabet to write Arabic in their IM exchanges. They found that employment of the Latin alphabet instead of the Arabic alphabet is shaped by "linguistic, technological and social factors." The influence of the American Standard Code for Information Interchange (ASCII) on online communication can partly explain why young people engage in this digital practice. Palfreyman and Al Khalil recognize ASCII as "a kind of lingua franca of the Internet" (2003). Globally, the ASCII computer character set is the technological default. There is a general lack of support for Arabic script in keyboards, computers, and operating systems. The standard mainly covers Latin letters, which are most commonly used in European languages, and excludes Arabic script (among other non-Latin scripts).

However, the practice of using Latinized Arabic, dubbed "ASCII-ized Arabic" (AA) by Palfreyman and Al Khalil, is not only shaped by constraints of computer character sets. ASCII-ized Arabic has also been taken up as an everyday informal writing style. In their casual IM conversations with peers, the students participating in the study by Palfreyman and Al Khalil wrote in ASCII-ized Arabic because of its "ease of typing." However, they also reported using it because of privacy concerns (their parents would not be able to follow the conversation) and because they were interested in "writing in an unusual script" (2003).[9] Among Moroccan-Dutch youth,

9 Typing in ASCII-ized Arabic, students in the United Arab Emirates were seen to negotiate between localized, linguistically specific vernaculars and Modern Standard Arabic. Linguistic vernaculars in the United Arab Emirates were previously only used for genres such as poetry and cartoons. In their use of IM, these vernaculars are now actively transferred and translated

this writing style has likewise grown into an informal and generationally specific symbolic resource invested with shared meanings. The style is used to articulate a bounded collective identity with an in-group that recognizes its principles, and allows its users to exclude outsiders such as teachers and other adults. In a similar vein, Yi noted that his Korean-American interviewee Mike came to think of reading and writing Korean as "cool" after his peers complimented his use of Korean in diary writing and web-posting. "[H]e seemed to (re)learn the value of his heritage language and to construct a positive self-image" (2009, p. 108). IM was also a significant safe space for our interviewees to find acknowledgement of their heritage language as a positive, empowering resource.

These insights allow me to intervene in two scholarly debates. In the Netherlands, youngsters with a Moroccan background have been recognized as linguistic trendsetters in creating and distributing slang (Vermeij, 2004). Lotte Vermeij, however, added that their language-crossing practices are very limited and that interethnic language use is chosen as a way to express the liking or disliking of others: "the interethnic language users do not use this way of talking for conversations about ordinary topics" (2004, p. 164). In MSN expressive culture, apart from signaling religious and ethnic affiliations in display names, non-Dutch words are also used in IM conversations, for instance, to express liking each other ("*zina*"), thanking one another ("*besaha*," "*hmdl*"), doubt ("*swia swia*," "*ze3ma*") and, for instance, to talk about preferred drinks (on MSN seventeen-year-old Fatiha invited her friend to come over for "*3assir*," a fruity drink). The analysis of the corpus displays that interethnic language use is quite rich; it is interspersed in everyday conversations to establish a shared common ground and to symbolize gender, diasporic and youth cultural affiliations. Second, earlier research established that boys use more slang in their everyday speech than girls (Gordon, 1993). In Moroccan-Dutch young people's use of IM, however, slang is not restricted to the male domain; girls are avid slang producers in the conversations and display names I analyzed.

The display pictures and display names discussed above indicate how the lived experience of difference among Moroccan-Dutch youth – who are sometimes made hyper visible as absolute Others – is not always an oppressive one, but can also be an empowering "positive difference" (Modood, 2007, p. 37). I observed the ways informants take the stage to gain solidarity from various peer groups by foregrounding various community memberships,

for the purpose of everyday informal computer-mediated communication (Palfreyman & Al Khalil, 2003).

belongings and loyalties. Becoming active agents over their own representation, the interviewees go beyond a singular onstage articulation of identity; rather they perform a multiplicity of selves by remixing diasporic, gendered, youth cultural, Internet culture and religious affiliations.

3.5 Conclusions

Instant messaging has been immensely popular among young people since the 1990s. IM goes back to the purely text-based roots of the Internet, but outside of use in the workplace it has remained a relatively understudied and undertheorized social media technology because it is not straightforward to gather data within this private space. In the chapter, I opened up this private space. Although MSN Messenger, the field site considered as a case study for this chapter, does not exist anymore, the analysis does shed light on contemporary instant messaging practices taking place on Facebook Chat, Skype and especially smartphone apps like What's App, iChat and BlackBerry Messenger.

IM was shown to provide a window into the private engagements of teens with their peers that includes interaction with private/public spaces, interethnic language and slang use in the construction of selfhood, the negotiation of friendship and the production and consumption of sexuality. Focusing on performativity of self, remaining aware of how users adapt to the environment and by taking into consideration how the applications' interface, restrictions imposed by dominant computer character sets, and commercial incentives inscribe themselves upon the users' performance of self, I unraveled how in IM Moroccan-Dutch youth actively (re)position themselves in their personal networks. Together with survey and interview findings, the transcripts Fatiha, Naoul, Midia, Kamal, Khadija and Inzaf shared offer a glimpse of how that relatively safe backstage space is negotiated and how differential social belongings are communicated.

I analyzed two kinds of identity work IM is used for. MSN is taken up as an opportunity to perform diversified selves onstage and iterating a personal identity backstage resulting from multiple forms of negotiations with technical skills, digital literacies, net speak along with consuming and bending stereotypical gendered discourses, youth branding and localized forms of global connections. Moroccan-Dutch young people and especially girls, in their quotidian interaction with the digital realm, carved out a communicative space of their own. The interviewees maintain their own private networked territory as they themselves control its boundaries. Gatekeeping is done physically – offline – as well as digitally – online. Experimenting with relationships and rehearsing personal identities, interviewees are empowered, expanding the parameters of their social and physical worlds through IM, while navigating between conflicting familial, gendered, religious and ethno-cultural motivations. Said Graiouid similarly found that female chatters in Morocco build relationships with males and females with less fear of losing face, illustrating once more the impact digital media use has on spatial regulations of gender and social relations (2005, p. 84).

I have argued that for Moroccan-Dutch boys and girls instant messaging offered a space to negotiate these issues backstage and become active agents over their own multiaxial representations onstage. Despite all existing constraints that are related to gender restrictions, often disenfranchised family backgrounds, religious dictums, surveillance by parents, siblings and peers, and stereotypical youth cultural gender ideologies, which effect Moroccan-Dutch boys and especially girls in specific ways, IM was found to be a unique space for exerting their agency in playful and intimate ways. In tandem with discussion forums, using IM informants find themselves in a safe enough space to circulate self-narratives and appreciate their cultural and gendered trajectories. Unlike publicly accessible forums, in their own networked territory they are able to limit their communication to a self-chosen audience of friends. However, IM is no social vacuum disembedded from offline power relations. The example of sexual harassment raised by Inzaf and Naoul indicates girls remain susceptible to male domination in their personal territory. The relationship between IM and the offline world remains intricate and complex; at certain points, both worlds overlap and sometimes collide, at others they diverge and provide autonomy. In the following chapter the focus shifts from the mostly text-based space of IM to visually oriented social networking sites.

4. Selfies and hypertextual selves on social networking sites

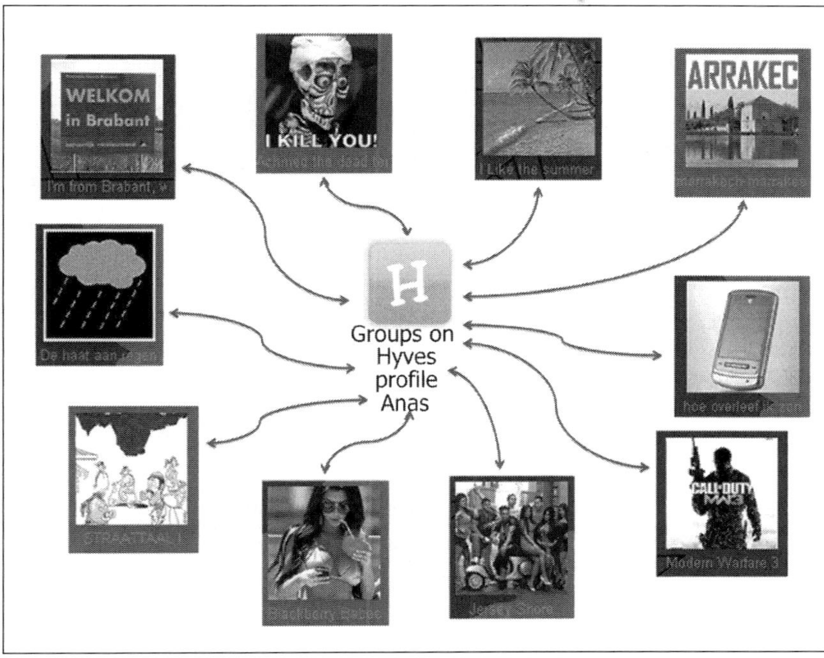

Fig. 12: Hyves groups thirteen-year-old Anas linked to on his Hyves profile page (July 22, 2011)

After joining a group on the Dutch social networking site Hyves, a hyperlinked icon appeared on the user's personal profile page. By joining these groups, users articulate hypertextual narratives of selves. Figure 12 shows the interest groups Anas, a thirteen-year-old rap fanatic, included on his profile page. From the top left he linked to "I'm from Brabant where the fack you from?," a group referring to the province where he lives in the south of the Netherlands. "Achmed the dead terrorist," refers to the comical incompetent suicide bomber act performed by Jeff Dunham, an American ventriloquist. With "I Like the summer" he indicated to prefer warm weather. By having joined the group "Marrakesh," he published symbolic diasporic affiliations. His parents were born in Marrakech, in Morocco, and by listing this group Anas shows he is proud of his migration background. He connects with global youth cultural forms with the groups "how do I survive without a mobile phone," "Modern Warfare 3," "Jersey

Shore," and "STREETLANGUAGE!." The hyperlinked groups showcase his attachment to his mobile phone, to a first-person shooter video game, the MTV reality TV series and his preference for slang and urban youth culture. "Blackberry Babes" is a page where girls posted selfies taken with their mobile phones. The site was used for dating purposes, as it is dedicated to exchanging BlackBerry PingChat! messenger contact details. The group icon is exemplary for stereotypically gendered selfies that meet the dominant perspective of the heterosexual male gaze. Lastly he linked to "Hate the rain" as another reminder of his preference for summery weather.

The example is included to draw attention to the distinct youth cultural dynamics of social networking sites (SNSs), in particular, to its visually gendered and multiaxial hyperlinked dimensions. Although SNSs – like forums and IM applications – share a given set of affordances, users appropriate them in various socio-culturally specific ways. In other words, the "key technological features are fairly consistent," however, the "the cultures that emerge around SNSs are varied" (Boyd & Ellison, 2008, p. 210). Nonetheless, scholars have noted there are "relatively few culturally specific online social network studies" (Grasmuck, Martin & Zhao, 2009, p. 161) and little research is done on "language-and-national-identity-specific" social networking practices (Siibak, 2009). Addressing the gap in the literature, in this chapter I develop two complementary partial perspectives to analyze social networking site user cultures of Moroccan-Dutch youth.

On social networking sites, users are expected to construct their digital identities by completing profile page interface and menu options. Users can, for instance, do so by publishing self-descriptions, status updates, selfies, hyperlinks, videos and music. Earlier empirical studies mostly focused on the typed narratives of SNS users (Siibak, 2009), in this chapter I focus on selfies and hyperlinking practices. Profile photos and hyperlinks are user-generated digital artifacts that can be taken into account as "objects to think with" (Turkle, 2007, p. 5), as they unlock sets of associations and layers of meaning. Selfies have been recognized to function as innovative ways to "see and shape ourselves" (Rettberg, 2014). Therefore, the following main question guides this chapter: how do Moroccan-Dutch youth perform their identities by publishing selfies and hyperlinks on their personal profile pages on Hyves and Facebook? As they become active agents over their own representation – bounded by the SNS habitus (profile template structures and peer norms) – I scrutinize which aspects of their identities they highlight in their profile photos and hyperlinked affiliations.

Besides the Wired Up survey findings, this chapter draws on in-depth interviews, a virtual ethnography of the digital SNS practices of six informants and interviews with eight SNS group page founders and moderators. First, as I will elaborate in Section 4.1, Wired Up survey findings show that gender is one of the most important dynamics Moroccan-Dutch young people include on their personal profile pages. In this chapter I therefore focus on gender as the primary analytical category when examining the use of personal profile photos. These profile photos are mostly self-taken self-portrait photographs or selfies. Guided by my analysis in the previous chapter of stereotypically gendered display pictures in IM, I continue exploring whether a fetishization of male and female bodies is also dominant in the ways in which users present themselves in SNS selfies. Secondly, not wanting to obfuscate other axis of differentiation in my scrutiny of the SNS expressive cultures of Moroccan-Dutch youth, I additionally concern myself with the implications of intercultural encounters on social networking sites by interpreting how Moroccan-Dutch youth perform hypertextual selves on their profiles. I assess whether informants homogenously emphasize their ethnic backgrounds on their profiles and corroborate dominant views of failed multiculturalism and ethnic segregation or whether they rather express heterogeneous selves and identify beyond the singular ethnicized positions to which they often find themselves allocated.

This chapter is structured as follows. In Section 4.1, I introduce the meanings of Hyves and Facebook in the lives of my informants. Next, I set out theoretical underpinnings to grasp the impetus of teenager and cultural industry logics that operate (in the background of) online social networking sites. In Section 4.3, I assess how social networking site profile photos are imbued with gender and sexuality among Moroccan-Dutch youth. Section 4.4 develops further the figuration of hypertextual selves, theorizing hyperlinks to acknowledge cosmopolitan processes of networked belonging across difference through the digital performativity of gender, ethnicity, religion, and youth cultural fandom.

4.1 Moroccan-Dutch youth on Hyves and Facebook

In this section I introduce the third field site I studied on a case study basis by describing Hyves and Facebook in the words of the informants. I list reasons for joining these platforms, dynamics of setting up a profile page and discuss how personal profile pages can be used to signal affiliations. At the time of the fieldwork the popularity of Facebook was beginning to outgrow Hyves, however Hyves remained especially popular among the younger informants. In July 2011 Facebook for the first time attracted more

Dutch members in comparison with Hyves (4.9 million versus 4.8 million). At that time, two-thirds of users made use of both platforms. However, on December 2, 2013, Hyves ceased to exist as a social networking site, it is now a child-oriented video game platform. However, the argumentation developed in this chapter holds both for Hyves and Facebook (and alternatives including MySpace and Ello). Hyves was set up in October 2004 and was "named after beehives. The users are bees and the social network is the hive." The space was developed to be nationally oriented and most content was posted in Dutch (Bannier, 2011, p. 587). During my fieldwork, its founders sold the site to owners of the Dutch conservative daily newspaper *De Telegraaf.* When that happened, fifteen-year-old Oussema mentioned he quit the site like a lot of other Dutch users, fearing the new owners would commercially exploit the site more extensively: "*I have deleted my account yesterday. I have heard that they will be sending a lot of advertisements.*"

Originally targeted toward students, Facebook became publicly accessible in September 2006, and a Dutch-language version was released in May 2008. On average, 829 million users across the world were active daily in June 2014 (Facebook, 2014), and in the Netherlands 8.9 million people were active on Facebook, of whom 6.1 million on a daily basis (Newcom, 2014, p. 7).

Table 6: The importance of social networking sites in the lives of Moroccan-Dutch youth (percentages, n = 344)

Would you miss Hyves and Facebook if you could not use them any longer?	*Completely not*	*Somewhat*	*Very much*	*Total*
Girls	38.7%	29.3%	32.0%	100%
Boys	42.3%	30.1%	27.6%	100%

Informants visited social networking sites on a daily basis. Ilana, a sixteen-year-old girl, said a profile page allows "*sharing your own photo's and videos, what you do in your daily life.*" seventeen-year-old Ferran made "*daily use of it. When I'm on the computer, I sign in to Hyves*" and he added his use is "*not an addiction but more of a habit.*" Sixteen-year-old Nevra felt it is "*standard*" to log on automatically. The Wired Up survey found that roughly two-thirds of Moroccan-Dutch young people reported they feel attached to the communication platform (see Table 6). Online social networking is interwoven into the fabric of everyday life, as is can also be illustrated with the verbs "facebooking" and "hyving," which were common parlance among the interviewees.

In general, the younger interviewees aged between twelve and fifteen years old primarily used Hyves, while informants aged sixteen years old and upward preferred Facebook. Both aesthetic and functional differences were experienced between the two sites. Hyves offered more opportunities for customization in comparison with Facebook. Fifteen-year-old Hatim felt, "*Hyves, you can do more things with it, such as changing your background. With Facebook, it's only white and blue; it's not so nice. You cannot change the background.*" Yethi, a fifteen-year-old boy, stated, "*Hyves is more colorful, Facebook is a bit dull.*" Digitizing the passages from childhood to adulthood, informants moved from Hyves to Facebook, as older adolescents seemed to prefer the clean, orderly and more professional look of Facebook. Furthermore, unlike Hyves which was mostly frequented by Dutch-speaking users, Facebook enabled users to establish transnational contacts with those living in the diaspora outside of the Netherlands, as fifteen-year-old Wafaa says: "*The whole world doesn't have Hyves. You don't have access to your family members living in Belgium, Morocco, etc. on it. It's more the Netherlands.*" In Hyves, a nationally bounded community was established, in contrast to the global reach of Facebook. Sixteen-year-old Ilana described this dynamic as follows: "*Hyves is mostly about what happens in the Netherlands. And on Facebook you have people from all over the world.*"

Wired Up survey findings showed that Moroccan-Dutch youth on average befriended 239 contacts, close to the average of 250-275 Facebook friends American college students connect with (Walther et al., 2011, pp. 28-29). I am aware that the definition of friendship is stretched, as these numbers exceed the ten to twenty close traditional relationships people sustain on average (Parks, 2007). It is interesting that informants note a delicate line between privacy and public access. Motives collide. On the one hand, informants are interested in attracting new friends while they also want to maintain the privacy of their personal information. Platform settings complicate this process further. Facebook and Hyves differed slightly in the privacy options they provide and this difference offers a window into the balancing acts between maintaining privacy and attracting new friends users engage in. Friend lists impact upon one's popularity and attractiveness. In Hyves, informants noted they appreciated being able to allow the friends of their friends to access their profile page. This way, they could get in touch with new contacts from the networks of their friends. This option is not available on Facebook. Oussema illustrates this lack in privacy settings poses a problem: "*On Facebook I have opened up my profile page, because you cannot chose 'only visible for friends of your friends' – only 'for friends' or 'for everyone. On Hyves, the settings are 'not visible for anyone,' 'for friends,' 'for friends of friends,' 'for all Hyvers' and 'for everyone.'*"

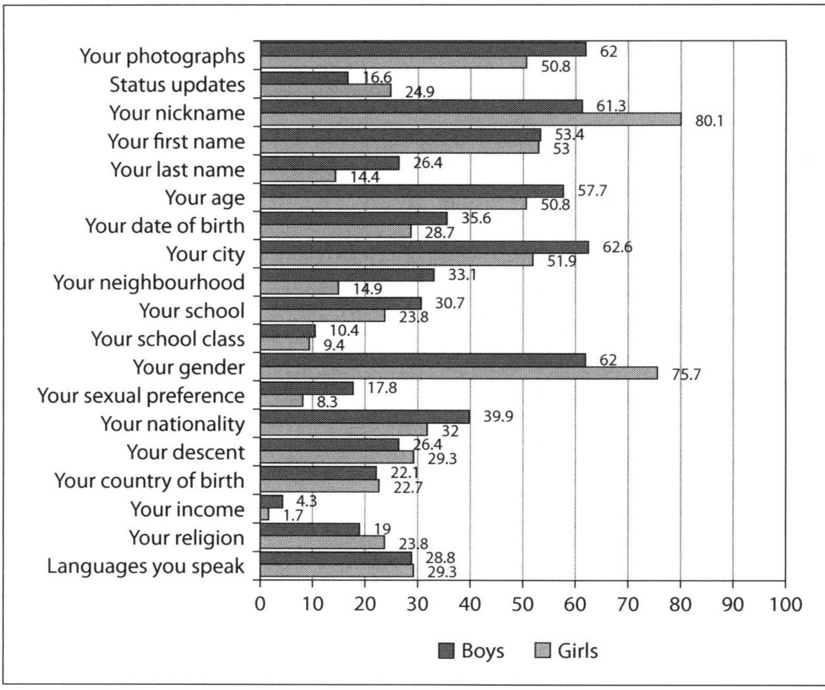

Diagram 7: Moroccan-Dutch youth self-reporting SNS profiling attributes (graph shows percentages, n = 344)

Self-profiling attributes

In the Wired Up survey, respondents were asked what self-profiling options they would make use of on their personal profile pages. Nicknames, gender and photos were the three most important self-profiling attributes Moroccan-Dutch youth reported using. More than two-thirds of respondents noted including those on their profile pages. Girls, in particular, frequently noted adding their gender and nicknames while boys reported showing location markers such as their city, neighborhood and school. Other markers that were frequently mentioned are age, first name, nationality, birthday, languages one speaks, and one's descent (see Diagram 7).

In Chapter 3 I argued that IM users updated their multilayered display names in the onstage. Similarly on Hyves and Facebook, users can post nicknames and status updates on their personal profile wall for their friends to see. Sixteen-year-old Naoul saw her profile page on Hyves as her public presence on the web: "*It feels like your own sort of blog, your own site.*" On Hyves, users can enter a "w.w.w." (who, what, where?), says thirteen-year-old

Tariq: "*so you can say where you are at the moment, what you are doing, and which places you will go.*" Likewise, Facebook asks it users to write about "What are you doing?" in status updates. For instance, Oussema said he likes to update his status with his "*favorite phrases.*" He engaged in various antiracist acts. For example, on August 26, 2011, he wrote "*don't be racist, be like a panda, they're black, white and asian.*" His next update was during the night of August 30 "*sugar sugar sugar sugar parteeeee!*" referring to the festive conclusion of the fasting month of Ramadan.

Some users include a nickname on their page. Thirteen-year-old Inas said, "*Often users put, for instance, 'Moroccan' and this and that as their name.*" Moroccan-Dutch youth engage in specific naming practices as on October 31, 2011, for instance, 3,724 users in Hyves included "Mocro" in their nickname, often combining it together with age, gender, sexual preference, religious, sport, music and other youth cultural affiliations. As I described in the introduction, the term "Mocro" is a Moroccan-Dutch honorary nickname stemming from Dutch-language rap and hip-hop culture. Through acts of bricolage, this term is innovatively combined with other markers of distinction in nicknames, such as "Mocro^boy-96," "^mocro^girlsZz^," "MY OWN_MOCRO_STYLE" and "MocroLiciouz." In the following section I address motivations for self-profiling.

Motivations

Informants explained they especially valued the opportunity to visually represent themselves on social networking sites. Twelve-year-old Soufian noted that with Hyves profiles "*at a glance you see what people are like,*" which was different from platforms such as instant messaging: "*With MSN it's just talking, but with Hyves it's more about photos. You'll see more and get a chance to know more about a person.*" Fifteen-year-old Hatim specified setting up a profile on Facebook "*is like introducing myself to someone, only on the Internet.*" Fifteen-year-old Oussema said that users can include "*photographs of your friends, of yourself, your pet, your family, where you live,*" and that users can show "*what you like, where you are interested in, your sexual preference, males or females.*"

In the interviews, being able to socialize was mentioned as the key reason to join social networking sites. Informants felt the urge to follow in the footsteps of their peers and set up a profile of their own. Fourteen-year-old Loubna, for instance, joined Facebook because she noticed her sisters having fun using it: "*My sisters always went on Facebook, so I thought, 'Yes, I'll set up a Facebook account, too.*" Similarly, thinking aloud about why he

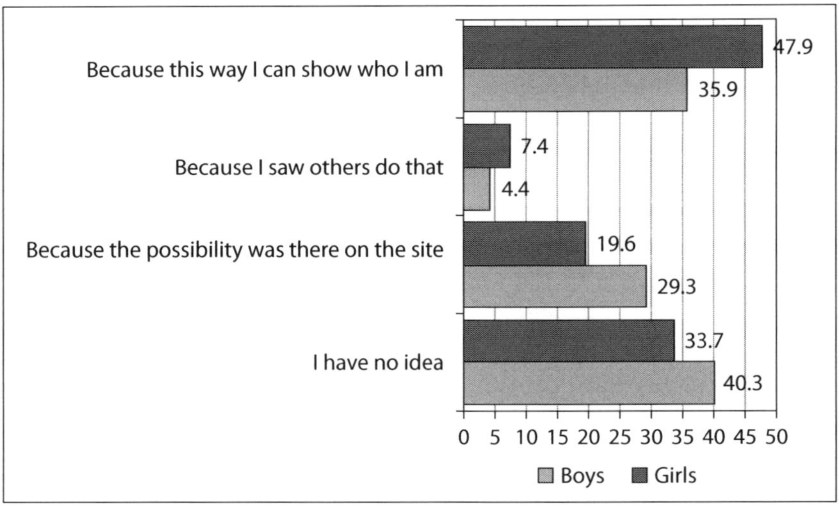

Diagram 8: Reasons for participating in self-profiling on SNSs (multiple answers possible, graph shows percentages, n = 344)

set up a profile on Hyves, fifteen-year-old Ryan said, *"I think I have made it because many children had one. And I thought 'why don't I make one,' and then I made one."*

In the survey, with the question "Why do you include things like music and photographs on your website?," respondents were invited to reflect on the reasons why they include certain attributes on their profile pages (see Diagram 8). More than girls, Moroccan-Dutch boys reported that profiling options such as photographs allow them to show who they are. Also they did so more often because of seeing others doing so. Girls more often responded they had no idea why they include certain things on their personal page. They also more frequently noted including elements on their profile pages after seeing the site offered the chance to do so. In sum, this section showed there is a variety of ways Moroccan-Dutch youth can articulate their individuality using online social networking sites. Different profiling opportunities give the user the opportunity to make visual statements about their ethnic, religious, gendered and youth cultural situatedness to an extended group of connected friends.

The red thread of the remainder of the chapter is woven from two specific dynamics. In Section 4.3, I focus on photographs and the portrayal of gender, the main themes in self-profiling. I study photographs and gender in tandem by analyzing the gendered gaze manifested in the profile pictures informants use. As the example I gave in the beginning of this chapter of the groups

Anas links to on his personal profile page implies, users are linked up with people beyond their own friend list on social networking sites. Upon joining a group, not only is the group icon included on individual personal profile pages, individual users are also linked together as their membership is made visible on the group page itself. Anas's example indicates users can simultaneously become an audience member across a variety of spaces. I unravel this dynamic further in Section 4.4 by considering cosmopolitan, intercultural encounters in hypertext networking. Below I first theorize the tension between desiring to articulate one's individuality and being guided by prestructured profiling options.

4.2 Theorizing the politics of online social networking sites

Social networking sites have been defined "as web-based services that allow individuals to (1) construct a public or semi-public profile within a bounded system, (2) articulate a list of other users with whom they share a connection, and (3) view and traverse their list of connections and those made by others within the system" (Boyd & Ellison, 2007, p. 211). Constructing a profile on social networking sites is bound by technological restrictions, neoliberal incentives, and peer norms and expectations. In this section I explore these three dimensions one by one to situate informants' practices in the wider context of the intricate politics of social networking sites and their specific appeal for teenagers.

Templates and user cultures

Profiles on social networking sites provide a template within which users can act. This template structures, and thus bounds their behavior around "heavily politicised identity categories" (Cover, 2012, p. 182). Users can publicly disclose how they want to present themselves in a preformatted way by making use of the provided "templated biographical categories." How the template "is actually used, however, varies considerably" (Davis, 2010, p. 1111). Templated choices in Western-oriented platforms are essentially restricted to "cultural signs rooted in mainstream Western culture" (Donnelly, 2011, p. 173). These signs are ideological indicators of particular age group, gender and religious norms. Furthermore, interface decisions produce and reflect hierarchical ethnic and racial categorizations. By providing a limited set of options to chose from in the form of drop-down menu boxes to select, interfaces narrow "choices of subject positions available to the user," as users are required "to choose 'what' they are" from a limited set of options. Lisa Nakamura added: "When race is put on the menu," limited options render "mestiza or other culturally ambiguous identities" invisible when they are not "given a 'box' of their own" (2002, pp. 104, 120). In response to limited menu options, minorities have been found to publish elaborate ethno-racial narratives of self, for example, on Facebook. By doing so they can resist being silenced by "dominant color-blind ideologies" (Grasmuck, Martin & Zhao, 2009, p. 158).

The informants also noted menu-options in discussing their self-profiling. When asked how users can show their cultural or religious preferences, Oussema reflected that in Facebook "*there is a special box to publish your religion and I find it important to let that show*," but he described there are alternatives when there is no menu option that suits profiling preferences: "*You can, for instance, type, 'Yes, I have just had couscous'*[1] *– that is possible, but there is not really a box to register your culture.*"

Templated biographical categories and interface decisions – but also dynamic (and not fully controllable) user behavior – result in particularly embodied social networking spaces. Particular configurations of ethnic, gendered, and classed ways of being become dominant. For instance, Amanda Lenhart analyzed the differences between typical Facebook and Myspace users and noted "typically, MySpace users are more likely to be women, Hispanic or black, to have a high school education or some experience with college," while "Facebook users are more likely to be men and to have a college degree" (2009, p. 6). American teenager preference for either one of these spaces reflects a reproduction of dominant social categories of ethnicity and social-economic status. Analogues to the 1960s "white flight" by white American families from city centers to suburbs, danah boyd observed a recent "networked exodus" of white, affluent teenagers toward Facebook (2012). Facebook started as a social network for Harvard University students and in the beginning year access remained intentionally limited to college students. In the years to follow, college-bound teenagers aiming for university are seeing access to Facebook and its "highbrow aura" as part of their rite of passage, while subculturally identifying teenagers are drawn to MySpace. While Facebook was seen as "mature," "mainstream," "safe" and "clean," MySpace in turn became increasingly seen as "hyper-sexual," "bling-bling," "ghetto," "unsafe." Mainstream fears over the digital space of the "other" mirrors and magnifies societal divisions (boyd, 2012, pp. 203-220).

1 Couscous is a popular dish across North Africa and it is said to be a Berber invention (Escher & Wüst, 2010).

To a certain extent, a parallel can be drawn between these observations and the preferences for SNSs among the young people I interviewed. Those informants who noted having transferred from Hyves to Facebook mostly framed their move in terms of an age-based decision; in this way access to Facebook for them indicated a rite of passage from teenage life toward a more professional one. The younger informants considered Facebook dull, the older one's found Hyves too colorful.

Neoliberal SNS logics

The decisions over technological affordances and restrictions of the platforms the interviewees use are designed to meet commercial interests. Social networking sites are structured on the basis of commercial decisions, and their "code is law," channeling the behavior of people using their services (Mitchel, 1995, p. 111). SNSs are constructed as an "approximation of the social" designed to be commercially exploited (Ippolita, Lovink & Rossiter, 2009). Weighing costs and benefits for the young consumer is difficult as the terms of services of SNSs are extreme lengthy and complex. Although Facebook officially asks for parental consent and guidance for users under thirteen and Hyves asked parental permission for users under the age of sixteen, most survey respondents and interviewees, for instance, reported they had the autonomy to decide what they like to publish online. During the interviews it occurred to me that like most users, informants knew little about the conditions under which they exchange their time and personal information that gets monitored and monetized in return of their goals: access to communication, sharing of information and being able to socialize with their friends (see Shepherd, 2012). Besides having to pay for special features in Facebook games (like *Candy Crush Saga*), user activities are transferred into "commercial commodities" and "marketing campaigns" (Andrejevic, 2011, pp. 97-99). Although many considered privacy settings important, most were unaware of how Facebook connects advertisers to a specific relevant target audience on the basis of individual users' personal preferences, their behavior and their friends' behavior on the platform. The following exchange I had with fifteen-year-old Yethi is exemplary:

> Koen Leurs: look, take this Facebook page
> On this side [pointing to my Facebook profile which I have opened on my laptop]
> *Yethi: Ah here, like Nike and so on.*

Koen Leurs: yes, this is because I have mentioned running, and next you'll see a Nike advertisement.
Yethi: Wajoo that's quite irritating heey [*wajoo*: slang for wow, pfft].
Koen Leurs: yes it is
Yethi: for real
Koen Leurs: yes its especially, they monitor all your data. They see who you befriend, and what all those people put online. They know quite a bit about you.
Yethi: those [people] from the advertisements?
Koen Leurs: yes
Yethi: I had not really considered that
Koen Leurs: so for instance if you talk about swimming, it might be that the next day you'll get an ad saying buy this jogging pants or something like that.
Yethi: For real? I didn't know that.
Koen Leurs: yes Facebook before did not really know how to make money, but they started to connect all those personal details, the things you become a fan of and you'll get specific
Yethi: advertisements directed at you personally, yes

The advertisements shown in Figure 13 illustrate how direct marketing algorithms may slot the digital profiling practices of the informants. The figure is a compilation of advertisements that appeared on my personal Facebook profile page. After a friend sent me a message about a new Red Hot Chili Peppers record coming out, advertisements from a Dutch company selling Red Hot Chili Peppers concert tickets appeared on my profile page. Processes of niche marketing along ethnic lines are visible in the top two advertisements. After I made reference to Morocco on my profile page and joining Facebook groups pertaining Morocco, my behavior was made knowable by the Facebook system.

As Facebook algorithms assigned advertisements of Prepaidunion.com and Etnoselect.nl to appear on my profile it shows I was recognized as a member of a marketable ethnic category (Gajjala & Birzescu, 2010). Using an image of the Moroccan flag and the question, "Are you looking for a nice gift?," Prepaidunion.com aimed to attract Moroccan-Dutch users of Facebook to its website: "Give call-credit to your family and friends in Morocco. Surprise them with an original gift and get up to 400% bonus. Order now." Using Facebook advertisements, the company sought entrance in the lucrative transnational telephone market. Similarly, using an image of the Moroccan flag, asking, "Are you also Moroccan?" Etnoselect.nl, a

Fig. 13: Facebook advertisements (advertisements appeared on October 16, 2011, and January 11, 2012)

commercial research company, sought to attract Moroccan-Dutch people to participate in survey taking and product testing: "Receive surveys in your mail and complete them whenever it suits you. Maximum reward: five euro per survey!" Facebook algorithms transfer practices and user-generated content into a value-generating ethnic niche-marketing opportunity.

Similarly, having joined groups related to Islam, an advertisement for Islamic products appeared. The company Islamproducten.nl used an image of a headscarf-wearing girl with the tagline "20% discount on our whole stock. Use the code actiejan2012." The advertisement, from "the largest islam webshop in the Netherlands," presented users with a particular gendered configuration of religious preferences. These examples demonstrate how user practices are machine-readable as algorithms channel them into monetizable categories of ethnicity, religiosity and gender. The corporate logic of technological disciplining is a power relational field that seeks to place individual subject positions into knowable, slottable positions. This process, however, leaves room for agency, as Gajjala and Birzescu theorize: although "appropriation occurs" in corporate mainstreaming of subaltern identities through interface design and templates, "there is also a certain kind of empowerment also occurring simultaneously" (2010, pp. 77). Little is known about the relationship between the cultural industry and the use of social media among ethnic and religious minorities.

Teenager SNS logics

Considering the dense web of power relations unraveled above, one may wonder why adolescents invest significant time and effort in setting up and updating their profile pages after all. Their preferences can partly be understood by considering the desires, needs and expectations that may arise during their life phase of coming-of-age. The bottom-line is that the services social networking sites provide are appealing for teens, as they might feel empowered by them in having a say over their own identity representations and to facilitate peer verification, teen sociality, becoming (more) attractive and achieving a higher status (Boyd, 2007, 2008, 2014; Ünlüsoy, De Haan & Leander, 2012; De Ridder, 2014). Young people put in an effort in updating their profile pages hoping their peers will notice it. The amount of information American college students upload on their Facebook profile, for example, can predict the number of contacts they attract (Lampe, Ellison and Steinfield, 2007, p. 441). The more information users publish on their profile, the more traffic they generate to their page and the more people they befriend. Additionally, research on impression management in Facebook demonstrates that users who list a large number of friends on their profile page are perceived as being more "attractive," "self-confident" and "popular" than users with a small number of friends (Kleck et al., 2007, p. 2).

By observing the ways in which their peers construct their identities on their personal profile pages, adolescents learn which social expectations and norms they need to meet in order to be accepted and liked (Boyd, 2007, p. 76; De Ridder, 2014, p. 24-26). Performing one's identity in order to receive attention and verification from peers is a highly competitive activity; "it is a means to improve one's reputation and status," which might result in "access to resources and social and practical solidarity" (Tufecki, 2008, p. 546). Hyves is used among young users to market themselves to their peers (Utz, 2008, pp. 236-237). For example, on SNSs selfies and other photos are used as identity building blocks that assist in sustaining peer groups (Van Dijck, 2008). Such online photo sharing transforms the boundaries between publicity and privateness (Lasén & Gómez-Cruz, 2009).

Attention-seeking activities – for example, through the use of particular selfies – on social networking sites are not gender neutral. Ashley Donnelly argues profile pictures are problematically gendered and sexualized and cultivated by masculine fantasies that dominate the Internet. In the United States, she noted, teens on Facebook are expected to "sell" themselves through their personal profiles to gain friends and access social capital. Young women in order to do so often have to "subscribe to heteronormative, patriarchal ideals" by engaging in "submissive presentations of self" in their profile pictures (Donnelly, 2011, p. 179). Meanwhile, among Muslim girls in Qatar, Rodda Leage and Ivana Chalmers found these girls use Facebook to practice juggling the conflicting gendered, religious and cultural norms they need to deal with. First, some girls opted out of social networking sites completely in fear of damaging their reputations; others participated minimally, for instance, refraining from the use of selfies in order to abide by stringent religious and cultural norms. Others used creative approaches, such as digitally manipulating their facial features in photographs, only showing parts of their body in pictures or crafting complete fantasy identities. A final group rebelled and disregarded strict cultural mores; taking a risk, they circulated personal photographs and befriended boys, while trying to keep their parents away from their digital profiles (Leage & Chalmers, 2010, pp. 31-40).

Feeling confident, accepted, attractive and popular are of particular relevance during the informants' life stage of adolescence. Publishing specific information and visual material may assist in attracting a wider group of friends. An increase in the number of friends in turn may render the person behind the profile page more popular and attractive in the eyes of his/her peers and potential lovers. This investment is a form of labor that is of interest for the platform owners; the growth in personal information published on the site and an increase of site users imply commercially exploitable value gets added to the social network. In the end the user performs this labor for herself: "the future rewards of which include improved standing and greater opportunity" (Gregg, 2007). Below I consider two different perspectives to consider further the wider implications of the field site of social networking. I first focus on the gendered gaze in profile pictures, before considering hypertextual networking and intercultural encounters.

4.3 Selfies and the gendered gaze

In my discussion of MSN display photos I argued selfies are used to construct a gendered identity. Informants noted that display pictures used in instant messaging reflect ideals of masculinity and femininity through stereotypical poses: boys aim for looking "*tough*" while girls aim to show themselves as "*sensual*" and "*emotional*." The interviewees discussed how they use display photos to show certain parts of their bodies. Girls, for instance, used pictures where they show their pouted lips while boys exhibited their muscled "six-packs." This way, bodies are fragmented into sexualized objects. Analyzing the Wired Up survey findings, I discussed in Section 4.1 that gender and visual representation are considered key to self-profiling on social networking sites, too. Gender and photographs were singled out as two of the most popular attributes used among the respondents to decorate their personal profiles pages. In this section I explore further how the two are related.

"*You'll see more and get a chance to know more about a person.*" This statement made by twelve-year-old Soufian is exemplary of the seeing-is-knowing motive many informants shared. On a social networking site, the profile picture of a user "stands in" for his/her body (Strano, 2008). Besides technological constraints that inscribe themselves upon user self-profiling, the ways in which users stand in for themselves in selfies put on social networking sites is also partly influenced by gendered peer norms and expectations. Guided by this assumption I focus in this section on gender as the primary analytical category in my analysis of how informants (perceive the) use of profile images.

Selfie ideals

In the Wired Up survey respondents were asked how they would show themselves in their profile pictures in order to be liked by their friends. With the question we aimed to learn more about the norms of online photographic self-depictions among young people. In designing the survey, we acknowledged that display pictures do not carry singular meanings. Therefore, respondents were invited to choose a maximum of three self-presentation labels. This opportunity was used, as the percentages add up to well over 100% for both girls and boys. The respondent's answers enable reflection on impression management, expectations of appropriate self-presentations and ideal beauty standards among Moroccan-Dutch youth.

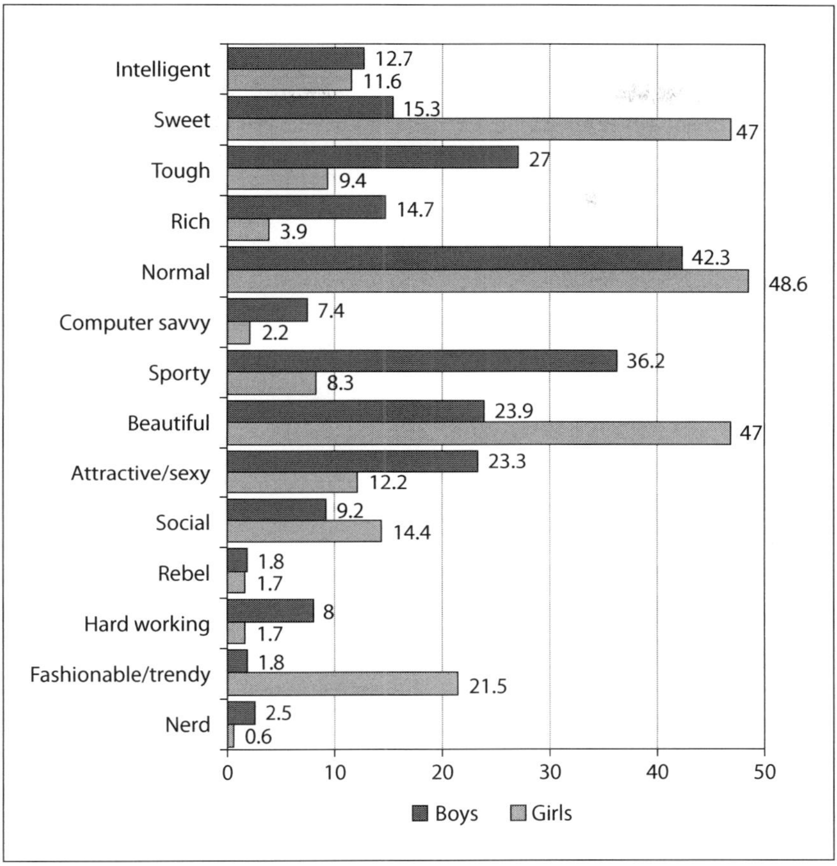

Diagram 9: Selfie ideals reported by Moroccan-Dutch youth (multiple answers possible, percentages, n = 344)

Most importantly, nearly half of the Moroccan-Dutch girls and boys in the survey sample reported they ideally would like to present themselves as "normal" in their selfies (Diagram 9). Besides wanting to being normal, boys and girls chose varying additional labels to report on their aspired self-presentation. Commonly chosen labels indicate that participating girls specifically desire to look "beautiful," "sweet" or "fashionable/trendy" and "social" and to a lesser extent "attractive/sexy," "intelligent" and "tough." Boys want to come across as "sporty," "though," "beautiful,' "attractive/sexy," and to a lesser extent "sweet," "rich," "intelligent," "hard working" and "computer savvy" (Leurs & Ponzanesi, 2012, pp. 446-447).

By asking respondents how they would like to show themselves in order to be liked by their friends, the survey findings revealed how Moroccan-Dutch youth would ideally represent themselves. The informants reported seeking to meet expectations of what is normal and appropriate in selfie culture. Aiming for the appropriate standard was combined with dichotomous gender ideals. Girls reported their ideals were being beautiful and sweet, while boys aimed for a sporty image and toughness. Being expected to showcase certain attributes, these ideals reveal self-regulatory values young people negotiate with (Siibak, 2009). Each of these labels covers a distinct configuration of femininity and masculinity. Andra Siibak in Estonia (2009) and Michele Strano in the US (2008) have found similar self-presentation labels, for instance, girls aim to display ideals of female beauty on their online profile pages. These findings suggest shared (youth cultural) norms of gender that go beyond distinct locations and ethnic groups.

During the interviews, informants described a stereotypically gendered practice of profile photo selection. Oussema described that most boys showed themselves as follows: "*Look at how pretty I am. Look at how nice my eyes are as a ray of light shines in them,*" or they posed in their pictures with "*pumped up chests*" and aimed to go for a "*look at how tough I am, look at how muscled I am*" impression or, while girls "*lean forward,*" to show off their bodily curves and "*blow a kiss to the camera.*" Fourteen-year-old Ziham said boys "*put up tough photos, where they put up their middle-fingers and so on,*" she adds that among her friends "*girls don't do that. They just show themselves wearing tight clothes or so, with untied hair.*" According to sixteen-year-old Bibi, in some photos "*girls show their boobs almost popping out of their bras.*" Fourteen-year-old Ayoub noted, "*girls put lots of make-up on*" or post selfies taken "*when they have just come from the shower.*" Although individual informants often nuanced their own positioning, the majority of the informants gave a highly stereotypically gendered description of self-photograph ideals.

Andra Siibak found strikingly similar patterns in her visual analysis of photos posted to Rate.ee, the most popular social networking site in Estonia. She notes that stereotypes of the "porno-chic" are the source for dichotomous gender identities. In their attempt to meet social expectations of female physical attractiveness she found that girls met the norms and emphasized sexuality by smiling (which can be interpreted as a submissive position in the power/status hierarchy), stressing their slenderness, exposing their bodies and wearing clothes to stress their perfect body shape. Additionally, the majority of women were posing from a position of inferiority, submissively looking up at the viewers with canted heads "so that the viewer was placed in a position of superiority." Emphasizing manliness, the "macho man," for instance, posed next to a car or motorcycle (signs of hyper-masculinity) and exposes his bare athletic body for "the female gaze" (Siibak, 2007).

The particular ideal ways of showing noted by the informants signal hierarchical power relations. Girls desiring to come across as sweet and beautiful are more submissive and inferior to the tough and sporty image boys desire to project. Contrasting feminine and masculine self-presentational repertoires exposes forms of patriarchal subordination that get perpetuated and magnified online. In expressing themselves on social networking sites, users build on cultural signs of desirability that originate from a patriarchal belief system:

> Collective, societal ideologies that favor youth, Western standards of beauty (thin, white, tall, able-bodied, etc.), and conformity are dominated by a patriarchal system that genders traits as either "masculine" or "feminine" empowering the masculine while devaluing the feminine. (Donnelly, 2011, p. 174)

Although users themselves decided to publish certain selfies exposing their naked bodies, their choices are to a certain extent guided by the ideals and expectations of an imagined audience of peers. SNSs are "heavily peer-controlled normative spaces" and their habitus constructs "what types of self-representations are socially acceptable" (De Ridder, 2014, p. 24). Informants frequently brought up their audiences during the interviewees, and getting reactions from peers was highly valued. For example, sixteen-year-old Bibi noted she is always eager to read reactions and learn about others' opinions when she posts a photo on Facebook: "*It is so interesting, because on Facebook you can react on pictures. And I'm really like 'Oh, someone is reacting to my photo.' You know, I am very curious.*" Photographs are used to attract attention. Fifteen-year-old Hajar noted that boys go on Facebook where they "*search for girls that they like,*" and they will then "*react to photos, you know, to ask the girl out on a date and so on.*" And they allow users to gain status. Fourteen-year-old Ayoub noted you could become very popular when you post good photos. His friend uploaded a photo and asked everyone "*to give respect to the photo.*" Similar to the "Like" button on Facebook, on the social networking site Hyves, users could click a "Respect" button that allows friends to express their acknowledgement of a photo. Ayoub added this is done because "*when you have a photo, and a lot of people have reacted to it, on that day, it will appear on 'The Story of the Day,' the opening page of your Hyves friends.*"

Meeting the gaze: Objectification and/or representation

The question arises whether female submissive self-portrayals and the objectification of selfies must be understood purely as a lack of empowerment. Can it also be a strategic decision by users to publish distinctly feminine photographs to their profile page? Online, a complex dialectic can be recognized between disempowering objectification and agentic representation: "images of women on the Web exist along a continuum from objectification to representation" (Blair & Takayoshi, 1999, p. 7). The objectification of women cannot be fully attributed to the male gaze only, as women themselves also navigate the continuum "consciously and unconsciously in their own production of electronic discourse" (ibid.). In the blogosphere, some female writers participate consciously in the objectification of their bodies in their attempt to secure a large audience: they "purposefully use their sexuality and beauty as a way to attract readers" (Ratliff, 2007, p. 3). Similarly, on social networking sites, young female users who conform to and identify with vanity and beauty ideals in their profile images might feel pleasure and empowerment when receiving attention and attracting a large audience to their personal profile pages. For example, Kathrin Tiidenbeg describes how sexy selfies allow their makers to reclaim their bodies. One of her informants, for example, appropriated a new gaze: "self-shooting gave her a way to care for herself" which "taught her to feel sexy in her body" (Tiidenbeg, 2014). In addition, historically, based on restrictive cultural and Islamic principles women and girls were rarely allowed to be photographed in Morocco (McMurray, 2001, p. 78). This still holds for some Arab Muslim girls, as, for instance, Leage and Chalmers found to be the case in Qatar (2010, pp. 34-35). Uploading selfies, Moroccan-Dutch girls can take up self-expression liberties they may lack offline.

These forms of power and agency also have their obvious wide-ranging drawbacks, including exploitation and narcissism. Facebook may encourage "narcissistic behavior": "narcissists appear to be attractive on Facebook because they are strategically posting pictures that make them appear sexy and attractive" (Buffardi & Campbell, 2008, p. 1311). Other critics argue that selfie poses are mostly based on real-time viewing instead of autonomous self-contemplation. Increasingly self-taken with smartphones, the distance between camera and subject is restricted to an arm's length, lacking opportunities for "meaningful self-reflection," it can therefore be argued that the habitus of social networking sites may be "conditioning users to look at themselves as surface objects, rather than encouraging them to engage in meaningful self-reflection" (Wendt, 2014, p. 24).

The tension between being either a subject of the gaze or object of the gaze can be drawn out further with feminist psychoanalytic theory. This framework reminds us that the

> sexual economy of looking at a photograph (not just erotic or pornographic ones) represents the heterosexual male gaze. Psychoanalytic terms, such as scopophilia (the pleasure in looking), voyeurism, and fetish are theoretically structured around a male viewer and his pleasures/traumas. (Zarzycka, 2009, p. 159)

In feminist film theory, presuming an asymmetrical relation between the "active" men and "passive" women, the male viewer derives his pleasure from a voyeuristic objectification of female bodies. Male fantasies are projected on female bodies, which are styled accordingly for erotic and sexual impact (Mulvey, 1975). In the case of uploading selfies to one's profile page, a girl's internalization of the gaze might indicate she seized the opportunity "to be in charge of her to-be-looked-at-ness" (Smelik, 2009, p. 185). This opportunity, however, becomes increasingly difficult as the celebrated visual ideals of youth, fitness and beauty are becoming more and unrealistic and unattainable, especially in the present era of widespread digital manipulation. In a search for conformity, this entails disciplining the body with dieting, fitness, and consuming products from the beauty industry as well as managing certain poses, the "duck face" and other facial expressions besides learning to use smartphone filters and digital photo processing software (cf. Foucault, 1978). In their attempts at gender stereotypically inscribing themselves in the desiring gazes of masculinist objectification, girls' aspirations to meet the male fantasy may be impossible to completely fulfill. Again punctuating the myths of utopian digital disembodiment, when falling victim to the heterosexual male gaze and sensing their digital photographic self-depictions do not meet its ideals, girls might not feel valued as full human beings.

Victimization and cautionary measures

A statement seventeen-year-old Ferran made can be taken to further nuance the potential for agency in the Moroccan-Dutch context. He thought some Moroccan-Dutch "*girls are a bit more loose, because they do not really have contact with boys, real contact*" away from the Internet. Taking the opportunity to have more freedom and befriend boys online, Ferran added, "*some Moroccan girls put up crazy pictures that they shouldn't have done.*" He hints at the fact that acts of online experimentation may have very serious consequences. The discussion in the prior chapter of Naoul and Inzaf's friend who was severely beaten up after engaging in MSN webcam intimacy is an exceptional, but brutal reminder of negative repercussions. As seventeen-year-old Sadik noted, users are not always conscious of the consequences of the ways they depict themselves in their profile images, they do not "*realize what can happen*":

> *Sometimes you see the craziest things on Hyves, weird things that make you wonder, "Okay, if your dad know about this, you would not have Hyves anymore." Some people take nude pictures and put them on their Hyves. Thinking that is a fun thing to do until the wrong person comes across them.*

Girls, but also boys, feeling urged to upload revealing profile pictures may fall victim to being "broomed" ("*bezemen*" in Dutch). In Dutch sexist and homophobic street language, the dismissive label "*bezem*" stands for "hooker" in the case of girls and "homosexual" in the case of boys (Hamer, 2010). Fifteen-year-old Hatim explained: "*People can take your image, and save it to their computer, and edit it and put it on a site. For instance, people put up a video on YouTube called* Hookers of the City *which included a lot of photographs.*" Figure 14 is a still taken from a "*bezem*" YouTube video. The maker's nickname "Bezemswalla," includes a reference to brooming, but also "*walla*," Arabic and Berber for "I swear." The video consists of a compilation of photographs displaced from profile pages of Moroccan-Dutch boys and girls. The photos are accompanied with abusive commentary such as "blowjob slut" and "homo." The still shown in Figure 14 displays a girl who looks upward at the viewer from the corner of her eyes and she leans on a tough-looking guy. The maker of the video clip has edited the photograph by including the statement "hooker of twelve" years old.

Even though the video was deleted from the YouTube servers shortly after its publication, the 62,000 plus people who have watched *Bezems 2010.!!* illustrate video circulation is rapid. YouTube users flagged the video as inappropriate, and eighty-one people clicked the "Dislike" button, versus thirty people who clicked the like button. When trying to access the video, users are now shown the following message: "This video has been removed because its content violated YouTube's Terms of Service. Sorry about that" (Bezemswalla, 2010). Such materials, however, can spread across video-sharing sites with great speed making it difficult to completely remove them from the Internet. Victimizing young people through brooming is a new semi-anonymous form of cyberbullying, hostile behavior which reshifts power balances. Similar to the disturbing example discussed in the previous

Fig. 14: Still from *Bezems 2010.!!* uploaded by user Bezemswalla on YouTube (February 8, 2010)

chapter, for example, ex-lovers carry out these practices to digitally take revenge after relationship breakups. Once profile photos are lifted from their original intimate, yet semi-public contexts, feelings of empowerment in successfully attracting friends and achieving popularity thus might also rapidly dissolve after being victimized and rendered helpless.

Judging from the informants' descriptions and YouTube search results this practice is observable among young people of a variety of backgrounds in the Netherlands but it seems to be especially prevalent among Moroccan-Dutch youth, indicating how conflicting gender and sexual morals affect migrant girls in specific ways (which also became apparent in Chapter 3 on instant messaging). Hyves cofounder Raymond Spanjar wrote in his book on the history of the social networking site that virtual bullying seemed to be "especially prevalent among allochthonous girls and the victim is portrayed as a slut." This is not without dangers, as he cited from a desperate e-mail he received from Hyves user Fatima: "Raymond you have to help me. Please delete that fake profile of mine, the one on which I'm doing a striptease. My brothers will kill me once they see me" (2011, p. 133).

Similar to how Qatari Arab girls were found to employ creative methods to safely express themselves on Facebook (Leage & Chalmers, 2010, p. 41), interviewees report to take cautionary measures to monitor their privacy and reputation. For instance, fourteen-year-old Senna shared she restricted herself in publishing personal photos, selecting only a few, and publishing them not publicly but only for her friends to see: "*I have put up only some photos, but it's not like anyone can see them, I don't like that.*" She kept a close watch over the people she befriends, and she unfriended contacts whenever she felt it was necessary to control her reputation. On most social networking sites, by default, information published to profile pages is public. Sixteen-year-old Nevra, who shared her fear of the phenomenon of brooming. She also became more cautious about placing photographs on Hyves, and she made sure to "*make the profile invisible, only visible for my friends.*" Fourteen-year-old Kenza listed fictive personal information while fifteen-year-old Meryam shared she chose a creatively spelled pseudonym instead of her real name when she set up her profile page on Facebook.

In this way, Meryam renders it more difficult for nonfriends to locate her personal profile page. She noted fearing being easily traceable on Facebook, as people with bad intentions would be able to download her pictures and digitally manipulate them: nowadays people "*can take your head and paste it onto another body,*" adding "*I have heard from girls in other cities that they have completely been ruined on the Internet.*" Subverting Facebook's "real name culture" policy, a number of other female interviewees chose to adopt a similar strategy of choosing pseudonyms in order to make it more difficult for their profile page and photos to be found. Joe Sullivan, Facebook's chief security officer, argues that Facebook promotes a "real name culture," arguing that "Facebook's real name culture creates accountability and deters bad behavior since people using Facebook understand that their actions create a record of their behavior" (2010, p. 2). Some informants claimed to adapt the space to their own preferences. They were of the opinion that policy instilled forms of peer accountability were insufficient. They argued that pseudonyms, fictive information, making one's profile invisible and consciously choosing what pictures to upload were better ways to monitor one's reputation and deter bad behavior.

In-betweenness

Lastly, I want to offer a final nuance to the ways in which profile photos are imbued with gender and sexuality by noting that their norms do remain open to subversion. Niels van Doorn recognized the constructedness of networked performance of gender and sexuality in the social networking site MySpace. Similar to how Moroccan-Dutch youth uploaded stereotypical selfies for their peers to see, he argued that a shared social context is established through the circulation of artifacts that invoke particular meanings for a specific imagined audience. Building on Judith Butler, he noted a citation and reiteration of gender and sexuality norms in social networking site practices. Following the digitally articulated sexual encounters of gay, lesbian and hetero people he found that in their resignification of norms of "decent behavior" the constructedness of gender and sexuality can be unmasked and the "gender binary" can be transgressed (Van Doorn, 2009, pp. 5, 17). In a similar way, informants did underline that they do not necessarily always conformed to the dominant gender stereotypical modes of visual representation I have described so far. For instance, Oussema specified that he positioned himself "*in-between, always in-between*" in his profile images. He stated:

> *I like sports a lot, but I also like computer games a lot, so I'm a bit in-between.... I'm not a chubby kid, but also not super muscled. I'm not like "look at how tough I am," but also not like "look at how nice my eyes are in the photo," it's more a bit in between.*

In the next section I shift the focus from using selfies to perform an attractive stereotypically gendered self, to using hyperlinks for a more multiaxial performance. Besides photos, hyperlinks are visual statements that are part of the larger visual narrative of self users compose on their personal profile pages. On profile pages, users can use hyperlinks to communicate their associations to their friends. In the following section, the articulation of hypertextual selves is analyzed as a micro-political act.

4.4 Hypertextual selves and the micro-politics of association

Selfies are only one element of the rich visual narrative of self users can construct on their profile page. I argue in this section users author their hypertextual selves by publishing hyperlinks on their profile pages. Following the adage "you are what you link" (Adamic and Adar, 2001), mapping hypertextual selves reveals users' micro-politics of association. The informants chose to express themselves mostly as cosmopolitan individuals through performing a variety of identifications. Their engagement with various alignments may subsequently involve a growing reflective awareness of different trajectories.

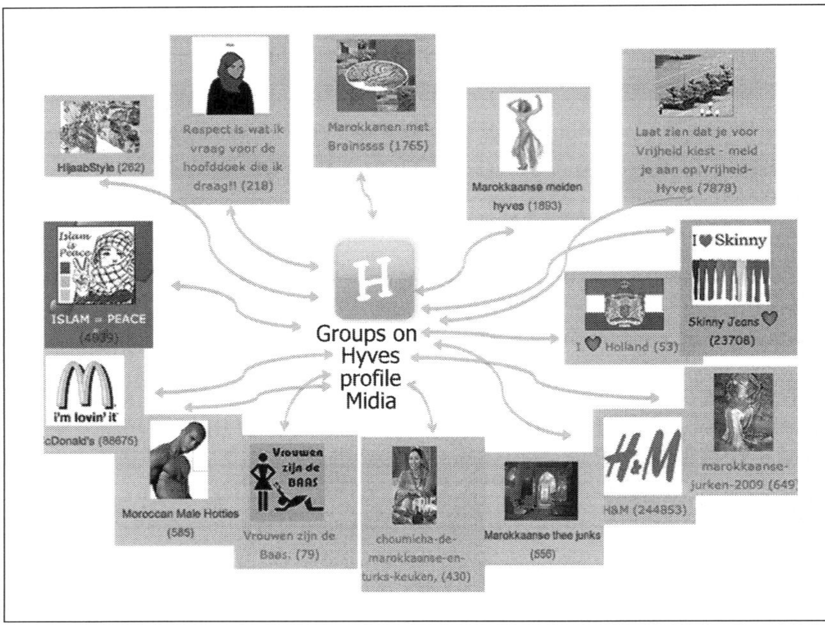

Fig. 15: Hyves groups Midia linked to on her Hyves profile page (April 15, 2009)

For example, in Figure 15, the icons of the groups thirteen-year-old Midia hyperlinked to on her Hyves profile page are shown. She connected to a variety of groups ranging from feminist interests ("Women in Charge"), gendered ethnic solidarity ("Moroccan girls hyves"), Dutch nationalism ("I love Holland"), to food cultures relating to both migration backgrounds ("choumicha-the-Moroccan-and-Turkish-kitchen," "Moroccan tea junkies") as well as global junk food ("McDonald's"). She expressed her religious affinity ("ISLAM = PEACE") and claimed recognition of her headscarf ("Respect is what I ask for the headscarf that I'm wearing!!"). She published preferences for clothing styles ranging from stylish headscarves ("HijaabStyle"), Moroccan dresses ("moroccan-dresses-2009") and global fashion trends ("Skinny Jeans love" and the brand "H&M"). Additionally she joined the groups "Moroccan Male Hotties" and "Show you chose for Freedom – sign up for the Freedom-Hyves." These groups varied in member-size from fifty-three members who joined the group "I love Holland" to nearly 250,000 members who joined "H&M." Joining these groups, hyperlinked icons are published on Midia's profile. The icons that appear on her profile page can be compared to buttons and badges with statements that may be worn as fashion accessories. Taken together, these different visual statements cover a cosmopolitan spectrum of interests, belongings and affiliations (Leurs & Ponzanesi, 2014a).

As an example of a space invader tactic, hypertextual selves operate on three levels. Empirically, mapping out the hyperlinks is exemplary for how to "diagnose cultural change" by means of digital methods (Rogers, 2013, p. 5). Theoretically, hypertextual selves are meaningful cultural signifiers as they allow for the expression of fragmentation, discontinuity, multiplicity, layering and bricolage. In the specifically grounded context of migrant youth, the hypertextual affordances of SNS's can be taken up as a multicultural assemblage to relate to local, transnational and global contexts. Politically, mapping hypertextual selves provide grounds to intervene in mainstream discourse on migration, multiculturalism and integration by acknowledging the micro-politics of intercultural encounter. Following hyperlinks provides a new mapping of the ways in which migrant youth mobilize various resources to establish the grounds for defining themselves and for relating to the local, transnational and global contexts around them, particularly those contexts that are cultural, social and political.

Midia's links provided a glimpse at how she acquired taste for difference, showing her wordliness. She navigated the intersectional multiplicity of her personal gender, sexual, diaspora, religious, ethnic and youth cultural trajectory. Actively revaluing her contextual fields, she connected the categories of Islam and Dutch nationalism. Dutch right-wing politicians dominantly frame these two as irreconcilable. Simultaneously, she countered negative perceptions of Islam as a violent religion and she advocated for greater tolerance of veiling practices among Muslim girls. Dialoguing with her Muslim female peer group, she reframed the veil as a stylish fashion element. The representative profile page linking practices show unexpected hypertextual coalitions of second-generation migrant youth as space invaders: they align with majority groups through affiliating with global youth food preferences, activism and clothing styles.

The literature also suggests hyperlinking provides insight into migrant identification processes. For example, on the online social networking site Hi5, Nikkei youth (second-generation Japanese-Peruvians) were found to express their individuality by decorating their personal profile page with texts, audio, photos, and videos. "A starburst" of diverse affiliations was thus created, including those that signal Japanese-ness such as the Hello Kitty brand, anime videos, Kanji writing, kimonos, and Japanese celebrities. Nikkei also hyperlinked to "Latino" and "Chino" (Chinese) elements (Aoyama, 2007, pp. 104-110). Aoyama concluded that the groups to which Nikkei youth link on their profile pages "stretch across a large and varied scope of topics, including that of national, racial/ethnic, and cultural identities" (ibid., p. 2). Nikkei youth, similar to Anas's and Midia's linking practices, published hypertextual selves that illustrates the dynamics of a joyful convivial heterogeneity. Thus, rather than simply continuing migrant cultural legacies, migrant youth are actively transforming those in ways that resonate with the dominant local and global youth cultures in which they grow up.

Profile pages consist of a dynamic hypertext based on Hypertext Markup Language (HTML) coding. HTML is the protocol enabling online pages to be linked to one other, constituting the backbone of the Web. These linked files are in essence at equal distance from each other. As well as being a technological device, hypertext is also a metaphor to think with. Hypertext incorporates multiplicity as the examples of groups Midia linked up with display. Simultaneously different pathways are possible, as hypertext allows "multiple entryways and exits" and it "connects any point to any other point" (Landow, 2006, pp. 58-61). Already in the early days of the Internet, Donna Haraway recognized that hypertext implies making connections, but it does not foreground or forecloses certain areas of the Internet. Borrowing Haraway's words, approaching profile pages from the perspective of hypertext enables me to make an "inquiry into which connections matter, why, and for whom" (1997, pp. 128-130).

In this section I develop my understanding of hypertextual selves further to shed light on cosmopolitan, convivial networked belonging in social networking sites. First, I recognize self-profiling (including hypertextual linking) as a fandom practice. I ground my analysis in Wired Up survey findings and informants' discussions of cultural self-profiling on social networking sites. Subsequently I zoom in on intercultural encounters by detailing how Moroccan-Dutch and ethnic-majority Dutch youth both report to express affiliations to food, celebrities and music artists that pertain to their own ethnic backgrounds. However, these groups also express the desire to publish international food, celebrities and music artists' affiliations. Subsequently, I turn to hypertextual performativity of self and argue informants' linking to group pages is an example of conviviality that allows me to rethink multiculturalism from below.

Cultural self-profiling as fandom

In expressing a variety of affiliations, Anas and Midia actively revalued her ethnic, religious and gendered embeddings. Users on Hyves actively branded themselves toward their peers (Utz, 2008). Similar to how on Facebook users can press the "Like" button to show their appreciation of a page, video or uploaded selfie, people performed their affiliations on Hyves. Here I want to consider, in particular, digital fandom practices. Investigations of fan cultures stress the relevance of studying how individuals as dedicated and participatory audience members select from the repertoires of popular culture. Deliberative consumption of cultural and media artifacts enable pleasure, individuality and identity construction. Fans use media products to express their own culture, by selectively "poaching" media texts and favored significations (Jenkins, 1992). Fandom is an ongoing process of "capital accumulation" (Fiske, 1992, p. 42): Fans are active consumers who become often, and especially in digital settings, also producers and distributors of content. Fandom arises from engagements and confrontations with "dominant value systems" and it can therefore be associated "particularly with those disempowered by any combination of gender, age, class and race" (Fiske, 1992, p. 30). In studies of digital fandom, the focus has, however, mostly been on "the default fanboy," which presumes a geeky, young, white, middle-class, heterosexual male (Gatson & Reid, 2012).

Hyperlinking to groups and pages is one example of engaging in fandom practices on social networking sites. The dynamics of performing ethnicity as fandom practice can be illustrated by considering how belonging to the Berber culture is made public. Sixteen-year-old Bibi, for instance, noted she joined the "Imazighen Hyves group" to include a Berber flag icon on her profile page: "*an Amazigh flag of the Berbers, these kind of things I do have, so people will see what my culture is.*" In my interview with Rafik, the twenty-one-year-old moderator of the "Imazighen" group on Hyves, he shared that he started the group in April 2007. He compared his group to the Hyves group celebrating the famous Dutch football club PSV Eindhoven. "*On your personal profile page within the social networking site, you can list your interests, but you can also do this through a Hyves group. A PSV fan would join a PSV Hyves group, for instance.*" The difference with the football group site lays in the fact that the Imazighen Hyves group concerns ethnic or diasporic affinity. Rafik describes the goal of his site as follows:

> *My Hyves group concerns a group of people from North Africa, who are known as Imazighen.* "Imazighen" *means "free people" and is a reaction to colonists, the Arabs, who wanted to impose their culture to the indigenous people of North Africa (the Imazighens). In almost all of North Africa this assimilation succeeded, however in Morocco and Algeria there are still Imazighen people who are conscious of their identity and history. Lots of them are in the Netherlands (and whose forefathers worked here in the Netherlands as guest workers) and to stimulate their search of identity (which is restricted in Morocco and Algeria) I have started this Hyves.*

Fig. 16: "I'm a Berber Soldier," archived from http://imazighen.hyves.nl (September 19, 2009)

Rafik is himself aware of the fact that he provides Hyves users an avenue for ethnic identity expression. Instead of or next to becoming a fan of a famous sports club, Hyves users can opt to join the "Imazighen" page to perform their ethnic affiliation online. On this page, Moroccan-Dutch youth expressed the Berber elements of their identities. The following English-language exclamations posted on the message board are illustrative: "😃💗IMAZIGHENNNNN!!! 💗😃" (June 3, 2009), "I LOVE AMAZIGH AMAZIGH IS THE BOOOOOOOM" (March 6, 2009), "Amazighen!! 4-Evaah" (August 18, 2008) and "Amazigh. My Pride. My Life" (April 11, 2008).

Figure 16 is an image uploaded to the Imazighen page that clearly displays how attributes are lifted from their original contexts to create new meanings. This act of visual poaching illustrates the intertextual dimensions of digital fandom. The image shows a cartoon figure of a fair-skinned youngster holding a gun with the saying "I'm a Berber Soldier." The picture presents a complex hybrid of symbols. Strikingly, the Aza, a central Berber symbol, is included.[2] It has traveled far. The Aza derives from an ancient alphabet and was taken up in the Berber alphabet. The Berber movement included the Aza in the blue, green and yellow Berber flag. Moroccan-Dutch youth have mixed the Aza with other expressions of global youth culture. The gun and textual exclamation are, for instance, expressions lifted from the

2 The Aza is a letter from the Tifinagh Berber alphabet. The letter is included in the blue, green and yellow Berber flag. In parallel with the meaning of the Berber word "Amazigh," the letter symbolizes Berbers to be "free people" (Sache, 2009).

contexts of global (English language) hip-hop toughness. This exemplifies how ethnicity is performed through a detour of youth cultural reembedding. The observed group page is considered safe enough to circulate textual and visual statements to an intended audience of fellow Berber-identifying youth or interested individuals. Digital Berber fandom identification is one example of cultural self-profiling. Other hyperlinked groups include "the Netherlands was partly made possible by allochthonous people," that, for example, Ryan linked to. This group aimed to emphasize the hard work carried out by non-Western guest workers in the Netherlands. The group was set up "for all allochthonous and autochthonous who support a multicultural society."[3] As I noted in the introductory chapter, Ryan masked Moroccan affiliations while playing computer games, however, by linking to this group Ryan showed he felt confident enough to identify with the guest-worker history of his parents on the territory of his personal profile page. Reversing the labels "allochthonous" and "guest worker" from negative stigmas to a positive affiliation, Ryan proudly showed the icons of the group on his personal page. By joining the "Michael Jackson," "Nike Air Max" and "South Park" groups, he connected with global youth cultural forms of popular music, sneakers and TV-series, respectively. Also he signaled his support for various causes by joining groups that range from countering racism and Islamophobia with "The Anti-Wilders Hyves," to "Stop Aids Now!," "Unite Against Cancer" and "anti-animal cruelty."

Wired Up survey respondents were asked to reflect on how they engage in various forms of online cultural self-profiling. From piloting and participant observations, a list with cultural self-profiling options was generated. The respondents were asked to select from this list which things they would

3 Page visited on October 19, 2011. According to Dutch government definitions, the term "*allochtonen*" ("allochthonous" in English) concerns inhabitants of the Netherlands who were born in a "non-Western country" (they are labeled as the "first generation") or people from which at least one of the parents was born in a "non-Western" country (the "second generation"). Defined against allochthonous people, autochthonous are those of Western descent. The constructed binary opposition between autochthonous and allochthonous Western and non-Western groups is problematic. In every dichotomy one side is favored over the other, resulting from the presentation of particular kinds of information in particular kinds of ways. The side not favored is Othered. In this case, migrants hailing from "Western countries" are on the good side of some sort of divide, while migrants from "non-Western countries" come from the "wrong" side of this divide. As such, people coming from the first are seen as the standard and the norm, as being more advanced and sophisticated, while people in the latter category are seen as backward, exotic, primitive, uncivilized, "oriental" Others (Said, 1979). The label "allochthonous" is now increasingly also a substitute for speaking about Muslims (Leurs, Midden & Ponzanesi, 2012, p. 156).

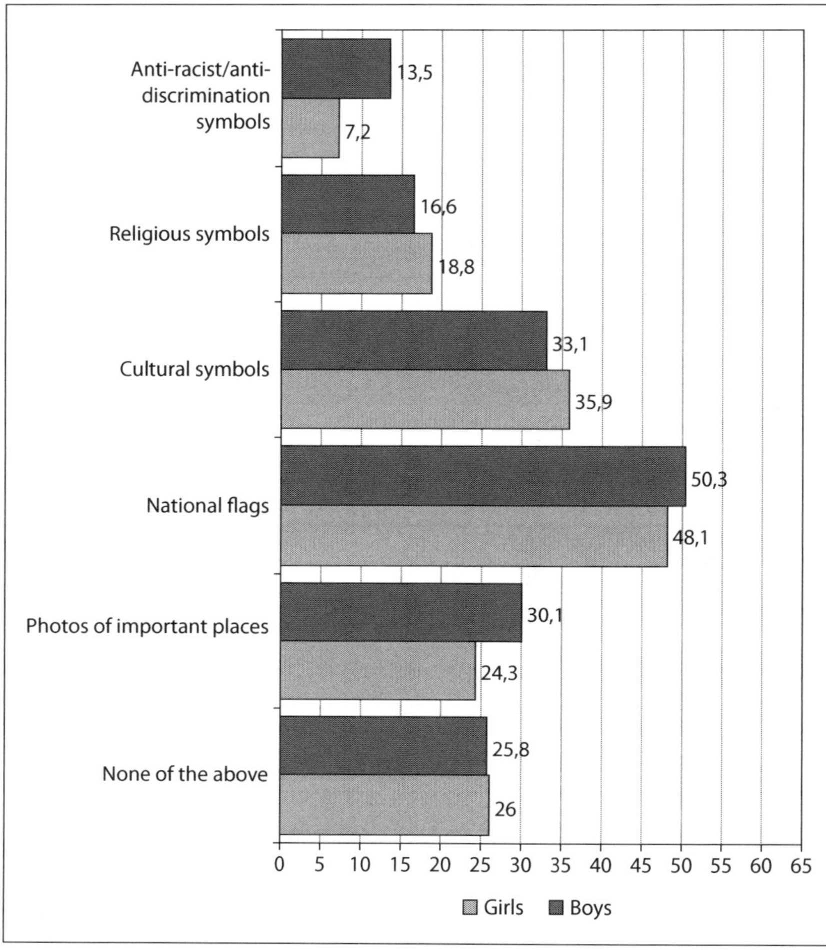

Diagram 10: Moroccan-Dutch youth cultural self-profiling on SNSs (multiple answers possible, graph shows percentages, n = 344)

link to and include on their profile page. Diagram 10 displays cultural self-profiling preferences among Moroccan-Dutch girls and boys.

A quarter of Moroccan-Dutch youth reported they do not put any of these cultural self-profiling things on their personal page. The option to include national flags was popular among boys and girls. Roughly half of them reported incorporating their national flag on their profile page. Girls listed they would include cultural symbols like the Aza discussed above, while boys more often listed they include pictures of important places on their page. Furthermore, religious symbols were more frequently listed by girls, while antiracist or antidiscrimination signs or texts, were more popular among boys.

During the follow-up interviews, informants reflected further on their self-presentations. Underlining ethnic pride and wearing the headscarf as an important identity marker, thirteen-year-old Inas described her construction of a personal profile page as follows, "*It's like, I'm wearing a headscarf. When I post a photo of me wearing a headscarf, you can, so to say, see that I have an Islamic background. And with my name and so on.*" Furthermore, interviewees report highlighting their attachment to Islam by showing they are a member of groups pertaining to Islam on their online profile page. Similarly, Facebook allows minorities to affirm their self-expressions, which is important as a "positive adjustment to diverse environments depends on the development of healthy cultural identities among adolescents" (Grasmuck, Martin & Zhao, 2009, p. 180). However, Eighteen-year-old Safae reported that signaling Muslim affinities sometimes backfires: "*I have a girlfriend, and she wears a headscarf. On Hyves she got a message from someone stating, 'We live in 2010 – a headscarf is outdated, it's something from the past.' That was bad – you can't say that. I feel that is discrimination.*" This remark once again emphasizes how offline social divisions also color digital behavior. As such, minorities may remain space invaders in social networking sites. When informants engage in digital fandom practices and mark their ethnic or religious background they remain vulnerable to being dismissed as backward. However, in return, Moroccan-Dutch Hyves users actively respond to such acts of racism by disrupting stereotypes, a process which shows similarities to the typed contestations of allocated positions on online discussion boards.

Consider, for example, the Hyves groups Ryan links to on his profile page. Having joined the "Allochthonous Hyves group" an image appeared on his page that read "Netherlands was partly made possible by Moroccans."

Fig. 17: "Error," archived from http://trotsopmarokko.hyves.nl (October 23, 2009)

Fig. 18: "100% Marokaan," archived from http://trotsopmarokko.hyves.nl (October 23, 2009)

Similarly, by linking to "Proud to be Moroccan," Ryan made an additional visual statement. Figures 17 and 18 are other examples of images that ironically and reflexively play with Dutch mainstream representations of Moroccan-Dutch young people. The figures were downloaded from the "Proud to be Moroccan" group page. On the page, a large collection of similar images was collected, as Hyves users were invited to share their personal profile images there. Cultural profiling is taken up to publish being proud of one's minority background.

Figure 17 reads, "ERROR, this Moroccan is too dangerous to be depicted in a picture." Figure 18 is a critical reading of what it means to be allocated a position as Moroccan-Dutch: "10% are thieves, 15% are poor, 45% are illegal, 10% are on welfare, 20% are unemployed, in sum 100% Moroccan." The figure reveals some of the ways Moroccan-Dutch youth perceive to be stereotyped. In my interview with Abdelilah Amraoui, the founder and moderator of the "Proud to be Moroccan" group, he noted that he started the page as a joke in response to Trots op Nederland (Proud of the Netherlands), a Dutch conservative party lead by right-wing politician Rita Verdonk, and to be able to gather information and remind fellow Moroccan-Dutch youth of Moroccan-Dutch role models such as footballers and musicians. These examples display agency on the side of ethnic-minority youth to create alternative fandom positions by circulating new signifiers of Moroccan-Dutchness. As I illustrated with the notion of carnivalesque I used to analyze the field site of discussion forum discussions, distinct normative frameworks guide humor.[4] Ethnic jokes are mostly only accepted when made by a member of the

4 In the art scene similar counterinitiatives emerged where Moroccan-Dutch artists ironically and reflexively played with negative stereotypes. Consider, for instance, the 2005-2006

group joked about: "Blacks joke about Blacks, Turks about Turks" (Kuipers, 2008, p. 8). They establish a bond of mutual understanding by circulating jokes about themselves as being dangerous, thieves or poor on the "Proud to be Moroccan" Hyves group page where fellow Moroccan-Dutch youth congregate. Through their participation in this fandom counterculture, they establish a shared identity and a mutual sense of belonging.

Differential networking

Inspired by the notion of hypertextual selves, the Wired Up survey was designed to capture differential profiling activities that stretch across and mix local, migratory and global affiliations. More specifically respondents were asked whether they showed food, music and celebrity preferences on three locality dimensions (host, migrant or transnational cultures) on their profile page (see Table 7). For instance, on the topic of celebrities the survey asked respondents to tick a box indicating whether they would show Dutch celebrities, famous migrants and international stars.

I zoom in on two themes in the self-profiling of Moroccan-Dutch and ethnic-majority Dutch youth. Firstly, the table shows that compared to Moroccan-Dutch respondents, majority Dutch respondents participate relatively more in all three strands of Dutch self-profiling. More than girls, boys list Dutch food preferences, while girls favor Dutch music and celebrities. Conversely, Moroccan-Dutch respondents are more active in all three forms of migrant cultural self-profiling. Moroccan-Dutch boys list migrant background food and celebrities preferences more than girls, while they equally participate in migrant-background music profiling. Migrant self-profiling allows informants to highlight migrant identity alignments. One way to do so is joining a group related to Berber culture (as I have discussed in the prior subsection). This feeling of affirmation both holds for Moroccan-Dutch as well as ethnic-majority Dutch young people who report including Dutch cultural food, music and celebrities on their page. It should thus be noted that opportunities to manifest ethnic dimensions of one's identity are taken up by both Moroccan-Dutch as well as majority Dutch youth. Singling out migrant affiliations among Moroccan-Dutch youth and Dutch affiliations among majority Dutch youth does, however, not paint the full picture.

Kunstmarokkanen (Art Moroccans) contemporary art project. The name is a pun that hints at the negative label of "*Kutmarokkanen*" (Moroccan cunts), commonly used when dismissing Moroccan-Dutch boys who misbehave (see https://web.archive.org/web/20080904070633/http://www.kunstmarokkanen.nl/index.php?page = 10).

Table 7: Self-profiling cultural affiliations (n = 344 Moroccan-Dutch and 448 ethnic-majority Dutch respondents)

Self-profiling cultural affiliations		*Moroccan-Dutch girls*	*Moroccan-Dutch Boys*	*ethnic majority-Dutch girls*	*ethnic majority-Dutch boys*
Self-profiling *Dutch* culture	Food	6.6	12.9	31.4	41.6
	Music	4.4	4.9	19.7	19.1
	Celebrities	8.3	12.9	24.7	19.1
Self-profiling *migrant* cultures	Food	40.3	48.5	16.3	18.2
	Music	**61.3**	**61.3**	17.2	**24.4**
	Celebrities	48.6	51.5	7.1	12
Self-profiling *international* cultures	Food	**30.9**	**36.2**	**32.6**	**34**
	Music	**61.9**	**40.5**	**82.8**	**71.3**
	Celebrities	**30.9**	**28.2**	**40.2**	**34.4**
I do not include the following preferences	Food	16	23.3	55.2	44
	Music	48.6	41.7	21.2	14.2
	Celebrities	37.6	36.8	48.1	53.1

Politically relevant, the differences between how the two groups engage with global cultural affiliations are generally smaller and more ambiguous. The results indicate (printed bold in the table) that international affiliations constitute the liminal space of intercultural encounter for ethnic-majority Dutch and Moroccan-Dutch young people. Almost one-third of every Moroccan-Dutch boy or girl and ethnic-majority Dutch boy or girl participates in profiling international food and celebrities preferences. The category of music preferences is a more prominent space of intercultural grouping as two-thirds of Moroccan Dutch girls and 40% of boys and over two-thirds of ethnic-majority Dutch boys and girls selected it.

Cosmopolitan perspectives

The hyperlinking practices discussed above were found to cover a wide spectrum of affiliations. Moroccan-Dutch youth link across cultural difference and geographical distances. As an example of bottom-up multiculturalism, the SNS profiling practices of migrant youth indicate "transnational activities and identifications do not need to constitute an impediment to integration" (Snel, Engbersen & Leerkes, 2006, p. 304). In contrast to claims over digital exclusion and segregation, they can become space invaders by articulating a multiplicity of identifications. The ways in which they perform their digital identities in the form of hypertextual selves provides grounded, empirical evidence of the actually existing everyday realities of digital conviviality. Beyond political, governmental, scholarly and mainstream media understandings of the failure of top-down multiculturalism, multiculture is in action from the bottom up in convivial perspectives and forms of cohabitation. There is potential for empowerment in such interactional processes that render "multiculture an ordinary feature of social life" (Gilroy, 2005, p. xv). Users may each express their individual cultural identifications on their profile pages. For example, on Facebook, the selfies, status updates and videos used to express identifications show up on the timeline of their friends. As these postings may include a wide variety of affiliations, SNS users may have to navigate a situation of being digitally thrown together with difference (Leurs, 2014b). The articulation of hypertextual selves exemplifies how users negotiate a situation of digital throwntogetherness in a progressive way. By combining various ethnic, gender, religious and youth cultural affiliations, hypertextual selves published by the informants empirically sustain their cosmopolitan perspectives.

The aesthetic of hypertext has been theorized to resonate strongly with migrant multiple identifications. Jaishree Odin argued that border subjects operate in contact zones. In their engagement with digital practices, they establish a hypertext aesthetic characterized by discontinuity, fragmentation, multiplicity, assemblage and technocracy (2010). She proposed this hypertext aesthetic

> represents the need to switch from the linear, univocal, closed, authoritative aesthetic involving passive encounters characterizing the performance of the same to that of non-linear, multivocal, open, non-hierarchical aesthetic involving active encounters that are marked by repetition of the same with and in difference. (Odin, cited in Landow, 2006, pp. 356-357)

Her theoretical reflection on hypertext can also inform an empirical mapping of actual online linking practices of migrants. Hyperlink practices on social networking sites allow Moroccan-Dutch youth to express innovative networked forms of belonging in their dealing with oppositional ethnic, gendered, religious and youth cultural motivations of continuity and change. Intercultural encounters take place in the networked space of global cultural belongingness. (Dis)located between the local and the global, such spaces arise form "the point at which boundaries of inclusion and exclusion, of belonging and otherness, of 'us' and 'them,' are contested" (Brah, 1996, p. 205).

On Hyves and Facebook, users can stake out their differential positionalities. In the words of my informants, thirteen-year-old Ilham compared SNSs with MSN and argued that on MSN "*you see one side of someone*" while a profile page "*allows you to show more of yourself.*" Eighteen-year-old Mustafa noted, "*You see how open a person can be, that he has a lot of fun, because a whole lot of information can be put up about a person.*" He added that personal profile pages allow users to show different sides of themselves: "*may provide a better glance at the life of a person, so you cannot really dismiss someone like 'Oh, yeah, that's him and he is like that.'*" Analyzing hypertextual narratives of selves reveals how identities are neither fixed nor singular but are dynamically constructed at the crossroads of different affiliations.

Online social networking sites such as Hyves and Facebook therefore may offer a glimpse at how migrant youth articulate cosmopolitan perspectives. Anas's and Midia's hypertextual outlook illustrates their cosmopolitanism positionining "which involves crossing the borders of separate worlds (nations, religions, cultures, skin colors, continents, etc.) and whose oppositions must or may lodge in a single life" (Beck, 2000, p. 75). Informants were found to hyperlink to cultural affiliations that are generally seen as incompatible. The space where hypertextual selves gather is space of digital interaction where heterogeneity and diversity can become ordinary. As an example of how youth cultures include intercultural encounters, joining groups in social networking sites offer ethnic-minority and -majority youth a platform for self-expression, cross-cultural exchange and active encounter. Fostering multiplicity by bringing different orientations together, youth culture may offer grounds for the contestation of racisms, nationalisms and ethnic absolutisms.

Hypertextual performativity of self in the production of digital space in social networking sites is, however, not always simply enabling. Users are economically exploited as online social networking sites collect personal data, including the hyperlinks user make, which are sold for niche-marketing purposes. Safae's remarks on online discrimination remind us that ethnic-cultural and religious expressions such as wearing a headscarf did not meet the mainstream norm of Hyves's expressive culture. Also, peer pressure impacts on the ways young people articulate their hypertextual selves, comparable to how peer expectations have an influence over the way users self-photograph themselves along the lines of gender and sexuality. From a reaction by Mustafa I learned that peer-pressure dynamics are also at work in joining groups:

> *When many people have joined something, you may think, "Oh, that is [OK]" or "I don't really think it would be nice to belong to it, but I do join after all, because many people have joined." [Sometimes you may feel as if] you do not do it for yourself, but for someone else.*

Trinh T. Minh-ha states that fragmentation denotes a way of living with differences at the margins, where "one finds oneself, in the context of cultural hybridity always pushing one's questioning of oneself to the limit of what one is and what one is not" (1992, pp. 156-157). This process of questioning oneself is complicated further as teenagers with a migration background also have to negotiate whether or not to conform to – sometimes demanding – varying peer norms and expectations.

Finally, as the digital realm is increasingly policed, certain minoritarian practices become restricted as well. Especially with the recent scares over Islamic State's online recruitment of disenfranchised Muslim youth, authorities treat digital Muslim/migrant networks as risks to society: "Migrant digital networks are increasingly conceptualised as an Internet security threat, in particular after September 11th and the rise in Islamophobia" (Kambouri & Parsanoglou, 2010, p. 30). New technologies thus also present new tools for the monitoring, surveillance and disciplining of migrant bodies (ibid., p. 10, 30). For instance, when Facebook administrators were asked by Israeli Public Diplomacy and Diaspora Affairs Minister Yuli Edelstein to take down an Arabic-language page calling for a third Intifada against Israel to liberate the Palestinian territory, they first prided themselves on the Facebook "Terms of Service" for promoting freedom of expression and deliberation:

> While some kinds of comments and content may be upsetting for someone – criticism of a certain culture, country, religion, lifestyle, or political ideology, for example – that alone is not a reason to remove the discussion. We strongly believe that Facebook users have the ability to express their opinions. (Cited in Protalinski, 2011)

Under increased Israeli government pressure, the page was, however, deleted soon after by Facebook administrators (Protalinski, 2011). Similarly, political activity was restricted within Hyves. Its founder, Raymond Spanjar, chose to forbid anti-groups such as "Anti Geert Wilders" because these acts also flood the screens of the advertisers. Advertisers do not want their product to be associated with political struggles (2011, pp. 137-138).

In sum, hypertextual selves performed on personal profile pages may be taken to reflect the cosmopolitan multiplicity of Moroccan-Dutch youth identification. Hypertext as an in-between space where different points of articulation can meet and in-between identities can be expressed presents a strong example of how emancipation can be fostered through bottom-up multicultural interaction. However, racism, victimization, peer pressure, surveillance and commercial incentives leave their imprint on the ways Moroccan-Dutch youth articulate their hypertextual selves and engage in intercultural encounters with various social networking site users.

4.5 Conclusions

In this chapter, I focused on visual representations and hyperlinking practices as two distinct ways the self is performed on social networking sites. I described how technological restrictions, user cultures, corporate motives and peer norms shape a particular age, gender, and religiosity-based habitus on social networking sites. The informants follow critical cues of their peers about what to show in their profile photos and I argued that popularity and attractiveness (key facets to the life stage of adolescence) explain the ideals of stereotypically gendered selfies. Certain versions of femininity and masculinity were found to be hegemonic. These are powerful ideological models, to which users aspire in order to achieve social acceptance, make new friends, find romance and gain popularity. Achieved through interactions but abiding by hegemonic standards, some young people may find empowerment by being in charge of their to-be-looked-at-ness and may feel self-confident in successfully attracting a wide audience to their profile page. For girls I argued this means taking a narcissistic and submissive pose reflecting awareness of the heterosexual masculine gaze. Bodies are disciplined to meet these expectations, but versions of femininity are increasingly becoming unattainable, leading to frustration and a loss of (peer-generated) self-worth. Additionally, exposing oneself implies susceptibility to victimization practices ("brooming") that may put an end to the sense of agency users may have affectively felt.

Secondly, I analyzed in-between forms of identification on social networking sites. I assessed how hypertextual selves are articulated through fandom forms of cultural self-profiling. Forming a response to discrimination and exclusion, Moroccan-Dutch youth turn to more positive experiences such as identification with their descent and/or their religion in social networking sites. They are also inspired by global youth culture. In their cultural self-profiling online, the younger generations not only tap into migrant heritage elements. Second-generation migrant youth are actually actively transforming the legacies of their parents in connection with the dominant global youth cultures in which they grow up. The analytic lens of hypertext is useful to consider bottom-up representations of decentered, cosmopolitan identities that signal the bankruptcy of the clichéd images of

Islamic, migrant youth as backward, radicalized or oppressed. Furthermore the links imply that intercultural encounters with multiple others take place in the space of social networking sites. Considering the hypertextual in-between positioning of Moroccan-Dutch youth in their interaction with young users of a variety of backgrounds as a form of convivial networked belonging not only helps to produce a new understanding of multiculturalism, but also assists in discovering the emancipatory possibilities in everyday culture. In the next chapter I consider affective identification in the field site of YouTube.

5. Affective geographies on YouTube

From time to time I watch videos, self-made ones, showing different Moroccan scenes. I kind of enjoy watching those. They make me go back in my mind to Morocco, and every once in a while I like that.
– Nevra, a sixteen-year-old girl

Me at the Zoo is the first file ever uploaded on YouTube. In this nineteen-second video set in the San Diego Zoo in the United States, we see Jawed Karim – one of YouTube's founders – in front of an elephant enclosure stating, "Alright, so here we are in front of the elephants. The cool thing about these guys is that they have really, really, really long trunks, and that's cool. And that's pretty much all there is to say" (Jawed, 2005). By viewing such videos on their screens, users may affectively presence themselves at a distant location. In this chapter I map out what emotions may be evoked in the bodies of Moroccan-Dutch youth as they watch YouTube videos. The interviewees mostly watched two genres: user-generated videos shot in Morocco that may sustain feelings of transnational diaspora belonging, and commercial music videos that may produce feelings of attachment to local, national and global youth culture. In particular, I will argue that YouTube video-viewing practices of migrant youth provide insights into how affective belongings across transnational geographies are audiovisually sustained.

Nevra, a sixteen-year-old girl, stated she travels back to Morocco in her mind when watching YouTube videos shot in Morocco. She feels moved when watching these videos. Nevra and other informants use YouTube as a way to emotionally reconnect to their childhood histories and recent holiday visits. Nevra was born in the Netherlands and thus imaginings of her Moroccan home are mainly virtual and are sustained through holiday travel, stories and pictures, music and videos (Stock, 2014; Turan Hoffman, 2014; Alinejad, 2013). Besides watching Moroccan-themed videos, informants turned to YouTube to access music videos from artists from various parts of the world. When asked why informants used YouTube, they commonly stated watching videos shot in Morocco made them feel "*nostalgic*" and "*emotional,*" while music videos made them feel "*happy.*"

YouTube played two roles in the lives of the majority of the informants. Thirteen-year-old Ilham explained: "*You can watch anything you want there, by searching for a key word. You will find video clips of songs, and real videos.*" She juxtaposed "*video clips*" and "*real videos.*" With "*video clips*" she referred to professional music videos from American, Moroccan and Middle-Eastern artists she enjoys listening to. With "*real videos*" she referred to amateur, user-generated content such as travel videos shot in Morocco. The distinguishing of the informants between the two genres echoes scholarly divisions made between mainstream materials uploaded by commercial corporate and/or institutional players, and user-generated video content (Burgess & Green, 2009; Jean Christian, 2009). From the forty-three interviewees, thirty-eight young people turn to YouTube to watch music video clips, while eighteen look up user-generated videos about Islam and twelve informants watch diasporic videos taken in Morocco.

Cultural theorists are increasingly taking affective bodily sensations seriously in recent years, a development that has been described to constitute an "affective turn" (Clough & Halley, 2007). A substantial amount of critical scholarship has emerged that probes the cultural politics of affectivity (Ahmed 2004, 2010; Brennan 2004; Fortunati & Vincent, 2009; Jones, Jackson & Rhys-Taylor, 2014; Leurs, 2014a; Sedgwick, 2003; Turan Hoffman, 2014). However, affectivity remains understudied in migration and media studies: most previous research "on migration rarely captures the affective and emotional dimensions of global processes" (Boehm & Swank, 2011, p. 1). Others have lamented the scarce attention for affectivity in studies on digital technologies: "We are at the infancy of studies on emotion and ICTs" (Fortunati & Vincent, 2009, p. 15). Migration and media scholars have previously focused more on issues of representation such as framing and identity construction (Madianou, 2014, p. 324). This chapter contributes to filling the gaps in the literature by taking YouTube video-viewing practices as an entry point to address the intersection between affectivity and media use experiences across transnational and local spaces (Leurs, De Haan & Leander, 2015). The affective encounter of bodies with media objects shifts attention from understanding viewing as processes of symbolic meaning making, toward apprehending them as sparking emotions, feelings and experiences that matter. I posit, in particular, that by charting second-generation Moroccan-Dutch youth's affective geographies of belonging that may arise from watching YouTube videos, the generational-specific experiences of second-generation migrant youth can be highlighted.

Below, I first introduce the use of YouTube among Moroccan-Dutch youth in the wider context of the Netherlands. Second, I reflect on the politics of YouTube. Third, I review prior scholarship on affectivity, belonging and digital practices. Fourth, YouTube video-viewing practices that spark affective senses of nostalgic and home-making "rooted" diaspora belonging (Gilroy, 1993a) are scrutinized. In the final section viewing practices that affectively shape feelings of belonging to "routed" (Gilroy, 1993a) international/local orientations are analyzed.

5.1 Moroccan-Dutch youth using YouTube

Globally, YouTube is the third most frequented site on the web (Alexa, 2014). At the time of the interviews, the informants considered YouTube the second most valuable platform online after MSN, based on the number of times YouTube was included in the Internet maps. The Wired Up survey data also showed that among the Moroccan-Dutch respondents YouTube was the second most frequented space online. Together with MSN they valued YouTube the highest (see Diagram 3 and Diagram 4, pp. 68-69). Of the Moroccan-Dutch survey takers, 77% reported going on YouTube four days per week or more. Additionally, over half of the respondents noted they would miss the platform when they would not be able to use it anymore. Two-thirds of Moroccan-Dutch girls and over half of boys reported they would miss using YouTube very much (see Table 8).

Table 8: The importance of YouTube in the lives of Moroccan-Dutch youth (percentages, n = 344)

Would you miss YouTube if you could not use it any longer?	*Completely not*	*Somewhat*	*Very much*	*Total*
Young women	8.3%	32.6%	59.1%	100%
Young men	11.0%	36.8%	52.2%	100%

Illustrative for her fellow informants, thirteen-year-old Ilham perceived YouTube as platform with a global reach, where a wide variety of videos can be accessed. During the interview that took place in 2010 she also explained that videos that do not meet YouTube's moderation policy can be deleted.

> *It is a site, very much global. It has been a great success. It has existed for five years, I recently read about it. You can upload all sorts of videos there. They can be about many different things. Some will be deleted when they are really dirty or when they hurt people.*

Informants made use of YouTube for a variety of reasons. Seventeen-year-old Sadik saw YouTube as a good place to learn new guitar tricks: "*The advantage with YouTube is that you don't have to take guitar lessons, because they are given for free there*" (see Lange, 2014, p. 189). Using a website such as Keepvid.com, fourteen-year-old Mehmet Ali downloaded Moroccan-Arabic and Berber songs from YouTube to his mobile phone, a Nokia N95.

Besides the actual videos, the informants also related to the comment section where discussions take place. Flaming and other forms of antisocial behavior are not uncommon there: "insulting, swearing or using otherwise offensive language… appears to be very common on YouTube" (Moor, Heuvelman & Verleur, 2010, p. 1536). Like most informants, sixteen-year-old Inzaf shared she has accepted that comments can hurt: "*Yes, they can post [whatever they want], as freedom of speech applies there.*" Comments affect her only when the videos are dear to her heart, as is the case when videos are about things "*or people I know.*" She mentioned in such cases "*I do have a look at what people have to say about it.*" One of sixteen-year-old Naoul's statements reminds us that Moroccan-Dutch youth are space invaders on YouTube. Naoul said that the comment sections below videos about Morocco fill up with verbal abuse and hostility: "*When you watch a video on YouTube, they shout 'Moroccan cunts' and this and that about Moroccans.*"

The *Ummah*

Eighteen interviewees (seven boys and eleven girls) discussed watching videos pertaining to Islam. Eighteen-year-old Mustafa, for instance, reflected on how he turned to YouTube during the fasting month of Ramadan to look up videos of people reciting suras "*Of course, for me it can get very emotional when hearing someone state these words in a beautiful voice.*" Similarly, fifteen-year-old Meryam – the informant who showed her *Handbook for Muslim Women* during fieldwork – praises the platform as she feels able to find exalting material there: "*There are children that have learned the whole Quran by heart; I think they are very bright, that they can do it. And yes, I have a look at those.*" She added: "*It gives me inspiration to better commit myself to my religion.*" Fifteen-year-old Oussema discussed turning to YouTube together with his father before his parents embarked on their hajj pilgrimage to Mecca: "*I'm not a practicing Muslim, but for my dad it was useful. He wanted to learn more before he went on his pilgrimage.*" Oussema acted as a knowledge broker, assisting his father to view pilgrimage videos.

Some of the younger informants, for example, twelve-year-old Soufian, thirteen-year-old Hanan and fourteen-year-old Sahar, look up "*anasheed*" movies. *Anasheed* are songs typically performed in Arabic but increasingly also in Dutch that offer young people an accessible way to incorporate a sense of Islam in their everyday life (Razzaqi, 2011, p. 272).[1] Hanan argues that she listens

1 *Anasheed* is Islamic vocal music, a cappella or accompanied by instruments that references Islamic history, beliefs and interpretations but also politics and current events. *Anasheed* songs

to such "*songs that deal with the peacefulness of Islam. For instance,* [*songs*] *by Maher Zain. He has a very pretty voice. I don't know, his songs have a soothing effect on me.*" Videos are thus experienced as affective objects, informants note feeling touched by them, providing an inspirational boost, a sense of authority vis-à-vis their parents, guidance or moving them to the brink of tears.

Videos are taken up to learn more about Islam. Fourteen-year-old Ziham shared: "*Say, when I did not know how to pray yet, I turned to YouTube to learn about the steps to take and later I turned to books, and now I just pray every day.*" YouTube for her was a fun way to follow instructions on Islamic devotion. Sixteen-year-old Nevra learns more about what is halal or haram, "*what you are supposed and not supposed to do according to Islam.*" Seventeen-year-old Sadik, too, shared he learns more about Islam and his role as a Muslim through YouTube: "*For example, they talk about Islam in English, which I understood better, because Arabic I don't understand that well. They, for instance, discuss the state of the world, and how Islam is seen across the world and how it started.*" He gave the example of watching a series called *The Arrivals*, "*about the dangers that go around the world.*" (Islamic authorities have dismissed this series as deceitful conspiracy theories.)

In the introduction and Chapter 2 I argued that digital media are taken up as "a missing middle" between the textual studies of Islam by elite intellectuals and Islam as a socio-cultural force among the mass of followers (Leurs, Midden & Ponzanesi, 2012, p. 162). In YouTube, alternative conventions of religious authority arise, being partly shaped by prior user behavior and algorithms that translate prior viewer and search practices in key word search rankings (Bunt, 2009, p. 31). Online performances of Islam decentralize religious authority and provide interpretative opportunities to a wider range of actors, but this democratization may also result in the circulation of problematic content, as is evident from the videos Sadik watched. Some insist that when religious education and the credibility of Imams and Muslim scholars are undermined the dangers of extremism, offensive jihad and legitimating violence may grow. This issue is especially pertinent given the recent attention paid to online recruitment by extremist groups including Al-Qaeda and the Islamic State (IS), which aim to attract European Muslims to join their fight (Leurs & Ponzanesi, 2014c). Therefore, there is an urgency to provide young people with the tools of media literacy to balance, contextualize and judge the materials they encounter online (Ryan, 2007; Lange, 2014).

can be compared to nursery rhymes, and they can also be understood to be analogous to psalms and hymns sung in Christian contexts (Razzaqi, 2011, p. 272).

Overall, consuming Islamic sermons, lectures and *anasheed* provide informants with an affective sense of belonging to the "*Ummah*" (the worldwide Muslim community). Instead of being passive members, searching out the Islamic videos they feel personally moved by, they affectively enact and claim belonging to this community (Roy, 2004, p. 183). Especially during the Islamic month of Ramadan, the Internet can be seen to offers a space for identity-formation and cohesion as information, rituals and norms are easily shared among like-minded users (Bunt, 2009, p. 97). During the fast, believers abstain from eating, drinking, smoking and sexual intercourse but not from browsing the Internet. For Mustafa YouTube sermons offered emotional support during Ramadan, and Bunt contextualizes that more broadly "the Net helps bring iMuslims together during this sacred month, especially those living outside of established Muslim communities" (2009, p. 97). Imagining an audience of fellow Muslim video viewers, informants sense a shared frame of reference that goes beyond the borders of the Netherlands.

Fitna

One video in particular, *Fitna* – and the video responses it provoked – has dominated recent Dutch public and scholarly debates over digital video, Muslims and YouTube (Leurs, Hirzalla & Van Zoonen, 2012). The anti-Islamic visual pamphlet *Fitna* was made by Dutch right-wing Member of Parliament Geert Wilders. *Fitna* is a 17-minute cut-n-mix collage that includes excerpts from the Quran, crosscut with suras,[2] blurry video segments and newspaper clippings portraying acts of violence carried out by Muslims across the globe. The video opens with a cartoon by Kurt Westergaard depicting Prophet Muhammad wearing a turban in the shape of a lighted bomb, which was a central image in the *Jyllands-Posten* Muhammad cartoons controversy (Blaagaard, 2010; Kuipers, 2008). Centering on perceived negative influences of Islam in the Netherlands, the film implies that Islam promotes terrorism, anti-Semitism, and violence against women, homosexuals and nonbelievers. *Fitna* is an example of how those in positions of power in the Netherlands – Wilders was a member of the Dutch parliament at the time the video was released – hail Muslim identities in negative terms. Ryan, a fifteen-year-old interviewee, shared his frustration with Geert Wilders and *Fitna*:

2 A sura refers to one of the 114 particular sections or chapters of the Quran.

> *He had just made* Fitna*, and I got very angry with him. I really did not like that. He combined all sorts of outrageous stuff. He included strange things, I found it outrageous. He says that many [Muslim] people wear a burqa, but in my family no one wears a burqa, I never see a burqa in the streets. Why does he make such a fuss about it, that Geert Wilders? I believe he also has some good ideas. Like, that we should have to pay lower taxes. But he has a lot of nonsensical ideas, such as about Islam.*

Fitna was followed up by an intensive video battle that has not gone unnoticed by scholars. Thousands of users from across the globe posted their own videos to critique or show their support of the film. For example: people recorded video messages offering their personal apologies for Wilders's making of *Fitna*; satirical and parodying cut-n-mix videos were uploaded, and finally, as a form of activism and culture jamming, users tagged unrelated videos with keywords pertaining to *Fitna* to make Wilders's video more difficult to find online. These acts have been recognized as performances of dispersed citizenship (Van Zoonen, Vis & Mihelj, 2010, p. 260). Young Muslim women from Egypt, in particular, were found to be active in uploading videos that critiqued Wilders for speaking for them and presenting Islam as an oppressive religion (Vis, Van Zoonen & Mihelj, 2011, pp. 123-127). The *Fitna* video battle has also been analyzed in terms of humor, however some comedians defending their Islamic faith through vlogs have been critiqued for being excluding instead of fostering constructive and uniting dialogue (Hirzalla, Van Zoonen & Müller, 2011). The battle is still going on, and Geert Wilders is rumored to be working on a sequel to *Fitna*.

The video *Kop of Munt* (*Heads or Tails*), mentioned by the informants, is one example of a comical response to *Fitna*. *Kop of Munt* is a film that can be positioned in the video debate that unfolded after Wilders released *Fitna*. The video was made in October 2009 by MUNT, a collective of Moroccan-Dutch young professionals, and by November 2014 it had attracted 235,000 views (MUNT, 2009). This short, 9-minute movie is accompanied by the following tagline on YouTube: "*Kop of Munt* depicts the day the Moroccans have deserted the Netherlands en masse" (my translation). In the video some of the stereotypical consequences of what the Netherlands would look like without Moroccan-Dutch inhabitants are visualized: newspaper delivery stagnates, Moroccan-Dutch shows in the theaters are canceled, barbershops close down, newspaper commentary and opinion sections are left empty, taxis become scarce, social housing projects are abandoned, prisons are put up for sale because they are untenanted, requests for social services decline and there are major traffic jams in Belgium, France and Spain in

Fig. 19: "Prison for sale", still from *Kop of Munt*, YouTube video uploaded by MUNT (October 20, 2009)

the direction of Morocco. The film counters Islamophobia by exaggerating what the Netherlands would look like without Moroccan-Dutch inhabitants, exposing the absurdities in the debates on Moroccan-Dutch people. Videos that similarly satirically showcased what would happen if a particular ethnic-minority group would leave a country include *The City without Jews*, a prophetic expressionist film about what would happen if all Jews left Vienna (Breslauer, 1924) and *A Day without a Mexican* depicting what would happen if all the Mexicans abandoned the US state of California (Arau, 2004). Dialoguing with these previous films, MUNT subverts normative ideas about race relations, migration, multiculturalism and Islam and promotes greater intercultural understanding (Leurs & Ponzanesi, 2014a, p. 632).

After he first saw *Kop of Munt* Oussema wrote to me in a Facebook Chat conversation. He reflected on the video from two perspectives: "*as a [video] editor I think it is well composed and I think the color balance (magic bullet looks) is well done,*"[3] and "*as a Moroccan I find it quite funny and I believe they are so right*" in addressing these topics. He admired the satire: "*I love how you see the hairdresser taking off, taking the dish with him.*" The satellite dish Oussema mentioned has become a symbol of alterity. Because migrants can tune in to channels from their country of origins, satellite television is increasingly seen as a reason why ethnic minorities fail to integrate in Dutch society (Scheffer, 2007, p. 40). On YouTube, a flood of verbal abuse is visible in the comment

3 Magic Bullet is a video-editing software plug-in which enables filmmakers to edit digital video to make it look like a professional film.

section below. Oussema was quite offended by the amount of negative responses and reactions left by other viewers, as he wrote to me "*172 dislikes:S* ," adding a shocked and sad face emoticon. A large number of people had clicked the YouTube "Dislike" button, while 231 users pressed the "Like" button. He dismisses the many negative, discriminating and painful comments; he felt such hateful views were coming from the margins of Dutch society.

In the worldview set forward by Wilders in *Fitna* the religion of Islam is equated with violence and oppression, and Muslim believers are framed as violent, backward and frightening. This way, at the mercy of being hailed by those in power, Muslim people from around the globe and the Netherlands, in particular, are denied their status as full human subjects; they are not seen as equal. Rather, Muslims become dehumanized objects deviating from the norm, and are allocated positions as inferior citizens, being somehow less than fully human. As a form of humorous agency, *Kop of Munt*, displays how such injurious hailing acts can begin to be subverted and resignified by returning a gaze through video parody. *Kop of Munt* received major exposure in mainstream news coverage (such as on NOS op 3, a Dutch public broadcaster, and in major national newspapers, including *De Volkskrant* and *NRC Next*). The video shows how humor may "transcend cultural boundaries" as specific *Kop of Munt* elements address audiences inside and outside the ethnic-specific normative community it arose from (Kuipers, 2008, pp. 7-8).

The *Fitna* video battle is a significant feature of digital video culture among Muslim and Moroccan-Dutch youth, however in this chapter I focus, in particular, on those videos that informants mentioned more often. When informants discussed their uses of YouTube during the in-depth interview, they were asked to write down the titles of videos they frequently looked up, and did so by variously listing one to six videos. Interviewees were also asked to provide background information on the videos they listed. For example, when discussing music videos, informants were prompted to situate the artists in terms of genre, gender, language use and geographical location. Thus, the informants explicitly mentioned the videos discussed in this chapter. Before analyzing the affective attachments interviewees reported having of particular videos, I describe the politics of YouTube and position myself in theories on affectivity below.

5.2 Theorizing the politics of YouTube

Before elaborating affectivity on YouTube, in this section I focus first on the politics of the platform itself. YouTube users search and select the videos they want to watch: people "no longer watch films or TV; we watch databases" (Lovink, 2007, p. 11). Watching databases has its downsides, as user behavior on the platform is monitored and made into a valuable economic asset that is exploited by YouTube's owner, Google. User behavior such as viewing, uploading, tagging, sharing and commenting enables YouTube to grow as these practices stimulate YouTube's audience to grow (Kessler & Schäfer, 2009, pp. 278-285). Such profit-oriented motives increasingly coshape user behavior, because with the advent of social media the previously private sphere of emotions is increasingly intertwined with public monetization. Although commodified through the culture of capitalism, the communication of emotions fosters "sociability" between people as well as selfhood (Illouz, 2007, p. 21). Affective user practices are quantified and remain subject to profit-oriented motives of measurement and control.

Personal viewing preferences, for instance, provide unique personally targeted advertising opportunities that Google can sell to corporations. YouTube viewing practices have been noted to mirror those of television audiences, with the difference that they do leave "material traces on the YouTube network, and this evidence of an attentive audience is essential to demonstrating the value of YouTube to advertisers" (Burgess, 2011, p. 327). Every user's interaction with the site leaves a trace in the YouTube database; this is an act of "implicit participation," as the tracing of users is built into the software design (Kessler & Schäfer, 2009, p. 285). Corporations pay to tap into YouTube's database of user profiles; this way they are able to individually target users with advertisement banners and commercial videos.

YouTube's orientation toward attracting a particular, more profitable, segment of users from around the globe also has its consequences. Infrastructure decisions and user preferences result in "hegemonic masculinity" (Hendrick & Lindgren, 2011, p. 165), and the cultural traits embedded in the platform reveal a distinct "Anglo-Western stance" (Pauwels & Hellriegel, 2009). Illustratively, Melissa Wall researched YouTube videos featuring the countries of Ghana and Kenya, exploring whether these videos might circulate alternative representations of African countries. She found several issues impact on the potential to subvert dominant Western gazes. Most of the content about Ghana and Kenya is posted by Western tourists, international aid agencies and Kenyans and Ghanaians who posted entertainment content. She found that historical inequalities are perpetuated on YouTube and those from the West remain dominant:

> YouTube enables the average westerner in particular to become a chronicler of other peoples in faraway lands just as travelers and missionaries

> "discovered" Africa in previous centuries. Most of these westerners, although not the official voices of the past, do not offer a remedy to the Othering of Africa. Indeed, many of their contributions to YouTube reinforce and naturalize stereotypes. (Wall, 2009, p. 405)

The YouTube structure and search algorithms also make user-generated videos more difficult to find in comparison with corporate, government or institutional videos that appear higher in search results rankings. This becomes apparent when considering the videos YouTube suggests to users as related with Morocco. After carrying out a search in the YouTube interface using the keyword "Morocco," the vast majority of videos coming up on the first page of results are not user-generated but videos uploaded by Western-oriented travel agencies, retail exporters, Western corporate news outlets, government institutions, and Western artists.[4] Although user-generated content is provided on the subsequent pages of search results, the order of results hurts the chances of user-generated views on Morocco being located by a wider audience, as "80 percent to 90 percent of browsers do not look beyond the first page of results after a search" (Levinson, 2007, p. 250). The promotion of nonuser-generated content is also the result of the search algorithm, which lists high-definition videos higher in the list of search results. However, beneath the surface of the profit-driven Anglo-Western stance, a heterogeneous user base exists that appropriate YouTube in ways that they seem fit (Pauwels & Hellriegel, 2009, p. 395).

User preferences do coshape YouTube, which is already clear when considering the platform started out as an online dating site. When the makers observed different than expected user behavior they repositioned the platform as a video repository. With this change, YouTube of course also sought to expand its market. Other examples of tactical behavior through which power exercised from the top down is resisted include circumventing

4 Illustratively, at the top and bottom of the first YouTube search results page, I was presented with "promoted videos" about "Group Tours and Tailor Made Trips" in Morocco by the company On the Go Tours. This company makes use of YouTube's "Promoted Video Ads," a service YouTube offers to boost user viewing counts making use of "keyword-based targeting" for video promotion to enable advertisers to reach more customers, "drive community engagement" and "engage with an audience" (Google, 2011, p. 1). To contextualize this result, I carried out an exploratory search using the YouTube search engine. I carried out a search with the keyword "Morocco," and this returned 26,800 results. The first page displayed twenty-six results, containing five corporate transportation-oriented videos, five non-Moroccan corporate news videos, five corporate videos by music artists, three travel organizations videos, two tourism board videos uploaded by the Moroccan government, one retail importer video, and one international festival video. This left four videos (or 15.4% of the total) on the first page of results that were possibly user-generated.

YouTube's policy that forbids hyperlinks outside of the site and providing mock descriptions and false information to resist direct-marketing techniques, to protest against its content as was the case in response to the publication of *Fitna* as described in the section above and to maintain one's individual privacy (Pauwels & Hellriegel, 2009, p. 389). The media-sharing practices of migrants show how they creatively work around standards and restrictions of the platform. For example, in 2009, the time limit for uploading videos was 10 minutes, and Turkish and Filipino migrants innovatively circumvented this restriction: "the uploading of Philippino or Turkish soap opera episodes, divided into pieces to get around YouTube's content limits, can be seen as acts of cultural citizenship" (Burgess & Green, 2009, p. 81). In the next section, I develop affect theory further to improve our understandings of the cultural politics of multilocational flows of migrants, digital media and feelings.

5.3 Theorizing affective geographies and YouTube use

> Mediation is the common way in which second or third generation diaspora tourists form attachment to their ancestral homeland. Their bond to that particular land is based on stories they had heard and photographs they had seen as opposed to first-hand experiences of the actual landscape.
>
> – Turan Hoffman (2014, p. 144)

In her analysis of Armenians touring eastern Turkey, Turan Hoffman argues that second- and third-generation Armenians who were born in the diaspora develop an affective sense of attachment to their homeland through mediation. Besides other axes of identification including gender, ethnicity and religion, she argues that "place attachment," provides a distinct window into diaspora identification: "group diaspora identity is usually based on their one enduring commonality – their homeland" (Turan Hoffman, 2014, p. 154). Affectivity is used here to address the ways in which YouTube videos showing places, people or objects on a computer screen may trigger certain responses in the body of a user. By being affected by watching a video, the emotional state of the user may change.

Most YouTube research has focused on video production (Burgess, 2011; Burgess & Green, 2009; Lange, 2014), I address a gap in the literature by focusing on how informants feel when viewing videos as members of an audience:

> [W]hile much popular and scholarly discourse imagines casual viewing of content as the lowest level of engagement, with creation as the highest level, perhaps it is time we took more seriously once again the question of the audience – asking what is involved in being an audience for user-created and user-distributed content, in media ecologies that also include television content, as in YouTube. (Burgess, 2011, p. 328)

Approaching YouTube viewers as audience members that actively engage with content, a focus on affectivity generates insights on what happens in between online content and user signification practices, a process that cannot be reduced solely to either meanings or bytes. Affectivity broadens the scope to consider how meaning making also involves embodied affective responses. Bringing into focus affectivity in the study of mediated communication is urgent, as prior scholarship in the field has too often relied on "sociological theories without heart" (Fortunati, 2009, p. 5).

The term "affect" is a translation from the Latin word "*affectus*," which can be understood as "passion," "emotion," or "desire" (Brennan, 2004, pp. 3-4). Building on Gilles Deleuze (1988), I understand affectivity as the process where bodies, spurred by interactions on screens, attain a different emotional state. Deleuze theorized affectivity by drawing out the relationships between images, corporality and emotional passages:

> [T]hese image affections or ideas form a certain state of the affected body and mind, which implies more or less perfection than the preceding state. Therefore, from one state to another, from one image or idea to another, there are transitions, passages that are experienced, durations through which we pass to a greater or a lesser perfection. (1988, p. 48)

Affectivity concerns a passage in a body's experiential state, while emotion concerns how that passage is made meaningful through one's biographical experiences (Jones, Jackson & Rhys-Taylor, 2014). Sara Ahmed theorized the cultural politics of affectivity, as processes that "work on and in relation to bodies" (Ahmed 2004, 194). She argued that affectivity is produced through "circulation," "accumulation" and "endurance" (2004, pp. 45, 46, 91). The question arises, How we can understand affectivity in relation to digital practices? Affect works as an evaluative orientation, a judgment accompanied by a "physiological shift," such as a growth of intensity, attention or attachment. Affectivity can be coded in signs that can be "transmitted" from one person to another (Brennan, 2004, pp. 5-6). As a database of coded signs, YouTube can be considered "an archive of feelings," a repository of mediated sensations that "are encoded not only in the content of the texts themselves but in the practices that surround their production and reception" (Cvetkovich, 2003, p. 7). Signs do not causally determine a feeling, but the affective relationship of an individual with particular signs can make them matter. Affect theory has been used to understand user experiences of online pornography: people may develop a "fondness for specific images" that result in particular sensory effects (Paasonen, 2010, p. 58). Other studies show that the affective pleasures of women's diary blog reading may emerge from gender, age, race, and education-based "sameness" and "recognition" (Karlsson 2007, 138).

Using these insights in combination with Ahmed's conceptualization of affect (2004), I argue the production of affectivity arising from viewing YouTube videos can be analyzed by disentangling three interrelated processes: (1) "circulation": sensations are encoded by people producing audiovisual texts, these texts flow through digital networks, and they are decoded and viscerally experienced by audience members, (2) "accumulation": the affective response to certain videos may grow through repetitious viewing and (3) "endurance": affective responses may stick with audience members. In this way, in contrast to earlier utopian beliefs on the disembodied workings of cyberspace, theories of affectivity readdress relations between phenomenology and technology, semiotics and materiality, and the body and the mind. In particular, I explore the ways in which young migrant subjects are moved by videos as they sense connections and disconnections with people and places across distances.

Media users share their audiencehood with an "imagined community" of fellow audience members, and this relation may span wide geographical distances (Anderson, 1983). The notion of "transnational affect" was developed to understand how affectivity coshapes practices of transnational belonging among migrants (Wise & Velayutham, 2006). Wise and Velayutham describe transnational affectivity as a "circulation of bodily emotive affect between transnational subjects and between subjects and symbolic fields which give qualitative intensity to vectors and routes thus reproducing belonging to, and boundaries of, transnational fields" (2006, p. 3). Their examples focus on the offline world and include moral economies of shame and pride, symbolic identification and belonging. Online, migrants are known to digitally construct "mobile networks of belonging" (Diminescu, 2008, p. 574). When migrant subjects take up technologies like YouTube to watch videos shot in their homeland and elsewhere, they can develop an attachment to multiple geographical locations.

YouTube allows for the circulation of affective diaspora attachments. For example, Matteo Vergani and Dennis Zuev observed two ways YouTube is used among the Uyghur people, a Muslim minority population in northwest China (2011). Music is shared among the group for the purpose of diaspora identification and entertainment. However, after the September 11, 2001, attacks in the United States, mainstream Chinese news reporting about Uyghurs changed from "Uyghur separatists" to "Muslim terrorists." Sharing and viewing Uyghur-themed YouTube videos became politicized. Uyghur videos were found to play two roles: they are consumed in ways that establish "spatial togetherness" as a form of "transnational loyalty" by linking together members of the community, and at the same time they insert alternative representations into the public domain, "broadcasting a positive image of the Uyghurs to a wide audience" (2011, pp. 1, pp. 227-228). The circulation of transnational loyalty through videos among Uyghurs in the diaspora can be understood as an example of transnational affectivity. Transnational affectivity generated through digital practices may be highly valued among migrants, as it potentially offers the means to regain a sense of stable self-identity and "ontological security" (Giddens, 1990). The positive feelings migrants may get by engaging with "happy objects" (Ahmed, 2010) such as diasporic videos can be recognized as a form of "transnational affective capital" (Leurs, 2014a, pp. 89-92). Good feelings, as triggered by digital practices, for example, may become one of the scarce forms of capital available to migrants to tap into to cope with difficulties of living an often precarious life.

However, singling out transnational affectivity would leave crucial additional networks of belonging untouched. Prior research on migration has demonstrated that identifications among subjects in the diaspora are not purely geared toward transnational migratory orientations. In the introduction I already drew on Paul Gilroy and Stuart Hall to unpack different dimensions to belonging and expand the focus from transnational ties toward traversal imaginaries, multilocality, circulation and hybriditization. Two positions of cultural identification were distinguished. On the one hand, affiliations with one's "roots" concern those feelings of connection with people, artifacts, representations and ideas pertaining to where migrants imagine to be coming from (Gilroy, 1993a). On the other hand, the concept of "routes" acknowledges the active process of cultural identification, acknowledging ongoing dynamic positioning and active encounters with contemporary influences (Gilroy, 1993a). Oriented toward the future it sees belongings also as a "matter of 'becoming'" (Hall 1990, p. 225). Connecting these theories with affective geographies of belonging, it is similarly important to distinguish between the ways in which "emotions show us how histories stay alive" and how feelings "also open up futures, in the ways they involve different orientations to others" (Ahmed, 2004, p. 202). Therefore, in the empirical analysis (Sections 4 and 5 below) I report how migrant youth as YouTube audience members feel connectedness to multiple places and people. In particular, I explore the affectivity of rooted and routed belonging, respectively.

5.4 Rooted belongings: Transnational affectivity

This section focuses on the use of YouTube among the informants for continuous orientation on migratory homelands and "rootedness" (Gilroy, 1993a). The affective search for rootedness emerged as a theme when analyzing the ways in which the informants spoke about user-generated YouTube videos shot in Morocco. Moroccan-Dutch youth shared feeling "*less homesick*," "*emotional*" and "*nostalgic*" from watching videos shot in Morocco. Stuart Hall described rooted cultural identification as a way to maintain membership and belonging to a community of "one people" (1990, p. 223). Identifying with a territory, "roots signify emotional bonds with the physical environment" (Gustafson, 2001, p. 670). In line with this definition, feelings of rootedness can be said to provide a sense of a cohesive collectivity, an "anchor point" (Stock, 2014, p. 175) beyond the constraints of time and space. By exploring the links between affective community and transnational affectivity, videos shot in Morocco can be said to operate in two ways: diasporic home making in response to feeling Othered and nostalgic desires for shared cultural codes and feelings.

For example, thirteen-year-old Anas brought up the video *Marrakech, Morocco City Drive* (see Figure 20). He spoke about watching the video before he went on holidays to Marrakech, the city where his parents were born. *Marrakech, Morocco City Drive* was made by the Moroccan-American adult male YouTube user eMoroccan. He shot the video with a digital handheld camera from a moving car on Avenue Mohammed V in Marrakech. The video was shot from a first-person point of view and consists of one single take of 78 seconds. Only synchronous, diegetic sounds are audible; besides the engine of the car the filmmaker is driving in, noise of a passing motorcycle and birds chirping in the palm trees the car passes can be heard. The first-person perspective adds to Anas's feeling of being able to immerse himself in the scene. In the video, following the single trajectory of the road, the viewer gradually approaches the city's fortifications. Although in the

Fig. 20: Still from *Marrakech, Morocco City Drive*, YouTube video uploaded by eMoroccan (October 8, 2010)

distance the Koutoubia Mosque is featured, the video mostly shows the journey of driving through the streets of Marrakech. Various elements in the video are familiar to Anas. Seeing these familiarities may "accumulate" value and "stick" a sense of transnational affection to the video (Ahmed, 2004, p. 91), which in turn may strengthen Anas's symbolic attachment to the city.

> *I looked up the YouTube video* Marrakech, Morocco City Drive. *A while back I was really looking forward to the holidays and by coincidence I spotted that clip on YouTube. I had not been to Morocco for some time back then. That's why I looked up some videos. With the two of them they are in a car, and they film the city. I recognized many things; I saw all the famous things in my city.* (Anas, thirteen years old)

Nostalgia and homeland are central notions in migration studies. In migrant literature, the "poetics of home" operate as symbols for stability, belonging and safety (Buikema, 2005, p. 168). Home-making practices are organized around patterns of inclusion and exclusion. Homelands are exclusive, and therefore they establish difference. Home, next to axes such as gender, sexuality and class, "acts as an ideological determinant of the subject"

(George, 1999, p. 2). Home-making concerns the human desires all humans share: boundedness, stability and belonging. People long to belong.

Another participant, fifteen-year-old Meryam, expresses how she imagines Morocco: "*You think of the country like I would want to stay there forever, because, yeah, my parents are from there, and a piece of it is in you.*" For members of diasporic communities, longing for home concerns feelings of having a safe place elsewhere in the world. Feeling able to occupy a welcoming location, in the presence of significant likeminded others, it concerns an individual as well as collective idea based on ideas of origins. "As an idea it [a home] stands for shelter, stability, security and comfort" (McLeod, 2000, p. 210). And for the informants, this idea may be based on feelings of connectedness with the house and areas where they or their parents grew up. Watching YouTube videos, second-generation migrant youth, born in the diaspora, heavily rely on such mediations to affectively construct a sense of homeland.

Diasporic videos can be consumed as symbolic anchors of migratory affiliations. For Moroccan-Dutch youth, apart from stories told by their parents and their holidays, YouTube is one of the few other ways to experience Morocco. Abdelsammad, a fifteen-year-old boy, who migrated to the Netherlands at young age, explained this dynamic as follows:

> *I watch movies about where we come from. On YouTube there are movies about where we lived, that is nice to see. There is much to find about Nador. Many, many movies. For instance, clips that show the roads, the shopping malls, the boulevard. Lots of things that you are familiar with. I was born there and lived there until I was three years old, but I know it better from holidays. [Moroccan-Dutch] people from the Netherlands, who go there on holidays, when they get back they put the video they took there online.*

eMoroccan, a Moroccan-American adult male, is a major producer of the genre of videos that Abdelsammad and other informants takes pleasure in. With over 400,000 people having viewed one of his thirty-nine movies, eMoroccan plays a key role in producing videos and "circulating" transnational affectivity (Ahmed, 2004, p. 60) for Moroccans in the diaspora. His videos include *Athan (Call to Prayer) in Morocco*; *Autoroutes du Maroc*; *Casablanca Street View*; *Agadir Morocco: Entering City*; *Hassan II Mosque*; *Landing in Morocco onboard Royal Air Maroc*; *Marina Agadir*; *Traditional Berber Folklore Music*. His main aim is welcoming YouTube users to "virtual Morocco." In an interview conducted via YouTube's personal messaging system, I invited eMoroccan to describe his motivations for sharing videos shot in Morocco:

> *A common theme among Moroccans living abroad is their continual attachment to their country* (l'blad) *and their hometowns. Some have been living abroad for years and haven't been able to return to Morocco due to several reasons. I wanted to create a virtual outlet for these individuals so that they may experience Morocco visually and hopefully fill some void. But I also enjoy making videos in general and have a keen interest in Morocco. By using the Internet a Moroccan individual becomes an "eMoroccan" who can experience "virtual Morocco."*

The video producer eMoroccan touches upon the issue of user-generated video being consumed by people in the Moroccan diaspora as a way to connect to their homeland, literally "visually experiencing" the country when physical travel is unattainable. YouTube allows Moroccans living abroad the means to become "eMoroccans." Watching videos such *Landing in Morocco onboard Royal Air Maroc* provide Moroccans living in the diaspora an opportunity to relive prior experiences they had traveling to their homeland. "Accumulating" value in the body of viewers (Ahmed, 2014, p. 91), these videos may prompt affective transnational belongings; making digital visits to Morocco users can become "electronic Moroccans." Such diasporic videos can be recognized as a separate YouTube video genre, with their particular subject and aesthetic choices. The topical preference and aesthetics most likely appeal to those in the diaspora more than Western tourists, for example. eMoroccan's videos do not conform to the mainstream tourist imagery of beaches, handicraft markets, camels and exotic desert oases, and people who do not share the habitus of migration will thus experience these videos very differently.

Moroccan diasporic videos, mostly filmed with camera-phones and hand-held digital cameras, generally include low resolution, unedited shots taken while flying, in the train or driving around the country in cars showing the roads, traffic in all its variety, cities and towns and seemingly random living areas and structures. Usually, no sound is added; viewers overhear people speaking in the taxi or airplane interspersed with the noises of traffic and car engines. Videos generally include scenes taken from everyday life that can have an important social meaning for migrants. The main tourist highlights of sandy beaches, palm trees, museums, luxury and splendor are not necessarily the main focus points in these pieces.

During the interviews, informants explicitly mentioned turning to YouTube when they felt "*heimwee*" – the Dutch word for homesickness or nostalgia. Videos shot in Morocco helped them to combat feelings of homesickness. Fourteen-year-old Kenza shared that she highly values YouTube in order to look up videos that make her think about Morocco "*because sometimes I do get quite strongly filled with a feeling of nostalgia, because I'm missing Morocco.*" Watching videos such as *Marrakech, Morocco City Drive* has affective nostalgic workings, as physiological shifts take place in the bodies of the viewers – the videos make these migrant youth feel better.

Johannes Hofer coined the word "nostalgia" in a medical dissertation to describe sad moods that can arise from desires to go back to one's native land. The word "nostalgia" combines two words with Greek roots, "*nostos*," meaning "homesickness" or "returning home" and "*algia*," meaning "longing" or "pain." Nostalgia now stands for "a longing for a home that no longer exists or has never existed. Nostalgia is a sentiment of loss and displacement, but it is also a romance with one's own fantasy" (Boym, 2001; pp. xiii, 3). Feelings of nostalgia can become especially pertinent among descendants of those who have migrated who were born in the diaspora: "first-wave immigrants are often notoriously unsentimental, leaving the search for roots to their children and grandchildren" (ibid., p. xv). Looking up videos shot in Morocco evoke feelings of happiness in second-generation informants, and this practice illustrates how this particular form of transnational affectivity shapes a generationally specific "transnational habitus" (Nedelcu, 2012).

The specific materialities of the videos are valued among diasporic youth as they encode and circulate nostalgia. Similarly, Hamid Naficy found that Iranian migrants living in exile enjoy Iranian music videos that show everyday life on the streets and bazaars because of their "live ontology" that create an alluring "reality effect" (1998, p. 58). Consisting of low-resolution, unedited, single camera position shots, without the addition of nondiegetic sounds and music, the videos construct a sense of authenticity. The viewer can follow the footsteps of the video producer who has been present in the filmed location. These features serve as reminders that filmmaker and camera were actually present in Morocco and bestow these videos with authenticity, trustworthiness and power as emotionally touching, transnational diaspora objects carrying a sense of subjectivity-in-place.

Nostalgia may be conceived of as a return to one's origins or as an escape from the multicultural tensions of one's host country. For those migrants disenchanted with aspects of their surroundings, many find in nostalgia an escape to a temporary secure place of oppositional belonging: "nostalgic communication provides individuals with a means of symbolically escaping cultural conditions that they find depressing and/or disorienting." In this way nostalgia can be experienced as "a sanctuary of meaning," as migrants may sense being "safe from oppressive cultural conditions" (Aden, 1995, 35). Nostalgic diasporic affinity provides informants with a temporary escape to the sanctuary of an affective, imagined community. When she misses Morocco and feels "*nostalgic*," Kenza explained, she looks up amateur videos shot in Morocco, music videos of Moroccan artists, and also sometimes watches highlights of the national Moroccan football. After feeling down, she adds viewing such videos make her feel "*happy*" again (see Ahmed, 2010). Fourteen-year-old Ayoub mentions he lifts his mood by looking up videos in which his Moroccan dialect is spoken: "*Most often I watch funny videos in Berber, my own language.*" Similarly, Sixteen-year-old Nevra noted user-generated videos make her "*go back*" to Morocco in her mind. As members of an imagined wider audience, interviewees experience a sense of belonging and feelings of reassurance they are not left on their own.

Holiday travel and thinking back about the good times spent on the Moroccan beaches or in the mountains may work as a coping mechanism to deal with the polarizing tensions in Dutch society. Traveling to Morocco entails going about daily life without being constantly singled out as someone who is Moroccan-Dutch or Muslim (Meijerink, 2009, pp. 64-68). Fifteen-year-old Ryan describes that his parents were born in the low-profile coastal city of Kenitra, however he adds that "*we do not often go there* [*to Kenitra*]. *When we go on holidays we go to other places* [*in Morocco*], *where the nature is beautiful, in the mountain areas and so on.*" In this case holiday travel is adjusted to meet a desired exoticized imagination of one's homeland, rather than an actual, historical homeland. Fourteen-year-old Badr shared that he enjoys visiting Morocco, "*but only for two or three weeks. After that I want to go back, because I'm more used to being here*" in the Netherlands. Back in the Netherlands, Badr shared that he wants to hold on to the images of his holiday experiences, for instance, by posting pictures on his personal social networking site profile page. In the utopian fantasies of their homeland, informants can imagine commonality with inhabitants of Morocco and their everyday life, however, once they are traveling there, nostalgic imaginings of their Moroccan "*home*" may prove to differ greatly from the everyday realities on the ground.

Imagined dreamscapes serve to construct many different "*Moroccos of the mind*," using eMoroccans terminology. Fourteen-year-old Mehmet Ali, who was born in Nador but migrated to the Netherlands at the age of four, reveals the double-sidedness of nostalgic affectivity. On the one hand he emphasizes that while in the Netherlands he misses being in Morocco: "*You miss everything that's there.*" Watching YouTube videos with images of the homeland helps him alleviate such feelings. While the experience of visiting Morocco and being in Nador during the holidays differs from his fantasy of home that may have been sustained through watching videos: "*It is really,*

really hot most of the time, and busy, very, very busy in the city." Everyday realities can differ from the affective nostalgic sanctuary. Nostalgic longings may continue to "haunt" diasporic subjects (Naficy, 1998, p. 58). Among the second-generation, the location of one's roots becomes "a home to refer to rather than a place to live" (Stock, 2014, p. 175).

Finally, ethnic outsiders can also perceive virtual tourism to Morocco on YouTube as a threat. The sanctuary of transnational affectivity is not safe from disruption from outsiders who might feel excluded by material they perceive as different. Upon encountering vernacular diaspora video, outsiders might not understand the content or aim of the video. As Wise and Velayutham noted, transnational affectivity may produce boundaries (2006, p. 3) and videos shot in Morocco can operate as inclusionary and exclusionary mechanisms. Interviewees share how flaming and trolling, as acts of hostility, can abruptly punctuate nostalgic feelings. Sixteen-year-old Naoul reports, "*They shout 'Moroccan cunts'*" in the YouTube comment sections while fourteen-year-old Ayoub notes that "*similar to how some people give me a dirty look outdoors, under videos dealing with Morocco, they write 'Get out of the country' and so on. It does not really bother me; there is not much I can do.*" Notwithstanding, as the informants are being touched by vernacular videos of nostalgia, transnational affectivity enables them to renew and reimagine bonds with their diasporic identities. In the next section, I shift my attention from videos shot in Morocco toward music videos.

5.5 Routed affective belongings across geographies

Next to watching videos spurring affective "rooted" geographical referentialities, informants engaged in viewing practices that indicate affective connections with global youth cultural orientations or "routes." The concept of "routes" acknowledges dynamic positioning and active encounter (Gilroy, 1993a). YouTube is a preferred space to access music for the majority of the informants. From the forty-three interviewees, twenty-five young people mentioned they visit the platform mainly to watch and listen to music videos. With the advent of YouTube, and its growing database of (often pirated) music videos that can be played on demand, music videos have become easily accessible. YouTube music videos become affective "landing points" of youth cultural texts. These may be a source of agency for young people, allowing them to redefine who they are and with whom they want to affectively affiliate. These landing points allow young people to individually attribute value and position themselves in affective relations with others

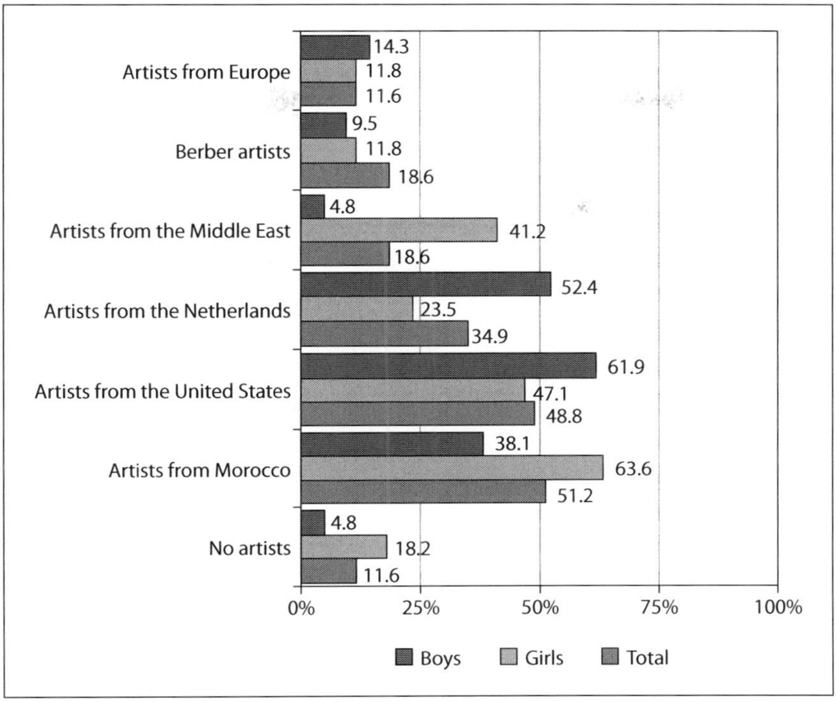

Diagram 11: Geographical locations of music artists interviewees look up on YouTube (percentages, multiple answers possible, n = 43)

by grounding YouTube videos as resources for the negotiation of "identities and relationships" (Androutsopoulos, 2010, pp. 204-206). YouTube, as a repository of "circulating" sensations (Ahmed, 2004, p. 60), becomes politically meaningful when considering young migrants' cosmopolitan viewer practices that span across nations.

Interviewees usually employed language-specific and geographic labels when asked to describe their music video-viewing practices. For example, they used categories such as "American," "Moroccan," "Dutch" and "Turkish" when describing the music videos of their favorite artists.

Diagram 11 provides an overview of all the geographic locations of the music artists the interviewees mentioned. More than half of the informants – in particular, two-thirds of the young women – watch videos of Moroccan artists. These videos may also spur feelings of nostalgia. Fourteen-year-old Ziham explains "*Most of the time I listen to Moroccan music. I prefer that sort, especially Mohamed Sami, Morad Salam, Laila Chakir and Amazrine. They sing about love stories.*" Fourteen-year-old Mehmet Ali discusses his inclination toward looking up Moroccan videos: "*Most often I look up Moroccan songs.*" The artists sing "*about love, about the country Morocco itself, about its cities and its history, by artists that are famous in Morocco.*" CDs of these artists are difficult to find in shops in the Netherlands.

Amir shared that consuming music videos of two Moroccan rap groups gives him a feeling of being unique, as it is an original way to stand out from others: "*I listen to H-Kayne and Fnaïre, these are two Moroccan rap groups. They only have shows in Morocco, and they rap in Arabic. They are famous in Morocco. I haven't heard anything about them here*" in the Netherlands. H-Kayne and Fnaïre are rap crews who create music that is not part of the mainstream global circuits of youth culture (yet), and these groups have not been embraced by most fellow Moroccan-Dutch youth. Knowing these groups gives Amir a sense of being special. Providing status and admiration, this knowledge is a form of "subcultural capital" (Jensen, 2006, p. 263) that allows him to mark out his individuality as he discovered their music while on holidays in Marrakech, the city where his parents where born. These connections are suggestive of the ways in which the affective practices of music video and "*real video*" consumption are interwoven.

Showing his affinity with American forms of youth culture, Sixteen-year-old Ryan prefers to listen to international, English-language music: "*Dutch music, for instance, I find it so boring, I always fall asleep listening to it. Moroccan music I also don't really like – as a matter of fact I like only English, international music.*" Ryan's self-positioning and musical preference is indicative for a belonging that goes beyond the nation and diaspora. Thirteen-year-old Inas is a devout Muslim, and during our interview she highlighted she's also a "Belieber." She shared her attachment to international youth icon Justin Bieber, while beginning to giggle she said, "*Justin Bieber, I like him. Just to watch videos of him, yes him especially.*" To download his songs from YouTube to her Samsung Wave mobile phone she uses the website YoutubeConverter.org. Engaging with Justin Bieber music videos she becomes part of the global affective youth cultural community of fellow Justin Bieber fans ('Beliebers'), a fan-base that consists mostly of young women. Next to artists from Morocco, and the United States, Inas and other young women prefer videos from artists hailing from countries in the Middle East and the Netherlands. Next to artists from the United States, young men preferred music videos that feature artists from the Netherlands, from Morocco and to a small extent other countries in Europe. However, singling out emotional attachment to artists from one of these geographical locations does not do justice to the multigeographical complexity of the informants' favorite music videos. Affective belongings are both transnationally rooted as well as routed across global youth cultures.

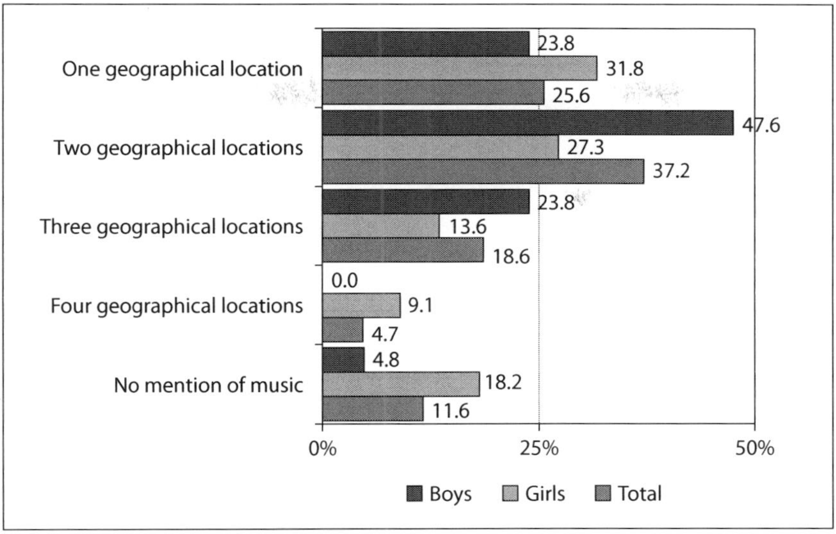

Diagram 12: Geographical locations of artists interviewees combine in their YouTube viewing practices (percentages, n = 43)

As Diagram 12 shows, the affective belonging to singular geographical locations is observable among one-fourth of the interviewees who reported looking up music videos from recording artists coming mainly from one geographical location. This includes looking up videos by artists from either Morocco or the US that were considered in the prior section. However, the viewing preferences of the majority of the informants surpass the singular. The group that views only music by artists from one of the above-mentioned geographical locations is smaller than the group of informants who turn to YouTube to listen to music by artists from at least two different geographical locations. Moreover, almost one out of every four interviewees reported listening to artists from three or more areas across the world. For instance, fifteen-year-old Hajar told me, "*I listen to all sorts of things, Moroccan and English. Just a mix of all these things.*"

Sixteen-year-old Bibi mentions her favorite artists are from four different locations across the world. Her description is indicative for attachments to a multiplicity of geographical affinities:

> *I'm addicted to the new song by Rihanna, "What's My Name" or something like that. I'm fully hooked on Drake, I listen to him 24 hours [a day]. Other artists are [Moroccan], such as Daoudi or Douzi or Sabah and Rola, you know, from "Yana yana," from Mourad Salam, from Laila Chakir. Just those really famous artists.*

A variety of affiliations are combined. Rihanna is an American R&B artist from Barbados, while Drake is a Canadian rapper of mixed African-American and Jewish descent. Both sing in English. Daoudi is a *shaabi* musician singing in Darija (Moroccan-Arabic). The genre *shaabi* (Arabic for "of the people") concerns popular Moroccan folk music that may give rise to feelings of nostalgia. Douzi is a Moroccan rapper singing in English and Darija, and he collaborates with the Moroccan-Dutch rapper Appa. Sabah and Rola are Lebanese singers singing in Arabic, while Mourad Salam and Laila Chakir sing in Berber. Bibi thus signaled affective relations with different geographies and groups of people. She combines Berber, North American, Middle-Eastern and Dutch artists, English, Darija, Arabic and Dutch languages, genres of R&B, *shaabi* and rap. Bibi moves beyond singular affective attachments to either nationalism or diaspora affiliation, her preferences bring together different geographies, languages and genres. Watching these videos and negotiating multilocational landing points can be understood as a form of banal cosmopolitanism demonstrating how migrant youth make the cosmopolitan "passage from place-monogamous to place-polygamous ways of living" (Beck, 2000, pp. 74-75).

Illustratively, sixteen-year-old Amir argued that his attachments go beyond singular notions of affective group belonging:

> *I just have my own style, I think. I don't belong to any group. Everyone is different. [People say] one person is Turkish, another is Moroccan and yet another is Dutch, but for me it's not like that. It's not really like I [fit] into one particular group. It's more multiculti, I think.*

Multilocational engagements across geographies provide a glimpse at the layered affective identity construction beyond expectations of narrowly defined, stereotypical Moroccan-Dutch identities. Consider Inas, for example, a thirteen-year-old young woman who feels strongly about covering her hair in public and also strongly values Justin Bieber music videos. In contrast to dominant stereotypes, these two affiliations are not mutually exclusive. Her affective engagement with global girl culture does not meet the expectations of dominant stereotypical Orientalist discourses of headscarf-wearing Muslim women as backward and/or oppressed (Said, 1979; Piela, 2012). Furthermore, YouTube music video consumption may counter ethnic absolutism, as it is in the consumption of music from different youth cultural scenes that young people of various backgrounds – as geographically dispersed members of a global cosmopolitan imagined audience – can convivially connect (Gilroy, 2005).

5.6 Conclusions

In this chapter, an affective optic on digital videos was developed to shed light on how digital practices implicate an active reembodiment of the user across online and offline geographies. YouTube videos were analyzed to "circulate," "accumulate" and "stick" affective value (Ahmed, 2004). Understanding affectivity as the potential of digital media artifacts to alter the emotional states of user bodies, I focused on how video viewing by Moroccan-Dutch youth enables affective belongings across geographies. In particular, I explored how these second-generation migrant youth dialogically negotiate the horizons of homeland, host country and youth culture as audience members watching YouTube videos. Videos may provide an alternative but contested location of familiarity for Moroccan-Dutch young people to work through their feelings.

The focus was on transnational "rooted" and the multilocational geographies of "routed" belongings (Gilroy, 1993a). As most informants were born in the diaspora, Morocco is mostly a virtual entity; second-generation migrant youth experience their homeland mostly through mediation. Viewing diasporic user-generated content shot in Morocco was understood to produce transnational affectivity, these sensations were argued to foster mediated home-making and nostalgic belonging. Watching music videos of recording artists coming from cross-national locations, informants land youth cultural material as a source for hybridity and multiplicity. As a form of micro-politics, the affective belongings of Moroccan-Dutch youth in their viewing of wide-ranging music videos are multilocational and show cosmopolitan sensibilities. Sustaining abstract theories on the ordinariness of multiculture and "vernacular cosmopolitanism" (Werbner, 2006), engaging with these videos implies the informants show an open disposition toward cultural difference. They counter ethnic absolutism and nationalism by affectively belonging across different geographies.

Conclusions

By making a cartography of identity performativity across Internet applications, I have detailed how relationships between diaspora, gender, youth culture and digital media are articulated in the specific case of second-generation Moroccan-Dutch youth in the Netherlands. With the title of this book, *Digital Passages*, I drew an analogy between mid-nineteenth-century arcades or commercial passageways that were developed in European cities like Bologna, Brussels and Paris and early-twenty-first-century Internet applications like discussion forums, instant messaging, YouTube and Facebook. In the words of Walter Benjamin, arcades were "the most important architecture of the nineteenth century" (1999, p. 834). Nowadays, digital platforms play a fundamental role in the daily lives of millions of people. Benjamin recognized that passageways had an ambivalent meaning; they captured collective utopian and dystopian views. New in their era, they offered pleasure by promising "a new world" of safe urban excitement, however passages also implied oppression by their promotion of commodity fetishism (1999, pp. 637, 939, 943). Passages played a double-faced role, which Benjamin explained with the following example: "During sudden rainshowers, the arcades are a place of refuge for the unprepared, to whom they offer a secure, if restricted, promenade – one from which the merchants also benefit" (1999, p. 31). Neither skepticism nor evangelism fully captured the dynamics of arcades fully, and Benjamin pleaded to consider them as a "constellation saturated of tensions" (1999, p. 475).

A passage was seen as a miniature world (Benjamin, 1999, p. 32). Not only was it a new space where commodities were exchanged, but it also became a comfortable urban environment where people could find shelter from rainy weather, observe others, do window-shopping, stroll around and spend their time in an enjoyable way. In this study I considered digital platforms as present-day arcades. They offer their users an enjoyable miniature world, one that at times works as a shelter from undesired external circumstances. Digital spaces offer users a chance to enjoy themselves, observe other people and do some (window) shopping. They are not public domains; they serve private interests and they have been developed to make profit. As digitized passageways, Internet applications offer advertisers a chance to market their products and monitor consumer preferences. Digital spaces have become "walled gardens" (Zittrain, 2008) that, similar to offline arcades, concentrate commercial establishments in a single-bordered space.

In tandem with the ambivalent meanings of arcades, scholars have either applauded Internet applications as utopian, inclusionary and participatory spaces of disembodiment or criticized them for their profit-oriented and exclusionary character. These extreme perspectives, however, cannot fully capture the dynamics of digital space. Building on transdisciplinary theories of new media, postcolonial and gender studies I therefore developed a middle-ground perspective by combining medium-specific analysis with a commitment to political engagement and social justice. I argued that identity performativity in digital space revolves around a complex process of material, representational and affective interactions. The in-between position I advanced is attuned to the mutual constitution of identity and technology in everyday, situated, and power-laden medium-specific contexts. Invisible to those who meet their requirements, each field site was found to reserve certain dominant gendered, ethnic, age-specific positions and mainstream users reinforce those habituated dispositions. Such a platform-specific habitus restricts but does not fully determines user behavior.

When having to assert themselves against the grain, users become invaders of online territories. I developed the optic of space invaders to empirically trace and theorize digital spatial biases and their subversion but also to intervene in dominant thinking about digital media potentialities. With the notion of digital passages, I referred, however, not only to the navigation of Moroccan-Dutch youth across demarcated digital spaces, but also sought to capture their digital identity formation processes at the interstices of online and offline relations that included coming-of-age, rites of passage and the generational-specific negotiation of gendered, diaspora, religious and youth cultural expectations. These processes were shown to revolve around a politics of hybridization in which multiple minority and majority legacies, belongings and loyalties were enacted. As a process of subversion from below, their participation can be taken to refute emerging views of failed multiculturalism and ethnic segregation.

I have empirically sustained my arguments by innovatively bringing together a variety of data-gathering approaches. The extensive fieldwork combined surveys, qualitative in-depth interviews and virtual ethnography. The fieldwork took place in the context of Wired Up, an international, collaborative research project that brought together scholars from the humanities and social sciences to critically explore the multifarious implications of digital media use among migrant youth. The computer-based survey was developed together with other researchers in the project. A total of 1,408 young people, contacted through seven secondary schools in five Dutch cities, completed the questionnaire in classrooms or computer labs. The central database of their answers, shared among Wired Up researchers, was used in this study to get a general impression of digital media use frequencies, attachments to platforms and online self-presentation practices. Furthermore in-depth interviews were carried out with a group of forty-three young Moroccan-Dutch individuals consisting of twenty-one girls and twenty-two boys. In order to ground the study in a broader context, I also spoke with Moroccan-Dutch parents, website founders, moderators and artists. During the virtual ethnography, digital narratives of self were gathered, archived and analyzed.

From the survey findings, interviews and Internet maps I learned that Moroccan-Dutch youth consider online discussion forums, instant messaging (IM), online social networking sites (SNSs) and YouTube the most important platforms. These four field sites were studied on a case study basis. Although digital culture is in constant flux, which is obvious when considering the demise of MSN and Hyves, the analytical framework and insights generated on the basis of the different field sites are transferable to consider other recent platforms including What's App, Twitter, Snapchat, Instagram and Ello, to name a few. In the case studies I have achieved a complex variety of layered insights.

In this concluding chapter I bring these different insights together in order to revisit my main research question: How do Moroccan-Dutch youth participate in and appropriate digital spaces in order to convey their belongings across multiple axes of identification such as gender, sexuality, diaspora, religion, generation and youth culture? In the following, I first consider the theoretical and methodological issues I encountered and tackled. In Section 1, I address the ways in which new media, gender and postcolonial theory worked together to unearth the complex dynamics of digital identity performativity. In Section 2, I describe how I have produced new knowledge on digital identity construction in my creative collision of methodological approaches from the humanities and social sciences. In Section 3, I discuss how offline exclusionary mechanisms such as gender, ethnic, religious and age-based norms travel online, structure digital spaces and create new digital divides. In Section 4, I reflect on the implications of space invader tactics that Moroccan-Dutch youth employ to cope with digital forms of inequality.

1. Transdisciplinary dialogues

My transdisciplinary journey through different fields of critical inquiry assisted me to select a specific focus and acknowledge the contestedness and multilayeredness of identity performativity and belonging in digital space. Now it is time to take stock of how this research speaks to those fields

I have tapped into. Rather than moving beyond or against disciplines, I take transdisciplinarity to denote a reflexive discussion of an interdisciplinary research endeavor (Lykke, 2011). By virtue of its transdisciplinary approach, this study touches on various debates across multiple disciplines, and in the following I reflect on the relevance my journey may have for different disciplines. Therefore, I consider what the study does – in terms of issues that can now be addressed – for the fields of new media, gender and postcolonial studies, migration and transnationalism, religion, media and communication studies, cyber feminism, studies of girlhood and studies on the Moroccan-Dutch community in particular. Also I point out possible future points of inquiry.

In theoretically staking out and empirically sustaining a position between utopian and dystopian perspectives on digital embodiment and identity, I brought new media studies, feminist technoscience and postcolonial theory into dialogue. Gender and postcolonial theories allowed me to be attentive to social injustices, the reproduction of gendered, ethnic and religious unevenness as well as agency and empowerment across the various field sites. New media studies allowed me to anchor the ways in which medium-specific characteristics coconstruct identity performativity and a platform-specific habitus. Studying medium-specific practices and experiences as spatial power relations, I positioned myself in the "spatial turn" that is finding resonance across the humanities and social sciences (Shome, 2003; Soja, 2010; Warf & Arias, 2009). A focus on space also brings out the potential of combining gender, postcolonial and new media studies. Combining them culminated in my extending of the notion of space invaders to empirically map out, conceptually reflect on and transform digital spatial hierarchies (Puwar, 2004).

This contribution contributes to the broader ongoing shift toward de-Westernization and internationalization in media and Internet studies (Thussu, 2009; Goggin & McLelland, 2009). In particular, it presents a timely contribution to the fields of communication, media and migration studies, given the recent growing interest in digital diasporas. A number of monographs, anthologies and special issues on the topic have recently been published (e.g., Fortunati, Pertierra & Vincent, 2012; Ponzanesi & Leurs, 2014; Madianou & Miller, 2012; Oiarzabal, 2013; Trandafoiu, 2013) and the number of panels addressing diaspora, migration and media use is rapidly growing in conferences such as the European Communication Research and Education Association (ECREA), the International Association for Media and Communication Research (IAMCR), the International Communication Association (ICA), and the International Migration, Integration and Social Cohesion network (IMISCOE). However, even though there have been calls for the "establishment of a European Research Area on ICT and migrations" (Borkert, Cingolani & Premazzi, 2009, 25), there remains "a dearth of nuanced research on digital diasporas in Europe" (Ponzanesi & Leurs, 2014, p. 11).

The study adds to prior scholarship on information and communication technologies (ICTs) use in the field of migration studies and transnationalism by focusing mostly on the digital performativity of identity of European second-generation migrant youth. The specific situation of the generation of young people born in the diaspora – descendants of those who have migrated – demands more attention (Wessendorfer, 2013), and especially their digital media use has been largely left unaddressed (Green & Kabir, 2012). Earlier work has shed light on how migrants use ICTs for transnational communication purposes with people in their country of origin (e.g., Georgiou, 2006; Leurs, 2014a; Miller & Slater, 2000; Vertovec, 2009). Besides transnational Skype and MSN Messenger conversations between the near and far connecting those who have migrated, those who have stayed and those in the diaspora, my focus on the particular configurations of age and generation revealed that second-generation migrant youth who are born in the diaspora were more concerned with the digital remediation of diaspora as an affective, symbolic marker. Digital media were appropriated to reimagine and exert pride in one's migratory roots by producing, circulating and viewing representations of transnational belonging across IM display names, SNS group pages and diaspora YouTube videos.

Taking a feminist, postcolonial approach enabled me to bring to the forefront the paradoxes of hybridized local, transnational and global orientations in digital media practices (Fernández, 1999; Ignacio, 2006). By considering how multiple axes of differentiation intersect in the everyday conveyal of belonging by Moroccan-Dutch youth, I gave an example of how intersectionality can be a promising way to diversify studies of technology use. This is pressing because cyberfeminism has been oriented toward young, white, middle-class, Christian, North American women (Consalvo, 2003; Leurs, 2012). Similarly, the study demonstrates how ethnicity, age, generation and religion differently impact upon processes of coming-of-age, and how an intersectional perspective can inform future feminist studies of girl cultures and understudied cultures of boys (Durham, 2004; Lemish, 2010).

Scholars of religion find in the study insights into the role of the Internet in the lives of young European Muslims. In Chapter 2, I argued that religious top-down authority is decentered through the construction of postsecular digital identities. Informants turned to online discussion forums to voice and share religious interpretations of what they feel are allowed ("halal") or forbidden ("haram") practices, choosing their righteous path at the crossroads of gender, sexuality and generation. Digital practices also revealed affective dimensions of faith, as viewing Islamic sermons, lectures and *anasheed* music videos on YouTube was noted to be a mode of affective belonging to the wider community (*Ummah*) of Muslims. Considering the engagement of young, urban, Muslim migrants with digital culture provided an uncharted entry point to explore the complex trajectories of European metropolitan postsecularism. Their reflections can be taken to contests the "secularization myth" as a prerequisite for European democracy and progress (Leurs & Ponzanesi, 2014c, p. 153). In considering the emotional bonds informants established with (and through) YouTube videos, I offered an example of how to bring in affectivity to study processes of migration and the use of ICT, which is also generally lacking in the fields of migration and media/communication studies (Boehm & Swank, 2011; Fortunati & Vincent, 2009).

This study intervened in the debates about Moroccan-Dutch youth in the context of the Netherlands. Moroccan-Dutch youth have become the primary locus of fear over ethnic and religious otherness in the Netherlands (Ghorashi, 2010; Leurs, Midden & Ponzanesi, 2012). The majority of news reporting and scholarly work covers issues around juvenile delinquency, mental health problems, radicalization and Islam and unemployment, educational underachieving and social security reliance. Bringing these four themes together, a so-called "Moroccan drama" has been diagnosed (Jurgens, 2007). There is a widening gap between this discourse and the facts of increasingly successful immigrant integration in the Netherlands (Entzinger, 2014). Aiming to nuance the heated rhetoric, this book adds to an emerging alternative body of work on the everyday experiences of Moroccan-Dutch youth (Stock, 2014; Gazzah, 2009; Brouwer, 2006a). In particular, I contribute to a greater understanding of ethnic, diaspora, religious, gendered and youth cultural dimensions of their everyday Internet use.

Finally, this research also raises new questions related to digital embodiment, migration and digital forms of micro-politics. Future research can continue exploring the fissures emerging from the embedding of offline identities online by assessing, for instance, issues around love, queerness and heteronormativity that I have left untouched. More research juxtaposing digital practices of young asylum seekers and refugees, guest laborers and expats is needed to grasp the implications of class differences in relation to borders and boundaries. The role of ICTs (and their relationships with gender) in both forced migration and human trafficking also largely remains uncharted. Furthermore, empirical scrutiny of the role of diaspora subjects in political activism might be useful to ground and develop nuanced understandings of recent uprisings in the Middle East and elsewhere that have been overtly celebrated in Western news reporting as rosy social media revolutions. Finally, the relationship between migration and transnational communication needs to be unpacked to reconsider long-distance digital radicalization, conflict, religious extremism and terrorist recruitment as well as local urban digital practices of multiculturalism, cultural citizenship and intercultural encounters.

2. Methodological considerations

Finding a middle way between the extremes of hard-boiled empiricism and postmodern rejections of essentialism, this research resulted from a creative collision of different methodological approaches. Although quantitative and qualitative approaches to research are often dualistically separated out, I did not consider them as mutually exclusive. Different methodological approaches can be used to construct differently "situated knowledges" (Haraway, 1988). Combining quantitative and qualitative methods, I gathered different accounts of everyday digital identity performances. From large-scale surveys I learned what to focus on during in-depth interviews and the interviews subsequently directed me to ethnographically focus on specific digital practices. Combining these partial, situated and contingent accounts allowed me to conduct a multilayered study.

I have suggested measures to consider the pitfalls of speaking for informants and advanced several initiatives to study identities and digital practices with informants (Spivak, 1993a). I have sought to share my power of definition over the lives of the informants, as interviewees were invited to come up with pseudonyms to include their voice on their own terms. Also, throughout the text I have used the label "Moroccan-Dutch," as this was the label the majority of informants used when asked to introduce themselves at the beginning of the interviews. Advancing a way to share interpretational power, I studied digital practices together with the informants by encouraging them to reflect on what their Internet looks like and to draw out this mental picture in an Internet map showing their favorite Internet destinations. I built on their reflections to demarcate this study. By focusing on forums, instant messaging, social networking sites and YouTube, I chose to analyze those field sites that were most important for the informants. Circumventing ethical issues that may arise from anonymously lurking and gathering materials from publicly accessible Internet applications, I restricted my virtual ethnography by only participating in, observing and archiving those discussion topics, IM conversations, social networking profiles and YouTube videos that my informants specifically spoke to me about or shared with me via e-mail, IM or Facebook Chat. In this way, the preferences of informants were also taken to limit my online fieldwork (Hine, 2013; AOIR, 2012).

Carrying out offline fieldwork together with Fayrouz Boulayounne, a Moroccan-Dutch research assistant, brought to the fore the shifting gendered, ethnic, religious, age and education-based power relations in interviewer-interviewee positioning. There were instances where informants joined up the facets of Fayrouz's identity so they she was perceived as an insider in their world on the basis of a sensed shared ethnic background, gender, or religious upbringing. However, I noted that being seen as different or an outsider means multiple things. It may hinder interaction but it may also promote exchange: this became apparent as informants sometimes made an extra effort to explain issues that might be left uncovered or taken for granted among insiders. In some instances informants allowed me into their worlds especially because I was an outsider and appeared to them to be someone who was nonjudgmental in regards to their behavior in light of their ethnic or religious background, in others they did so when they considered me an insider to their world on the basis of me being male, being interested and/or knowledgeable about digital media, youth culture, fashion, sports or music or my outspoken commitment to antiracism and social justice. The issue of trust also emerged as a locus of power struggles, with paradoxically experienced allowances and restrictions across school, noninstitutional and online interviewing settings. Among the interviewees, there were some who preferred to disclose their personal opinions in the setting of school instead of online, or online instead of elsewhere.

Finally I proposed poststructuralist discursive analysis, attentive to medium-specific narratives, as a way to deconstruct how multiple axes of identifications intersect and perpetuate and/or contest hierarchical power relations. The multispatial micro-politics of power and its subversion were brought out in informants' narratives by taking an agency-sensitive approach combined with attentiveness to multiperspectivism, polyphony and fragmentation. To convey these strategies I, for instance, adopted a reflexive writing style. Avoiding the "God-trick" of assuming a position of an external objective observer (Haraway, 1988, p. 581), I made my own presence clear in the text, and I italicized statements by informants to distinguish between their voice and my own reasoning. Italicization was also chosen to highlight my awareness of the politics in my translation into English of Dutch (and some Moroccan-Arabic and Berber words). These methodological considerations may provide useful for researchers working in media and communication studies, gender studies and youth studies interested in grasping the meanings young people attribute to digital media practices.

3. Digital inequality and spatial hierarchies

Reflecting on prior strands of scholarship on inequality and digital media, I argued digital divides need to be addressed in a novel way. I learned from Wired Up survey findings that computer ownership and Internet access is widespread among Moroccan-Dutch youth, as 98.3% of girls and 96.9% of boys reported they have a computer in their homes with Internet access. These figures are similar to the national averages in the Netherlands, Europe, the US and other parts of the overdeveloped world (Madden, Lenhart, Duggan, Cortesi & Gasser, 2013; D'Haenens & Ogan, 2013). However, digital divides go beyond ownership and access. The first studies on digital gaps focused on uneven distribution of computer ownership and Internet access along geographic scales (the level of development of a country) and social categories (hardware was found to be mostly owned by young, white, affluent, males). The second wave of research analyzed divides between so-called information haves and have-nots caused by a similar asymmetrical distribution of skills and literacies. I have proposed digital gaps should be assessed in a novel way. To put the recent celebratory discourses surrounding Web 2.0 in perspective, more attention is needed to examine how the profit-driven and peer production of the digital divide cocreate uneven opportunities for nonmainstream groups to participate in digital culture. In this section, I recap how habituated dispositions and normative ways of being – sustained by profit-driven computer algorithms, interface templates and majority user cultures – operate as exclusionary mechanisms in digital participation.

Norms and hierarchies in digital space emerge from the interplay of technological decisions and the preferences of the majority of users. Young, white, masculine and middle-class bodies are the main target group of the profit driven cultural industry that develops Internet applications. Invisible to those who meet its requirements, each platform revolves around a dominant gendered, ethnic, age-specific habitus for its defining users. In their digital participation, the majority of users also occupy and produce certain structured ideal types. These hegemonic, mainstream positions and norms may restrict subaltern users in their ability to become active agents in their own representation.

In Chapter 1, I gave the example how computer algorithms can establish norms. I discussed the auto-search complete suggestions the Google Netherlands search engine gives when typing the Dutch word for Moroccans in the search box. The suggestions Google provides after typing "*Marokkanen*" revealed some of the ways Moroccan-Dutch youth are allocated positions of "negative difference" (Modood, 2007, p. 37). The auto-search complete example demonstrated how an ethnic-minority group was algorithmically be slotted in positions of negative hypervisibility. By conveying particular suggestions, algorithmic associations magnify these views, slandering reputations (boyd, 2011a).

In a similar vein, I found that YouTube's profit-driven search engine, guided by a filtering algorithm that demotes amateur, user-generated content pertaining to Morocco, while promoting sponsored and professional high definition videos, further perpetuates Western perspectives (Pauwels & Hellriegel, 2009; Wall, 2009. Algorithms are thus power-ridden. Options for self-presentation offered by preformatted template structures on social networking sites are limited in order to channel behavior and facilitate the generation of consumer profiles (Andrejevic, 2011). Fifteen-year-old Oussema reflected that in Facebook "*there is a special box to publish your religion and I find it important to let that show*," however, he adds that additional categories cannot so easily be included: "*there is not really a box to register your culture.*" Emphasizing the limitations of templates that perpetuate dominant color-blind ideologies (Nakamura, 2002; Grasmuck, Martin & Zhao, 2009; Cover, 2012), template structures do not offer users the opportunity for hybridization and multilayered identification.

Financial motives also guide the policing of ethnic-minority activities online. Consider, for instance, the Anti-Wilders Hyves group. The icon of the group consists of a crossed-out photograph of the Dutch anti-immigrant and anti-Islam Member of Parliament Geert Wilders. As a form of protest, everyone who joins this group includes this image on their profile page. However, when such groups grow large, they were marked as a security risk. Large-scale political activity eventually was restricted within Hyves, because these acts also flooded the screens of the advertisers. Advertisers did not want their product to be associated with political struggles (Spanjar, 2011, pp. 137-138). Upon deletion of the Anti-Wilders Hyves group users were again made to feel out of place, being disempowered by the tools that they had manipulated in order to make a political statement and empower themselves.

The habitus of a majority of users may also cause people to feel unwelcome on a specific platform. In different digital spaces informants felt out of place, or got the feeling as if they were trespassing. Besides certain aged-based expectations, ethnic and religious norms also characterize digital space. As informants grew older they moved from the Dutch social networking site Hyves to Facebook. The latter is considered to be a more professional platform. Exchanging the one for the other is indicative of a rite of passage away from what older informants described as the childish, bright, colorful and messy Hyves toward the more serious young adulthood of Facebook. Exclusionary majority norms were, for instance, apparent in computer game culture. A fan of the game *Counter-Strike*, Oussema shared that he had bad experiences after he disclosed his ethnic and religious background: "*When saying I am Moroccan, I am a Muslim, I get called a terrorist.*" Discussing comments made on YouTube videos pertaining to the country of Morocco, sixteen-year-old Naoul said: "*When you watch a video on YouTube, they shout 'Moroccan cunts' and this and that about Moroccans.*" Eighteen-year-old Safae told me after her friend who covers her hair uploaded a picture on the Dutch social networking site Hyves, somebody sent her a message typing, "*a headscarf is outdated, it's something from the past'.*" Once inside, the interviewees have to actively work against being Othered and struggle to acquire a desired position.

Consider, for example, the illustrative Facebook status update Oussema published on October 3, 2014. He aimed to counter the growth of Islamophobia resulting from global fears over Islamic State (IS) terrorism by sharing a news item on pedophilia in the Roman Catholic Church. Together with the link, he posted the following explanation: "*With that I would like to say that not every Muslim is a terrorist when a few are. Just like not all Christians are pedophiles when only a few are.*" When having to assert themselves against the grain, users become invaders of online territories. Having mapped out how digital spaces are constructed as prescriptive, normative spaces the question arises how they can be subverted, invaded or transformed by the contributions of subaltern subjects, as they create diversity in spaces that were previously defined as neutral and universal.

4. Space invader tactics and digital belonging

In this section I reflect further on the subversive space invader tactics that Moroccan-Dutch youth use to cope with digital forms of inequality. Space invaders are considered to be bodies out of place that cross, trespass and invade institutional settings where the norm is to be populated by mainstream, white, male, élite bodies. Women and minorities have, however, permeated those through top-down governmental practices (like the integration of minorities through multicultural policies) and bottom-up approaches by creating countercultures and entering the no-go spaces through social climbing, education and other tactics to decolonize the dominant spaces (Puwar, 2004; Leurs & Ponzanesi, 2014b). Following Puwar, the question arises, What happens when Moroccan-Dutch youth take up "'privileged positions' which have not been 'reserved' for them" across digital space? (2004, p. 144). How do subjects on the wrong side of the template and peer-produced digital divide invade prescriptive spaces transforming them from within but also creating alternative platforms for communication and belonging? The notion of trespassing digital space brought the new media, gender and postcolonial and approach to the fore again, proven useful to unearth the complex dynamics of how the body was reinscribed online and how online gender/ethnicity/age/nationality/language/sexual preferences and their offline counterparts influence in different ways the invasion of normative digital spaces.

The first space invader tactic I consider here is the masking of difference. Fifteen-year-old Ryan engages in various acts of ethnic impersonation or racial passing. His desire to be included in my study under the pseudonym Ryan can already be seen as an act of passing, as he did not chose a Moroccan name, as most other interviewees did, but an English given name. Talking about the Dutch online social networking sites Hyves, he noted, "*When someone sees me there, they say I do not look like a Moroccan, but obviously I am one, but I do not let it show.*" Masking Moroccanness, he passed as an ethnic-majority Dutch boy. As a gamer, he felt he acted "*very different from what normal Moroccan youth in my school do.*" He experienced playing computer games as "*Dutch culture,*" as it was mostly "*Dutch kids who play games.*" He made an effort to be accepted in Dutch gaming culture by backgrounding Moroccan affiliations during in-game interaction "*when I talk I do not appear to be Moroccan.*" An act of racial passing is a performance that reveals much about how users negotiate their embodiment online. Homi Bhabha recognized the ambivalence of passing as an act of "mimicry": it may offer camouflage and it also may offer resistance and transgression. By passing, subaltern subjects may achieve "partial presence" by passing for something one is not and "becoming a subject of a difference that is almost the same, but not quite" (1994, pp. 122-123). Ryan took up the space invader tactic of passing by strategically employing dominant cultural repertoires and making less visible the ways he diverts from the norms of user majorities. Digital tactics of racial impersonation, however, leave the foundations of dominant exclusionary, white national identities intact.

Appropriating a space to become the majority is a second space invader tactic. More popular among Moroccan-Dutch youth than ethnic-majority Dutch youth, online discussion forums such as Marokko.nl and Chaima.nl are used to publish alternative collective voices. Online discussion forums foster hopes for transformation, as they allow Moroccan-Dutch youth to gather and become the ethnic majority in their own digital space. Forums enable them to counter stereotypes, speak for themselves and develop their own normative ways of being. Discussion forums are used to acquire new positions in response to narrow-fitting allocated ethnic, gender and religious positions. These spaces are considered as safe loci for multiple forms of discursive contestation. The medium-specific sense of anonymity fuels disinhibition as the forum participants felt they could safely articulate views that may violate offline norms with a smaller risk of sanctions, repercussions or disapproval than elsewhere. Forming a "subaltern counterpublic" (Fraser, 1990, p. 67) that felt hushed away from the mainstream, Moroccan-Dutch youth participated in an innovative form of digital multiculturalism and spoke back to allocated ethnic positions and "negative difference" (Modood, 2007, p. 37). Gender is of central concern in these ethnic boundary countering processes as boys and girls relate differently to both Dutch society and Islam, for example, because the stereotypical allocated positions and racisms they experience are not the same (boys are depicted as criminals, girls as headscarf-wearing and therefore backward and oppressed). Furthermore, their position in the public debates in the Netherlands about Islam differs, as female Islamic dress is more heavily discussed than most male traditions are (Leurs, Midden, & Ponzanesi, 2012, p. 173). Moreover, girls could circulate counterviews online toward two of the prejudiced discourses that discipline Muslim women: (neo) Orientalist representations of backwardness and oppression by Muslim men and conservative Islamist discourses that criticize Western women's roles as sex objects (Piela, 2012, pp. 2-3).

Seeking a middle ground between familial, Dutch societal and global youth cultural notions of gender and sexuality, Moroccan-Dutch girls shared feeling less restricted in disclosing themselves on online forums and because of that they dared to bring up personal experiences they have difficulties with sharing elsewhere. They used forums to negotiate "*hchouma*" topics connected to love, relationships, marriage and sexuality, which would be shameful or taboo to discuss offline (Skalli, 2006; Sadiqi, 2003). By doing so, they expanded their radius of action and achieved greater autonomy. By bringing gender issues and sexuality into the public digital space of discussion forums, they also breached the dichotomy of masculine public and feminine private space that is noted in Moroccan socialization (Mernissi, 1987; Graiouid, 2005; Sadiqi, 2003; Brouwer, 2006a; Pels & De Haan, 2003).

As a form of digital postsecularism, online forums were also used to negotiate Islamic codes of conduct. By performing Islam, religious authority is digitally reconfigured and decentered. Although most informants considered it a space of their own, forums were increasingly monitored and surveilled. Politicians and public news media linked discussion sites frequented by Moroccan-Dutch individuals to radicalism and these sites were dismissed as segregated ghettos, unknown grimy spaces disconnected from mainstream society. Nonetheless, my analysis of the interview narratives emphasized the value of forums were minority subjects could appropriate definitional power over collective self-identification away from Dutch societal, Moroccan-Dutch community and familial social norms as well as religious authorities that ascribed singular identity positions (Leurs, Midden & Ponzanesi, 2012; Leurs, Hirzalla & Van Zoonen, 2012).

Besides the collective voices on forums, informants noted they felt they could control the boundaries to the space of instant messaging, where gender boundaries were drawn and erased in additional ways. Away from their parents and siblings, and actively monitoring their contact list, they felt a great sense of autonomy over their private communicative space, which is of great appeal during the life phase of adolescence (Bradley, 2005, p. 62; Leurs & Ponzanesi, 2011a, p. 206). Informants spoke of being less inhibited about sharing their personal feelings. Such feelings posed both risks and opportunities. Boys and girls took the opportunity to get to know each other personally, but on the other hand personal typed conversations were found to be prone to being copied and pasted to other contacts and similarly, while also the circulation of intimate webcam images beyond its original contexts was reported to have very serious consequences. A friend of two interviewees, sixteen-year-old Naoul and fifteen-year-old Inzaf, was, for instance, seriously beaten up after the girls' father and nephew were confronted with nude images she had decided to privately share in good faith with her boyfriend over MSN (Leurs & Ponzanesi, 2011c, pp. 70-72). Furthermore, the gender stereotypical ways girls and boys posed in instant messaging and social networking sites display photos reveals the hegemonic functioning of shared gender norms to achieve a desired level of attractiveness and attention. In their gendered peer economies, youth were found to tap into stereotypical dichotomous feminine and masculine conventions. Furthermore, the example of sexual harassment raised by Inzaf and Naoul as well as the manipulation of personal profile images and republication on YouTube ("brooming") indicates girls remain susceptible to male domination.

The conveyal of hybridized belongings across Internet applications indicates informants also opt for a third space invader tactic. Scholars like Paul Scheffer and anti-immigrant political parties have argued that transnational communication opportunities such as satellite television and Skype that enable migrants to stay in contact with their family and friends in their homeland and diaspora is detrimental to integration. They are of the opinion that ethnic minorities become encapsulated ethnic enclaves when they can remain connected to their homeland, religion and diaspora instead of interacting with ethnic-majority Dutch people (Scheffer 2007, p. 40). I observed that Skype and MSN were used among the informants for transnational communication purposes. Their practices, however, indicate second-generation migrant youth contribute to a generationally distinct "transnational habitus" (Nedelcu, 2012). Having grown up with technologies their parents are unfamiliar with, such as MSN and Skype, Moroccan-Dutch youth mainly acted as technology brokers, assisting their parents in crossing a digital divide by brokering diasporic instant messaging and Skype connections. Complicating intergenerational relations, the bounded roles of parent as educator and child as learner get reversed (Orellana, 2009, p. 19-21; De Haan, 2012). These acts sustain the Moroccan diaspora as a distinct group (Slade, 2010; Backx, 2010).

However, I also noted a distinct generational specificity. Rather than a straightforward continuation of cultural legacies of their parents, Moroccan-Dutch individuals are actively transforming these in ways that resonate with the dominant youth cultures in which they grow up. In contrast to their parents, the informants, who are mostly born in the diaspora, invoke transnationalism more as an affective, symbolic representation by including references to Morocco in their instant messaging display names and including Berber symbols in display photos on their personal profile page on Hyves rather than using Skype to talk to family members. Growing up in the Netherlands, most speak better Dutch than they speak Moroccan-Arabic and/or a Berber language. Rather than having telephone conversations and person-to-person transnational contacts, symbolic diaspora attachments were published online as a way to signal ethnic pride. Also, amateur videos shot in Morocco viewed on YouTube sustained feelings of nostalgia and promoted emotional bonds with an imagined homeland. Symbolic transnationalism as such sparks a sense of affective belonging to a community, which is more imagined and virtual than a physically grounded connection.

The digital identification of Moroccan-Dutch youth went beyond the maintenance of singular migratory ties. Inspired by Stuart Hall, who noted, "when I ask people where they are from, I expect nowadays an extremely long story" (Akomfrah, Gopaul & Lawson, 2013), I asked the informants how they would normally introduce their backgrounds to people they did not know. Fifteen-year-old Inzaf introduced herself by stating: "*I am born here, but my parents are from Morocco. I would not say that I am Moroccan because I was born here.*" Thirteen-year-old Ilham laughed about her differential positioning and shared: "*I am Moroccan, Berber and Muslim, but as you see I do have the Dutch nationality as well.*" Sixteen-year-old Naoul explained her positionality by stating, "*I follow my own path.*" Similarly, sixteen-year-old Amir went beyond ethnic categorizations by stating, "*I just have my own style, I think. I don't belong to any group..*" And fifteen-year-old Oussema specified, "*I can't be pinned down to something specific. I am a bit of everything,*" he positioned himself "*in-between, always in-between.*" In their countering of positions of marginality informants expressed "new ethnicities." These hybrid identities exceed the sum of its positioning parts

(Hall, 1996c). The examples of informants' narrating of self outside the Internet resonated in their differential digital identity performativity.

Informants extended the boundaries of their ascribed position as Moroccan-Dutch people beyond the "rooted" form of identification (Hall, 1990, p. 225; Gilroy, 1993a, p. 19). For example, while instant messaging, Inzaf expressed her affiliation with Al Hoceima, the city in Morocco where her parents were born, but does so by tapping into international repertoires of youth culture, rhyming in English: "*El Hoceima is the bom, that's the place where I come from so just tell everyone thats the city number ONE.*" Explaining its significance she shared: Al Hoceima "*means a lot to me because that is the town in Morocco where I am from and I want to show that I am proud of it.*" She added that "*it rhymes in English*" and it is "*nicer to say it in English than in Dutch.*" Such acts of hybridization reflect active intercultural encounters. Different loyalties are brought together, as she "routes" and embeds her identity performance in the youth culture in which she grows up (Gilroy, 1993a, p. 19). She signals transnational affiliations with the city of Al Hoceima in Morocco where her father was born, but she symbolically mediates it through the vocabulary of English-language global hip-hop youth culture. It becomes a way to emphasize one's individuality to peers, but also to connect with others.

In addition, street language and slang spoken among urban youth in the Netherlands of various backgrounds includes Moroccan-Arabic and Berber words. Instant messaging also revealed a breaching of a teenage gender habitus: while scholars have argued boys use more slang in their everyday speech than girls (e.g., Gordon, 1993), among the informants the use of slang on IM was not restricted to boys. Creatively working around the medium-specific constraints of the American Standard Code for Information Interchange (ASCII) Latin computer character set on their Dutch keyboards; informants use the Latin alphabet to write Moroccan-Arabic and Berber dialect words. Typing words such as "*ze3ma*" to express doubt and "*3assir*" to refer to a fruity drink, youth develop a generational-specific, hybrid style. They not only borrow from youth cultural styles. The styles that they develop and infuse are also taken up by non-Moroccan-Dutch youth. Music produced by Moroccan-Dutch rappers is consumed by the mainstream; Ali B.'s 2006 hit single "Crazy Mocro Flavour," for example, topped Dutch music charts. Girls were avid slang producers in the conversations and display names I analyzed. Also ethnic-majority Dutch youth tap into the repertoire of "Moroccan flavored Dutch" (Nortier & Dorleijn, 2008, pp. 132-139). For instance, nearly one in four ethnic-majority Dutch survey respondents reported including migrant-background artists on their profile pages.

I observed another tactic of space invasion in the articulation of hypertextual narratives of selves. The examples of how thirteen-year-old Midia and thirteen-year-old Anas link to different groups on their SNS profile pages showed affiliations with issues ranging from Dutch nationalism, global consumerism, sexism, feminist interests, ethnic affiliations, religious concerns, gadgets, political activism and youth culture. Likewise, in their preference for music videos, informants mostly listened to recording artists from more than one location in the world. Informants emotionally bonded with music videos as a source of multiplicity, as their viewing reflects affective belongings that stretch across geographies. In the hyperlink practices and viewing strategies of Moroccan-Dutch youth, the multiplicity of their personal cultural trajectories and their cosmopolitan perspectives becomes visible. These findings provide new leads to consider how second-generation migrant youth who have been shown to be more concerned with identity issues and belonging than their parents, digitally rearticulate their selfhood (Boym, 2001; Berry, Phinney, Sam & Vedder, 2006; Brouwer, 2006a; Mainsah, 2011; De Leeuw & Rydin, 2007; Green & Kabir, 2012).

The digital practices Moroccan-Dutch youth engage in showed unexpected coalitions of ethnic-minority youth as space invaders: minoritarian subjects align with majority groups through a variety of shared affiliations. Not only immigrant heritage was highlighted. I have empirically sustained what Eliezer Ben-Rafael and Yitzhak Sternberg have theorized earlier: "diaspora communities in Western societies may remain involved in networks of varying amplitude, across borders and continents, and this does by no means preclude them from to invest their best in efforts to integrate into their actual society (2002, p. 11). On the basis of binary thinking between modes of cultural continuation versus assimilation of minoritarian cultures, scholars such as Paul Scheffer and European politicians like David Cameron, Angela Merkel and Geert Wilders have argued that multiculturalism has failed. My study on Moroccan-Dutch digital passages provides theoretical and empirical fundaments to challenge this binary view.

In sum, considering how Moroccan-Dutch youth as invaders of digital space are simultaneously empowered and disempowered, digital spaces prove to be promising entry points to discern various intersecting issues of identity construction and belonging, and they raise new questions about everyday multiculturalism. Away from state-organized initiatives of multiculturalism, Paul Gilroy saw everyday multiculture or conviviality in action in the "liberating ordinariness" of everyday "heteroculture" that ranged from art, music, food, transport and consumption (2005, p. 119). In their everyday mediation of lived experiences through digital practices, Moroccan-Dutch youth are thrown together with people, representations and ideas from a variety of backgrounds (Leurs, 2014b). The key to a culture of conviviality lies in the recognition that European culture is more than a monolithic, homogeneous white culture. A greater insight into everyday dwelling of minority groups such as second-generation Moroccan-Dutch youth – beyond the manipulations of political leaders and commerce – may serve to counter anti-immigrant and racist perspectives in European societies. These counter-histories can not only help to produce a new understanding of multicultural and postcolonial Europe, but also assist to discover the emancipatory cosmopolitan possibilities of convivial culture to remedy xenophobia and neoimperialism. More research on digital throwntogetherness, intercultural encounters and cosmopolitanism is urgent to continue speaking back to pessimists that argue multiculturalism and integration have failed.

My cartography of the multispatial digital identity performativity of Moroccan-Dutch youth provides a history of the present full of promises but also full of personal experiences of struggle. The relationship between digital templates, habituated dispositions and conveying belonging across multiple offline axes of identification remains intricate and complex. At certain points, the online and offline world overlap or augment one another and at others they collide, providing room for resignification. The boys and girls I interviewed are constantly confronted with various aspects of Dutch multicultural society: while they are often considered the other, they nevertheless also constantly create and connect new passages between their Dutch, Moroccan-Dutch, Muslim, generational, and multilocational youth cultural belongings.

Bibliography

Adamic, L.A. & Adar, E. (2001). You are what you link. Paper presented at the 10th International World Wide Web Conference, Hong Kong, May 1-5. Retrieved from: http://www10.org/program/society/yawyl/YouAreWhatYouLink.htm (accessed October 17, 2014).

Aden, R.C. (1995). Nostalgic communication as temporal escape. *Western Journal of Communication* 59(1), 20-38.

Afshar, H. (2008). Can I see your hair. Choice, agency, and attitudes: the dilemma of faith and feminism for Muslim women who cover. *Ethnic and Racial Studies*, 31(2), 411-427.

Ahmed, S. (2004). *The Cultural Politics of Emotion*. New York: Routledge.

Ahmed, S. (2010). Happy Objects. In M. Gregg and G.J. Seigworth (eds.), *The Affect Theory Reader* (pp. 29-51). Durham, NC: Duke University Press.

Ahmed, S. (2012). *On Being Included: Racism and Diversity in Institutional Life*. Durham, NC: Duke University Press.

Akomfrah, J. (director) & Gopaul, L., Lawson, D. (producers). (2013). *The Stuart Hall Project* [documentary film]. United Kingdom: Smoking Dogs Films.

Albero-Andrés, M. (2004). The Internet and adolescents. In J. Goldstein, D. Buckingham & G. Brougere (eds.), *Toys, Games and Media* (pp. 109-129). Mahwah, NJ: Lawrence Erlbaum.

Alexa (2014). YouTube.com site info, September 30. *Alexa*. Retrieved from: http://www.alexa.com/siteinfo/youtube.com (accessed September 30, 2014).

Alinejad, D. (2013). Locating home in a 'digital age': *An Ethnographic case study of second-generation Iranian Americans in LA and their use of internet media*. Iranian Studies, 46(1), 95-113.

Allagui, I. & Kuebler, J. (2011). The Arab Spring & the role of ICTs. *International Journal of Communication* 5. Retrieved from: http://ijoc.org/ojs/index.php/ijoc/issue/view/6 (accessed October 15, 2014).

Anderson, B. (1983). *Imagined Communities: Reflections on the Origin and Spread of Nationalism*. London: Verso.

Andrejevic, M. (2011). Social network exploitation. In Z. Papacharissi (ed.), *A Networked Self* (pp. 82-101). London: Routledge.

Androutsopoulos, J. (2006). Multilingualism, diaspora, and the Internet. *Journal of Sociolinguistics* 10(4), 520-547.

Androutsopoulos, J. (2007). Language choice and code-switching in German-based diasporic web forums. In B. Danet & S.C. Herring (eds.), *The Multilingual Internet* (pp. 340-361). Oxford: Oxford University Press.

Androutsopoulos, J. (2010). Localizing the global on the participatory web. In N. Coupland (ed.), *The Handbook of Language and Globalization* (pp. 203-231). Oxford: Wiley-Blackwell.

Ang, I. (1996). *Living Room Wars: Rethinking Media Audiences for a Postmodern World*. London: Routledge.

Antias, F. (2002). Where do I belong? Narrating collective identity and translocational positionality. *Ethnicities* 2(4), 491-514.

AOIR (2012). Ethical decision-making and Internet research. Association of Internet Researchers. Retrieved from: http://aoir.org/reports/ethics2.pdf (accessed October 13, 2014).

Aoyama, S. (2007). *Nikkei-Ness: A Cyber-Ethnographic Exploration of Identity among the Japanese Peruvians of Peru*. MA thesis. Department of Anthropology, Mount Holyoke College, South Hadley, MA.

Appadurai, A. (2006). *Fear of Small Numbers: An Essay on the Geography of Anger*. Durham, NC: Duke University Press.

Arau, S. (Producer) (2004). *A Day without a Mexican.* Los Angeles, CA: *Jose & Friends.*
Backx, Q. (2010). Bicultural media use: Amsterdam. *Journalism* 11(6), 733-737.

Bakhtin, M.M. (1984). *Rabelais and His World.* H. Iswolsky (trans.). Bloomington, IN: Indiana University Press.
Balibar, E. & Wallerstein, I. (1991). *Race, Nation, Class: Ambiguous Identities.* London: Verso.
Banaji, S. & Buckingham, D. (2013). *The Civic Web: Young People, the Internet and Civic Participation.* Cambridge, MA: MIT Press.
Bannier, S. (2011). Netherlands. In G. Barnett (ed.), *Encyclopedia of Social Networks* (pp. 586-588). Los Angeles, CA: Sage.
Bargh, J., McKenna, K. & Fitzsimons, G. (2002). Can you see the real me? Activation and expression of the "true self" on the Internet. *Journal of Social Issues* 58(1), 33-48.
Baron, N. (2004). See you online: Gender issues in college student use of instant messaging. *Journal of Language and Social Psychology* 23(4), 397-423.
Baron, N. (2008). *Always On: Language in an Online and Mobile World.* Oxford: Oxford University Press.
Baxter, J. (2008). Feminist post-structuralist discourse analysis: A new theoretical and methodological approach? In K. Harrington, L. Litosseliti, H. Sauntson & J. Sunderland (eds.), *Theoretical and Methodological Approaches to Gender and Language Study* (pp. 243-255). Basingstoke: Palgrave.
Bazeley, P. (2007). *Qualitative Data Analysis with NVivo.* London: Sage.
Beck, U. (2000). *What Is Globalization?* Cambridge: Polity Press.
Beck, U. & Grande, E. (2010). Varieties of second modernity: The cosmopolitan turn in social and political theory and research. *British Journal of Sociology* 61(3), 409-443.
Becker, C. (2009). Gaining knowledge: Salafi activism in German and Dutch online forums. *Masaryk University Journal of Law and Technology* 3(1), 79-98.
Bel Ghazi, H. (1986). *Van souk naar arbeidsmarkt, Marokkaanse migranten en hun kinderen in Nederland* [From the souk to the job market: Moroccan migrants and their children in the Netherlands]. Houten/Amsterdam: Unie Boek BV.
Benjamin, W. (1999). *The Arcades Project.* H. Eiland & K. McLaughlin (trans.). Cambridge, MA: Harvard University Press.
Ben-Rafael, E. & Sternberg, Y. (2002). Analyzing our time: A sociological problématique. In E. Ben-Rafael & Y. Sternberg (eds.), *Identity, Culture and Globalization* (pp. 3-20). Leiden: Brill.
Bernstein, M.S., Monroy-Hernández, A., Harry, D., André, P., Panovich, K. & Vargas, G. (2011). 4chan and /b/: An analysis of anonymity and ephemerality in a large online community. *Proceedings of the Fifth International AAAI Conference on Weblogs and Social Media*, 50-57. Retrieved from: http://www.aaai.org/ocs/index.php/ICWSM/ICWSM11/paper/view/2873/4398 (accessed October 15, 2014).
Berry, J.W., Phinney, J.S., Sam, D.L. & Vedder, P. (2006). *Immigrant Youth in Cultural Transition.* Mahwah, NJ: Lawrence Erlbaum Associates.
Bezemswalla (producer) (2010). *Bezems 2010!!* YouTube. Retrieved from: http://www.youtube.com/watch?v=33fQre3zNIE (accessed October 27, 2011).
Bhabha, H. (1994). *The Location of Culture.* New York, NY: Routledge.
Blaagaard, B.B. (2010). Media and multiplicity: Journalistic practices and the resurgence of xenophobia in Europe. *Translocations: Migration and Social Change* 6(2). Retrieved from: http://www.translocations.ie/Vol%206%20Issue%202%20-%20Europe%20-%20Blaagaard.pdf (accessed September 30, 2014).

Blair, K. & Takayoshi, P. (1999). Introduction: Mapping the terrain of feminist cyberscapes. In K. Blair & P. Takayoshi (eds.), *Feminist Cyberscapes: Mapping Gendered Academic Spaces* (pp. 1-18). Stanford, CT: Ablex.

Bloom, J.M. (1989). *Minaret, Symbol of Islam*. Oxford: Oxford University Press.

Boehm, D.A. & Swank, H. (2011). Introduction. *International Migration* 49(6), 1-6.

Boelstorff, T. (2010). A typology of ethnographic scales for virtual worlds. In W.S. Bainbridge (ed.), *Online Worlds: Convergence of the Real and the Virtual* (pp. 123-133). London: Springer.

Boneva, B.S., Quinn, A., Kraut, R., Kiesler, S. & Shklovski, I. (2006). Teenage communication in the instant messaging era. In R. Kraut, M. Brynin & S. Kiesler (eds.), *Computers, Phones, and the Internet* (pp. 201-218). Oxford: Oxford University Press.

Borghuis, P., De Graaf, C. & Hermes, J. (2010). Digital storytelling in sex education: Avoiding the pitfalls of building a "haram" website. *Seminar.net* 6(2), 234-247. Retrieved from: http://seminar.net/index.php/home/75-current-issue/148-digital-storytelling-in-sex-education-avoiding-the-pitfalls-of-building-a-haram-website (accessed October 15, 2014).

Borkert, M., Cingolani, P. & Premazzi, V. (2009). *The State of the Art of Research in the EU on the Uptaker Use of ICT by Immigrants and Ethnic Minorities (IEM)*. Luxembourg: Office for Official Publications of the European Communities. Retrieved from: http://ipts.jrc.ec.europa.eu/publications/pub.cfm?id=2560 (accessed February 03, 2015).

Boubekeur, A. (2005). Cool and competitive: Muslim cultures in the West. *ISIM Review* 16, 12-13. Retrieved from: http://openaccess.leidenuniv.nl/bitstream/handle/1887/10076/Review_16.pdf (accessed October 14, 2014).

Boumans, L. (2002). Meertaligheid op Marokkaanse elektronische prikborden [Multilinguality on Moroccan electronic forums]. *Levende Talen* 3(1), 11-21.

Boumans, L. (2003). Ze3ma. Een Noordafrikaans epistemisch partikel dat zich verspreidt [A North African epistemic particle that is spreading]. *Gramma/TTT* 10(1), 1-26.

Bourdieu, P. (1977). *Outline of a Theory of Practice*. Cambridge: Cambridge University Press.

Bourdieu, P. (1991). *Language and Symbolic Power*. Cambridge, MA: Polity Press.

boyd, d. (2007). Why youth heart social network sites: The role of networked publics in teenage social life. In D. Buckingham (ed.), *Youth, Identity and Digital Media* (pp. 119-142). Cambridge, MA: MIT Press.

boyd, d. (2010a). Personal communication: E-mail correspondence on carrying out interviews with teenagers about social media, June 10-October 11.

boyd, d. (2010b). Friendship. In M. Ito (ed.), *Hanging Out, Messing Around and Geeking Out* (pp. 79-115). Cambridge, MA: MIT Press.

boyd, d. (2011a). Guilt through algorithmic association. *Apophenia*, September 12. Retrieved from: http://www.zephoria.org/thoughts/archives/2011/09/12/guilt-through-algorithmic-association.html (accessed October 17, 2014).

boyd, d. (2011b). Social networked sites as networked publics: Affordances, dynamics, and implications. In Z. Papacharissi (ed.), *A Networked Self: Identity, Community, and Culture in Social Network Sites* (pp. 39-58). New York, NY: Routledge.

boyd, d. (2012). White flight in networked publics? In L. Nakamura & P.A. Chow-White (eds.), *Race after the Internet* (pp. 203-222). New York, NY: Routledge.

boyd, d. (2014). *It's Complicated: The Social Lives of Networked Teens*. New Haven, CT: Yale University Press.

boyd, d. & Ellison, N. (2007). Social network sites: Definition, history, and scholarship. *Journal of Computer-Mediated Communication* 13(1), 210-230.

Boym, S. (2001). *The Future of Nostalgia*. New York, NY: Basic Books.

Bradley, K. (2005). Internet lives: Social context and moral domain in adolescent development. *New Directions for Youth Development* 108, 57-76.

Brah, A. (1996). *Cartographies* of *Diaspora: Contesting Identities*. London: Routledge.

Braidotti, R. (2006). *Transpositions: On Nomadic Ethics*. Cambridge: Polity Press.

Brandist, C. (2001). The Bakhtin circle. *The Internet Encyclopedia of Philosophy*. Retrieved from: http://www.iep.utm.edu/bakhtin/ (accessed January 23, 2012).

Brennan, T. (2004). *The Transmission of Affect*. Ithaca, NY: Cornell University Press.

Breslauer, H.K. (Producer) (1924). *The City without Jews*. Vienna: H.K. Breslauer-Film.

Brouwer, L. (2002). Marokkaanse jongeren en virtuele discussies [Moroccan youth and virtual discussions]. *Sociologische Gids* 49(2), 121-135.

Brouwer, L. (2006a). Giving voice to Dutch Moroccan girls on the Internet. *Global Media Journal* 5(9), n.p. Retrieved from: http://lass.purduecal.edu/cca/gmj/fa06/gmj_fa06_brouwer.htm (accessed September 18, 2014).

Brouwer, L. (2006b). Dutch-Moroccan websites: A transnational imagery? *Journal of Ethnic and Migration Studies* 32(7), 1153-1168.

Brouwer, L. (2011). Jokes, raps and transnational orientations: Protests of Dutch-Moroccan youths in the debate on Islam. In M. de Theije & T. Salman (eds.), *Local Battles: Global Stakes* (pp. 175-194). Amsterdam: VU University Press.

Buckingham, D. & Kehily, M.J. (2014). Introduction: Rethinking Youth Cultures in the Age of Global Media. In D. Buckingham, S. Bragg & M.J. Kehily (eds.), *Youth Cultures in the Age of Global Media*, (pp. 1-18). New York, NY: Palgrave Macmillan.

Buffardi, L.E. & Campbell, W.K. (2008). Narcissism and social networking sites. *Personality and Social Psychology Bulletin* 34, 1303-1314.

Buikema, R. (2005). A poetics of home. In S. Ponzanesi & D. Merola (eds.), *Migrant Cartographies* (pp. 177-187). Lanham, MD: Lexington Books.

Buikema, R. (2009). Crossing the borders of identity politics. *European Journal of Women's Studies* 16(4), 309-323.

Buitelaar, M. (2007). Staying close by moving out: The contextual meanings of personal autonomy in the life stories of women of Moroccan descent in the Netherlands. *Contemporary Islam* 1(1), 3-22.

Buitelaar, M. (2008). De Islamisering van identiteit onder jongeren van Marokkaanse afkomst. [The Islamization of identity among youth of Moroccan descent]. In M. ter Borg (ed.), *Handboek religie in Nederland: Perspectief, overzicht, debat* [Handbook of religion in the Netherlands: Perspective, overview, debate] (pp. 239-252). Zoetermeer: Meinema.

Buitelaar, M. & Stock, F. (2010). Making homes in turbulent times: Moroccan-Dutch Muslims contesting dominant discourses of belonging. In H. Moghissi & H. Ghorashi (eds.), *Muslim Diaspora in the West* (pp. 163-180). Farnham: Ashgate.

Bunt, G.R. (2009). *iMuslims: Rewiring the House of Islam*. Chapel Hill: University of North Carolina Press.

Burgess, J. (2011). User-created content and everyday cultural practice: Lessons from YouTube. In J. Bennett & N. Strange (eds.), *Television as Digital Media* (pp. 311-331). Durham, NC: Duke University Press.

Burgess, J. & Green, J. (2009). *YouTube: Online Video and Participatory Culture*. Cambridge: Polity Press.

Burkhalter, B. (1999). Reading race online: Discovering racial identity in Usenet discussions. In M.A. Smith & P. Kollock (eds.), *Communities in Cyberspace* (pp. 60-75). New York: Routledge.

Butler, J. (2003). Performative acts and gender constitution. In A. Jones (ed.), *The Feminism and Visual Culture Reader* (pp. 392-402). London: Routledge.

Byrne, D.N. (2008). The future of (the) "race": Identity, discourse, and the rise of computer-mediated public spheres. In A. Everett (ed.), *Learning Race and Ethnicity: Youth and Digital Media* (pp. 15-38). Cambridge, MA: MIT Press.

Campbell, H. (2012). *Digital Religion: Understanding Religious Practice in New Media Worlds.* New York: Routledge.

Castells, M. (2001). *The Internet Galaxy.* Oxford: Blackwell.

Castells, M. (2009). *Communication Power.* Oxford: Oxford University Press.

CBS (2012). *Jaarboek onderwijs in cijfers.* The Hague: Statistics Netherlands. Retrieved from: http://www.cbs.nl/NR/rdonlyres/3036B4E1-A671-4C9E-95BF-90C0493B4CD9/0/2012f162pub.pdf (accessed September 16, 2014).

CBS (2014a). Population: Sex, Age, Origin and Generation, 1 January. Retrieved from: http://statline.cbs.nl/Statweb/publication/?DM=SLEN&PA=37325ENG&D1=0&D2=0&D3=0&D4=0&D5=139&D6=l&LA=EN&VW=T (accessed 28 October, 2014).

CBS (2014b). ICT gebruik van personen naar persoonskenmerken [ICT use and personal characteristics]. Retrieved from: http://statline.cbs.nl/StatWeb/publication/?DM=SLNL&PA=71098ned&D1=33-133&D2=0-3&D3=a&HDR=G1&STB=T,G2&VW=T (accessed September 17, 2014).

CBS (2014c). VO, onderwijssoort, leerjaar, herkomstgroepering, generation [secondary education, educational track, year, ethnicity, generation]. Retrieved from: http://statline.cbs.nl/Statweb/publication/?DM=SLNL&PA=80043NED&D1=3&D2=a&D3=0&D4=5&D5=0&D6=0&D7=0&D8=l&HDR=G7,G5,G4,G2,G1,G6,G3&STB=T&VW=T (accessed October 14, 2014).

CBS (2014d). Bevolkingstrends 2014. Allochthonen en geluk [Population trends 2014: Allochthnous people and happiness]. Retrieved from: http://www.cbs.nl/NR/rdonlyres/72DBD1AF-B71A-4972-B108-30B69995C6D2/0/20140110b15art.pdf (accessed October 17, 2014).

Chaima.nl (2011). Registratie [Registration]. *Chaima.nl.* Retrieved from: http://www.chaima.nl/register.php?do=register (accessed September 30, 2011).

Christensen, N.B. (2003). *Inuit in Cyberspace: Embedding Offline Identities Online.* Copenhagen: Museum Tusculanum Press.

Church, K. & De Oliveira, R. (2013). What's up with WhatsApp?: comparing mobile instant messaging behaviors with traditional SMS. In M. Rohs & A. Schmidt (eds.), *Proceedings of the 15th International Conference on Human-Computer Interaction with Mobile Devices and Services* (pp. 352-361). New York: ACM.

Clough, P.T. & Halley, J. (eds.) (2007). *The Affective Turn.* Durham, NC: Duke University Press.

Codagnone, C. & Kluzer, S. (2011). *ICT for the Social and Economic Integration of Migrants into Europe.* Seville: JRC-IPTS. Retrieved from: http://ftp.jrc.es/EURdoc/JRC63183.pdf (accessed October 14, 2014).

Code, L. (1991). *What Can She Know? Feminist Theory and the Construction of Knowledge.* Ithaca, NY: Cornell University Press.

Consalvo, M. (2003). Cyberfeminism. In S. Jones (ed.), *Encyclopedia of New Media* (pp. 108-109). Thousand Oaks, CA: Sage.

Cooke, M. (2007). The Muslimwoman. *Contemporary Islam* 1(2), 139-154.

Cottaar, A. & Bouras, N. (2009). *Marokkanen in Nederland. De pioneers vertellen* [Moroccans in the Netherlands: The pioneers tell their stories]. Amsterdam: Meulenhoff.

Couldry, N. (2003). *Media Rituals: A Critical Approach.* London: Routledge.

Couldry, N. (2010). *Why Voice Matters.* Los Angeles, CA: Sage.

Couldry, N. (2012). *Media, Society, World: Social Theory and Digital Media Practice.* Cambridge: Polity Press.

Cover, R. (2012). Performing and undoing identity online: Social networking, identity theories and the incompatibility of online profiles and friendship regimes. *Convergence* 18(2), 177-193.
Crul, M. & Doomernik, J. (2003). The Turkish and Moroccan second generation in the Netherlands. *International Migration Review* 37(4), 1039-1064.
Cvetkovich, A. (2003). *An Archive of Feelings: Trauma, Sexuality, and Lesbian Public Cultures*. Durham, NC: Duke University Press.

Dagevos, J., Huijnk, W. & Gijsberts, M. (2014). Labour market position of migrant groups in times of economic recession: Summary, conclusions and policy implications. In W. Huijnk, M. Gijsberts & J. Dagevos (eds.), *Jaarraport integratie 2013. Participatie van migranten op de arbeidsmarkt* (pp. 182-202). The Hague: SCP.
Dahlberg, L. & Siapera, E. (eds.) (2007). *Radical Democracy and the Internet*. New York: Palgrave MacMillan.
Davis, J. (2010). Architecture of the personal interactive homepage: Constructing the self through MySpace. *New Media & Society* 12(7), 1103-1119.
Davis, K. (2012). Friendship 2.0: Adolescents' experiences of belonging and self-disclosure online. *Journal of Adolescence* 35(6), 1527-1536.
De Certeau, M. (1984). *The Practice of Everyday Life*. Berkeley, CA: University of California Press.
De Jong, J. (2007). *Kapot moeilijk: een etnografisch onderzoek naar opvallend delinquent groepsgedrag van "Marokkaanse" jongens* [An ethnographic study of the delinquent behavior of "Moroccan" boys]. Amsterdam: Amsterdam University Press.
De Haan, M.J. (2012). Immigrant learning. In K. S. Gallagher, R. Goodyear, D. Brewer & R. Rueda (eds.), *Urban Education: A Model for Leadership and Policy* (pp. 328-341). New York, NY: Routledge.
De Haan, M.J., Leander, K., Ünlüsoy & A., Prinsen, F. (2014). Challenging ideals of connected learning: The networked configurations for learning of migrant youth in the Netherlands. *Learning, Media and Technology* 39(4), 507-535.
De Koning, M. (2005). Dit is geen poep wat ik praat. De Hirsi Ali Diss nader belicht [This is no bullshit: Assessing the Hirsi Ali Diss]. *ZemZem* 1(1), 36-41.
De Koster, W. (2010). Contesting community online: Virtual imagery among Dutch orthodox Protestant homosexuals. *Symbolic Interaction* 33(4), 552-577.
De Leeuw, S. & Rydin, I. (2007). Migrant children's digital stories. *European Journal of Cultural Studies* 10(4), 447-464.
Deleuze, G. (1988), *Spinoza: Practical Philosophy*. Trans. Robert Hurley. San Francisco, CA: City Lights Books.
Deleuze, G. & Guattari, F. (2004). *A Thousand Plateaus*. Brian Massumi (trans.). London: Continuum.
De Ridder, S. (2014). *Unfolding Intimate Media Cultures*. PhD dissertation. Faculty of Political and Social Sciences, Ghent University, Belgium.
Derrida, J. (1978). *Writing and Difference*. Chicago: University of Chicago Press.
De Valk, H. & Crul, M. (2008). Education. In M. Crul & L. Heering (eds.), *The Position of the Turkish and Moroccan Second Generation in Amsterdam and Rotterdam* (pp. 63-85). Amsterdam: Amsterdam University Press.
De Waal, M. (2003). Soms op de kaasmanier, soms op onze manier [Sometimes in the Dutch cheese way, sometimes in our way]. In H. Blanken & M. Deuze (eds.), *De mediarevolutie. 10 jaar www in Nederland* [The media revolution: 10 years of the WWW in the Netherlands] (pp. 146-167). Amsterdam: Boom.
D'Haenens, L. (2003). ICT in multicultural society: The Netherlands: A context for sound multiform media policy. *Gazette: The International Journal for Communication Studies* 65(4-5), 401-421.

D'Haenens, L. & Ogan, C. (2013). Internet-using children and digital inequality: A comparison between majority and minority Europeans. *Communications: The European Journal of Communication Research* 38(1): 41-60.

D'Haenens, L., Summeren, C. van, Saeys, F. & Koeman, J. (2004). *Integratie of identiteit? Mediamenu's van Turkse en Marokkaanse jongeren* [Integration or identity? Media menus of Turkish and Moroccan youths]. Amsterdam: Boom.

Diminescu, D. (2008). The connected migrant: An epistemological manifesto. *Social Science Information* 47(4), 565-579.

Donnelly, A.M. (2011). Read my profile: Internet profile culture, young women, and the communication of power. In M. Ames & S. Burcon (eds.), *Women and Language: Essays on Gendered Communication across Media* (pp. 167-181). Jefferson, NC: McFarland.

Dorleijn, M. & Nortier, J. (2009). Code-switching and the Internet. In B.E. Bullock & A.J. Toribio (eds.), *The Cambridge Handbook of Linguistic Code-Switching* (pp. 127-141). Cambridge: Cambridge University Press.

Duimel, M. & Haan, J. de (2007). *Nieuwe links in het gezin.* [New links in the family]. Den Haag: Sociaal en Cultureel Planbureau.

Duits, L. & Van Zoonen, L. (2006). Headscarves and porno-chic: Disciplining girls' dress in the European multicultural society. *The European Journal of Women's Studies* 13(2), 103-117.

Dunyahenya (2011). Kanker hoofddoek [The headscarf is a cancer]. *Dunyahenya: A Moslima Living in the Big World!* blog, April 23. Retrieved from: http://dunyahenya.wordpress.com/2011/04/23/kanker-hoofddoek/ (accessed January 11, 2011).

Durham, M.G. (2001). Adolescents, the Internet and the politics of gender. *Race, Gender & Class* 8(4), 20-41.

Durham, M.G. (2004). Constructing the "new ethnicities": Media, sexuality and diaspora identity in the lives of South Asian immigrant girls. *Critical Studies in Media Communication* 21(2), 140-161.

Eagleton, T. (1986). *Against the Grain: Essays, 1975-1985*. London: Verso.

Eickelman, D.F. & Anderson, J.W. (2003). *New Media in the Muslim world.* 2nd ed. Bloomington: Indiana University Press.

Elahi, J. (2014). *Etnische websites, behoeften en netwerken. Over het gebruik van internet door jongeren* [Ethnic websites, needs and networks: About the use of the Internet among young people]. Delft: Eburon.

Entzinger, H. (2014). The growing gap between facts and discourse on immigrant integration in the Netherlands. *Identities: Global Studies in Culture and Power* 21(6), 693-707.

eMoroccan (2010). *Marrakech, Morocco City Drive.* YouTube. Retrieved from: http://www.youtube.com/watch?v=hbQGveCIcaU (accessed October 17, 2014).

Ennaji, M. (2005). *Multilingualism, Cultural Identity and Education in Morocco.* New York: Springer.

Escher, A. & Wüst, M. (2010) Couscous, tajine und bastilla. Ein Versuch über die marokkanische Küche [Couscous, tagine and pastilla: A study of the Moroccan kitchen]. In I. Schütze (ed.), *Über Geschmack lässt sich doch streiten. Zutaten aus Küche, Kunst und Wissenschaft* (pp. 61-81). Berlin: Kulturverlag Kadmos.

Essed, P. & Hoving, I. (eds.). (2014). Dutch racism. Amsterdam: Rodopi.

Everett, A. (2009). *Digital Diaspora: A Race for Cyberspace.* Albany: State University of New York Press.

Facebook (2014). Company info. *Newsroom.* Retrieved from: http://newsroom.fb.com/company-info/ (accessed October 3, 2014).

Fernández, M. (1999). Postcolonial media theory. *Art Journal* 58(3), 58-73.

Fiske, J. (1992). The cultural economy of fandom. In L.A. Lewis (ed.), *The Adoring Audience: Fan Culture and Popular Media* (pp. 30-49). New York, NY: Routledge.
Fortunati, L. (2009). Theories without heart. In A. Esposito & R. Vích (eds.), *Cross-Modal Analysis of Speech, Gestures, Gaze and Facial Expressions* (pp. 5-17). Berlin: Springer Verlag.
Fortunati, L., Pertierra, R. & Vincent, J. (eds.) (2012), *Migration, Diaspora and Information Technology in Global Societies*. New York, NY: Routledge.
Fortunati, L. & Vincent, J. (2009). Introduction. In L. Fortunati & J. Vincent (eds.), *Electronic Emotion* (pp. 1-25). Bern: Peter Lang.
Foucault, M. (1978). *The History of Sexuality: Volume 1: An Introduction*. New York: Pantheon Books.
Foucault, M. (1980). *Power/Knowledge*. Brighton: Harvester Press.
Foucault, M. (1982). The subject and power. In H.L. Dreyfus & P. Rabinow (eds.), *Michel Foucault: Beyond Structuralism and Hermeneutics* (pp. 208-226). New York: Harvester Wheatsheaf.
Franklin, M.I. (2003). I define my own identity: Pacific articulations of "race" and "culture" on the Internet. *Ethnicities* 3(4), 465-490.
Fraser, N. (1990). Rethinking the public sphere: A contribution to the critique of actually existing democracy. *Social Text* 25/26, 56-80.
Freishtat, R. & Sandlin, J. (2010). Shaping youth discourse about technology: Technological colonization, manifest destiny, and the frontier myth in Facebook's public pedagogy. *Educational Studies* 46, 503-523.

Gajjala, R. & Birzescu, A. (2010). Voicing and placement in online networks. In M. Levina & G. Kien (eds.), *Post-Global Network and Everyday Life* (pp. 73-91). New York, NY: Peter Lang.
Gajjala, R. & Gajjala, V. (eds.). (2008). *South Asian Technospaces*. New York, NY: Peter Lang.
Galasińska, A. (2010). Leavers and stayers discuss returning home: Internet discourses on migration in the context of post-communist transformation. *Social Identities: Journal for the Study of Race, Nation and Culture* 16(3), 309-324.
Gatson, S.N. & Reid, R.A. (2012). Race and ethnicity in fandom. *Transformative Works and Cultures* 8. Retrieved from: http://journal.transformativeworks.org/index.php/twc/article/view/392/252 (accessed October 17, 2014).
Gauntlett, D. & Holzwarth, P. (2006). Creative and visual methods. *Visual Studies* 21(1), 82-91.
Gazzah, M. (2009). European Muslim youth: Towards a cool Islam? In J.S. Nielsen (ed.), *Yearbook of Muslims in Europe* (pp. 403-425). Leiden: Brill.
Gazzah, M. (2010). Maroc-Hop: Music and youth identities in the Netherlands. In L. Herrera & A. Bayat (eds.), *Being Young and Muslim* (pp. 309-323). Oxford: Oxford University Press.
Geense, P. & Pels, T. (2002). Allochtone jongeren op het Internet [Allochthonous youth on the Internet]. *Migrantenstudies* 18, 2-19.
Geertz, C. (1988). *Works and Lives: The Anthropologist as Author*. Stanford, CA: Stanford University Press.
George, R.M. (1999). *The Politics of Home: Postcolonial Relocations and Twentieth-Century Fiction*. Berkeley, CA: University of California Press.
Georgiou, M. (2006). *Diaspora, identity and the media*. Cresskill, NJ: Hampton Press.
Georgiou, M. (2012). Seeking ontological security beyond the nation: The role of transnational television. *Television & New Media* 14(4), 304-321.
Ghorashi, H. (2010). From absolute invisibility to extreme visibility: Emancipation trajectory of migrant women in the Netherlands. *Feminist Review* 94(1), 75-92.
Giddens, A. (1990). *The Consequences of Modernity*. Stanford, CA: Stanford University Press.

Giddens, A. (1991). *Modernity and Self-Identity: Self and Society in the Late Modern Age*. Cambridge: Polity Press.
Gilbert, M. (1994). The politics of location: Doing feminist research at "home." *Professional Geographer* 46(1), 90-96.
Gilbert, M. (2010). Theorizing digital and urban inequalities: Critical geographies of "race," gender and technological capital. *Information, Communication & Society* 13(7), 1000-1018.
Gillespie, T. (2010). The politics of "platforms." *New Media & Society* 12(3), 347-364.
Gilroy, P. (1993a). *The Black Atlantic: Modernity and Double Consciousness*. London: Verso.
Gilroy, P. (1993b). Between Afro-centrism and Euro-centrism: Youth culture and the problem of hybridity. *Young* 1(2), 2-12.
Gilroy, P. (2005). *Postcolonial Melancholia*. New York: Columbia University Press.
Goffman, E. (1959). *The Presentation of Self in Everyday Life*. Garden City, NY: Doubleday.
Goggin, G. & McLelland, M. (eds.) (2009). *Internationalizing Internet Studies: Beyond Anglophone Paradigms*. Oxon: Routledge.
Gokdemir, O. & Dumludag, D. (2011), Life satisfaction among Turkish and Moroccan Immigrants in the Netherlands: The role of absolute and relative income. *Social Indicators Research* 106, 407-417.
Gómez-Peña, G. (2000). Chicano Interneta: The search for intelligent life in cyberspace. *Hopscotch: A Cultural Review* 2(2), 80-91.
Google (2015). Autocomplete. Retrieved from: https://support.google.com/websearch/answer/106230?hl=en (accessed January 29, 2015).
Google (2011). Welcome to promoted videos. YouTube. Retrieved from: https://ads.youtube.com/pdf/YouTube-Promoted-Videos.pdf (accessed August 09, 2011).
Gordon, M. (1993). Sexual slang and gender. *Women and Language* 16(2), 16-21.
Graham, M. (2011). Time machines and virtual portals: The spatialities of the digital divide. *Progress in Development Studies* 11(3), 211-227.
Graiouid, S. (2005). Social exile and virtual Hrig: Computer-mediated interaction and cybercafé culture in Morocco. In M. Wilberg (ed.), *The Interaction Society: Practice, Theories and Supportive Technologies* (pp. 57-92). Hershey, PA: Information Science Publishing.
Grasmuck, S., Martin, J. & Zhao, S. (2009). Ethno-racial identity displays on Facebook. *Journal of Computer-Mediated Communication* 15, 158-188.
Green, L. & Kabir, N. (2012). Australian migrant children: ICT use and the construction of future lives. In L. Fortunati, R. Pertierra & J. Vincent (eds.), *Migration, Diaspora and Information Technology in Global Societies* (pp. 91-103). London: Routledge.
Gregg, M. (2007). Thanks for the ad(d): Neoliberalism compulsory friendship. *Online Opinion*. Retrieved from: http://www.onlineopinion.com.au/view.asp?article=6400&page=0 (accessed October 17, 2014).
Griffin, G. (2011). Writing about research methods in the arts and humanities. In R. Buikema, G. Griffin & N. Lykke (eds.), *Theories and Methodologies in Postgraduate Feminist Research* (pp. 91-104). New York, NY: Routledge.
Grinter, R. E. & Palen, L. (2002). Instant messaging in teen life. In *Proceedings of the 2002 ACM Conference on Computer Supported Cooperative Work* (pp. 21-30). Retrieved from: http://doi.acm.org/10.1145/587078.587082 (accessed October 17, 2014).
Grosz, E. (1995). *Space, Time and Perversion*. New York, NY: Routledge.
Gubrium, A., and Harper, K. (2013). *Participatory Visual and Digital Methods*. Walnut Creek, CA: Left Coast Press.
Gustafson, P. (2001). Roots and routes: Exploring the relationship between place attachment and mobility. *Environment and Behavior* 33(5), 667-686.

Habermas, J. (2002). The public sphere. In P. Marris & S. Thornham (eds.), *Media Studies: A Reader.* 2nd ed. (pp. 92-97). Edinburgh: Edinburgh University Press.

Hahner, L.A. (2012). Constitutive intersectionality and the affect of rhetorical form. In K.R. Chávez & C.L. Griffin (eds.), *Standing in the Intersection: Feminist Voices, Feminist Practices in Communication Studies* (pp. 147-168). Albany: State University of New York Press.

Hall, S. (1990). Cultural identity and diaspora. In J. Rutherford (ed.), *Identity: Community, Culture, Difference* (pp. 222-237). London: Lawrence and Wishart.

Hall, S. (1996a). When was the "post-colonial"? Thinking at the limit. In I. Chambers & L. Curtis (eds.), *The Post-Colonial Question*: *Common Skies Divided Horizons* (pp. 242-260). London, Routledge.

Hall, S. (1996b). Introduction: Who needs identity? In S. Hall & P. du Gay (eds.), *Questions of Cultural Identity* (pp. 1-17). London: Sage.

Hall, S. (1996c). New ethnicities. In H.A. Baker, M. Diawara & R.H. Lindeborg (eds.), *Black British Cultural Studies: A Reader* (pp. 163-172). Chicago, IL: University of Chicago Press.

Hall, S. (1996d). Minimal selves. In H.A. Baker, M. Diawara & R.H. Lindeborg (eds.), *Black British Cultural Studies: A Reader* (pp. 114-119). Chicago, IL: University of Chicago Press.

Hall, S. (1997a). The local and the global: Globalization and ethnicity. In A. McClintock, A. Mufti & E. Shohat (eds.), *Dangerous Liaisons: Gender, Nation, and Postcolonial Perspectives* (pp. 173-187). Minneapolis, MN: University of Minnesota Press.

Hall, S. (1997b). Old and new identities, old and new ethnicities. In A.D. King (ed.), *Culture, Globalization, and the World-System: Contemporary Conditions for the Representation of Identity* (pp. 41-68). Minneapolis, MN: University of Minnesota Press.

Hall, S. (1997c). *Representation: Cultural Representation and Signifying Practices.* London: Sage.

Hamer, H. (2010). "Bezemen" treft docenten en leerlingen ["Brooming" affects teachers and students]. *Trouw*, September 17. Retrieved from: http://www.trouw.nl/tr/nl/4324/Nieuws/article/detail/1792176/2010/09/17/Bezemen-treft-docenten-en-leerlingen.dhtml (accessed October 17, 2014).

Haraway, D. (1988). Situated knowledges: The science question in feminism and the privilege of partial perspective. *Feminist Studies* 14(3), 575-599.

Haraway, D. (1991). *Simians, Cyborgs, and Women: The Reinvention of Nature.* New York: Routledge.

Haraway, D. (1997). *Modest_Witness@Second_Millenium.FemaleMan_ Meets_OncoMouse: Feminism and Technoscience.* New York, NY, Routledge.

Harchaoui, S. & Huinder, C. (2003). Inleiding [Introduction]. In S. Harchaoui & C. Huinder (eds.), *Stigma: Marokkaan. Afstoten en insluiten van een ingebeelde bevolkingsgroep* [Stigma: Moroccan, excluding and including an imagined community] (pp. 7-22). Utrecht: Forum.

Hård af Segerstad, Y. & Hashemi, S.S. (2006). Learning to write in the information age. In L. Waes, M. Leijten & C.M. Neuwirth (eds.), *Writing and Digital Media* (pp. 49-64). Amsterdam: Elsevier.

Harding, S. (1991). *Whose Science? Whose Knowledge? Thinking From Women's Lives.* Ithaca, NY: Cornell University Press.

Hartley, J. (2010). Homo nuntius – Messaging humanity. *Popular Communication* 8(4), 293-311.

Hebdige, D. (1979). *Subculture: The Meaning of Style.* London: Methuen.

Heering, L. & ter Bekke, S. (2008). Labour and income. In M. Crul & L. Heering (eds.), *The Position of the Turkish and Moroccan Second Generation in Amsterdam and Rotterdam* (pp. 87-104). Amsterdam: Amsterdam University Press.

Hendrick, S.F. & Lindgren, S. (2011). YouTube as a performative arena. In E. Dunkels, G.M. Franberg & C. Hallgren (eds.), *Youth Culture and Net Culture* (pp. 153-169). Hershey, PA: IGI Global.

Herring, S.C. (2003). Gender and power in on-line communication. In J. Holmes & M. Meyerhoff (eds.), *Handbook of Language and Gender* (pp. 202-28). Oxford: Blackwell.

Hillis, K. (2009). *Online a Lot of the Time.* Durham, NC: Duke University Press.

Hine, C. (2008). How can qualitative Internet researchers define the boundaries of their projects? In. A. Markham & N. Baym (eds.), *Internet Inquiry: Conversations about Method* (pp. 1-32). London: Sage.

Hine, C. (2013). *The Internet: Understanding Qualitative Research.* Oxford: Oxford University Press.

Hine, C. (2015). *Ethnography for the Internet.* London: Bloomsbury.

Hirschkind, C. (2006). *The Ethical Soundscape: Cassette Sermons and Islamic Counterpublics.* New York, NY: Columbia University Press.

Hirzalla, F., Van Zoonen, L. & Müller, F. (2013). How funny can Islam controversies be? Comedians defending their faith on YouTube. *Television & New Media* 14(1), 46-61.

Højsgaard, M.T. & Warburg, M. (eds.) (2005). *Religion and Cyberspace.* London: Routledge.

Hoover, S.M. (2006). *Religion in the Media Age.* New York, NY: Routledge.

Hosen, N. (2008). Online fatwa in Indonesia: From fatwa shopping to googling a Kiai. In G. Fealy & S. White (eds.), *Expressing Islam: Religious Life and Politics in Indonesia* (pp. 159-173). Singapore: ISEAS Publishing.

Hulsman, B. (2005). Getto's op het web. Op Internet heeft elke groep zijn eigen waarheid [Ghettos on the web: On the Internet, every group creates its own truth]. *NRC Handelsblad*, January 8, p. 33.

Human Rights Watch (2010). Morocco/Western Sahara: More freedom to name their children. *Human Rights Watch*, December 14. Retrieved from: http://www.hrw.org/news/2010/12/14/moroccowestern-sahara-more-freedom-name-their-children (accessed October 15, 2014).

Ignacio, E.N. (2006). E-scaping boundaries: Bridging cyberspace and diaspora studies through ethnography. In D. Silver & A. Massanari (eds.), *Critical Cyberculture Studies* (pp. 181-193). New York, NY: New York University Press.

Illouz, E. (2007). *Cold intimacies. The making of emotional capitalism.* Oxford: Polity Press.

Immigration and Refugee Board of Canada (2000). Morocco: Brief history of the Berbers including their origins and geographic location, 16 November, MAR35753.E, Retrieved from: http://www.refworld.org/docid/3df4be668.html (accessed December 16, 2011).

Ippolita, Lovink, G. & Rossiter, N. (2009). The digital given: 10 Web 2.0 theses. *Fibreculture* 14. Retrieved from: http://fibreculture.org/journal/issue14/issue14_ippolita_et_al_print.html (accessed October 17, 2014).

Jacobs, G. (2003). Breaking down virtual walls. Paper presented at the annual meeting of the American Educational Research Association, April, Chicago, IL.

Jacobs, G. (2005). *"Ur part of it": Portfolio People and Adolescent Use of Instant Messaging.* PhD dissertation. Department of Teaching and Curriculum, University of Rochester, Rochester, NY.

Jaikumar, P. (2011). Postface. In S. Ponzanesi & M. Waller (eds.), *Postcolonial Cinema Studies* (pp. 233-242). London: Routledge.

James, A. (2007). Giving voice to children's voices: Practices and problems, pitfalls and potentials. *American Anthropologist* 109(2), 261-272.

Jawed (Producer) (2005). *Me at the Zoo.* Retrieved from: http://www.youtube.com/watch?v=jNQXAC9IVRw (accessed October 17, 2014).

Jean Christian, A. (2009). Real vlogs: The rules and meanings of online personal videos. *First Monday* 14(11). Retrieved from: http://firstmonday.org/htbin/cgiwrap/bin/ojs/index.php/fm/article/view/2699/2353 (accessed September 25, 2014).

Jenkins, H. (1992). *Textual Poachers: Television Fans and Participatory Culture*. New York, NY: Routledge.

Jensen, S.Q. (2006). Rethinking subcultural capital. *Young* 14(3), 257-267.

Jones, H., Jackson, E. & Rhys-Taylor, A. (2014). Introduction: Moving and being moved. In H. Jones & E. Jackson (eds.), *Stories of Cosmopolitan Belonging: Emotion and Location* (pp. 1-14). New York: Routledge.

Jurgens, F. (2007). *Het Marokkanendrama* [The Moroccan drama]. Amsterdam: Meulenhoff.

Kahn, R. & Kellner, D. (2007). Globalization, technopolitics and radical democracy. In L. Dahlberg & E. Siapera (eds.), *Radical Democracy and the Internet* (pp. 17-36). New York: Palgrave MacMillan.

Kambouri, N. & Parsanoglou, D. (2010). Transnational digital networks, migration and gender: Literature review and policy analysis. *Mig@Net Deliverable* 3 (pp. 1-45). Retrieved from: http://www.mignetproject.eu/wp-content/uploads/2011/02/MIGNET_Deliverable_No3_Literature_review_and_policy_analysis_Final1.pdf (accessed October 17, 2014).

Karim, K.H. (2003). Mapping diasporic mediascapes. In K.H. Karim (ed.), *The Media of Diaspora* (pp. 1-17). Oxford: Routledge.

Karlsson, L. (2007). Desperately seeking sameness. *Feminist Media Studies* 7(2), 137-153.

Kelly, D.M., Pomerantz, S. & Currie, D.H. (2006). "No Boundaries"? Girls' interactive, online learning about femininities. *Youth & Society* 38(1), 3-28.

Kendall, L. (1999). Recontextualizing "cyberspace": Methodological considerations for online research. In S. Jones (eds.), *Doing Internet Research* (pp. 55-74). London: Sage.

Kessler, F. & Schäfer, M. (2009). Navigating YouTube. In P. Vonderau & P. Snickars (eds.), *The YouTube Reader* (pp. 275-291). New York, NY: Wallflower Press.

Ketner, S. (2010). *Marokkaanse wortels, Nederlandse grond. Jonge moslims over opgroeien in Nederland* [Moroccan roots, Dutch soil: Young Muslims speaking about growing up in the Netherlands]. Utrecht: Verwey-Jonker Instituut.

Kleck, C. A., Reese, C., Ziegerer-Behnken, D. & Sundar, S. (2007). The company you keep and the image you project: Putting your best face forward in online social networks. Paper presented at the annual meeting of the International Communication Association, San Francisco, CA, May (pp. 1-30). Retrieved from: http://citation.allacademic.com/meta/p_mla_apa_research_citation/1/7/2/7/5/pages172756/p172756-1.php (accessed October 17, 2014).

Knaap, J., Stoepker, S. & Wegloop, O. (2011). *Hoofdboek. Onthullend magazine over de hoofddoek* [: Revealing magazine about the headscarf]. Haarlem: Cup of Culture.

Knijff, C. (2009). Marokko.nl: Nuttige kijk op de onderbuik [Marokko.nl: A useful glance at gut feelings]. *Volkskrant*, November 6. Retrieved from: http://www.volkskrant.nl/vk/nl/2694/Media/article/detail/364713/2009/11/06/Marokko-nl-Nuttige-kijk-op-de-onderbuik.dhtml (accessed October 15, 2014).

Knott, K. (2010). Space and movement. In K. Knott & S. McLoughlin (eds.), *Diasporas: Concepts, Intersections, Identities* (pp. 79-83). London: Zed Books.

Kozinets, R.V. (2010). *Netnography: Doing Ethnographic Research Online*. Los Angeles, CA: Sage.

Kristeva, J. (1986). Word, dialogue and novel. In T. Moi (ed.), *The Kristeva Reader* (pp. 34-61). New York, NY: Columbia University Press.

Kuhn, T. (1970). *The Structure of Scientific Revolutions*. 2nd ed. Chicago, IL: University of Chicago Press.

Kuipers, G. (2008). The Muhammad cartoon controversy and the globalization of humor. *Humor* 21(1), 7-11.

Kunstman, A. (2008). Contested borders and the politics of passing in Israel/Palestine and in cyberspace. *Feminist Media Studies* 8(3), 267-283.

Kvasny, L. (2005). The role of the habitus in shaping discourses about the digital divide. *Journal of Computer-Mediated Communication* 10(2). Retrieved from: http://jcmc.indiana.edu/vol10/issue2/kvasny.html (accessed December 1, 2011).

Labovic, S. (2005). Marokkaanse websites vormen uitlaatklep, zeggen beheerders [Moroccan websites form an outlet, administrators say]. *Het Parool*, October 22, p. 27.

Lam, E. (2009). Multiliteracies on instant messaging in negotiating local, translocal, and transnational affiliation: A case of an adolescent immigrant. *Reading Research Quarterly* 44(4), 377-397.

Lampe, C.A.C., Ellison, N. & Steinfield, C. (2007). A familiar face(book): Profile elements as signals in an online social network. *Proceedings of the ACM CHI 2007 Conference on Human Factors in Computing Systems*, San Jose, CA, 28 April-3 May 2007. Retrieved from: http://dl.acm.org/citation.cfm?doid=1240624.1240695 (accessed October 17, 2014).

Landow, G.P. (2006). *Hypertext 3.0: Critical Theory and New Media in an Era of Globalization*. Baltimore, MD: Johns Hopkins University Press.

Lange, P.G. (2014). *Kids on YouTube: Technical Identities and Digital Literacies*. Walnut Creek, CA: Left Coast Press.

Lanier, J. (2010). *You Are Not a Gadget: A Manifesto*. London: Penguin Group.

Lasén, A. & Gómez-Cruz, E. (2009). Digital photography and picture sharing: Redefining the public/private divide. *Knowledge, Technology & Policy* 22(3), 205-215.

Lawson, V. (1995). The politics of difference: Examining the quantitative/qualitative dualism in post-structuralist feminist research. *Professional Geographer* 47(1), 449-457.

Leage, R. & Chalmers, I. (2010). Degrees of caution: Arab girls unveil on Facebook. In S. Mazzarella (ed.), *Girl Wide Web 2.0* (pp. 27-44). New York, NY: Peter Lang.

Leaman, O. & Ali, K. (2008). *Islam: The Key Concepts*. Oxon: Routledge.

Leander, K.M. (2003). Locating Latanya: The situated production of identity artifacts in classroom interaction. *Research in the Teaching of English* 37, 198-250.

Lefebvre, H. (1991). *The Production of Space*. Oxford: Blackwell Publishers.

Lemish, D. (2010). Foreword. In S.R. Mazzarella (ed.), *Girl Wide Web 2.0* (pp. ix-xiii). New York: Peter Lang.

Lenhart, A. (2009). Adults and social networking sites. Washington, DC: Pew Internet & American Life Project Retrieved from: http://www.pewinternet.org/files/old-media//Files/Reports/2009/PIP_Adult_social_networking_data_memo_FINAL.pdf.pdf (accessed January 30, 2015).

Lenhart, A., Rainie, L. & Lewis, O. (2001). *Teenage Life Online: The Rise of the Instant-Message Generation and the Internet's Impact on Friendships and Family Relationships*. Washington, DC: Pew Internet & American Life Project. Retrieved from: http://www.pewinternet.org/Reports/2001/Teenage-Life-Online.aspx (accessed October 17, 2014).

Leurs, K. (2012). *Digital Passages: Moroccan-Dutch Youths Performing Diaspora, Gender and Youth Cultural Identities across Digital Space*. PhD dissertation. Faculty of Humanities, Utrecht University, the Netherlands. Retrieved from: http://dspace.library.uu.nl/handle/1874/242468 (accessed September 17, 2014).

Leurs, K. (2013). "Ow god, die snobs zien ons weer aan voor een levend laboratorium." Participatief internet onderzoek over/met Marokkaans-Nederlandse jongeren. *Kwalon. Kwalitatief Onderzoek* 18(2), pp. 106-112.

Leurs, K. (2014a). The politics of transnational affective capital: Digital connectivity among young Somalis stranded in Ethiopia. *Crossings: Journal of Migration & Culture* 5(1), 87-104.

Leurs, K. (2014b). Digital throwntogetherness: Young Londoners negotiating urban politics of difference and encounter on Facebook. *Popular Communication* 12(4), 251-256.

Leurs, K. (2015a). Digital divides in the era of widespread Internet access: Migrant youth negotiating hierarchies in digital culture. In M. Walrave, K. Ponnet, E. Vanderhoven, J. Haers & B. Segaert (eds.), *Youth 2.0. Connecting, Sharing and Empowering: Affordances, Uses and Risks of Social Media*. Cham: Springer.

Leurs, K. (2015b). European migrant youth and their micro-politics of being and becoming. In S. Ponzanesi & G. Colpani (eds.)., *Postcolonial Transitions in Europe*. Lanham: Rowman & Littlefield.

Leurs, K., De Haan, M. & Leander, K. (2015). Affective belongings across geographies: Locating YouTube viewing practices of Moroccan-Dutch youth. In B. Aslinger & G.R. Halegoua (eds.), *Locating Emerging Media*. New York, NY: Routledge.

Leurs, K., Hirzalla, F. & Van Zoonen, L. (2012). Waar moslimjongeren hun eigen koers kunnen varen [Where Muslim youth can go their own way]. In A. Benschop & C. Menting (eds.), *ZinZoekers op het Web. Internet en verandering van geloofsbeleving* [Searching for faith on the web: The Internet and changing religious experiences] (pp. 129-139). Vught: Skandalon.

Leurs, K., Midden, E. & Ponzanesi, S. (2012). Digital multiculturalism in the Netherlands: Religious, ethnic, and gender positioning by Moroccan-Dutch youth. *Religion and Gender* 2(1), 150-175. Retrieved from: http://www.religionandgender.org/index.php/rg/article/view/36 (accessed October 15, 2014).

Leurs, K. & Ponzanesi, S. (2011a). Gendering the construction of instant messaging. In M. Ames & S. Burcon (eds.), *Women and Language: Essays on Gendered Communication across Media* (pp. 199-214). Jefferson, NC: McFarland.

Leurs, K. & Ponzanesi, S. (2011b). Mediated crossroads: Youthful digital diasporas. *M/C Journal* 14(2), Retrieved from: http://journal.media-culture.org.au/index.php/mcjournal/article/viewArticle/324 (accessed October 14, 2014).

Leurs, K. & Ponzanesi, S. (2011c). Communicative spaces of their own: Migrant girls performing selves using instant messaging software. *Feminist Review* 99, 55-78.

Leurs, K. & Ponzanesi, S. (2012). Dutch Moroccan girls performing their selves in instant messaging spaces. In K. Ross (ed.), *The Handbook of Gender, Sex and Media* (pp. 436-454). Hoboken, NJ: Wiley-Blackwell.

Leurs, K. & Ponzanesi, S. (2013). Bits of homeland: Generational and gender transformations of Moroccan-Dutch youth using digital technologies. In C. Ponte & M. Georgiou (eds.), *Observatorio (OBS*)* 7(1), 89-110. Special issue on Media, Technology and the Migrant Family: Media Uses, Appropriations and Articulations in a Culturally Diverse Europe. Retrieved from: http://obs.obercom.pt/index.php/obs/article/view/666 (accessed November 20, 2014).

Leurs, K. & Ponzanesi, S. (2014a). Intersectionality, digital identities and migrant youths: Moroccan-Dutch youths as digital space invaders. In L. Steiner, L. McLaughlin & C. Carter (eds.), *The Routledge Companion to Media and Gender* (pp. 632-642). New York, NY: Routledge.

Leurs, K. & Ponzanesi, S. (2014b). Norms and contestations: Ethnicized and minoritized students as space invaders in Dutch higher education. *Etnofoor* 25(2), 73-98.

Leurs, K. & Ponzanesi, S. (2014c). Remediating religion as everyday practice: Postsecularism, postcolonialism, and digital culture. In R. Braidotti, B. Blaagaard, T. De Graauw & E. Midden (eds.), *Transformations of Religions and the Public Sphere. Postsecular Publics*, (pp. 152-174). New York, NY: Palgrave Macmillan.

Leurs, K. & Olivieri, D. (eds.) (2014). *Everyday Feminist Research Praxis: Doing Gender in the Netherlands*. Newcastle upon Tyne: Cambridge Scholars Publishing

LeVine, M. (2008). *Heavy Metal Islam: Rock, Resistance and the Struggle for the Soul of Islam*. New York, NY: Three Rivers Press.

Levinson, J.C. (2007). *Guerilla Marketing*. New York, NY: Houghton Mifflin.

Levitt, P. (2009). Roots and routes: Understanding the lives of the second generation transnationally. *Journal of Ethnic and Migration Studies* 35(7), 1225-1242.

Lewis, C. & Fabos, B. (2005). Instant messaging, literacies and social identities. *Reading Research Quarterly* 40(4), 470-501.

Liberman, S. & Williams, L. (2010). Mektab and Sabr: Cultural and societal factors affecting mental health treatment for Moroccan adolescents. *Humanity in Action*. Retrieved from: http://www.humanityinaction.org/knowledgebase/314-mektab-and-sabr-cultural-and-societal-factors-affecting-mental-health-treatment-for-moroccan-adolescents (accessed December 13, 2011).

Livingstone, S. (2002). *Young People and New Media*. London: Sage.

Livingstone, S. (2003). Children's use of the Internet: Reflections on the emerging research agenda. *New Media & Society* 5(2), 147-166.

Lobe, B., Livingstone, S., Olafsson, K. & Simões, J.A. (2008). *Best Practice Research Guide: How to Research Children and Online Technologies in Comparative Perspective*. Deliverable D4.2. London: EU Kids Online. Retrieved from: http://eprints.lse.ac.uk/21658/ (accessed October 14, 2014).

Loukili, A. (2007). Moroccan diaspora, Internet and national imagination: Building a community online through the Internet portal Yabiladi. Paper presented at the Nordic Africa Days conference, Nordic Africa Institute, Uppsala, 5-7 October. Retrieved from: http://org.uib.no/imer/14Nordic/Papers%20fra%2014.%20Migrasjonsforskerkonferanse/Loukili.pdf (accessed February 12, 2012).

Lovink, G. (2007). The art of watching Databases. In G. Lovink & S. Niederer (eds), *Video Vortex Reader*, (pp. 9-12). Amsterdam: Institute of Network Cultures.

Lykke, N. (2011). This discipline which is not one. In R. Buikema, G. Griffin & N. Lykke (eds.), *Theories and Methodologies in Postgraduate Feminist Research* (pp. 137-150). New York, NY: Routledge.

Mack-Canty, C. (2004). Third-wave feminism and the need to reweave the nature/culture duality. *Feminist Formations* 16(3), 154-179.

Madden, M., Lenhart, A., Duggan, M., Cortesi, S. & Gasser, U. (2013). *Teens and Technology 2013*. Washington, DC: Pew Research Center's Internet & American Life Project. Retrieved from: http://www.pewinternet.org/files/old-media//Files/Reports/2013/PIP_TeensandTechnology2013.pdf (accessed October 17, 2014).

Maddy-Weitzman, B. (2011). *The Berber Identity Movement and the Challenge to North African States*. Austin, TX: University of Texas Press.

Madianou, M. (2014). Polymedia communication and mediatized migration: An ethnographic approach. In K. Lundby (ed.), *Mediatization of Communication* (pp. 323-348). Berlin: De Gruyter.

Madianou, M. & Miller, D. (2013). Polymedia: Towards a new theory of digital media in interpersonal communication. *International Journal of Cultural Studies* 16, 169-187.

Madianou, M. & Miller, D. (eds.) (2012). *Migration and New Media: Transnational Families and Polymedia*. New York, NY: Routledge.

Madison, S. (2012). *Critical Ethnography: Method, Ethics and Performance*. Los Angeles, CA: Sage.

Mainsah, H. (2011). Transcending the national imaginary: Digital online media and the transnational networks of ethnic minority youth in Norway. In E. Eide & K. Nikunen (eds.), *Media in Motion: Cultural Complexity and Migration in the Nordic Region* (pp. 201-219). Surrey: Ashgate.

Maira, S. (2002). *Desis in the House: Indian American Youth Culture in New York City*. Philadelphia, PA: Temple University Press.

Maliepaard, M., Lubbers, M. & Gijsberts, M. (2010). Generational differences in ethnic and religious attachment and their interrelation: A study among Muslim minorities in the Netherlands. *Ethnic and Racial Studies* 33(3), pp. 451-472.

Mallapragada, M. (2006). Home, homeland, homepage: Belonging and the Indian-American web. *New Media & Society* 8(2), 207-227.

Mamadouh, V. (2001). Constructing a Dutch Moroccan identity through the World Wide Web. *The Arab World Geographer* 4(4), 258-274.

Markham, A.N. (2004). Representation in online ethnographies: A matter of context sensitivity. In M.D. Johns, S. Chen & G. Hall (eds.), *Online Social Research: Methods, Issues and Ethics* (pp. 793-820). New York, NY: Peter Lang.

Marokko.nl (2011a). Registreer op Marokko community [Register of the Morocco community]. *Marokko.nl*. Retrieved from: http://forums.marokko.nl/register.php (accessed 30 September 2011).

Marokko.nl (2011b). Home. *Marokko.nl*. Retrieved from: http://home.marokko.nl/index.html (accessed 5 October 2011).

Marshall, J.P. (2010). Ambiguity, oscillation and disorder: Online ethnography and the making of culture. *Cosmopolitan Civil Societies Journal* 2(3), 1-22.

Massey, D. (2005). *For Space*. London: Sage.

Matsuda, M.J. (1991). Beside my sister, facing the enemy: Legal theory out of coalition. *Stanford Law Review* 43(6), 1183-1192.

McCall, L. (2005). The complexity of intersectionality. *Signs: Journal of Women in Culture and Society* 30(3), 1771-1800.

McLeod, J. (2000). *Beginning Postcolonialism*. Manchester: Manchester University Press.

McMurray, D.A. (2001). *In & Out of Morocco: Smuggling and Migration in a Frontier Boomtown*. Minneapolis, MN: University of Minnesota Press.

McRobbie, A. (1982). The politics of feminist research: Between talk, text and action. *Feminist Review* 12, 46-57.

McRobbie, A. (1994). *Post Modernism and Popular Culture*. London: Routledge.

Meijer, M., Buikema, R., Hoving, I., Lucassen, L., Vogel, J., Wekker, G. & Willems, W. (2005). Voorwoord bij de reeks [Series foreword]. In R. Buikema & M. Meijer (eds.), *Cultuur en migratie in Nederland. Kunsten in beweging. 1900-1980* (pp. i-x). Den Haag: Sdu Uitgevers.

Meijerink, D. (2009). *Dutch-Moroccan Youngsters and Morocco*. MA thesis. International Development Studies, Wageningen University, the Netherlands. Retrieved from: http://www.forum.nl/Portals/0/pdf/Dutch-Moroccan-Younsgster-and-Morocco-Dorien-Meijerink.pdf (accessed September 25, 2014).

Mernissi, F. (1987). *Beyond the Veil: Male-Female Dynamics in Modern Muslim Society*. Rev. ed. Bloomington, IN: Indiana University Press.

Merskin, D. (2005). Making an about-face: Jammer girls and the World Wide Web. In S.R. Mazzarella (ed.), *Girl Wide Web* (pp. 51-67). New York, NY: Peter Lang.

Metzger, M.J. & Flanagin, A.J. (eds.) (2008). *Digital Media, Youth and Credibility.* Cambridge, MA: MIT Press.

Miller, D. & Horst, H. (2012). The digital and the human: A prospectus for digital anthropology. In H. Horst & D. Miller (eds.), *Digital Anthropology*, pp. 3-38. London: Berg.

Miller, D. & Slater, D. (2000). *The Internet: An Ethnographic Approach.* Oxford: Berg.

Minh-ha, Trinh T. (1992). *Framer Framed.* New York, NY: Routledge.

Mitchel, W.J. (1995). *City of Bits: Space, Place, and the Infobahn.* Cambridge, MA: MIT Press.

Mitra, A. (2004). Voices of the marginalized on the Internet: Examples from a website for women of South Asia. *Journal of Communication* 54(3), 492-510.

Mitra, A. & Watts, E. (2002). Theorizing cyberspace: The idea of voice applied to the Internet discourse. *New Media & Society* 4(4), 479-498

Mocro_s (2007a). Gemiddelde Marokkaanse Jongens zien er zo uit! [foto] [Average Moroccan Boys look like this [PICTURE]!]. Marokko.nl. Retrieved from: http://forums.marokko.nl/showthread.php?t=3355237 (accessed January 30, 2015).

Mocro_s. (2007b). Gemiddelde Marokkaanse meisjes zien er zo uit [FOTO]! [Average Moroccan girls look like this [PICTURE]!]. Marokko.nl. Retrieved from: http://forums.marokko.nl/showthread.php?t=3357013&page=1 (accessed January 30, 2015).

Modood, T. (2007). *Multiculturalism: A Civic Idea.* Cambridge: Polity Press.

Moor, P.J., Heuvelman, A. & Verleur, R. (2010). Flaming on YouTube. *Computers in Human Behavior* 26(6), 1536-1546.

Morozov, E. (2011). *The Net Delusion: The Dark Side of Internet Freedom.* New York: Public Affairs.

Motivaction (2007). *Nieuwe Nederlanders zeer gehecht aan cultuurgebonden media* [New Dutch people attached to cultural media]. Retrieved from: http://www.motivaction.nl/content/nieuwe-nederlanders-gehecht-aan-cultuurgebonden-media (accessed October 15, 2014).

Mullings, B. (1999). Insider or outsider, both or neither: Some dilemmas of interviewing in a cross-cultural setting. *Geoforum* 30, 337-350.

Mulvey, L. (1975). Visual pleasure and narrative cinema. *Screen* 23(2-3), 6-18.

MUNT. (Producer), (2009) Kop of Munt. Retrieved from: https://www.youtube.com/watch?v=wNhiIe3g70s (accessed February 5, 2015).

Murelli, E. & Okot-Uma, R.W.O. (2002). *Breaking the Digital Divide: Implications for Developing Countries.* London: Commonwealth Secretariat.

Nabben, T., Yeşilgöz, B. & Korf, D.J. (2006). *Van Allah tot Prada. Identiteit, leefstijl en geloofsbeleving van jonge Marokkanen en Turken* [From Allah to Prada: Identity, lifestyle and religiosity among young Moroccans and Turks]. Utrecht: FORUM, Instituut voor Multiculturele Ontwikkeling.

Naficy, H. (1998). Identity politics and Iranian exile music videos. *Iranian Studies* 31(1), 51-64.

Nakamura, L. (2002). *Cybertypes: Race, Ethnicity and Identity on the Internet.* New York, NY: Routledge.

Nakamura, L. (2006). Cultural difference, theory and cyberculture studies. In D. Silver & A. Massanari (eds.), *Critical Cyberculture Studies* (pp. 29-36). New York: New York University Press.

Nakamura, L. (2008). *Digitizing Race: Visual Cultures of the Internet.* Minneapolis, MN: University of Minnesota Press.

Nakamura, L. (2011). Race and identity in digital media. In J. Curran (ed.), *Media and Society.* 5th ed. (pp. 336-347). New York, NY: Bloomsbury USA.

Nakamura, L. & Chow-White, P. (2012). Introduction-race and digital technology: Code, the color line, and the information society. In L. Nakamura & P. Chow-White (eds.), *Race after the Internet* (pp. 1-18). New York, NY: Routledge.

Nakamura, L. & Lovink, G. (2005). Talking race and cyberspace: An interview with Lisa Nakamura. *Frontiers: A Journal of Women Studies* 26(1), 60-65.

Narayan, K. (1993). How native is a "native" anthropologist? *American Anthropologist* 95(3), 671-686.

Nayar, P.K. (2010). *Introduction to New Media and Cybercultures*. Oxford: Wiley-Blackwell.

Nedelcu, M. (2009). *Le migrant online*. Paris: L'Harmattan.

Nedelcu, M. (2012). Migrants' new transnational habitus: Rethinking migration through a cosmopolitan lens in the digital age. *Journal of Ethnic and Migration Studies* 38(9), 1339-1356.

Nedelcu, M. & Wyss, M. (forthcoming 2016). "Doing family" through ICT-mediated ordinary co-presence routines: Transnational communication practices of Romanian migrants in Switzerland. *Global Networks*. Special issue on "Migration and ICTs: "Being Together" and "Co-presence" in Transnational Family Life," edited by M. Nedelcu & L. Baldassar.

Newcom (2014). Nationale Sociale Media Onderzoek 2014 [Dutch National Social Media Survey 2014]. Retrieved from: https://www.marketingoost.nl/dls/162 (accessed February 3, 2015).

Newman, N. (2009). "That's all concept; It's nothing real": Reality and lyrical meaning in rap. In S. Alim, A. Ibrahim & A. Pennycook (eds.), *Global Linguistic Flows: Hip Hop Cultures, Youth Identities, and the Politics of Language* (pp. 195-212). London: Routledge.

Nortier, J. & Dorleijn, M. (2008). A Moroccan accent in Dutch: A sociocultural style restricted to the Moroccan community? *International Journal of Bilingualism* 12(1-2), 125-142.

Nunes, M. (2006). *Cyberspaces of Everyday Life*. Minneapolis, MN: University of Minnesota Press.

Nunley, V. (2004). From the harbor to da academic hood: Hush harbors and an African American rhetorical tradition. In E. Richardson & R. Jackson (eds.), *African American Rhetoric(S): Interdisciplinary Perspectives* (pp. 221-241). Carbondale, IL: Southern Illinois University Press.

Nynäs, P., Lassander, M. and Utriainen, T. (eds.) (2012). *Postsecular Society*. New Brunswick, NJ: Transaction Publishers.

Odin, J. (2010). *Hypertext Aesthetic and the Female Imaginary*. Minneapolis, MN: University of Minnesota Press.

Oiarzabal, P. (2013). *Basque Diaspora Webscape: Identity, Nation, and Homeland, 1990s-2010s*. Reno, NV: Center for Basque Studies, University of Nevada.

Olivieri, D. (2012). *Haunted By Reality: Toward a Feminist Study of Documentary Film: Indexicality, Vision and the Artifice*. PhD dissertation. Faculty of Humanities, Utrecht University, the Netherlands. Retrieved from: http://dspace.library.uu.nl/handle/1874/221965 (accessed October 15, 2014).

OM (2014). OM to prosecute Geert Wilders on Charges of Discrimination. *The Public Prosecution Service*. Retrieved from: https://www.om.nl/algemeen/english/engelstalige/to-prosecute-geert/ (accessed January 29, 2015).

Oostveen, M. (2004). De knip- en plak-islam; Hoe jonge moslims in Nedelrand hun radicale wereldbeeld samenstellen [Cut-and-paste Islam: How young Muslims in the Netherlands compose their radical worldview]. *NRC Handelsblad*, November 27, p. 38.

Orellana, M.F. (2009). *Translating Childhoods: Immigrant Youth, Language and Culture*. Piscataway, NJ: Rutgers University Press.

Paasonen, S. (2010). Disturbing, fleshy texts: Close looking at pornography. In M. Liljeström & S. Paasonen (eds.), *Working with Affect in Feminist Readings* (pp. 58-71). New York, NY: Routledge.

Palfreyman, D. & Al Khalil, M. (2003). A funky language for teenzz to use: Representing gulf Arabic in instant messaging. *Journal of Computer-Mediated Communication* 9(1). Retrieved from: http://onlinelibrary.wiley.com/doi/10.1111/j.1083-6101.2003.tb00355.x/full (accessed October 17, 2014).

Papacharissi, Z. (2009). The virtual sphere 2.0: The Internet, the public sphere and beyond. In A. Chadwick (ed.), *Routledge Handbook of Internet Politics* (pp. 230-245). New York, NY: Routledge.

Papacharissi, Z. (2010). *A Private Sphere: Democracy In a Digital Age*. Cambridge: Polity Press.

Papacharissi, Z. & Easton, E. (2013). In the habitus of the new: Structure, agency and the social media habitus. In J. Hartley, J. Burgess & A. Bruns (eds.), *A Companion to New Media Dynamics* (pp. 171-184). Oxford: Wiley-Blackwell.

Parker, D. & Song, M. (2006). New ethnicities online: Reflexive racialisation and the Internet. *The Sociological Review* 54(3), 575-594.

Parker, D. & Song, M. (2009). New ethnicities and the Internet: Belonging and the negotiation of difference in multicultural Britain. *Cultural Studies* 23(4), 583-604.

Parks, M.R. (2007). *Personal Networks and Personal Relationships*. Mahway, NJ: Lawrence Erlbaum Associates.

Pauwels, L. & Hellriegel, P. (2009). A critical cultural reading of "YouTube." In S. Hatzipanagos & S. Warburton (eds.), *Handbook of Research on Social Software and Developing Community Ontology* (pp. 381-399). New York: Information Science Reference.

Pels, T. & De Haan, M.J. (2003). *Continuity and Change in Moroccan Socialization*. Utrecht: Verwey-Jonker Instituut/Utrecht University.

Pels, T. & De Haan, M.J. (2007). Socialization practices of Moroccan families after migration: A reconstruction in an "acculturative arena." *Young* 15(1), 71-89.

Peters, R. (2006). "A dangerous book": Dutch public intellectuals and the Koran. RSCAS Working Paper 39. Retrieved from: http://dare.uva.nl/document/225275 (accessed October 14, 2014).

Phalet, K. & ter Wal, J. (eds.) (2004). *Moslim in Nederland. Diversiteit en verandering in religieuze betrokkenheid* [Muslim in the Netherlands: Diversity and change in religious engagement]. Den Haag: SCP.

Phillips, N. & Hardy, C. (2002). *Discourse Analysis: Investigating Processes of Social Construction*. Thousand Oaks, CA: Sage.

Piela, A. (2012). *Muslim Women Online*. London: Routledge.

Pietersen, R. (2008). Forum waar beledigen mag [Forums where verbal abuse is allowed], *Trouw*, 21 January. Retrieved from: http://www.trouw.nl/tr/nl/4324/Nieuws/article/detail/1260775/2008/01/21/internetfora-Forum-waar-beledigen-mag.dhtml (accessed October 15, 2014).

Ponzanesi, S. & Leurs, K. (2014). On digital crossings in Europe. *Crossings: Journal of Migration & Culture* 5(1), 3-22.

Poorthuis, M. & Salemink, T. (2011). *Van harem tot Fitna. Beeldvorming over de Islam in Nederland 1848-2010* [From harem to *Fitna*: Representation of Islam in the Netherlands, 1848-2010]. Nijmegen: Valkhof Pers.

Press, A. & Livingstone, S. (2008). Taking audience research into the age of new media: Old problems and new challenges. In M. White & J. Schwoch (eds.), *Questions of Method in Cultural Studies* (pp. 175-200). Oxford: Blackwell.

Prins, B. (1997). *The Standpoint in Question: Situated Knowledges and the Dutch Minorities Discourse*. PhD dissertation. Faculty of Humanities, Utrecht University, the Netherlands.

Prins, B. (2010). From toleration to repression. The Dutch backlash against multiculturalism. In S. Vertovec & S. Wessendorf (Eds.), *The Multiculturalism Backlash: European Discourses, Policies And Practices,* (pp. 72-91). London: Routledge.

Prins, B. & Saharso, S. (2010). From toleration to repression: the Dutch backlash against multiculturalism. In S. Vertovec & S. Wessendorf (eds.), *The Multiculturalism Backlash: European Discourses, Policies and Practices* (pp. 72-91). New York, NY: Routledge.

Prinsen, F., De Haan, M.J. & Leander, K. (2015). Networked identity. *How immigrant youth employ online identity resources*. Young 23(1), 19-38.

Protalinski, E. (2011, March 29). Facebook backpedals: Removes Third Palestinian Intifada page against Israel. *ZDNET*. Retrieved from: http://www.zdnet.com/blog/facebook/facebook-backpedals-removes-third-palestinian-intifada-page-against-israel/1049 (Accessed January 30, 2015).

Puwar, N. (2004). *Space Invaders: Race, Gender and Bodies out of Place*. Oxford: Berg.

Rafje.nl, 2011) Overvaren. [Sailing across]. Retrieved from: http://rafje.nl/rafje/rafjes/349.png (Accessed February 3, 2015).

Raj, R. (2007). The festival of sacrifice and travellers to the City of Heaven (Makkah). In R. Raj & N.D. Morpeth (Eds.), Religious tourism and pilgrimage festivals management, (pp. 127-139). Cambridge, MA: Cabi.

Rana, J. (2011). Chicks, kicks & glory. De betekenis van kickboxen voor Marokkaanse meisjes [How Moroccan girls make meaning of kick boxing]. Amsterdam: Boom.

Ramazanoğlu, C. & Holland, J. (2002). *Feminist Methodology: Challenges and Choices*. London: Sage.

Ratliff, C. (2007). Attracting readers: Sex and audience in the blogosphere. *The Scholar and Feminist Online* 5(2), 1-4. Retrieved from: http://sfonline.barnard.edu/blogs/ratliff_01.htm (accessed October 17, 2014).

Razzaqi, Z. (2011). Performing arts. In F. Crowe, J. Goddard, B. Hollingum, S. MacEachern & H. Russell (eds.), *Islamic Beliefs, Practices, and Cultures* (pp. 270-289). Tarrytown, NY: Marshall Cavendish.

Rettberg, J. W. (2014). *Seeing Ourselves through Technology: How We Use Selfies, Blogs and Wearable Devices to See and Shape Ourselves*. New York, NY: Palgrave.

Rijksoverheid. (2009). Van der Laan: Afspraken met Marokko.nl voor beter beheer website [Agreements with Marokko.nl for better administration of its website]. *De Rijksoverheid. Voor Nederland*, October 29. Retrieved from: http://www.rijksoverheid.nl/nieuws/2009/10/29/van-der-laan-afspraken-met-marokko-nl-voor-beter-beheer-website.html (accessed October 15, 2014).

Rogers, R. (2013). *Digital Methods*. Cambridge, MA: MIT Press.

Rowe, A.C. (2008). *Power Lines: On the Subject of Feminist Alliances*. Durham, NC: Duke University Press.

Roy, O. (2004). *Globalised Islam: The Search for a New Ummah*. London: Hurst & Company.

RVD (2007). Toespraak van Prinses Máxima [Speech delivered by Princess Máxima], Het Koninklijk Huis. Retrieved from: http://web.archive.org/web/20071011154310/; http://koninklijkhuis.nl/content.jsp?objectid=20871 (accessed October 14, 2014).

Ryan, J. (2007). *Countering Militant Islamist Radicalization on the Internet*. Dublin: Institute of European Affairs.

Rybas, N. & Gajjala, R. (2007). Developing cyberethnographic research methods for understanding digitally mediated identities. *Forum: Qualitative Social Research* 8(3), art. 35. Retrieved from: http://www.qualitative-research.net/index.php/fqs/article/view/282 (September 19, 2014).

Sache, I. (2009). Berbers. Imazighen. *Flags of the World* website. Retrieved from: http://www.fotw.us/flags/xb.html (accessed October 17, 2014).
Sadiqi, F. (2003). *Women, Gender and Language in Morocco*. Leiden: Brill.
Said, E. (1979). *Orientalism*. New York, NY: Vintage Books.
Sánchez, M.C. & Schlossberg, L. (eds.) (2001). *Passing: Identity and Interpretation in Sexuality, Race and Religion*. New York, NY: New York University Press.
Sayad, A. (1999). *La double absence. Des illusions de l'émigré aux souffrances de l'immigré* [The double absence: Illusions of the emigrant to the suffering of the immigrant]. Paris: Seuil.
Saywitch, K., Camparo, L.B. & Romanoff, A. (2010). Interviewing children: Implications of research and policy. *Behavioral Sciences and the Law* 28(4), 542-562.
Schäfer, M. (2011). *Bastard Culture! How User Participation Transforms Cultural Production*. Amsterdam: Amsterdam University Press.
Scheffer, P. (2007). *Het land van aankomst* [The country of arrival]. Amsterdam: De Bezige Bij.
Schoorl, J. (2006). Demografische gegevens [Demographic figures]. In C. van Praag (ed.), *Marokkanen in Nederland: Een profiel* [Moroccans in the Netherlands: A profile] (pp. 3-13). Den Haag: Nidi.
Scott, J. (2014). Children's families: A child-centered perspective. In J. Treas, J. Scott & M. Richards (eds.), *The Wiley-Blackwell Companion to the Sociology of Families*. West Sussex: John Wiley & Sons.
Sedgwick, E.K. (2003). *Touching Feeling: Affect, Pedagogy, Performativity*. Durham, NC: Duke University Press.
Sedgwick, M. (2015). Families, governments, schools, alternative spaces and the making of European Muslims. In M. Sedgwick (ed.), *Making European Muslims* (pp. 1-20). New York, NY: Routledge.
Selwyn, N. (2004). Reconsidering political and popular understandings of the digital divide. *New Media & Society* 6, 341-362.
Shepherd, T. (2010). Personal communication, September 18.
Shepherd, T. (2012). *Persona Rights in Young People's Labour of Online Cultural Production: Implications for New Media Policy*. PhD dissertation. Faculty of Arts and Sciences, Concordia University Montréal, Canada. Retrieved from: http://spectrum.library.concordia.ca/973722/ (accessed October 17, 2014).
Shepherd, T. (2014). Gendering the commodity audience in social media. In L. Steiner, L. McLaughlin & C. Carter (eds.), *The Routledge Companion to Media and Gender* (pp. 157-167). New York: Routledge.
Shome, R. (2003). Space matters: The power and practice of space. *Communication Theory* 13(1), 39-56.
Siapera, E. (2010). *Cultural Diversity and Global Media*. Oxford: Wiley-Blackwell.
Siibak, A. (2009). Constructing the self through the photo selection. *Journal of Psychosocial Research on Cyberspace* 3(1). Retrieved from: http://www.cyberpsychology.eu/view.php?cisloclanku=2009061501 (accessed October 17, 2014).
Sims, C. (2013). From differentiated use to differentiating practices: Negotiating legitimate participation and the production of privileged identities. *Information, Communication and Society* 17(6), 670-682.
Skalli, L.H. (2006). *Through a Local Prism: Gender, Globalization, and Identity in Moroccan Women's Magazines*. Oxford: Lexington Books.
Slade, C. (2010). Media and citizenship: Transnational television cultures reshaping political identities in the European Union. *Journalism* 11(6), 727-733.

Slootman, M. & Tilly, J. (2006) *Processes of Radicalisation among Some Amsterdam Muslims: Why Some Amsterdam Muslims Become Radical.* Amsterdam: Imes. Retrieved from: http://home.medewerker.uva.nl/m.w.slootman/bestanden/Slootman%20Tillie%202006%20Processes%20of%20Radicalisation.pdf (accessed November 29, 2011).

Smelik, A. (2009). Lara Croft, *Kill Bill*, and the battle for theory in feminist film studies. In R. Buikema & I. van der Tuin (eds.), *Doing Gender in Media, Art and Culture* (pp. 178-192). Oxford, Routledge.

Snel, E., Engbersen, G. & Leerkens, A. (2006). Transnational involvement and social integration. *Global Networks* 6(3), 285-308.

Soja, E. (2010). *Seeking Spatial Justice.* Minneapolis, MN: University of Minnesota Press.

Somekh, B. & Mavers, D. (2003). Mapping learning potential: Student's conceptions of ICT in their world. *Assessment in Education* 10(3), 409-420.

Spanjar, R. (2011). *Van 3 naar 10.000.000 vrienden* [From 3 to 10,000,000 friends]. Amsterdam: Lebowski Publishers.

Spivak, G.C. (1990). Criticism, feminist and the institution. In S. Harasym (ed.), *The Post-Colonial Critic* (pp. 1-16). London: Routledge.

Spivak, G.C. (1993a). Can the subaltern speak? In P. Williams & L. Chrisman (eds.), *Colonial Discourse and Post-Colonial Theory* (pp. 66-111). Harlow: Longman.

Spivak, G.C. (1993b). The politics of translation. In G.C. Spivak (ed.), *Outside in the Teaching Machine* (pp. 179-200). New York, NY: Routledge.

Spivak, G.C. (1999). *A Critique of Postcolonial Reason: Toward a History of the Vanishing Present.* Cambridge, MA: Harvard University Press.

Stichting Maroc.nl (2001). *Maroc.nl. Digitaal lief en leed van Marokkaanse jongeren* [Maroc.nl: Digital joys and sorrows of young Moroccans]. Amsterdam: Uitgeverij Contact.

Stock, F. (2014). *Speaking of Home: Home and Identity in the Multivoiced Narratives of Descendants of Moroccan and Turkish Migrants in the Netherlands.* PhD dissertation. Faculty of Theology and Religious Studies, University of Groningen, the Netherlands.

Strano, M.M. (2008). User descriptions and interpretations of self-presentation through Facebook profile images. *Cyberpsychology: Journal of Psychosocial Research on Cyberspace* 2(2). Retrieved from: http://cyberpsychology.eu/view.php?cisloclanku=2008110402&article=5 (accessed October 17, 2014).

Strauss, A.L. & Corbin, J.M. (1998). *Basics of Qualitative Research: Techniques and Procedures for Developing Grounded Theory.* Thousand Oaks, CA: Sage.

Sullivan, J. (2010, July 28). Testimony of Joe Sullivan, Chief Security Officer, Facebook, July 28, 2010, Before the US House of Representatives Committee on the Judiciary, Subcommittee on Crime, Terrorism, and Homeland Security, Hearing on: Online Privacy, Social Networking, and Crime Victimization. Retrieved from: http://judiciary.house.gov/_files/hearings/pdf/Sullivan100728.pdf (accessed October 17, 2014).

Sultana, F. (2007). Reflexivity, positionality and participatory ethics: Negotiating fieldwork dilemmas in international research. *ACME: An International E-Journal for Critical Geographies* 6(3), 374-385. Retrieved from: www.acme-journal.org/vol6/FS.pdf (accessed October 15, 2014).

Sunier, T. (2010). Styles of religious practice: Muslim youth cultures in Europe. In H. Moghissi and H. Ghorashi (eds.), *Muslim Diaspora in the West: Negotiating Gender, Home and Belonging* (pp. 125-138). Farnham: Ashgate.

Tagliamonte, S. & Denis, D. (2008). Linguistic ruin? Lol! Instant messaging and teen language. *American Speech* 83(1), 3-34.

Thiel-Stern, S. (2007). *Instant Identity: Adolescent Girls and the World of Instant Messaging*. New York, NY: Peter Lang.

Thumim, N. (2012). *Self-Representation and Digital Culture*. New York, NY: Palgrave Macmillan.

Thurlow, C. (2006). From statistical panic to moral panic: The metadiscursive construction and popular exaggeration of new media language in the print media. *Journal of Computer-Mediated Communication* 11(3), 667-701.

Thussu, D.K. (ed.) (2009). *Internationalizing Media Studies*. Oxon: Routledge.

Tiidenberg, K. (2014). Bringing sexy back: Reclaiming the body aesthetic via self-shooting. *Cyberpsychology: Journal of Psychosocial Research on Cyberspace* 8(1). Retrieved from: http://cyberpsychology.eu/view.php?cisloclanku=2014021701&article=3. (accessed October 17, 2014).

Trandafoiu, R. (2013). *Diaspora Online: Identity Politics and Romanian Migrants*. New York, NY: Berghahn.

Tufecki, Z. (2008). Grooming, gossip, Facebook and MySpace: What can we learn from these sites from those who won't assimilate? *Information, Communication and Society* 11(4), 544-564.

Turan Hoffman, Z. (2014). Diaspora tours and place attachment: A unique configuration of emotion and location. In H. Jones & E. Jackson (eds.), *Stories of Cosmopolitan Belonging: Emotion and Location* (pp. 141-156). New York, NY: Routledge.

Turkle, S. (2007). The things that matter. In S. Turkle (ed.), *Evocative Objects: Things We Think With* (pp. 3-11). Cambridge, MA: MIT Press.

Ünlüsoy, A., De Haan, M. & Leander, K. (2012). Learning through network interaction: The potential of ego-networks. In V. Hodgson, C. Jones, M. de Laat, D. McConnell, T. Ryberg & P. Sloep (eds.), *Proceedings of the 8th International Conference on Networked Learning* (pp. 373-380). Lancaster: Lancaster University.

Urban Connect. (2011a). Welkom op onze homepage [Welcome on our homepage]. *Urban Connect BV.* Retrieved from: http://www.urbanconnect.nl/index.php?nav=static&pagina=Adverten tiecampagnes (accessed September 30, 2011).

Urban Connect. (2011b). Marokko.nl. *Urban Connect BV.* Retrieved from: http://www.urbanconnect.nl/index.php?nav=static&pagina=Marokko.nl (accessed September 30, 2011).

Utz, S. (2008). (Selbst)marketing auf Hyves [(Self)marketing on Hyves]. In P. Alpar & S. Blaschke (eds.), *Web2.0. Eine empirische Bestandsaufnahme* [Web 2.0: An empirical inventory] (pp. 235-258). Wiesbaden: Vieweg & Teubner.

Van den Boomen, M. (2000). *Leven op het net. De sociale betekenis van virtuele gemeenschappen* [Life on the net: The social meanings of virtual communities]. Amsterdam: Instituut voor Publiek en Politiek. Retrieved from: http://boom.home.xs4all.nl/boek/3ageo.htm (accessed October 15, 2014).

Van den Boomen, M., Lammes, S., Lehmann, A.S., Raessens, J. & Schäfer, M.T. (eds.) (2009). *Digital Material: Tracing New Media in Everyday Life and Technology*. Amsterdam: Amsterdam University Press.

Van der Stoep, J. (2009). The princess and the mushroom: Globalisation, existential insecurity and the search for a national identity. In I. ter Avest (ed.), *Education in Conflict* (pp. 117-136). Münster: Waxmann.

Van der Zee, R. (2006). Waarom moslimmeisjes graag een man zoeken via internet [Why Muslim girls prefer to find a man via the Internet]. *NRC Handelsblad*, March 25. Retrieved from: http://vorige.nrc.nl/krant/article1666058.ece (accessed October 15, 2014).

Van Dijck, J. (2008). Digital photography: Communication, identity, memory. *Visual Communication* 7(1), 57-76.

Van Dijck, J. (2013). *The Culture of Connectivity*. Oxford: Oxford University Press.

Van Doorn, N. (2009). The ties that bind: The networked performance of gender, sexuality and friendship on MySpace. *New Media & Society* 11(8), 1-22.

Van Doorn, N. & Van Zoonen, L. (2009). Theorizing gender and the Internet. In A. Chadwick & P.N. Howard (eds.), *Routledge Handbook of Internet Politics* (pp. 261-274). New York: Routledge.

Van Gemert, F. (1998). *Ieder voor zich: kansen, cultuur en criminaliteit van Marokkaanse jongens* [Everyone for themselves: Opportunities, culture and criminality among Moroccan youths]. Amsterdam: Het Spinhuis.

Van Heelsum, A.J. (1997). *De etnisch-culturele positie van de tweede generatie Surinamers* [The ethno-cultural position of second-generation Surinamese]. Amsterdam: Het Spinhuis.

Van Praag, C. & Schoorl, J. (2008). Housing and segregation. In M. Crul & L. Heering (eds.), *The Position of the Turkish and Moroccan Second Generation in Amsterdam and Rotterdam* (pp. 49-62). Amsterdam: Amsterdam University Press.

Van Stekelenburg, J., Oegema, D. & Klandermans, B. (2011). No radicalization without identification: How ethnic Dutch and Dutch Muslim web forums radicalize over time. In A.E. Azzi, X. Chryssochoou, B. Klandermans & B. Simon (eds.), *Identity and Participation in Culturally Diverse Societies* (pp. 256-274). Oxford: Blackwell.

Van Summeren, C. (2007). Religion online: The shaping of multidimensional interpretations of Muslimhood on Maroc.nl. *The European Journal of Communication Research* 32(2), 273-295.

Van Zoonen, L., Vis, F. & Mihelj, S. (2010). Performing citizenship on YouTube: Activism, satire and online debate around the anti-Islam video *Fitna*. *Critical Discourse Studies* 7(4), 249-262.

Veen, V., Stevens, G., Doreleijers, T., Ende, J. van der & Vollebergh, W. (2010) Ethnic differences in mental health among incarcerated youths. *European Child & Adolescent Psychiatry* 19(5), 431-440.

Vergani, M. & Zuev, D. (2011). Analysis of YouTube videos used by activists in the Uyghur nationalist movement: Combining quantitative and qualitative methods. *Journal of Contemporary China* 20(69), 205-229.

Verhagen, F. (2010). *Hoezo mislukt? De nuchtere feiten over de integratie in Nederland* [Failed in what way? The bare facts about integration in the Netherlands]. Amsterdam: Nieuw Amsterdam.

Vermeij, L. (2004). "Ya know what I'm sayin'?" The double meaning of language crossing among teenagers in the Netherlands. *International Journal of the Sociology of Language* 170, 141-168.

Vertovec, S. (2009). *Transnationalism*. Oxon: Routledge.

Verweij, A. & Bijl, R. (2012). Monitoring integration in the Netherlands. In R. Bijl & A. Verweij (eds.), *Measuring and Monitoring Immigrant Integration in Europe* (pp. 239-252). The Hague: The Netherlands Institute for Social Research.

Vis, F., Van Zoonen, L. & Mihelj, S. (2011). Women responding to the anti-Islam film *Fitna*: Voices and acts of citizenship on YouTube. *Feminist Review* 97, 110-129.

Wajcman, J. (2007). From women and technology to gendered technoscience. *Information, Communication & Society* 10(3), 287-298.

Wall, M. (2009). Africa on YouTube. *The International Communication Gazette* 71(5), 393-407.

Walther, J.B., Carr, C.T., Choi, S.S.W., DeAndrea, D.C., Kim, J., Tom Tong, S. & Van Der Heide, B. (2011). Interaction of interpersonal, peer, and media influence sources online. In Z. Papacharissi (ed.), *A Networked Self* (pp.17-38). London: Routledge.

Warf, B. & Arias, S. (eds.) (2009). The spatial turn: interdisciplinary perspectives. Oxon: Routledge.

Warshak, R. (2003). Payoffs and pitfalls of listening to children. *Family Relations* 52(4), 373-384.

Wekker, G. (2006). *The Politics of Passion: Women's Sexual Culture in the Afro-Surinamese Diaspora*. New York, NY: Columbia University Press.

Wendt, B. (2014). *The Allure of the Selfie. Instagram and the New Self-Portrait.* Amsterdam: Institute of Network Cultures. Retrieved from: http://networkcultures.org/blog/publication/no-08-the-allure-of-the-selfie-instagram-and-the-new-self-portrait-brooke-wendt/ (accessed October 10, 2014).

Werbner, P. (2006). Understanding vernacular cosmopolitanism. *Anthropology News* 47(5), 7-11.

Werdmölder, H. (2005). *Marokkaanse lieverdjes. Crimineel en hinderlijk gedrag onder Marokkaanse jongeren* [Moroccan darlings: Criminal and annoying behavior among Moroccan youths]. Amsterdam: Uitgeverij Balans.

Wessendorfer, S. (2013). *Second-Generation Transnationalism and Roots Migration: Cross-Border Lives*. Surrey: Ashgate.

Wilders, P. (2005). En wederom van die laffe kankermarokkanen. *Meetholland*, Retrieved from: https://web.archive.org/web/20120125074934/http://old.meetholland.com/message/708037.aspx. (accessed January 29, 2015).

Wired Up (2010a). Leuke bijbaan, assistant bij Wired Up Internet onderzoek. *Marokko Community* website, March 2008. Retrieved from: http://forums.marokko.nl/showthread.php?t=3132059 (accessed October 15, 2014).

Wired Up (2010b). Swia swia, ze3ma. *Maroc.nl. Community* website, February 16. Retrieved from: http://www.maroc.nl/forums/wie-schrijft-blijft/293645-swia-swia-ze3ma.html (accessed October 15, 2014).

Wired Up (2011). New media use among youth in migration: A survey-based account. Wired Up Technical Research Report. Utrecht: Utrecht University, December. Retrieved from: http://www.uu.nl/wiredup/pdf/Wired_Up_-_Technical_survey_report.pdf (accessed October 15, 2014).

Wise, A. & Velayutham, S. (2006). *Towards a Typology of Transnational Affect*. Sydney: Macquarie University, Centre for Research on Social Inclusion. Retrieved from: http://www.crsi.mq.edu.au/public/download.jsp?id=10615 (accessed September 25, 2014).

Yi, Y. (2009). Adolescent literacy and identity construction among 1.5 generation students. *Journal of Asian Pacific Communication* 19(1): 100-129.

Yuval-Davis, N. (2006). Intersectionality and feminist politics. *European Journal of Women's Studies* 13(3), 193-209.

Zarzycka, M. (2009). Cindy Sherman confronting feminism and (fashion) photography. In R. Buikema & I. van der Tuin (eds.), *Doing Gender in Media, Art and Culture* (pp. 151-161). Oxford, Routledge.

Zhao, Y., Liu, J. Tang, J. & Zhu, Q. (2013). Conceptualizing perceived affordances in social media interaction design. *Aslib Proceedings: New Information Perspectives* 65(3), 289-302.

Zittrain, J. (2008). *The Future of the Internet*. New Haven, CT: Yale University Press.

Appendix 1: Meet the informants

Abdel

Abdel (a pseudonym he chose himself) is a thirteen-year-old, second-year VWO student from Rotterdam. His parents migrated from Al Hoceima, his family is Berber and he also mainly speaks Berber with his parents. He described himself as "*tough but also a nice, spontaneous Moroccan boy*" and he feels connected to Muslim and hip-hop youth. He does not feel he belongs to a particular group, but "*he is just himself.*" He has three sisters, and his favorite subject in school is religious studies. Outside, Abdel likes to play football and other games. He connects to the Internet mostly using his desktop computer in his bedroom. He does not feel anyone has a say over his use of the Internet. He is into rap music, and he listens to both Moroccan-Dutch artists such as Yes-R and Ali B. and African-American rappers such as 50 Cent and Tupac. He includes the word "*mocro*" in his e-mail address. He uses the Internet mostly to log in to MSN, to send e-mails, to update his profile page and to watch videos on YouTube. He had befriended around 200 people, both on Hyves and MSN. He reports receiving overwhelming numbers of chain e-mails having to do with religion and current affairs, but he states he is especially interested in those that address ways to help people in wars across the globe, and mentions the specific case of Palestine. Abdel participated in the survey and Fayrouz and I interviewed him in a school multimedia center.

Abdelsammad

Abdelsammad is a fifteen-year-old MAVO student from Rotterdam. His parents migrated to the Netherlands from Nador in Morocco. His relatives live across Europe, in France, Spain, Belgium but also in Morocco. He speaks Dutch and Berber with his parents at home and he has three brothers and two sisters. His favorite subjects in school are Dutch language and athletics. In his spare time he likes to spend his time playing football and being at the computer. He describes himself as tough and sporty and says that he listens to rap music. Logging into his account, his parents makes use of MSN voice chat to keep in touch, next to almost yearly visits. His older sister helps him when something is not working on the computer. She also monitors what he downloads and whom he talks to online. He likes to put up his holiday pictures taken in Morocco on his Facebook profile page. Abdelsammad prefers Facebook because it is more international than Hyves, and he has around ninety friends there. He, for instance, talks to his nephew who lives in Spain on Facebook. On MSN, he has 350 friends, and on YouTube he likes to look up Dutch, Moroccan and American rap videos. Furthermore, he likes to relive his visits to Nador by watching YouTube videos showing the streets, shopping malls and the boulevard alongside the sea. Among other things, he has also included the name of the city in his e-mail address, together with a gendered affiliation "*nadorboy*." Furthermore he likes playing computer games such as *Grand Theft Auto* and the *FIFA Soccer* games. Abdelsammad participated in the survey and I interviewed him in a school multimedia center.

Anas

Anas is a thirteen-year-old old, second-year VMBO K/B student from 's-Hertogenbosch. He was born in the Netherlands while his parents are from Marrakech, and the family returns there during holiday trips. He has two older brothers who are both enrolled in the university. During the interview he was a bit shy, but with his friends he became very noisy afterward. His hobbies are being on the computer and going outside to play football. He also takes part in athletics. The majority of his family still lives in Morocco, and his parents make use of his MSN account to remain in touch with them. He uses Facebook to talk to his nephews in Morocco. He enjoys looking up R&B, hip-hop and house music on YouTube, but he also likes to watch videos shot in Marrakech. Recently he was mostly helping his dad to find out how to use Google Maps to print out driving directions, as his dad at the time was driving all over the Netherlands for job interviews. He is also attached to downloading music. Anas has fifty friends on FaceBook, but he just quit Hyves where he had befriended 158 contacts, just like he had on MSN. He participated in the survey. I carried out the interview with Anas in a school meeting room.

Amina

Amina (a pseudonym she chose herself) is a thirteen-year-old, second-year VWO student from Rotterdam. In describing her ethnicity, she stated her parents have migrated from Nador, stating, "*Yes, I am a Berber*," adding, "*I still remain Moroccan. I was born in the Netherlands, and I have a command over the Dutch language, but my Moroccan* [*Arabic*] *is not so good*." With her parents she speaks Dutch and Berber. Most relatives she knows best live in the Netherlands, but more distant relatives live in Spain, Germany and France but also in Morocco. She described herself as quite fashion-conscious and she sees herself as computer-savvy and added she is very eager to learn. Amina can access the Internet from her own room using her laptop, but she also uses the desktop computer in the living room. There she has to share the computer with her five siblings; she has one brother and four sisters. She is not interested in online social networking sites, but she logs in to MSN daily. On MSN, she had befriended around 130 people. Additionally she is connected to the Internet via her smartphone, and she checks her messages during our interview. She is a heavy user of what she says the *"girly online discussion board,"* Chaima.nl, to share sensitive, romantic and personal stories and to talk about nails, beauty and fashion. She is a fan of Maher Zain, a Swedish-Lebanese R&B singer whom she describes as an artist who sings in English *"about the peacefulness of Islam."* Amina participated in the survey. I conducted the interview in an empty classroom where Fayrouz was simultaneously interviewing Ilham in another corner.

Amir

Amir is a sixteen-year-old, fourth-year VMBO-B student from 's-Hertogenbosch. He was born in the Netherlands, and his parents migrated from Marrakech, in western Morocco. He has one brother and three sisters. With his parents he mainly speaks Moroccan-Arabic, and he stresses he does not feel Berber, but Arabic. He described himself as his own style. *"I don't belong to one particular group... I'm just multiculti, I think."* While some of his family members have moved to Algeria, most family still live in Morocco. Once every year he visits his family there. His favorite subject is tourism, an elective course he is following. He has a computer of his own, in his own bedroom. He likes to play football in his spare time. When he is at home he logs on to the computer, or he watches TV. He includes the word "*mocro*" in his e-mail address. Amir is a hip-hop fanatic and he listens to Moroccan-Dutch artists like Yes-R, Ali B., Ree B. and Soesi B. as well as Moroccan rap groups H-Kayne and Fnaïre. He is proud to know the last two groups, as they are not well known in the Netherlands yet. Amir had 349 Hyves friends and had over 200 MSN friends. To get in touch with girls he uses the international dating/social networking site Tagged.com and he likes to visit FRMF.ma, "Site Official de la Fédération Royale Marocaine de Football," to keep up-to-date on the proceedings of the Moroccan national football team. Amir participated in the survey, and I interviewed him in an empty classroom. After the interview we maintained extensive e-mail contact.

Ayoub

Ayoub is a fourteen-year-old, second-year VMBO B/K student from 's-Hertogenbosch. He described himself as a normal, sporty Muslim boy and he loves to surf the Internet, play football and chill with his friends. He has three sisters and one brother and he happily announced that his mother was pregnant. Ayoub speaks Dutch and Berber with his parents. He is born in the Netherlands, but his parents migrated from Haroun in east Morocco. At the time of the fieldwork he was very excited about the upcoming visit of his grandfather from Morocco. Most members of his father's side of the family live in the Netherlands, while most of his mother's relatives live in France, Germany, Belgium and Morocco. Besides annual holiday trips, he mostly is in touch with his nephew, who lives in Belgium. Together with his parents he uses video chat on MSN to talk to family in Morocco. He does not experience any restrictions in using the computer by anyone in his household and he uses MSN and PingChat! on his BlackBerry smartphone, too. His favorite online game is online billiards, which he played using the site gamzer.com. He had over 700 friends on Hyves, 500 MSN contacts and he is an avid Twitter user. Ayoub participated in the survey and was interviewed by me in a school meeting room.

Badr

Badr is a fourteen-year-old, third-year student VMBO K/B student from 's-Hertogenbosch. His parents are from Nador in Morocco and he is born in the Netherlands. At home he speaks Dutch and Berber with his parents and his younger brother and younger sister. His favorite subject in school is German because he can also practice it with his nephew, who is living in Germany. Badr likes to play sports, mainly football. He also frequently plays games on his PlayStation 3 and his desktop computer that he has to share with his siblings. He likes to go to Morocco, but only on holiday, because after two or three weeks he likes to go home, because he feels more at home in the Netherlands. His family has spread out across Europe, living in Belgium, Germany, France, Spain and Denmark. Mostly he keeps in touch with his nephews in Germany and Belgium. But he sets up Skype for his parents; they do not know how to use it. Everyday, he was online for a couple of hours and he liked to chat with one of his 500 MSN contacts or hang out in chat rooms, and update his profile page for his 500 Hyves friends to see. He also actively plays OSM.nl, an online soccer manager game. On YouTube he searches for highlight videos of his favorite football clubs, Ajax and Real Madrid. Above all, he is a Michael Jackson fan. Badr participated in the survey and I interviewed him. He appeared to feel a bit uncomfortable during the interview held in an empty classroom.

Bibi

Bibi (a pseudonym she chose herself) is a sixteen-year-old, fourth-year VMBO B/K student from 's-Hertogenbosch. Bibi is an openhearted girl who has much to share. Her parents migrated from Nador, a city on the Mediterranean coast in northeastern Morocco. She has two younger brothers and younger two sisters. With her parents she mainly speaks Berber. She speaks very fast and curses and swears every now and then. Bibi described she is one of the more lively girls in her school class; she jumps and dances, and is very active, adding, *"I am Moroccan, and I am proud of it."* Sometimes she clicks her tongue to say *"no."* Most of her family lives in the Netherlands, but there are also family members in Morocco. She only uses MSN and Hyves to keep in contact with nieces and nephews living in the Netherlands; the rest of her family she connects with only during yearly holiday trips when she likes to bring her nieces gifts. She thinks Dutch kids are more restricted in their use of the Internet, and she says, *"We Moroccan youth secretly take our laptops and hide them under our bed sheets and go on MSN and Facebook."* She admits she is always very curious to learn about what other people think about the pictures she puts up online. In her spare time, Bibi likes to play sports; she has joined indoor football and kickboxing clubs. Also she likes to help her mother out and to spend time with her friends. She has a laptop that she uses in her own room in the attic of the house. Her sisters also join her there when they want to use the computer. She likes to do her homework there, with her sisters. She listed 560 Hyves friends and 290 MSN contacts. Bibi participated in the survey and Fayrouz interviewed her in a school meeting room.

Carlos

Carlos (a pseudonym he chose himself), is a fifteen-year-old, third-year VMBO K/T student from 's-Hertogenbosch. Carlos calls himself a half-blood, adding, *"I have Dutch looks, but when I talk I talk like a Moroccan."* His father is Dutch and his mother is from Rabat, the capital city of Morocco. He has a younger brother and sister, and he has to share the desktop computer located in the living room with them. He wants to be seen as a normal, Muslim boy. In his household Dutch and Moroccan-Arabic are spoken. The majority of his mother's side of the family resides in Morocco, but he mentions a number of his aunts live in the Netherlands, France and Spain. He keeps in touch with them via MSN and Facebook. Interestingly, he speaks Italian with those family members that have migrated, as they first settled in Italy before moving onward toward other countries in Europe. The pseudonym he chose to have his voice included in the study also reflects his affinity with Italy. Athletics is his favorite subject in school, and in his spare time he plays sports in football and kickboxing clubs. At night he likes to be on the computer, connecting with his friends on MSN and

Facebook and to listen to music. However, he says he is also online "*24/7*." He connects to the Internet using his BlackBerry mobile phone, and he uses PingChat! a lot. He does not feel as if anyone in his household restricts him in his online behavior. Carlos had 900 friends on MSN and 850 friends on Hyves, he mentioned this was mostly to get in touch with girls, his 50 contacts on Facebook were mostly family in the diaspora. He includes the word "*badboy*" in his e-mail address. Like Senna, he spoke passionately about a page of remembrance on Hyves, an RIP page, set up for a friend of his who had recently passed away after a traffic accident. And he enjoys looking up information about motor scooters. He is into hip-hop; he listens to Moroccan-Dutch artists like Ali B. and Yes-R; Antillean-Dutch artists like Hef, Dio and Gio as well as and North American hip-hop artists like Eminem. Carlos participated in the survey and I interviewed him in an empty classroom.

Faruk

Faruk (a pseudonym he chose himself) is a sixteen-year-old, third-year MAVO student from Rotterdam. He describes himself as having Moroccan parents and he was born in the Netherlands. He adds he is interested in hip-hop and Islam. Sometimes he feels sad when he feels he and his friends are being more tightly monitored than other young people when they enter shops. He speaks Dutch, Moroccan-Arabic and Berber with his parents at home. He has one brother and two sisters. He has family in the Netherlands, but also in France, Spain and Morocco. In school, his favorite subjects are English, geography and physics. His favorite pastimes are hanging out with his friends, playing football and going to the shopping mall. Also he likes to be at the computer and play games on his PlayStation console. Faruk accesses the Internet from a laptop that is shared among the household, but he brings it to his own room and sits on is bed using the laptop. In his household they are most strongly connected to his aunt in France, and he logs on to MSN for his parents let them talk with her using their webcam. He feels that the ability to make voice and video calls to his family abroad for free is one of the biggest advantages of the Internet. He has around a hundred friends on MSN. He is not restricted by anyone in his household in his use of the Internet. His online interests resemble his offline interests, he likes to play Online Soccer Manager (OSM.nl), or watch football clips on YouTube. He also likes to search for music videos of the American rapper Eminem and has converted some of his songs into MP3s that he puts on his Samsung slider phone. Faruk participated in the survey and Fayrouz interviewed him in a school multimedia center.

Fatiha

Fatiha is a seventeen-year-old, fourth-year HAVO student from Eindhoven. She was born in the Netherlands, and both her parents were born in Morocco. She describes herself as Muslim and finds it important to present herself as a believer online as well, for instance, by choosing the following MSN display name "*Show remorse!!........ Allah (swt) will accept it from you and inchAllah will offer you goodness!!*" She has three sisters and one brother. At home she mostly speaks Dutch and Berber with her parents. She feels quite free in her use of the Internet, except for the school settings where she feels the schoolteacher monitors her. She says she is attached to MSN, Hyves, and YouTube, sites she visits on a daily basis. She had befriended around 115 people on MSN and on Hyves. Additionally, she often participates in online discussion boards, for instance, Marokko.nl, and the Moroccan-Dutch-girls-oriented Chaima.nl and the Islam-oriented Islaam.nl. The Islam portal website Al-Yaqeen.nl (meaning "trust in Islam") is also among her favorites. Fatiha shared MSN transcripts with me and participated in the piloting of the survey and the interview. I interviewed her through e-mail and MSN and we maintained e-mail contact.

Ferran

Ferran is a seventeen-year-old student in the second-year of his MBO degree (vocational education) in social work from Venlo. He describes himself as a "*Moroccan-Dutch boy.*" He mainly speaks Dutch and Berber with his parents. Most of his family lives in Morocco, Germany and the Netherlands, but he also has relatives in Spain. Quite frequently he meets his relatives at weddings; recently he attended one in Germany. It's mostly his mother who uses MSN and a webcam to talk to her brothers, sisters and her mother, who live outside the Netherlands. His most important hobby is playing football, which he does both for his club as well as on outdoor courts. He often turns to VI.nl, a site with football news, and he likes to use the Internet for entertainment purposes; he, for instance, watches funny videos gathered on Dumpert.nl. Other habits are browsing the profile pages of his 160 Hyves contacts and logging in to MSN talk to any of his 110 contacts. Also he looks up funny videos in Berber on YouTube as well as lectures on the Quran. He accesses the Internet in his own bedroom using his own laptop. Ferran participated in the piloting of the interview, and Fayrouz and I together interviewed him in a hotel lobby café.

Hajar

Hajar is a fifteen-year-old, third-year VMBO K/T student from 's-Hertogenbosch. Her parents migrated from the Berber city Meknès in northern

Morocco. She has two brothers and one sister. She describes herself as a normal and social Moroccan-Dutch girl, who stands up for herself, adding that she is of Moroccan descent but she was born in the Netherlands. She speaks Dutch, French and Moroccan-Arabic at home. Her hobbies are being on the computer and hanging out with friends either at home on the couch in the winter and outside in the summer. She says she is very tidy, and states she strongly asserts herself, when people gossip about her she gets very angry. Reflecting on her wearing of a double-wrap headscarf, she feels she stands out from others because of her faith. At home, she shares the desktop computer in the living room with her family, but she also connects to MSN on her mobile phone. Her father's side of the family lives in the Netherlands and her mother's side lives in Belgium. She keeps in touch with them via Skype and MSN, and she helps her mother set up connections. She thinks Moroccan-Dutch youth are active on the Internet because of the diasporic connections with grandmothers and uncles living in Morocco and elsewhere. She feels her parents and her brother control her Internet actions. Hajar enjoys looking up pictures of *takshitas* (Moroccan dresses) on the discussion board Marokko.nl and social networking sites. She had a hundred friends on Facebook, 487 on Hyves and 230 on MSN. She is into electronic dance music, and stresses she is addicted to mobile phone texting and to listening to Sami Yusuf, an Iranian-British singer. Hajar participated in the survey and Fayrouz interviewed her in a school meeting room.

Hatim

Hatim is a fifteen-year-old, third-year VMBO K/T student from 's-Hertogenbosch. He was born in Aklim in northeast Morocco and he migrated to the Netherlands with his parents at a young age. Hatim has three brothers and two sisters. His favorite subject in school is athletics and in his spare time he is occupied with football and kickboxing. He describes himself as "*someone who follows the mood of the moment and who is adventurous*," and added he is a Muslim. He likes electronic dance and house music. At home he speaks Dutch and Berber. His family lives in the Netherlands and in Morocco. He accesses the Internet from a desktop computer in his own bedroom, and first thing in the morning he turns on the computer to check whether he has received new messages. He does not feel anyone in his household monitors his actions online. He likes the Internet for MSN, watching videos on YouTube, downloading music and updating his profile page. He had 135 friends on Facebook, 556 on Hyves and 600 on MSN. Above all things he is an active gamer, specializing in *Call of Duty: Black Ops*, a first-person shooter video game on PlayStation 3. Hatim participated in the survey. The interview took place in a school meeting room. He was a bit reserved when answering, perhaps because Fayrouz, an adult female, interviewed him.

Ilana

Ilana is a sixteen-year-old, first-year student MBO (vocational education) in social work from Venlo. She describes herself "*as Dutch but of Moroccan descent.*" She has one older brother. Her relatives live in Morocco, Germany and the Netherlands. She uses MSN to talk to her cousins in Germany, and she likes to practice her German with them. Her favorite pastime is shopping. She accesses the Internet in her bedroom using her own laptop. She does not know by heart how many people are in her MSN or Hyves friend lists, but reckons that from her lists most often around ten people are online at the same time. Most of all she likes to surf to Marokko.nl and read stories that other people have posted. She is especially interested in reading about funny events and exciting experiences people have. She also sometimes goes to the thread on "Islam and I" to open topics to get more information about things in life related to Islam. On YouTube she likes to look up Moroccan-Arabic and English-language music. Ilana participated in the piloting of the interview and Fayrouz and I together interviewed her in a museum cafeteria.

Ilham

Ilham is a thirteen-year-old, second-year VWO student from Rotterdam. Her favorite subject is history, and her hobbies are football, swimming and reading books. She has four sisters. Ilham describes herself as embodyings "*opposite poles.*" She is social, sweet and companionable, but also quiet and at times overexcited. She is interested in politics, electronic dance music, hip-hop, Islam and religion. Furthermore she confidently stated, "*I'm Moroccan, Berber and Muslim, holding Dutch nationality.*" Different affiliations also become apparent from the e-mail address she chose, which includes "*miss*" and "*riff.*" "*Riff*" is an Arabic word meaning "the edge of a cultivated area" and it is commonly used to refer to the groups of Berber people occupying parts of northeastern Morocco, ranging from the dessert in the center of Morocco to the mountains to the Mediterranean coast. Her parents were among those people, having migrated from the coast city of Nador. Most of her mother's side of the family currently live in the Netherlands, while most of her father's side live abroad, in Spain, Belgium and Morocco. She speaks Dutch, Moroccan-Arabic and Berber with her parents. She mostly uses the laptop in the living room, where she has to share it with her siblings. She feels quite controlled in her use of the Internet – her parents and her sisters keep tabs on her behavior. But she says she, for instance, uses eBuddy.com to log on to get in touch with her MSN contacts. eBuddy is a web-based client that does not store any of her conversations on the computer as the MSN application does. She forms a clique with two of her best girlfriends, at school but also online. She also likes MSN because she uses it to maintain her friendships with girls she has befriended during holidays in Morocco. In total, she had 133 friends on MSN. She finds Google important and she likes to read stories on Marokko.nl. She likes listening to music using YouTube videos, especially music by the American pop singer Christina Aguilera. She was very curious also to know the background of Fayrouz, who interviewed her. Ilham participated in the survey, and the interview took place in the empty classroom where I was interviewing Amina in another corner.

Inas

Inas is a thirteen-year-old, second-year VWO student from Rotterdam. She has two brothers and one sister. She finds it important to have her own style and says that "*my origins are in Morocco, but I was born in the Netherlands*," adding that she is sweet and intelligent, but also rebellious at times. She sees her headscarf as a fashionable but also important identity marker, which she also shows in photographs she puts online on Hyves and MSN. In school, her favorite subject is math, and outside school she likes to hang out with her friends and practice swimming. She speaks Dutch and Moroccan-Arabic with her parents. She accesses the Internet from the family's desktop computer in the living room. Her relatives live in Morocco, Spain and the Netherlands. Her parents talk to family members using MSN and a webcam. She logs in to Hyves on a daily basis. On Hyves, she befriended ninety people, on MSN she had around 250 contacts. She is a fan of Justin Bieber and to download his songs from YouTube to her Samsung Wave mobile phone she uses YoutubeConverter.org. Her major passion is fashion; she spends a lot of her time browsing around different fashion web-logs and she also finds inspiration on the Moroccan-Dutch, girls-oriented discussion board Chaima.nl. She praises the Internet as a uniting force; underlining the fun she has in meeting people online who are also interested in sharing their thoughts on the latest fashion trends. Inas participated in the survey and I interviewed her in a school library.

Inzaf

Inzaf is a fifteen-year-old, fourth-year VMBO-T student from Eindhoven. In describing herself she says she is Muslim, but she adds: "*I follow my heart, I am not really someone who follows a group.*" In addition, she shared: "*I would not say I am Moroccan. My parents are from Morocco, but I was born here."* Her parents migrated from Al Hoceima in the north of Morocco, and other family members live in Belgium, France and Morocco. She has two sisters and one brother. At home she speaks Dutch and Moroccan-Arabic with her parents. She likes to be on the computer and to go to the city and hang out with her friends in shopping centers, or to go out for dinner. She logs on to the desktop computer in the living room, where she has to share it with her siblings. She is relatively free in her Internet activities, but occasionally her mother checks up on her. Discussion forums, chatting on MSN and watching videos are her main preoccupations online. Frequently she logs in to online discussion boards Marokko.nl and Yasmina.nl to find good recipes, *"most often Moroccan dishes – those dishes my mother does not know how to make."* And she likes to post and read online stories. She had befriended around 150 people on MSN and 120 on Hyves. Fayrouz and I interviewed Inzaf together with Naoul in a lunchroom. She participated in the piloting of the survey and interview and she shared MSN transcripts. We kept in touch via e-mail.

Kamal

Kamal is a fifteen-year-old, third-year VMBO-T student from Eindhoven. He was born in the Netherlands of parents who migrated from Morocco. He has three sisters. At home, he mainly speaks Berber with his parents. He describes himself as a sweet, Muslim, football fanatic, computer savvy, gamer boy. He connects to the Internet using his desktop computer in his bedroom, and he does not experience much supervision by anyone in his household. Every day he plays video games on his PlayStation. He likes to watch his favorite TV series online using the site RTLgemist.nl. Furthermore he likes to connect with fellow youngsters on the virtual hotel/social networking site Habbo.nl. He also likes to connect with Moroccan-Dutch youth on the online forum Marokko.nl. He had befriended around 600 people on Hyves, and 200 people on MSN. Kamal shared MSN transcripts and participated in the piloting of the survey and interview. I interviewed him via e-mail and MSN and we maintained e-mail contact.

Kenza

Kenza is a fourteen-year-old, third-year HAVO student from Rotterdam. She was born in Morocco and migrated to the Netherlands with her parents at young age. Kenza describes herself as being of *"Moroccan descent."* Members of her household are the only ones from her family who are living in the Netherlands; other family members live in Belgium, France, Spain, Italy and Morocco. She has one sister and one brother. At home, with her parents she mostly speaks Moroccan-Arabic. She does not understand Berber, only Arabic. In school, her favorite subject is French. She has also set up an e-mail address on the French e-mail provider *Hotmail.fr*. Outside of school she likes cycling and watching TV. She mostly accesses the Internet using her laptop in her own room. She feels computer-savvy, but adds that her sister asserts quite some control over her use of the laptop, monitoring what sites she visits and whom she talks to. Kenza uses Facebook to keep in touch with cousins in Belgium, France, Spain and Morocco. Most important for her is YouTube. She uses the site to look up *raï* music, especially the Algerian artist Cheb Khaled. Sometimes when she feels "*homesick*" for Morocco, she looks up Moroccan songs. Her best Internet experiences are when she puts up holiday pictures of Morocco on her profile page. Also she likes to play first-person shooter games online. She had fifty-three friends on Facebook and thirty-nine on MSN. Kenza participated in the survey and Fayrouz interviewed her in a school multimedia center.

Khadija

Khadija is a seventeen-year-old, fourth-year VMBO-K student from Eindhoven. She describes herself as a Muslim girl and adds she was born in the Netherlands. Her parents were born in Morocco. She mainly speaks Dutch and Moroccan-Arabic at home with her parents. In her spare time, she likes shopping, swimming, watching TV and assisting her mother with cooking. She mostly makes use of the desktop computer in the living room. She has to share the computer with her brother and her two sisters. She feels her mother keeps an eye on her Internet activities, especially concerning what she downloads from the Internet. She considers MSN, Marokko.nl and YouTube the most important spaces she engages with online. She reported to have fifty-three Hyves and IM contacts. MSN is used to have personal conversations with friends. She also likes the Internet for it enables her to buy stuff which she cannot find in the shops elsewhere and she uses it to download Moroccan-Arabic and Berber *raï* and *chaabi* music to her MP3 player. Khadija participated in the piloting of the survey and the interview mostly via e-mail and MSN and she shared MSN transcripts with me.

Loubna

Loubna is a fourteen-year-old, third-year VMBO K/T student from 's-Hertogenbosch. She describes herself as a confident, sweet, trustworthy girl, and admits she can sometimes be stubborn. She is into electronic dance and hip-hop music, fashion and Islam. Her favorite subject is math.

She comes from a large household; she has five sisters and one brother She speaks Dutch and Moroccan-Arabic at home. Loubna describes herself as being of Moroccan-Dutch descent, but adds that does not mean she does not like to go to the cinema and go shopping for clothes in the city. Apart from her parents, most family members live in Morocco. The family makes frequent visits to Morocco; she says she feels she "*cannot do without Morocco.*" Together with her mother she very frequently connects with her family in Morocco using Skype, especially at the time of the fieldwork, when her grandmother was seriously ill. Although she has her own laptop, her sisters restrict her activity, especially what she downloads from the Internet. As a great fan of *Twilight*, she shows her interest in the American series of vampire-themed fantasy romance novels and films with images and clips on her Hyves profile page. She had 232 friends on Hyves and 320 friends on MSN; a lot of people were added to her MSN friend list when she forgot to log out from her account in an Internet café in Morocco during a vacation. Her favorite musicians are North American R&B artists Beyoncé and Whitney Houston, Lebanese singers Nancy Ajram and Elissa and Moroccan artists Khalid Bennani and Sami Yusuf. Loubna likes to read books, but she also enjoys reading about other young peoples' trials and tribulations on the online forum Marokko.nl. Loubna participated in the survey and Fayrouz interviewed her in a school meeting room.

Mehmet Ali

Mehmet Ali is a fourteen-year-old, second-year VMBO B/K student from 's-Hertogenbosch. He describes himself as normal Moroccan boy. He was born in the city of Nador in Morocco, and at the age of four he migrated with his parents to the Netherlands. He has three younger brothers. In school, his favorite subjects are drama and athletics. Outside of school he has joined a football club, and he plays midfielder. Using the computer and browsing the Internet are also things he likes to do. Mostly, he speaks in Dutch and Berber with his parents. Most other family members live in Morocco, and his uncle lives in Spain. He shares the common laptop in the living room with his parents and his three younger brothers. He uses MSN to talk to his nephews who live in Morocco; his parents use the telephone more to connect with family members in the diaspora. He likes to joke around with his nephews. They log in to the Internet in a local Internet café in Nador and when he sees them behind the computer he relives his memories of Morocco. He had 570 people in his Hyves friend list and 195 in his MSN list. Badr is a fan of Moroccan-Dutch rappers Yes-R, Fouhadi as well as American rap artists like Jay-Z and the Moroccan singer Douzi. When he misses Morocco, he likes to look up photos and videos on YouTube from places he knows there. He has also included Morocco in his e-mail address. Badr participated in the survey and I interviewed him in a school meeting room.

Meryam

Meryam is a fifteen-year-old, third-year VMBO K/B student from 's-Hertogenbosch. Her parents migrated from Taourirt, near Oujda in north-eastern Morocco. She has one brother and one sister. In her family, Dutch, Moroccan-Arabic and Berber are spoken. During the interview it became apparent that she is heavily engaged with her faith. This became clear when she showed a book titled *Het Handboek voor Moslimvrouwen* (*The Handbook for Muslim Women*), which she bought at the mosque. Her favorite subject is math. She likes to spend her spare time with her friends, watching TV and using the computer. People in her school call her a gangster, because as she says she likes hip-hop and she sometimes comes over aggressive, but she notes, "*I do not mean to be like that at all.*" Besides Dutch and American music, she listens to Jalal El Hamdaoui on Mocro-place.nl. Her favorite musician is El Hamdaoui, who comes from Oujda like her parents. Currently, half of her family members have migrated to the Netherlands, France and Belgium, and the other half live in Morocco. She does not feel as if anyone in her family supervises her in her online activity. She is, however, very sensitive about putting information online. Meryam had sixty friends on Facebook and 400 on MSN. On MSN she writes in Arabic when talking to her nieces who live in France, and when talking to others she mostly writes in Dutch. She likes to read stories posted on the discussion board Marokko.nl. She feels bad that "a lot of people think that Moroccan youth are utterly bad and so on, but there are only a few who completely ruin it for the others." She includes the word "*mocrogirl*" in her e-mail address and she adds, "*I always say Morocco is the country of my dreams.*" Meryam participated in the survey and Fayrouz interviewed her in a school meeting room.

Midia

Midia is a thirteen-year-old, first-year VMBO-T student from Utrecht. She was born in the Netherlands; her parents were born in Morocco. She sees herself as a gamer and a Muslim. Occasionally she visits the mosque. She speaks Dutch and Moroccan-Arabic with her parents at home. She accesses the Internet from her bedroom using the desktop computer that she shares with her younger brother and sister. Her mother asserts influence over what she downloads and puts on her profile page. Her favorite online activities are browsing through profile pages on Hyves, chatting with her MSN friends and exploring the virtual hotel/social networking site Habbo Hotel. She is also into playing online games such as *World of Warcraft* and she likes to speak her mind on Marokko.nl. She had befriended 110 people on Hyves, and 400 people on MSN. Midia participated in the piloting of the survey and interview and she shared MSN transcripts with me. I interviewed her through e-mail and MSN and we maintained contact via e-mail.

Mohammed

Mohammed (a pseudonym he chose himself) is a thirteen-year-old, second-year VMBO K/T student from 's-Hertogenbosch. His parents migrated from Morocco, and he has one brother and two sisters. At home he speaks Dutch and Moroccan-Arabic. He describes himself a normal, intelligent and nice Moroccan-Dutch guy, who is into hip-hop, computers and Islam. He was reserved in his answers in the beginning of the interview but gradually opened up. He likes to play football and listens to hip-hop music a lot. He has to make use of his brother's laptop, mostly in his brother's bedroom. Also uses the computers at school daily, were he feels his schoolteacher restricts him in his online behavior. He often visits 101barz.bnn.nl and hiphopflow.nl, communities where members discuss and circulate rap songs. He downloads music by artists such as Ali B. Yes-R, Appa, Sjaak, Anu-D, and puts them on his iPod. He was most attached to MSN and YouTube, and he used the first to talk to family members living in the Netherlands, Belgium, France and Morocco or one of his 300 other contacts, while he enjoyed the latter to review football highlights. On his profile page, his 408 contacts could see he had put up pictures of his holiday trip to Morocco with his parents together with football and music. He participated in the survey and Fayrouz conducted the interview with Mohammed in a school meeting room.

Mustafa

Mustafa is an eighteen-year-old student from Venlo. He is in the second-year of his MBO (vocational education) degree in social work. He describes himself as *"born in the Netherlands, but still also of Moroccan descent, thus Moroccan-Dutch."* The largest part of his family lives in the Netherlands, but he also has family members living in France, Spain and Morocco. He mainly speaks Dutch and Berber with his parents. His household mainly keeps in touch with relatives living in the diaspora using their landline phone. Being at the computer, swimming and football are Mustafa's hobbies. He accesses the Internet in his bedroom using a desktop computer. He has around 100 friends on MSN and on Hyves. He likes to play video games, and he listens to R&B, electronic dance music and Moroccan music. He, for instance, subscribes to a channel dedicated to the African-American R&B singer Ryan Leslie on YouTube, which allow him to follow new music releases of his favorite artist. Using Keepvid.com he also downloads these songs to his MP3 player and mobile phone. During Ramadan, he turned to YouTube and found a number of inspiring recitations from the Quran. Also he browses the site Zoubida.nl for Berber artists. The site hosts music MP3s of artists from Morocco. Mustafa participated in the piloting of the interview and I interviewed him in a museum cafeteria.

Naoul

Naoul is a sixteen-year-old, MBO law student from Eindhoven. She describes herself as a Moroccan, a Muslim and an ambitious girl. She adds: "*I follow my own path. What other people think or do does not bother me.*" She speaks Dutch and Berber at home with her parents. Her parents migrated from Morocco, and other family members live in Morocco, Belgium, Germany, France and Spain. She sets up an MSN connection for her dad to connect with family members in the diaspora: "*We, the kids, have to prepare it and he comes in and sits in front of the camera and starts talking.*" Next to her school, she has a job on the side, and in her free time she likes to be on the computer and to hang out with her friends. Naoul works a lot on the computer for her studies. She has a laptop of her own, which she takes everywhere. She does not feel restricted in her Internet activities. At home she takes her laptop to her bedroom and logs on. Inzaf is also into playing online games such as *World of Warcraft* and she is interested in Marokko.nl. There, she finds support from what she describes as her "*own circle,*" to discuss "*Moroccan issues.*" She had around 110 friends on MSN and 190 on Hyves. Fayrouz and I interviewed Naoul together with Inzaf in a lunchroom. She participated in the piloting of the survey and interview and she shared MSN transcripts. We kept in touch via e-mail.

Nevra

Nevra is a sixteen-year-old, fourth-year VMBO-K student from 's-Hertogenbosch. Her parents migrated from the capital city of Morocco, Rabat. She has included the word "RABAT" in her e-mail address. She has three brothers and three sisters. Nevra sees herself as a sweet Moroccan-Dutch and Muslim girl. She likes to spend her free time with her girlfriends, shopping. She likes to play crazy tricks. She connects to the Internet from her own room using her own laptop, and she does not feel as if anyone in her household restricts her in her Internet usage. She also shared that she is online "*24/7*" by using her BlackBerry, to stay logged in to MSN all the time. Of all Internet applications she likes MSN and online discussion boards like Marokko.nl the most. About the latter she says young Moroccan-Dutch people "*can say what they want, and they can show it is not all bad*" there. She likes to download music from Mocro-place.nl such as *reggada*, an old genre of wedding music from the eastern parts of Morocco and *chaabi*, Moroccan folk music, and *raï* music, which blends African Spanish, French, and Arabic musical forms. She had 408 friends on Hyves and 450 on MSN. She lives in a middle-sized city in the southern part of the Netherlands. Nevra said she really enjoyed participating in our research. She completed the survey and Fayrouz and I interviewed her together in a school meeting room.

Oussema

Oussema (a pseudonym he chose himself) is a fifteen-year-old, third-year HAVO student from Rotterdam. His family migrated from near Nador in Morocco to "*various countries across the world, not India, but across Europe and the United States.*" He feels he is "*someone in between*" which he explains by stating, "*I listen to all sorts of music – rock, Dutch, R&B, electro, all of it. I love sports, but I love computer games a lot, too. I am Muslim. I am not a chubby kid, but also not super muscular. I can't be pinned down to something specific. I am a bit of everything.*" He feels his personally duty is to actively change the negative image of Moroccan-Dutch youth, and he does so, for instance, by assisting elderly people. He has two older brothers and a younger sister. He speaks Dutch, Moroccan-Arabic and Berber with his parents at home. His favorite subjects are biology and technology. His hobbies are judo, football and being at the computer. He uses Facebook to keep in touch with his cousins in the diaspora. He can access the Internet using the desktop computer in his bedroom, the computer in his brother's room and on his mobile phone. He also had a laptop but it recently crashed after he played too many computer games. He likes first-person shooter games such as *Call of Duty: Black Ops*, *Half Life 2* and *Counter-Strike* and he also likes to explore his creativity using video-editing and Photoshop image-editing software. He, for instance, makes "skins," visuals such as characters and news weapons for computer games. He also participates in online discussion board competitions, where his Photoshop creations get rated and he recently made it to the second place overall in the forum. At the time of the fieldwork his parents were on hajj, the pilgrimage to Mecca. He had just deleted his Hyves account, but he had 150 friends on Facebook and 300 friends on MSN. Oussema participated in the survey, and I interviewed him in a school multimedia center. After the interview we kept in touch via Facebook Chat.

Rachid

Rachid (a pseudonym he chose himself) is a thirteen-year-old, second-year VWO student from Utrecht. His parents were both born in Tangier and Driouche in northern Morocco. He has a younger brother and a younger sister. He tries to follow Islam as much as he can, adding, *"when I have time, I go to the Mosque – at least, I try to go every Friday."* With his parents he speaks Dutch, Moroccan-Arabic and Berber, mostly. He accesses the Internet from a shared desktop computer. He starts every day by going online to check whether there are any changes in his roster for the day. He is in touch with nephews and nieces living abroad on MSN, but when he is on the computer and his mother sees that family is also online she usually takes over the computer. His relatives live in the Netherlands, Germany and Morocco. Connecting to the Internet in Morocco is not commonplace for everyone, he says, and he also remarks that due to a recent flood in Morocco Internet connections got broken. In his spare time, he often goes to swimming practices at his club, he likes to be at the computer and he likes to play games on his PSP (PlayStation Portable). He had 266 friends on Facebook and similar number of contacts on MSN. On Facebook he also likes to play games, for instance, *Snake*, but he also uses it to find out about school exams and assignments and to circulate school texts. He is into both Dutch-language as well as English-language rap, hip-hop and R&B. He uses LimeWire and µTorrent software applications to download music and movies. Rachid proudly spoke about being able to circumvent Internet restrictions at school by visiting those blocked sites he likes using a proxy. Rachid participated in the piloting of the survey and interview, and I interviewed him in a university canteen.

Ryan

Ryan (a pseudonym he chose himself) is a fifteen-year-old, fourth-year VMBO-T student from 's-Hertogenbosch. He was born in the Netherlands, but his parents are from Kenitra, in the northwestern part of Morocco. He has one sister and one brother. He is a very spontaneous talker, and he wants to be seen as normal, but states he can also be rebellious. His favorite subjects are English and biology and he would like to continue his education in a laboratory school. Nine of his mother's siblings live in the Netherlands, while most family members from his father's side still live in Morocco. His parents speak Dutch and Moroccan-Arabic. Once a year he visits his family in Morocco with his parents, and he uses MSN and Skype to remain in contact with his nephews in Morocco. As his choice for an English pseudonym already signals, Ryan considers himself different from most other Moroccan-Dutch young people. On his Hyves profile page he, for instance, subverts the dominant image of Moroccan-Dutch youth: "*When someone sees me there, they say I do not look like a Moroccan, but obviously I am one, but I do not let it show.*" Also, he "*mostly only plays games on the computer*" which he thinks is "*very different from what normal Moroccan youth in my school do – they mostly use MSN, watch YouTube and listen to music.*" Gaming is more "*Dutch culture,*" he says, "*Dutch kids, I know a lot of them who play games.*" He likes electronic dance music and spends most of his spare time playing the third-person shooting game *GunZ: The Duel* and the online role-playing game *League of Legends*. He also plays *Modern Warfare* and *Call of Duty 2* on the PlayStation 3 and he likes to participate in online discussion boards, especially Worldwidegaming.org, to discuss the games he plays. However, Ryan is also an active swimmer for the local swimming club. He had 300 friends on Hyves and over 400 friends on MSN. Ryan participated in the survey and I interviewed him in a school meeting room.

Sadik

Sadik, from Venlo, is a seventeen-year-old student in the second year of his MBO (vocational education) degree to become a teaching assistant. He describes himself as Muslim, and both his parents migrated from Morocco, while he himself was born in the Netherlands. Apart from his household, and one uncle who lives in France, all his relatives live in Morocco. His favorite pastimes are playing the drums and swimming. He accesses the Internet from his bedroom using either his own laptop or his own desktop computer. His parents give him a lot of autonomy over his Internet activities; sometimes they come and have a look at what he is doing. But he says his father knows he handles the technologies well. Logging in to Hyves and MSN are daily routines. He had befriended 450 people on Hyves, and 150 on MSN Messenger. Just before the fieldwork he started using Twitter, and he finds it most interesting because he is now able to follow the personal experiences of people he admires from all over the world. Among his friends Twitter is used to arrange get-togethers and negotiate conflicting class schedules. Also he frequently surfs to Explosm.net, a site where funny cartoons are published. Finally, he likes to look up YouTube videos of musicians and Islam; he has saved them to a play list in his account. He likes videos of good drummers, guitarists and beatboxers. Sadik participated in the piloting of the interview and I interviewed him in a museum cafeteria.

Safae

Safae, from Venlo, is an eighteen-year-old student in the third year of her MBO (vocational education) degree in social work. She describes herself as Moroccan but adds, *"I was born and raised here, so in principle I am just an ordinary Dutch"* youth. Her hobbies are fitness and using the Internet. She accesses the Internet from her bedroom using her own laptop. She also has a mobile phone she uses to access to the Internet. Her favorite sites are MSN, Hyves, Facebook and Marokko.nl. She considers MSN as a sort of an addiction, because *"I automatically log in to MSN every day."* Sometimes her mother sits next to her behind the computer when she is talking to her friends on MSN or looking through the forum discussions on Marokko.nl. Marokko.nl she likes for reading *"true stories."* When her mother cannot answer questions she has about her background or questions relating to Islam, she considers Marokko.nl a good place to search for answers. She listens to Moroccan, English and Dutch artists. Safae participated in the piloting of the interview and Fayrouz interviewed her in a museum cafeteria.

Sahar

Sahar is a fourteen-year-old, third-year MAVO student from Rotterdam. She describes herself as *"a normal girl, and I am Moroccan. Yes, I was born in the Netherlands, and I wear a headscarf – most others don't."* She has one younger and one older brother and at home she speaks Dutch and Berber with her parents. English is her favorite subject. Her grandparents and some other family members still live in Morocco. She accesses the Internet from a desktop computer in her own room. She feels quite unrestricted in her use of the Internet; but her father does keep track of what she puts on her profile page. Outside school, she likes to hang out with her girlfriends and be at the computer and watch TV. She mostly uses MSN, browses YouTube and weblogs and visits Marokko.nl. She had 120 friends on MSN. She likes Marokko.nl for its capacity for people to say positive things about Moroccans in the Netherlands instead of the *"almost always negative things that people say."* She is also interested in discussing fashion and Islam. Her favorite artists are African-American R&B singers Auburn and Shontelle and the Moroccan singer Jalal El Hamdaoui, and she likes Islamic-oriented *anasheed* songs. She also keeps a virtual dog via the site Webpet.nl. Sahar participated in the survey and I interviewed her in a school multimedia center.

Salima

Salima (a pseudonym she chose herself) is a thirteen-year-old, second-year VWO student from Rotterdam. She describes herself as calm and Moroccan, coming from a large household of eight people; she has four brothers and one sister. Her parents have migrated from Al Hoceima in the north of Morocco. At home she mostly speaks Berber with her parents. She feels affiliated to Islam and fellow Muslims. Her favorite subject is Dutch, while her favorite pastimes are shopping and watching TV. She has to share the desktop computer in the living room with her siblings, and her parents and her sister restrict her in her use of the Internet. Her family has spread out from Morocco across Spain, France, Belgium and the Netherlands. Her household keeps in contact with family members mostly by calling them on the phone, and by making visits. She is most attached to MSN Messenger and to Google, which she uses to look up information and to download music. She had around fifty friends on MSN. Salima includes the word "*mocro*" in her e-mail address. To amuse herself she plays games on the website Funnygames.nl and she heads to Chaima.nl, a discussion board set up and frequented by Moroccan-Dutch girls. Also, she is a fan of the website Mocro-Place.nl, where she listens to Moroccan songs, wedding music and *raï* music such as Lella La3roussa. Salima participated in the survey and Fayrouz interviewed her in a school multimedia center.

Senna

Senna is a fourteen-year-old, second-year VMBO-K student from 's-Hertogenbosch. She describes herself as a normal girl who sometimes feels a bit shy. Senna was born in the Netherlands; her parents are from Berkane in the Rif in northeast Morocco. She speaks Dutch, Moroccan-Arabic and Berber with her parents at home. She has two brothers and three sisters. Her older brother knows most about computers. Accessing the Internet either on her mobile phone or by using her own laptop in her own room, she feels she is not restricted in her online action by anyone in her household. Her family lives in France, Morocco and the Netherlands, and she keeps in touch with her cousins abroad using MSN or her mobile phone, mostly. Senna uses ethnic identification markers, choosing symbols such as the Amazigh and Moroccan flag in her display image on MSN, but also for her avatars on the online forums Marokko.nl and Chaima.nl. On MSN and Hyves she had around 200 friends and on the latter platform she has joined groups such as "Takshita's" (a Moroccan dresses club), "I am proud of Morocco" and "RIP Faysel" to commemorate the tragic passing of one of her friends. On YouTube and websites such as Marokkia.nl and Mocro-Place.nl she looks up Moroccan artists like Hajja Hamdaouia and Rashid Kasmi. Furthermore she sends onward chain letters to her friends via e-mail on religion, such as prayers and *du'3as* (supplications) and issues around wearing the veil.

Senna participated in the survey and Fayrouz conducted the interview with her in a classroom.

Soesie

Soesie (a pseudonym she chose herself) is a thirteen-year-old, second-year VMBO student from 's-Hertogenbosch. She was born in the Netherlands, while both her parents were born in Tetouan in northern Morocco. During the summer holidays the family goes to Nador in northeast Morocco. At home and online, she speaks Dutch, Arabic and Berber. Soesie has two younger brothers (aged two and seven), and she likes to take pictures of them. For instance during the interview she spoke of a picture she took of the three of them together in the snow, which she uses as her profile picture on Hyves. She is quick to laugh; discussing personal things sometimes caused her to blush. Drama is her favorite subject in school. Outside school times she likes hang out with her friends or go on the computer and watch TV. She is interested in electronic dance and hip-hop music, and fashion trends. She admits she spends long hours behind the PC. Her mother keeps track of her use and tells her to go outside once she has used it for too long. Her mother also made her make her profile not visible for the public, she did not want pictures to circulate beyond Soesie's friends. Using her own laptop, she either goes online in her bedroom, or she does so downstairs on the couch while watching TV. When needed, she uses her Samsung touch screen phone to connect to the Internet, but she likes typing on the PC better. She has the Moroccan flag as the background image of her mobile phone, and she also uses it as a background of her Hyves profile page. She had around ninety friends on Hyves and 328 contacts on MSN. She enjoys talking with her friends on MSN, but she also likes to spend time in online chat room and playing online games. Sometimes she joins her dad when he uses Skype to speak to family members in Morocco, her uncle in Germany or other family members in the Netherlands. She participated in the survey. I conducted the interview with Soesie in a school library.

Soufian

Soufian (a pseudonym he chose himself) is a twelve-year-old, second-year HAVO student from Rotterdam. His parents are from Al Hoceima in the north of Morocco, while Soufian was born in the Netherlands. He has three brothers and one sister. Soufian sees himself as tough and sporty and describes himself as being both a gamer and a Muslim. He expresses his affinity with Berber culture by including the word "*Amazigh*" in his e-mail address. With his parents he speaks Dutch, Moroccan-Arabic and

Berber. Next to the Netherlands, his family members live in Morocco, Spain and France. His hobbies are playing football and kickboxing, and he does both at athletic clubs. He has to share the computer situated in the living room with his siblings. Of all people in his environment he feels he is most restricted in his use of the Internet by his schoolteacher. On his profile page on Hyves, he included a clock with a Moroccan flag that shows the one-hour time difference between the Netherlands and Morocco. He had around 200 friends on Hyves, but around 100 on MSN, because there he only includes people he knows well. His favorite site is YouTube, where he likes to go to look up comedy video clips and bloopers. Also he goes there to look up R&B and soul music but also *anasheed*. The latter is a type of Islamic vocal music, a cappella or music accompanied by instruments, that references Islamic history, beliefs and interpretations but also politics and current events. YouTube has become a place for the heavy circulation of such songs, and Soufian listens to English, Berber and Dutch *anasheed* songs on the site. It took some time for him to open up and share during the interview. Soufian participated in the survey, and Fayrouz interviewed him in a school multimedia center.

SouSou

SouSou (a pseudonym she chose herself) is a fifteen-year-old, third-year MAVO student from Rotterdam. Her parents migrated from Casablanca, Morocco's largest city. She has one young sister and two younger brothers. With her parents she speaks Dutch and Moroccan-Arabic. The majority of her family members live in Morocco, and she says the best thing about the Internet is that she and her parents can use MSN and a webcam to talk to family and friends who live there. She describes herself as witty but shy and she shared that she has little confidence, that's why she finds it difficult to built friendships. Her favorite subject in school is economics. She likes swimming and reading books. She feels affiliated with others interested in politics, Islam, and girl power. She likes to use her own computer in the living room. She feels free to use the Internet but her mother keeps track of what she downloads and what she puts on her profile page. While doing her homework, she likes to discuss what happened in school on MSN. Another favorite pastime is playing what she describes as "*games for girls*," web-based games on sites such as games2girls.com and girlsgogames.com. Also she enjoys being active on Marokko.nl. She mentions it is a useful site for people who find it difficult to get in contact elsewhere. She goes there to connect with other youngsters and read and contributes postings about relationships, Islam, the situation of Moroccans in the Netherlands, sexuality and friendships. She also downloads films and Nintendo DS games through LimeWire, and music using the YouTube converter application. She had 113 MSN contacts and somewhat fewer friends on Hyves. SouSou participated in the survey and Fayrouz interviewed her in a school multimedia center.

Tariq

Tariq is a thirteen-year-old, second-year VMBO-T student from Rotterdam. At different stages in the fieldwork he expressed enjoying participating in the study. His family has migrated to several countries across Europe. His grandparents, aunts and uncles live in Morocco but other relatives live in England and Italy. He describes himself as a normal young guy who sometimes is a bit boisterous. He has one brother and two sisters. With his parents he mainly speaks Berber. In school, his favorite subject is English. His family keeps in touch with webcam conversations on MSN, and they also make annual visits. Tariq's favorite applications are MSN and Hyves to keep in touch with his friends and he uses it to make plans for the weekends. He had around 120 friends on MSN, and 290 on Hyves. Tariq accesses the Internet from a desktop computer in his own room, and he does not feel anyone in his household supervises his actions online. After school hours he is active with Thai boxing. This has also posted on his Hyves profile page, next to videos of professional matches, a video of a Thai boxing match featuring himself. Next to his love of sports he is also proud of his descent, and he has put up a flag of Morocco on his profile page, which he says, shows "*where I am from.*" Also he includes the word "*mocro*" in his e-mail address. He does not like English or American rap groups, but he is a fan of Dutch groups and especially THC, a group formed in North Amsterdam which combines artists from Antillean, Armenian, Dutch, Indian, Moroccan, Surinamese, Tunisian and Turkish backgrounds. He also believes in the value of circulating protest and awareness e-mails, mentioning the case of protesting the Geert Wilders's "*kopvoddentaks*" initiative (to levy taxes on wearing the veil) through chain e-mails. He also remembers having donated money to victims of the Haiti earthquake after receiving a chain e-mail. Tariq participated in the survey and I interviewed him in a school multimedia center.

Yethi

Yethi (a pseudonym he chose himself) is a fifteen-year-old, third-year HAVO student from Utrecht. He describes himself as a "*Moroccan boy born in the Netherlands.*" He is a swimming fanatic but also plays other sports such as fitness and football. For him, "*the Internet is a part of my daily needs.*" He kept a profile on Hyves and Facebook, using Hyves for his friends in the Netherlands and Facebook for his nieces and nephews who live abroad. He had befriended around a hundred people on both sites. He does not feel restricted in his use of the Internet. When he was younger his parents kept a closer look at his online activities. He likes to visit sites having to do with swimming as well as voetbalprimeur.nl, which covers the latest developments in football. On his profile pages he posts images taken during swimming matches. Especially just before the summer he visits Marokko.nl to find out more about how other people are preparing for their holidays to Morocco and to read up on other people's experiences of traveling to Morocco. He mentions that there are many discussions about, for instance, *"being on the road to Morocco."* Yethi is into hip-hop, listening mostly to African-American artists such as Lil' Wayne, 50 Cent and Tupac. He uses LimeWire to download their songs to his BlackBerry smartphone. Yethi participated in the piloting of the interview, and I interviewed him in a university meeting room.

Ziham

Ziham (a pseudonym she chose herself) is a fourteen-year-old, second-year HAVO student from Rotterdam. She describes herself as a normal girl, adding that she feels *"I do not belong to anyone, I am just myself."* She was born in Morocco and migrated to the Netherlands with her parents at young age. She sees herself as *"Moroccan, very ordinary,"* and adds she *"is just proud of herself."* She speaks Dutch and Berber with her parents at home. She has two brothers and two sisters and her favorite subjects in school are French and the other languages she takes. Her main interest is playing football for her club, and she takes it very serious and practices a lot. Ziham is very proud of her accomplishments and tries to make the most of her talent. She has a laptop of her own, but her brother has changed the password, and he heavily controls her use of it. For instance, she is not allowed to delete her browser history and he forbids her to use Hyves. However, she makes use of her smartphone to circumvent her brother's restrictions. As a way to remember her football experiences, she likes to upload pictures of her football team on her profile page. Most of her family lives in the Netherlands, but her grandmothers live in Morocco. In her household, the phone is used to keep in touch with them. She likes Moroccan singers such as Mohamed Sami, Morad Salam, Leila Chaleir and Amazrine and she downloads their songs on her phone. She emphasizes her femininity by including the word "miss" in her e-mail address. She had 180 friends on Hyves, and nearly 800 friends on MSN. Ziham participated in the survey, and Fayrouz and I interviewed her together in a school library. I also remained in contact with Ziham through MSN.

Other informants

Abdelilah Amraoui

Abdelilah Amraoui was the founder of Geweigerd.nl, a site where ethnic-minority youth who are denied access to entertainment venues can share their stories and the "interactive Moroccan forum" Maghreb.nl. Amraoui believes digital technologies offer the opportunity to create media when it cannot be found elsewhere. The interview with Amraoui took place in a university meeting room.

eMoroccan

I interviewed eMoroccan about the videos he made in Morocco that he posted to YouTube. The interview took place via the YouTube personal messaging service.

Rabi'a Frank

In the early stages of recruiting informants for the research, this parent of three children aged eight, eleven and thirteen got in touch with me via e-mail. She is a Dutch Muslim woman, married to a Moroccan-Dutch man. She shared with me her views on the necessity of supervising children in their use of digital media.

Marocdelicious

Marocdelicious, a thirty-two-year-old male, was the founder of the "Marokkaanse Nederlanders hier melden" ("Moroccan-Dutch People Report Here") Hyves group (mijnmarokko.hyves.nl/). He started the site to allow Moroccan-Dutch youth to meet one another and engage in discussions on Hyves.

MintTea

MintTea, a twenty-nine-year-old woman, was the founder of the "Positive Muslim Newz?!" Hyves group (positivemuslimnewz.hyves.nl/). In response to the dominance of negative news about Muslims, she set up this page to give more attention to positive developments and news for and about Muslims. Our conversation took place via Hyves private messaging service.

NOONA

NOONA (a pseudonym she chose herself), a twenty-two-year-old woman, was the founder of the "Royals du Maroc" Hyves group (http://royalsdu-maroc.hyves.nl/). She set up this page in response to the Hyves group dedicated to the Dutch royal family. She highlighted the progressive developments spurred by the installment of Mohammed VI as the king of Morocco in 1999. Illustrating the difficulties of gaining access and trust, she shared her frustrations with the dominant negative reporting about Moroccan-Dutch people: "*You can write about this Hyves in your book, but I want to know what you will be writing, because there is enough negative news about Moroccans in the media already.*" Our conversation took place via Hyves private messaging service.

Rafik

Rafik was the founder of the "Imazighen" Hyves group. He set up this group to disseminate knowledge about Imazighen history and culture on Hyves. Our conversation took place via Hyves private messaging service.

Rafje

Rafje, a twenty-eight-year-old male, is an artist whose socially critical cartoons are published on the homepage of the discussion forum Marokko.nl. The interview with Rafje took place over the phone.

Index

MediaMatters

Maaike Bleeker
Anatomy Live. Performance and the Operating Theatre, 2008
ISBN 978 90 5356 516 2

Marianne van den Boomen, Sybille Lammes, Ann-Sophie Lehmann, Joost Raessens, Mirko Tobias Schäfer (eds.)
Digital Material. Tracing New Media in Everyday Life and Technology, 2009
ISBN 978 90 8964 068 0

Maaike Lauwaert
The Place of Play. Toys and Digital Cultures, 2009
ISBN 978 90 8964 080 2

Sarah Bay-Cheng, Chiel Kattenbelt, Andy Lavender, Robin Nelson (eds.)
Mapping Intermediality in Performance, 2010
ISBN 978 90 8964 255 4

Tanja Sihvonen
Players Unleashed! Modding The Sims *and the Culture of Gaming*, 2011
ISBN 978 90 8964 201 1

Mirko Tobias Schäfer
Bastard Culture! How User Participation Transforms Cultural Production, 2011
ISBN 978 90 8964 256 1

Imar O. de Vries
Tantalisingly Close. An Archaeology of Communication Desires in Discourses of Mobile Wireless Media, 2012
ISBN 978 90 8964 354 4

Nanna Verhoeff
Mobile Screens. The Visual Regime of Navigation, 2012
ISBN 978 90 8964 379 7

René Glas
Battlefields of Negotiation. Control, Agency, and Ownership in World of Warcraft, 2013
ISBN 978 90 8964 500 5

Valerie Frissen, Sybille Lammes, Michiel de Lange, Jos de Mul, Joost Raessens (eds.)
Playful Idenities. The Ludification of Digital Media Cultures, 2015
ISBN 978 90 8964 639 2

"Leurs' book, situated at the intersection of transnational cultural studies and new media studies, offers a compelling and theoretically rigorous examination of diasporas online. By locating communities and their emergent counterpublics within transnational studies – especially their affective politics, belongingness, citizenship and cultural affiliations – and then reenvisioning these same politics in the digital realm, Leurs demonstrates how identities, identifications, cultural crossings and memory projects are now indebted to digital spaces. Leurs also proves, conclusively, the materiality of digital cultures/spaces, by showing how the digital is constituted as space through social processes and cultural practices that are raced, gendered and sexualized. Our identities and affiliations, the book shows, are shaped by the media that now pervades our lives even as the media 'grows' through these same identities and affiliations."
– *Pramod Nayar, Professor in the Department of English, University of Hyderabad*

"Leurs's book reports on his intersectional study of the digital performativity of identity across gender, diaspora and Moroccan-Dutch youth culture. It provides exciting new insights into our understanding of the ways in which the web is providing spaces for the negotiation of new forms of digital belonging and greater cultural understanding in an increasingly multicultural world."
– *Cynthia Carter, Senior Lecturer in the Cardiff School of Journalism, Media and Cultural Studies, Cardiff University*

"This is a most timely intervention in the field of digital diaspora studies. Koen Leurs' book develops a substantial, well-supported argument about the reconfigurations of diaspora in the context of Moroccan Dutch communities, which engages with the intersections of different strands of identification on and offline. Leurs powerfully makes the case for the affective interrelationship between material, embodied spaces in an interdisciplinary text which makes significant contribution to this fast growing field of research, which has significant political and policy implications."
– *Kath Woodward, Emeritus Professor of Sociology, Open University*

15W36395/ T1/ 9789089646408